## This Book Belongs To:
# Alan L. Froelich

For him that steals,
or borrows and returns not,
a book from its owner,
let it change into a serpent in his hand
and rend him.
Let him be struck with palsy,
and all his members blasted.
Let him languish in pain crying
aloud for mercy,
and let there be no surcease to his
agony till he sing in dissolution.
Let bookworms gnaw at his
entrails in token of the Worm that dieth
not.
And when at last he goes to his
final punishment,
let the flames of Hell consume him forever.

# JAPAN'S LAST BID
# FOR VICTORY

## Also by Robert Lyman

*Slim, Master of War: Burma and the Birth of Modern Warfare*, Constable,
  London, 2004
*Iraq, 1941: The Battles for Basra, Habbaniya, Fallujah and Baghdad*,
  Osprey Publishing Ltd, Oxford, 2006
*First Victory: Britain's Forgotten Struggle in the Middle East, 1941*,
  Constable, London, 2006
*The Generals: From Defeat to Victory, Leadership in Asia 1941-45*,
  Constable, London, 2008
*The Longest Siege: Tobruk – The Battle that Saved North Africa*, Macmillan
  Ltd, London, 2009
*Kohima – The Battle that saved India*, Osprey Publishing Ltd,
  Oxford, 2010
*Bill Slim*, Osprey Publishing Ltd, Oxford, 2011

# JAPAN'S LAST BID FOR VICTORY

## The Invasion of India, 1944

### ROBERT LYMAN

PRAETORIAN PRESS

First published in Great Britain in 2011 by
**The Praetorian Press**
an imprint of
Pen & Sword Books Ltd
47 Church Street
Barnsley
South Yorkshire
S70 2AS

ISBN 978 1 84884 542 8

A CIP catalogue record for this book is
available from the British Library

Typeset in Ehrhardt
by Chic Media Ltd

Printed and bound in England
by CPI

*Pen & Sword Books Ltd incorporates the imprints of*
Pen & Sword Books Ltd incorporates the imprints of
Pen & Sword Aviation, Pen & Sword Family History, Pen & Sword Maritime,
Pen & Sword Military, Pen & Sword Discovery, Wharncliffe Local History,
Wharncliffe True Crime, Wharncliffe Transport, Pen & Sword Select,
Pen & Sword Military Classics, Leo Cooper, Remember When,
The Praetorian Press, Seaforth Publishing and Frontline Publishing

*For a complete list of Pen & Sword titles please contact*
PEN & SWORD BOOKS LIMITED
47 Church Street, Barnsley, South Yorkshire, S70 2AS, England
E-mail: enquiries@pen-and-sword.co.uk
Website: www.pen-and-sword.co.uk

# Contents

# Acknowledgements

Igratefully acknowledge the support of a wide range of people in the construction of this book: without their own research and experiences, published or otherwise, I could not have written this story. I want to start by recording my indebtedness yet again to the indefatigable Philip and Isla Brownless without whose constant encouragement and support the book would never have been written. Both read (and re-read) the manuscript in draft to offer opinion on both subject and construction, to its considerable benefit. Philip's memories of his long travails behind Japanese lines in the Naga Hills as part of 23 (Long Range Penetration) Brigade remain urgent and vital even after the passage of 65 years. I am grateful also to their son, Ben, who accompanied me on an adventure to Nagaland in 2008 and who has since become a trustee of the Kohima Educational Trust (www.kohimaeducationaltrust.net): this was set up by veterans of the battle to thank the Naga people for their unstinting support for the British, especially the wounded, during the war and also to offer ongoing help to younger generations of Nagas when peace returned to their land.

I wish also to record the help and friendship extended by the late Jon Latimer, whose early death aged forty-four in 2009, from an aortic aneurism, took from us a skilful and perceptive historian. Jon's book on the war in the Far East remains by far the best single volume on what is often called 'The Burma Campaign'. My profound thanks also goes to the Naga historian, Easterine Iralu, by whose endeavours many of the Naga memories of the battle have been preserved, and who introduced me to many of the survivors during my own journeys to Nagaland. She recorded the bulk of the Naga memories recorded in this book, particularly those of her great-aunt, Aviü. Alongside Easterine's work is that of the curator of the new Museum to the Second World War in Kohima, Kevi Nino Meru, who has undertaken the interviewing (and filming) of scores of aging Naga veterans to recover their invaluable memories of the war, some of which can be seen on my website, www.robertlyman.com. For talking to me about their experiences I am grateful to Khriezotijo Sachü, Khoienuo Keretsü, Ketsoü Sekhose and Shürhosielie Pienyü.

From a projector in the Imperial War Museum in London (JFU 90) and now, by virtue of digital technology on my website, one can watch grainy black and white images, taken by an Army cameraman, of the Viceroy of

India meeting Naga leaders at Kohima on 8 August 1944. Accompanying Wavell is the tall, gaunt figure of the Deputy Commissioner, Charles Pawsey MC. Wavell had arrived by plane into Imphal on 6 August, before driving north along the recently re-opened road to Kohima through the scenes of recent fighting. In his diary he writes:

> I was told that 15 or 20 Nagas would come to meet me at Kohima, actually 200 to 300 turned up, a picturesque sturdy looking people. They brought gifts of spears and headdresses and woven clothes and chickens and eggs. I had brought rum and cigarettes for them but there were a great many more than we had expected. The Nagas did us extraordinarily well in the recent fighting.

Given his penchant for understatement this was praise indeed. Wavell had been well briefed. In fact, without the support provided by the Nagas at Kohima it is unlikely that the British effort would have succeeded at all. At the very least, without the Nagas the battle would have been significantly more prolonged, and considerably more difficult.

A wide range of veterans and historians have helped me to understand the campaign's complexities and furies. These include my friend David Rooney (*Burma Victory*), the prolific air historian Norman Franks (*Air Battle for Imphal*), and John Nunneley, who has again allowed me to quote from his revelatory *Tales by Japanese Soldiers*, co-authored with Dr Kazuo Tamayama MBE. I wish to thank Mrs Hirakubo, for permission to quote from her late husband's memoirs; Major General Ian Lyall Grant, who has written the definitive account of the Tiddim Road battles in *Burma: The Turning Point*, battles in which he fought; Major Gordon Graham MC for the incomparable *The Trees are all Young on Garrison Hill* and George Forty for *XIV Army at War*. Michael Shipster has kindly allowed me to quote from his father's *Mist Over The Rice Fields*; and Bryan Perrett has done likewise from his *Tank Tracks to Rangoon*. Thanks are also due to Michael Lowry for his two quite excellent books (*An Infantry Company Commander in Arakan and Kohima* and *Fighting through to Kohima*); to John McCann for *Return to Kohima* and David Wilson for *The Sum of Things*, which was published just months before his death in 2001; to John Henslow for *A Sapper in the Forgotten Army;* to Mrs Paula Atkins, widow of the late David Atkins, for the use of the wonderful material from David's *The Reluctant Major* and *The Forgotten Major;* to Mrs John Hudson, widow of the late John Hudson (*Sunset in the East*); to Brigadier John Randle OBE MC (*Battle Tales from Burma*); to John Leyin (*Tell Them of Us*); to Arthur Freer (*Nunshigum*); to Ken Cooper (*The Little Men*); and to Bob Street for the story of his father, Raymond Street, one of the survivors of the gallant 4th Royal West Kents (*The Siege of Kohima*). Bob is also the author of *Another Brummie in Burma* which tells the story of Private Len Thornton RAMC, at Imphal. I am also grateful again to Major General Julian Thompson for allowing me fruitfully to mine his *War in Burma 1942-1945* and to Tim Molloy for allowing me to quote material from his father's (Terence Molloy) *The Silchar Track*. I also benefited enormously, as do all historians of the Far East from research undertaken by Louis Allen in *Burma: The Longest War*. All these people, and more, have helped me in many ways, but especially by providing insights into the war and for encouraging my efforts. All errors, of judgement or fact, remain, of course, entirely my own.

I am also indebted to my friend and fellow trustee of the Kohima Educational Trust, Lily Das, and her husband Smo, who helped in many different ways to make this book possible. Smo became my unofficial travel agent for my visits to Nagaland, smoothing the many bureaucratic inconveniences still encountered in trips to the subcontinent. But more importantly it was Lily who introduced me to her mother, Aviü ('Mari'), who lived through the battle and whose memories form an important part of this book.

I am grateful to the Second World War Experience Centre at the University of Leeds for permission to use material by Lieutenant Desmond Early. Likewise I wish to thank the many hundreds of Burma Star veterans and the stalwart supporters of both the Kohima Educational Trust and the Burma Campaign Society (successor to the Burma Campaign Fellowship Group) who have provided material for this book, and for permission granted to quote from material in the hands of either the Burma Star Association or the Burma Campaign Memorial Library. The memories of veterans have formed an important part of the telling of this story and I am grateful for the many men and women who have told me theirs. This includes contributions from David Murray; Peter Toole; John Burkmer James Evans; John Roberts; Thomas Joesbury; Stanley Hutson; Kenneth Keen; Len Hall; Bill Whalen; Gian Singh, Philip Malins MC; Ray Jackson; Basil French; Ron Bunnett; John Riggs; Clifford Wood; C. V. (Mike) Ball; Wilf Ogden; John Skene MBE; Roy Welland; Bob Allen and Alex Tiller. For help in many different practical ways I wish to thank Phil Crawley of the Burma Star Association, Rob and Sylvia May, Gordon and Betty Graham, Jerry Bird, Colonel Ted Shields, Bob Cook (Curator of the Kohima Museum, York) and Lieutenant Colonel Ingrid Hall. I am particularly beholden to the BBC Peoples War archive and for all its contributors who between 2004 and 2006 made it such a rich vein of information for historians of the Second World War. I wish to thank Dr Harry Good (A1968465); Fred Weedman (A5325518); Bob Blenkinsop (A2052181); Clifford Wood (A4254103); Deryck (Dick) Reynolds (A6432978); Howard Woodcock (A8766156) and Eric Forsdike (A6165623).

Likewise the treasure trove in the Department of Documents and the Sound Archives at the Imperial War Museum in London has once again proved immensely helpful to the narrative historian. I am honoured to have permission to quote from material provided by the late Paul Haskins (07/20/1); Pat Rome MC (DS/MISC/65); Jack F. Clifford (67/411/1); John Howard (99/21/1); Basil French (97/19/1); L. R. Mizen (71/63/1); Fred Hazell and V. F. S. Hawkins DSO MC (10520 P104). In the sound archives can be found dramatic, first-hand descriptions of the battles by John Randle (15335, 20457); Michael Marshall (11069); O. A. Parry (14742); Deryck Groocock (12559); Gerald Cree (10469); Arthur Freer (19822); 'Dicky' Richards (MAPC); F. G. Nields (MAPC); Harry Butchard (MAPC); John Winstanley (17955); Francis Boshell (15578); Martin McLane (10165); Alexander Wilson (20456); Sam Horner; 'Winkie' Fitt (16970); Walter Gilding (17534); Dickie Davies (17936); Lintorn Highett (15334); Dinesh Misra (187370) and James Evans (14841). The National Army Museum likewise has a substantial holding of useful documents including the diaries of Major Anthony Bickersteth (4/8th Gurkhas) and the War Diary of the 14/13th Frontier Force Rifles. Ian Kikuyu and his team in the Department of Film at the IWM were generous in the time and advice they gave to me, especially in identifying the unique cinematography of the battle and its aftermath in MWY23 and 26; ABY11 and 27; and JFU 90, 179, 225 and 230.

I pay tribute to the endeavours of a small but faithful group of friends who work diligently for the cause of reconciliation and remembrance across Nagaland. I would list here Mrs Grace Savino and her husband Kris, Pfelie Kesiezie, Atuo Angami, Charles Chasie, P Talitemjen Ao, Khrielie Kevichusa, Shurhozelie Liezietsu, Keluozie, and the Revd Khari Longchar. For various kindnesses I am grateful to Mr Neiphiu Rio (the Chief Minister for Nagaland) and Zhovehu Lohe (Speaker of the Legislative Assembly). To Kevichülie Meyase (of Alder Tours) and to Asanuo's wonderful guest house (Razhü Pru) in Naga Village I am very thankful. Anyone making the trek to Kohima is encouraged to enjoy the warm hospitality of this old family home. The email address is razhupru@yahoo.co.in.

It is a great regret that a vast treasure store of Japanese reminiscences remains locked out of view of international scholars because they have not been translated into English. Despite these difficulties I have managed to access a limited number of these accounts, through the assistance of Dr Kazuo Tamayama MBE. These include elements of Toshiro Takagi's *Imphal* (Tokyo, 1949), Takeo Komatsu's *Imphal Tragedy* (n.d.), Yukihiko Imai's *To and From Kohima* (Tokyo, 1953), Tochiro Imanishi's *Burma Front Diary* (Tokyo, 1961); the memoirs of Hirakubo Masao OBE and a collection of memories from the men of the *58th Regiment*, collated in Tokyo in 1964. In addition, the Imperial War Museum in London has a number of Japanese accounts including those of Lieutenant General Sato, Lieutenant Colonel Yamaki (*31st Division*), Lieutenant General Miyazaki, Major Masuda (CO, *2/214th Regiment*), Captain Nagao (Adjutant, *124th Regiment*, Lieutenant Sugiura, CO 5th Company of a battalion in *124th Regiment*, Colonel Shiraishi (CO, *31st Mountain Artillery Regiment*), Major Ishizuka (CO, *3/31st Mountain Artillery Battalion*), Captain Nishida (OC, 11th Company, *124th Regiment*). Recently the Japanese TV station NHK Niigata has conducted interviews in Japanese with veterans of the *58th Regiment*, under the direction of Eisuke Yamamori. I am grateful for the help of Kishi Yamamoto for making them available in English. I wish to pay tribute to the Burma Campaign Society, the successor to the Burma Campaign Fellowship Group, under their chairperson, Mrs Akiko MacDonald, and wish them all possible success in their continuing efforts to dispel the bitterness engendered by war through the reconciliation of the people of two great nations, once enemies, now friends.

Finally, I am grateful to the professionalism of the team at Pen and Sword who guided this book through to publication. To Richard Doherty, himself an accomplished historian, and Jamie Wilson: thank you!

## Notes to the Reader

I refer in the text to 'British' troops even though those of whom I write more often than not came not from Britain but from all over the Empire, not least from India itself. This device is to ensure simplicity in the telling of the story, and does not challenge the reality that at all times the troops from across the Empire – in particular Africa and un-partitioned India – comprised by far and away the largest proportion of 'British' fighting troops. By 1945 the 'British' Fourteenth Army, the largest army fielded by the United Kingdom during the war, was roughly 58 per cent Indian, 25 per cent West African and only 17 per cent British.

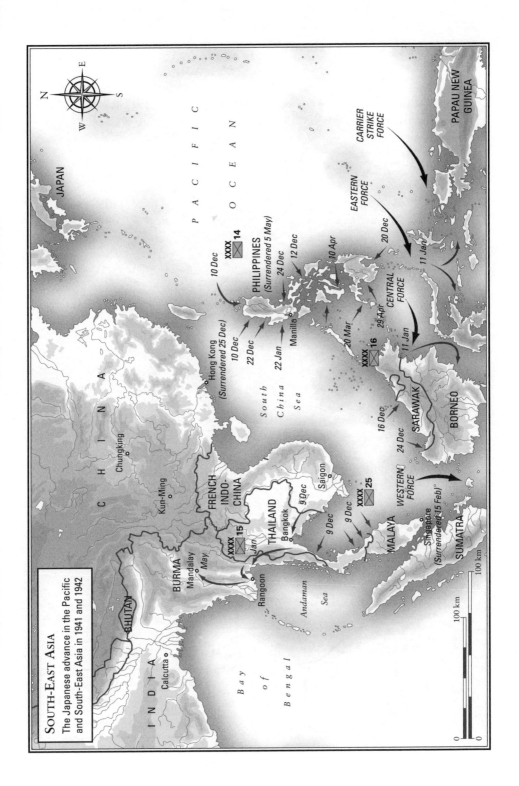

SOUTH-EAST ASIA

The Japanese advance in the Pacific and South-East Asia in 1941 and 1942

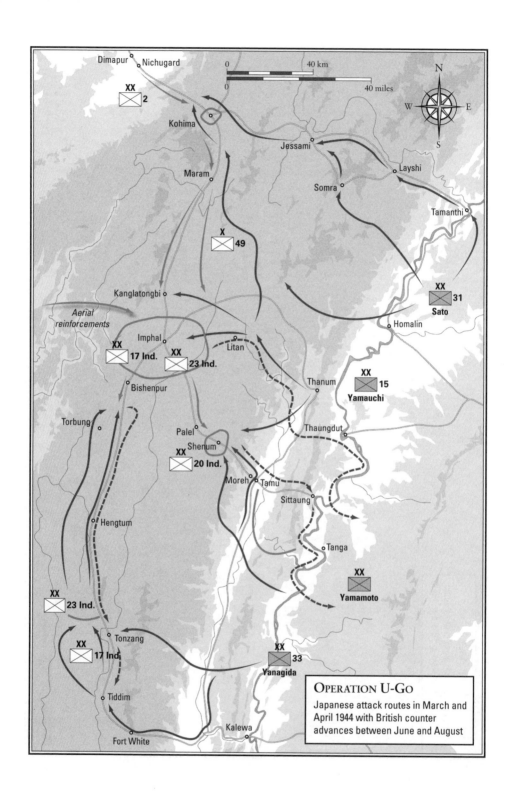

Dimapur ○ ● Nichugard

XX 2

Kohima

Jessami

Layshi

Maram

Somra

Tamanthi

X 49

Kanglatongbi

XX 31
Sato

Aerial
reinforcements

Imphal ○ ○ Litan

Homalin

XX 17 Ind. XX 23 Ind.

Thanum

XX 15
Yamauchi

Bishenpur

Torbung ○

Palel ○
Shenum

Thaungdut

XX 20 Ind.

Moreh ○ ○ Tamu

Sittaung

Hengtum

Tanga

XX 23 Ind.

XX
Yamamoto

Tonzang

XX 17 Ind.

Tiddim ○

Kalewa

XX 33
Yanagida

Fort White ○

**OPERATION U-GO**

Japanese attack routes in March and
April 1944 with British counter
advances between June and August

0 ___ 40 km
0 ___ 40 miles

N
W ✦ E
S

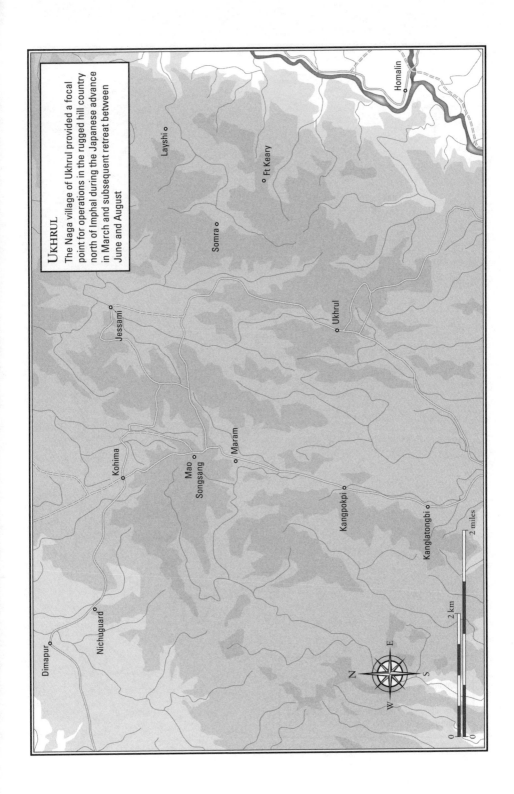

## UKHRUL

The Naga village of Ukhrul provided a focal point for operations in the rugged hill country north of Imphal during the Japanese advance in March and subsequent retreat between June and August

Homalin

Layshi

Ft Keary

Somra

Jessami

Ukhrul

Kohima

Mao
Songsang

Maram

Kangpokpi

Dimapur

Nichuguard

Kanglatongbi

N
W    E
S

2 km

2 miles

0

0

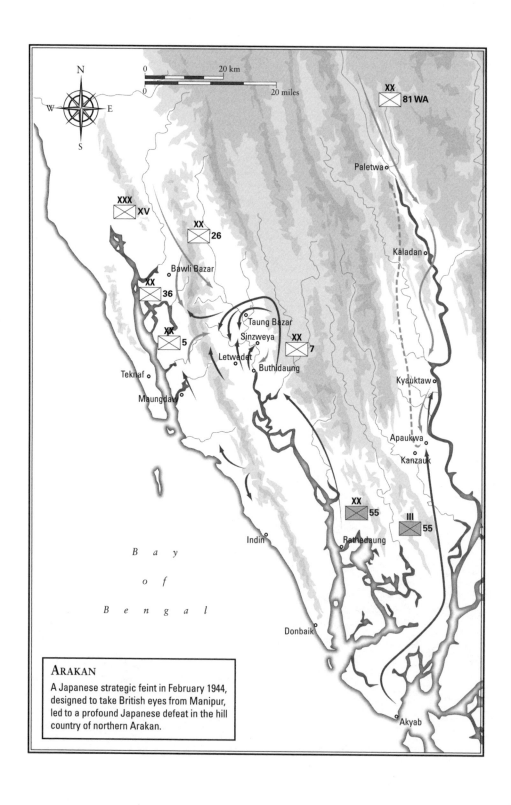

**N**
**W** **E**
**S**

0   20 km
0   20 miles

XX
81 WA

Paletwa

XXX
XV

XX
26

Kaladan

Bawli Bazar

XX
36

Taung Bazar

Sinzweya

XX
5

XX
7

Letwedet

Teknaf

Buthidaung

Maungdaw

Kyauktaw

Apaukwa

Kanzauk

XX
55

III
55

Indin

*B a y*

Rathedaung

*o f*

*B e n g a l*

Donbaik

Akyab

**ARAKAN**

A Japanese strategic feint in February 1944,
designed to take British eyes from Manipur,
led to a profound Japanese defeat in the hill
country of northern Arakan.

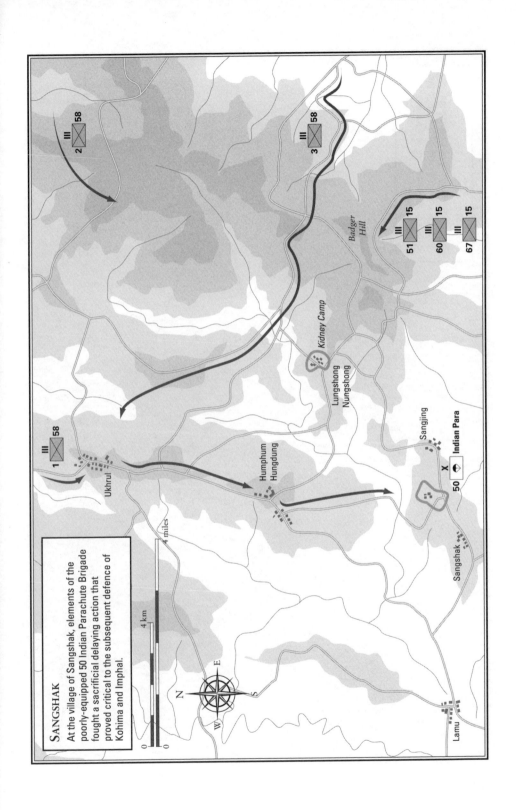

SANGSHAK

At the village of Sangshak, elements of the poorly-equipped 50 Indian Parachute Brigade fought a sacrificial delaying action that proved critical to the subsequent defence of Kohima and Imphal.

0    4 km

0    4 miles

N
E
S
W

III 58
1

III 58
2

III 58
3

Ukhrul

Badger Hill

III 15
51

III 15
60

III 15
67

Humphum
Hungdung

Kidney Camp

Lungshong
Nungshong

Sangjing

X 50
Indian Para

Sangshak

Lamu

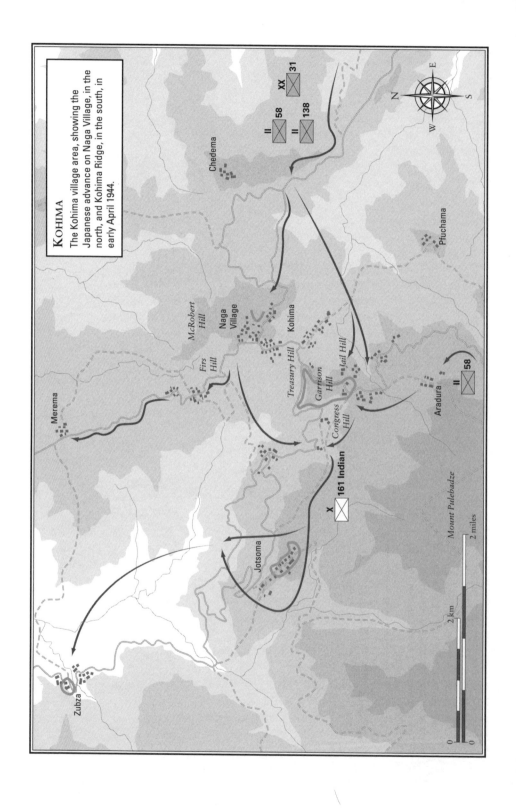

KOHIMA

The Kohima village area, showing the Japanese advance on Naga Village, in the north, and Kohima Ridge, in the south, in early April 1944.

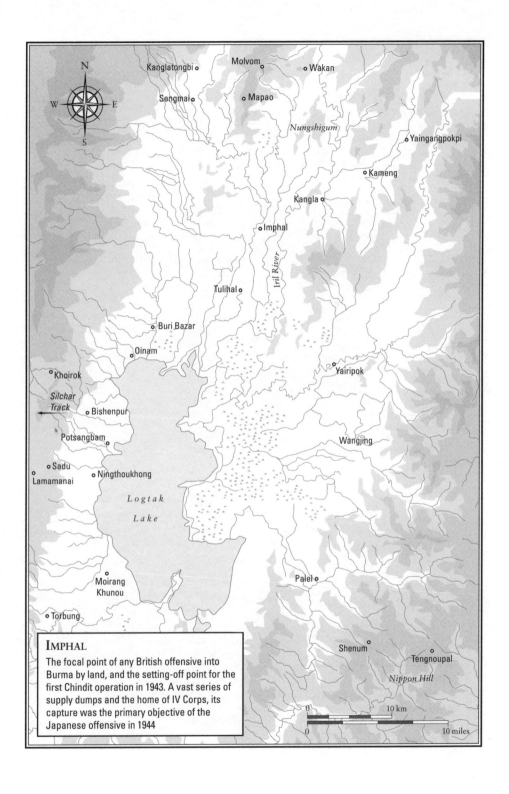

N

W    E

S

Kanglatongbi o     Molvom o     o Wakan

Sengmai o     o Mapao

*Nungshigum*     o Yaingangpokpi

o Kameng

Kangla o

o Imphal     *Iril River*

Tulihal o

o Buri Bazar

Oinam o

o Khoirok     o Yairipok

*Silchar Track*     o Bishenpur

Potsangbam

o Sadu     o Ningthoukhong     Wangjing

Lamamanai

*Logtak Lake*

Moirang Khunou     Palel o

o Torbung

## IMPHAL

The focal point of any British offensive into Burma by land, and the setting-off point for the first Chindit operation in 1943. A vast series of supply dumps and the home of IV Corps, its capture was the primary objective of the Japanese offensive in 1944

Shenum o     o Tengnoupal

*Nippon Hill*

0     10 km

0     10 miles

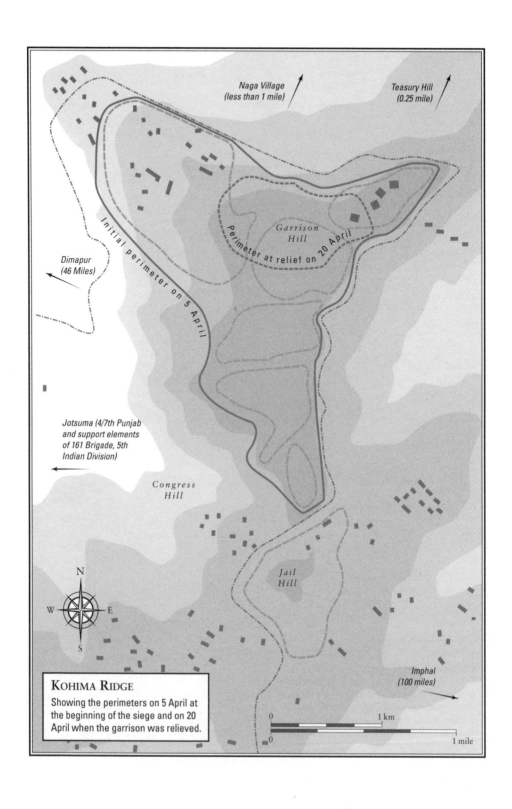

Naga Village
(less than 1 mile)

Teasury Hill
(0.25 mile)

*Initial perimeter on 5 April*

*Perimeter at relief on 20 April*

*Garrison
Hill*

Dimapur
(46 Miles)

Jotsuma (4/7th Punjab
and support elements
of 161 Brigade, 5th
Indian Division)

*Congress
Hill*

*Jail
Hill*

Imphal
(100 miles)

N
W    E
S

### KOHIMA RIDGE

Showing the perimeters on 5 April at
the beginning of the siege and on 20
April when the garrison was relieved.

0                    1 km

0                         1 mile

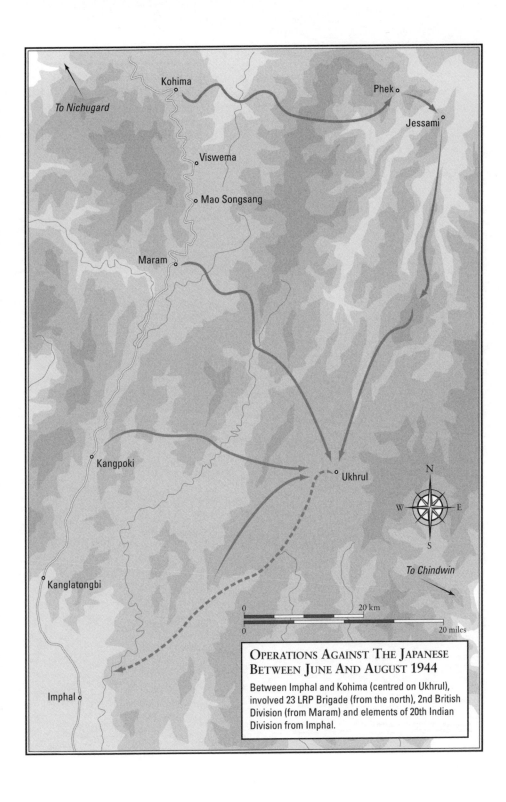

To Nichugard

Kohima

Phek

Jessami

Viswema

Mao Songsang

Maram

Kangpoki

Ukhrul

N
W E
S

To Chindwin

Kanglatongbi

0                    20 km

0                                      20 miles

Imphal

**OPERATIONS AGAINST THE JAPANESE
BETWEEN JUNE AND AUGUST 1944**

Between Imphal and Kohima (centred on Ukhrul),
involved 23 LRP Brigade (from the north), 2nd British
Division (from Maram) and elements of 20th Indian
Division from Imphal.

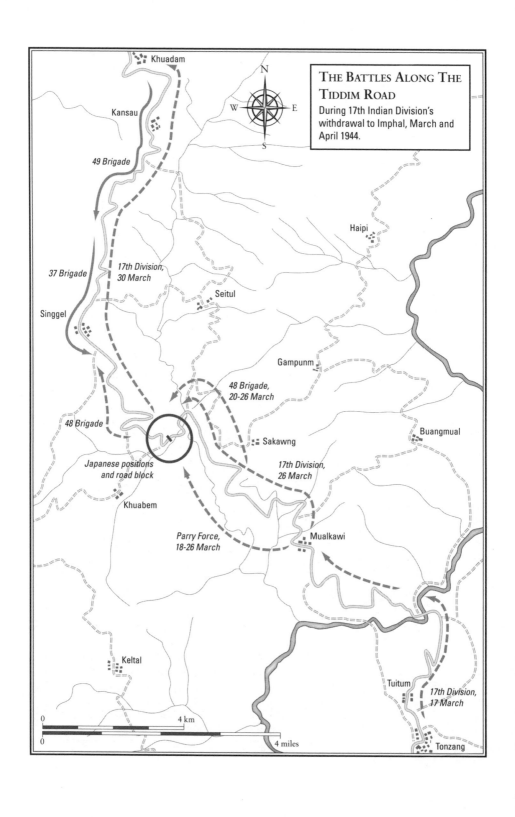

THE BATTLES ALONG THE
TIDDIM ROAD
During 17th Indian Division's
withdrawal to Imphal, March and
April 1944.

Khuadam

Kansau

49 Brigade

Haipi

37 Brigade

17th Division,
30 March

Seitul

Singgel

Gampunm

Buangmual

48 Brigade,
20-26 March

48 Brigade

Sakawng

Japanese positions
and road block

17th Division,
26 March

Khuabem

Parry Force,
18-26 March

Mualkawi

Keltal

Tuitum

17th Division,
17 March

0          4 km

0                            4 miles

Tonzang

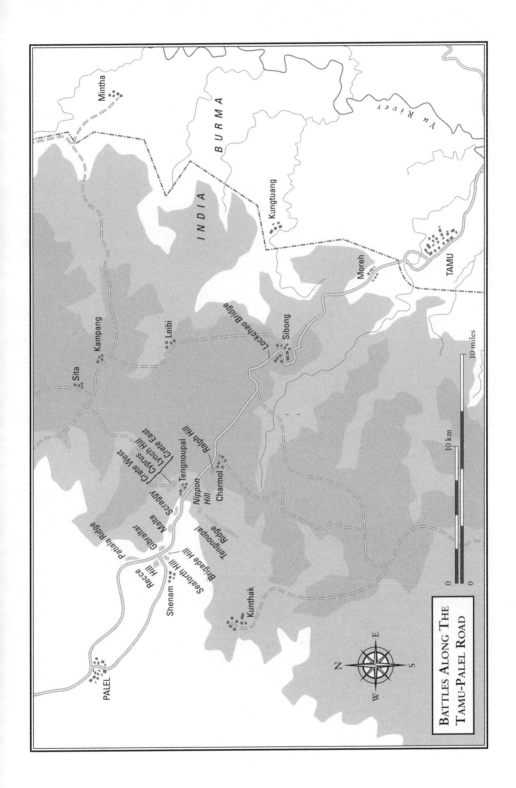

Mintha

BURMA

Yu River

INDIA

Kungtuang

Kampang

Leibi

Lockchao Bridge

Sibong

Moreh

TAMU

Sita

Crete East
Lynch Hill
Cyprus
Crete West
Scraggy
Malta
Gibraltar
Recce
Parala Ridge

Tengnoupal Hill

Ralph Hill

Nippon Hill

Charmol

Tengnoupal Bridge
Tengnoupal Ridge

Shenam
Seaforth Hill
Brigade Hill

Kunthak

PALEL

N
E
W
S

0        10 km

0        10 miles

BATTLES ALONG THE
TAMU-PALEL ROAD

# Prologue

The Air India Boeing 737 bumped its way through the turbulent air above the hills separating the Imphal Plain from Guwahati, whence we had departed an hour before. The dark green jungle-covered hills seemed threateningly close, rising up suddenly before falling away just as rapidly as the aircraft pitched and yawed its way eastwards, the rise and fall in altitude seeming to correspond with the endless, higgledy-piggledy terrain. When Private Len Thornton of the Royal Army Medical Corps first saw the rolling mountains around Imphal in 1943 from the window of a C-47 Dakota they seemed to him as 'though huge waves of an angry ocean had suddenly turned to rock and the covered themselves with primeval jungle which stretched for miles and miles'. Seeing these endless, jagged, green hills for the first time, I now knew what he meant. Then, without warning, the aircraft turned sharply to the left, dropping height at the same time and at a rate that was far too rapid to be comfortable. I grasped the side of the seat as from the windows on the other side of the aircraft I could see the ground below grow quickly closer. Then, just as suddenly, the aircraft jerked itself upright and a few seconds later we bounced heavily and rolled sluggishly to a stop on a long, grey tarmac runway. We had arrived at Imphal, capital of Manipur, the easternmost province of India. Sixty-six years ago this had been Tulihal Airfield, one of six on the bed of the ancient lake that forms the Imphal Plain, sunk deep below the surrounding mountains. Across the mountains to the east had marched an invading army intent on driving the British from Manipur and, if it were possible, initiating the collapse of the Raj. In 1944 the lumbering twin-engined Douglas Dakotas and Curtis Commandos of the RAF and USAAF spiralled down between the mountains day after day for four long, weary months giving sustenance to the force of Britons, Gurkhas and Indians fighting determinedly to turn back the Japanese invasion of India.

My journey was made in a modern aircraft, and yet I experienced in that short flight over the mountains something of the extremes of topography and climate enjoyed by this remote area of the world. The Imphal Plain is a flat alluvial basin some 2,500 feet above sea level stretching north to south some forty miles by twenty miles east to west. It sits deep within a vast and tangled mass of jungle-topped hills that provides a protective barrier for hundreds of miles in all directions and which separate Burma from India. From north to south the mountains stretch in a line along the Chindwin's left bank for some 600 miles into the depths of the Himalayas. Between the Chindwin in Burma to the east and the Brahmaputra Valley in India to the west they extend for some 200 miles. To the north of Imphal the Naga Hills cover some 8,000 square miles of hills. To the north-west lie the Somra Tracts, while the Angousham Hills rise to the east and south-east and then fall to the Chindwin and in the south and west lie the Chin Hills. In 1944, as now, the entire region boasted few roads and a scattered aboriginal population of perhaps 200,000 people, with the most significant population groupings at Imphal (little more than a small market town) and the tiny hill station at Kohima, which sits at 5,000 feet on the single road that links Imphal with Dimapur. The two tribes who inhabited this vast hill country were the Nagas – an animistic race, largely converted to Christianity after the arrival of American missionaries in the nineteenth century, comprising sixteen different tribes – and their unrelated neighbours, the Kuki, with whom there was often bad blood. A single-track road wound its way tortuously for 138 miles from the Brahmaputra Valley at Dimapur (also known as Manipur Road), where a vast array of depots were being constructed to supply Lieutenant General 'Vinegar Joe' Stilwell's American/Chinese forces beyond Ledo, through the mountains to IV Indian Corps at Imphal. The only viable road into Imphal, it was upgraded to a twin-track metalled road after many months of exhausting work in early 1943, but it still took a jeep some seven hours to travel between Imphal and Dimapur. It was also subject to regular mud slides and during the monsoon found itself regularly closed to traffic while repairs were undertaken. The only other access into Imphal was via a difficult mule track over the mountains from Silchar in Assam, which was never used as a supply route.

These mountains are the wettest in the world. They make the Imphal Plain a botanical paradise, fields of riotous colour, the bright sparkles of the many types and varieties of flowers brightening the otherwise monotonous hues of green and yellow of the ubiquitous rice fields, banana plantations and sugar cane. The variety and colour of tree-growing orchids is stunning. Between May and October the monsoon hits the region with astonishing power, the rain falling in ferocious torrents, up to 400 inches per annum, washing away roads and tracks and bringing transport on dry-weather roads to a standstill. The rain tends to fall during the night and early morning, but whole days can be lost to heavy downpours. The five inches of rain that plummets down each day during the wet season, recalled Major David Atkins of 309 General Purpose Transport (GPT) Company supporting 17th Indian Division, brought with it mould which grew everywhere, from boots to hairbrushes. Valleys and the low-lying areas around Imphal flood, heavy cloud descends and giant cumulus clouds gather in violent clusters in the skies to threaten the unwary. Aircraft caught up in these accumulations, which can rise from 2,000 to 40,000 feet were often violently thrown around, and sometimes destroyed, and tales were told of Dakota pilots exiting particularly turbulent cloud formations to find themselves flying upside down, with others entering at one altitude to come out facing an entirely different direction and at an entirely different height. Of the approximately 116 British aircraft lost between March and June 1944 during the air battle for Imphal, at least ten went down to storms. Warrant Officer Eric Forsdike of 117 Squadron RAF flew Dakota transport aircraft into the Imphal Plain during this time:

> If we could not find a way between these cumuli-nimbus clouds, developing into huge mushroom shapes, we reduced speed, sunglasses on to reduce the glare of the lightning flashes which were almost continuous, and hoped for the best. It said a lot for the design and strength of the aircraft that others and I survived, but unhappily our squadron losses were considerable: the squadron lost 143 aircrew flying operations in India and Burma.

There were some extraordinarily hair-raising experiences. On Thursday 6 April 1944, a Vengeance single-engined dive-bomber piloted by Pilot Officer Finnie was thrown into an involuntary loop: in the rear seat, finding himself upside down, and fearing that the aircraft was out of control, his colleague Pilot Officer Gabrielson pushed back the cockpit, released his seat harness and dropped out of the aircraft, parachuting safely to the ground. Finnie's aircraft in fact made it safely home, as did Gabrielson, after a six-day walk through the jungle, surviving through the kindness of Naga villagers.

For the troops on the ground, particularly in the hills and mountains, the entire period of the monsoon meant one of constant wetness and, if in the jungle or heavily-forested areas, one also of semi-permanent darkness. The rain, especially at night, came down in sheets, beating the ground, as Flight Lieutenant Wilcox of 23 Long Range Penetration Brigade described, 'like angry fists'. When not raining at this time of the year the mountains were continually shrouded in wet mists, often reducing visibility to zero. Even if one was fortunate enough to be under canvas in a rear area as Gunner Bill Johnson recalled, '... clothing, bedding, accommodation all became very damp with no chance of drying out. Food, if a fire could be kept going, tasted musty, cigarettes became soggy and tended to disintegrate, stamps and envelopes simply stuck together and footwear developed a thick mildew'.

In the low-lying areas around Imphal the immediate danger was flooding. The water table rose dramatically, flooding trenches and defensive positions. Major Henton-Wright of 19th Field Regiment recalled that the flooding was so extensive that at one track junction at Bishenpur on the edge of Logtak Lake some wag had put up a sign: 'Boats Only'. The wet weather was accompanied by a range of infirmities of which fungal infections around the crotch ('scrot rot') was the least life-threatening, unlike malaria, cholera and scrub typhus at the other end of the danger spectrum. The casualty rate for malaria in Major David Atkins' Transport Company in 1942 was 600 per cent. It was a scourge which came with the rains. Until strict anti-malaria discipline was instilled in the troops in late 1943, including the daily taking of Mepacrine tablets, it devastated the British armies. 'Malaria could strike very quickly,' noted Captain Charles Evans of the Royal Army Medical Corps: 'On 20 September [1944] I recorded that a British soldier lost consciousness at 1300 hours and was dead at 1530.' A field post-mortem a few hours later revealed that the brain was 'very much congested with blood and when we looked at sections we found it to be full of malaria parasites'. When the monsoon rains arrived in May 1943 Atkins found that his company had only ten fit men: the other ninety had fallen sick with malaria. Scrub typhus was also a devastating and indiscriminate killer. Between these extremes fell dengue fever, scabies, yaws, sprue and dysentery, which was endemic. No one was ever really free of 'the runs'. Lieutenant John Henslow, who worked on building and maintaining the mountain road between Imphal and Tamu in 1943, recalled that dysentery 'really knocked the stuffing out of you and sapped your will to live'. Cholera and dysentery were spread by flies that fed on raw sewerage, a serious problem in the plain where the water table sat only eighteen inches below the surface.

Leeches were legion and frighteningly large, lying on jungle ferns and attaching themselves to the unsuspecting men and animals brushing past, and making their way through the eyelets of boots to feast on feet until, bloodily sated, they fell off to be squashed by the movement of the marching boot. The more enterprising would make their way rapidly up the leg to gorge on the rich veins to be found under the testicles. Removing these nauseating though harmless limpets could best be achieved by applying the tip of a lighted cigarette although, as John Henslow recalled, this was never as easy as it sounded, as in pouring rain one 'could get through a week's cigarette ration and be left with a pile of sodden cigarettes for a poor return of dislodged leeches'. Pulling the leech off by force would leave the head embedded in the skin resulting in a foul-smelling blister called the 'Naga sore' which, if left untreated, could be fatal. In time the men got used to them.

~

In 1944 the Japanese, who had conquered Burma in a devastating blitzkrieg in 1942, pushing the British out in what was a profound humiliation for British arms, were nevertheless fearful of British intentions in Manipur. It was from Imphal in early 1943 that Brigadier Orde Wingate had launched his first 'Chindit' expedition into Burma, convincing some that the British were likely to try such a stunt again, but the next time in very much greater strength. This supposition was correct. The first demonstration of British offensive aspirations was a failed attempt to break into Arakan between December 1942 and May 1943 but this did not stifle British offensive plans. Indeed, the task of IV Indian Corps, based in Imphal and commanded by Lieutenant General Geoffrey Scoones, was to secure Manipur's mountain barrier against Japanese incursions and to prepare for an offensive across the Chindwin in the spring of 1944. This was intended to be a limited affair, designed to support both the insertion of a second expedition by Wingate (transported this time by air into central Burma rather than on their own legs), as well as an advance towards Myitkyina from Ledo of Stilwell's Chinese and American forces. By this time Scoones boasted 30,000 troops in three Indian infantry divisions (17th, 20th and 23rd Indian Divisions) and a tank brigade, which was the greatest number of troops that the difficult line of communication back to Dimapur could sustain. These forces were accordingly placed to prepare for an attack into Burma, not to receive one coming the other way. In the centre, based on Imphal itself, was Scoones' headquarters where, in anticipation of the forthcoming offensive, it was joined by a growing array of supply dumps, hospitals, workshops and airfields – the entire, complex paraphernalia of an army preparing to advance.

Far to the south of Imphal were positioned the two brigades (48 and 63) of the experienced and self-confident 17th Indian Division. With a total of about 7,000 soldiers it had moved to Tiddim, 164 miles south of Imphal in the Chin Hills, in November 1943. Here it continued a bitter struggle for areas of key terrain in the abrupt mountains that overlooked the Chindwin river valley to the east that had begun earlier in 1943. The division was under the able command of Major General 'Punch' Cowan, who had led it ever since the disaster of the Sittang Bridge in early 1942. Tiddim was connected to Imphal by a road which, even after many months of painful upgrading work by Cowan's troops during 1943, remained little more than a donkey track for much of its route, and which was to prove a serious problem for the division's maintenance. At the southern end of the Tiddim Road was the famous 'Chocolate Staircase', which rose 3,000 feet over seven miles on a gradient of one in twelve. During the wet season men and vehicles trampled it into ankle-deep mud and large chunks were often swept away by mud slides triggered by the monsoon.

These were all the forces available to Scoones in the south and west of Imphal. Or nearly all. Between Milestone 105 on the Tiddim Road and the Silchar Track, thirty miles to the south, a remarkable English anthropologist named Ursula Graham Bower led a widely dispersed group of V Force[1] Nagas in a 'Watch and Ward' scheme that covered over 800 square miles of jungle hills separating the Tiddim Valley from Silchar. These loyal Naga villagers, equipped initially with only their spears, but later with rifles, Bren guns and grenades, protected the hills from Japanese patrols, and warned of any enemy depredations into the hills. A woman of remarkable persistence and strength of character, Bower played a significant role in protecting the vulnerable right flank of the Imphal Plain, a huge area otherwise entirely devoid of military protection of any sort. The challenges she faced would have stumped most professional soldiers. Her 'Watch and Ward' system in North Cachar had, amongst her Zemi Nagas, 'a hundred and fifty native scouts, one service rifle, one single-barrelled shotgun, and seventy muzzle-loaders'. Nothing else protected the hill country in the vast rectangle of green matted mountains between Kohima and Imphal and the Brahmaputra Valley. When the Japanese arrived from across the Chindwin the Kuki members of V Force living in those easternmost hills betrayed their units shamelessly. Many British members, and natives loyal to the British, were hunted down and killed, their locations divulged to the Japanese for the equivalent of thirty pieces of silver. However, Ursula Graham Bower's Nagas remained loyal to a man, as did the Kukis in this region. 'After all,' one of her Naga leaders told her, 'which was the better thing? To desert and live, and hear our children curse us for the shame we put on them; or die with you, and leave them proud of us forever?'

The route from the Chindwin was guarded by Major General Douglas Gracey's 20th Indian Division (comprising 32, 80 and 100 Brigades), which was based sixty miles south-east of Imphal at Tamu. This was the route along which Lieutenant General Slim's tired but disciplined Burma Corps had retreated into India in May 1942. Twentieth Indian Division was not yet battle-tested but it was well trained and well led. Major General Douglas Gracey was highly capable and respected. The division, which had been raised in Ceylon in 1942 from British and Indian units specifically for the task of fighting the Japanese, arrived in Manipur in November 1943. Its task was both to guard the Chindwin, and to prepare to advance across it into Burma in due course. A large forward base, sufficient to supply two divisions in the advance, had been established close to the front at Moreh. Several miles square, Moreh included a hospital, light aircraft airstrip and vehicle park as well as the entire supply apparatus for the division.

The journey to Tamu from Imphal followed a metalled road for twenty-five miles to the key airfield at Palel, on the edge of the Imphal plain, after which it rose steeply to Shenam at the western edge of the 6,000-foot mountains which separate the Imphal Plain from the Kabaw Valley. Shenam was the final obstacle an invader would need to overcome in an attack on Imphal from the south-east. The position ran between Shenam Saddle and Nippon Hill three and a half miles further east. From Nippon Hill the road then ran for a further twenty-five miles to Tamu. Major John Henton-Wright travelled the route in December 1943, observing that the 'road' was so bad that the journey from Tamu to Imphal by jeep took six hours. When the monsoon rains fell landslides would often close the road for up to twenty-four hours.

Scoones' third division – ten thousand men of 23rd Indian Division (comprising 1, 37 and 49 Brigades) – had guarded Imphal since the start of the campaign in 1942. Commanded by the forty-one-year old Major General Ouvry Roberts, it was in reserve on the Imphal plain, supported by 254 Tank Brigade (equipped with American-built Stuart ('Honey' in British service) light tanks of 7th Indian Light Cavalry together with the sixty Lee Grants (also American) of 3rd Carabiniers (The Prince of Wales's Dragoon Guards). The first squadron of sixteen of these heavy tanks, armed with powerful 75mm and 37mm cannon, had been moved across India, then over the Naga Hills into Manipur in conditions of great secrecy and considerable difficulty, in October 1943.

During late-1943 and early-1944 the tempo of operations for both 17th and 20th Indian Divisions intensified. Both were tasked with continuous, intensive patrolling in order to maintain contact with the Japanese and to obtain intelligence of their moves and intentions. While neither side gained a decisive advantage in these operations they nevertheless raised the confidence of the troops. This period proved also to be an important learning experience for IV Corps, and especially for those units that had no direct experience to date of fighting the Japanese. At the time, among British and Indian troops (but less so the Gurkhas) Japanese soldiers had a fearsome and well-deserved reputation. They were hardy, aggressive, and, after two years of repeated success against the British, triumphant, even arrogant. Major 'Nobby' Clarke of 19 Battery, 25th Mountain Regiment, voiced a common nervousness among British soldiers being sent to fight the Japanese for the first time:

> The thought of the jungle and the Japs was a disturbing one and most British and Indian troops hoped they would be sent to the Eighth Army and not to Burma. Practically all our Indian troops had been in contact with survivors from one or other of the earlier Burma disasters, and had heard in the most lurid detail of the invincibility and savagery of the Japs. The tales of the shocking Jap atrocities put out as official propaganda did not make anyone feel particularly comfortable either, for being a living target for bayonet practice was a gruesome thought.

The Japanese certainly fought very differently from the Italians and Germans, as Clarke discovered. They used fear itself as a weapon. Observing for his mountain guns one day in early 1944, he watched four Japanese soldiers drag the dead bodies of fifteen British soldiers onto a path in the jungle, forward of positions held by the 1st Battalion, Queen's Royal Regiment in Arakan. That night plaintive cries came from the area of the bodies: 'Tommy! Tommy! Come and help me!' Forewarned by Clarke of the trap that had been set for them, the waiting Queensmen remained quietly in their slit trenches, scanning the darkness for hostile movement and refusing the bait that on previous occasions would have had troops going out to rescue their 'comrades', only to find themselves encountering the silent thrust of a Japanese bayonet. Rigorous fire discipline was required to ensure that unseasoned troops did not fire into the jungle at the slightest provocation, as this simply pinpointed their positions for Japanese counter-action, exacerbating nervousness and fear.

By 1944 British and Indian forces in eastern India had been strenuously retrained and prepared to withstand the extraordinary physical and mental demands required of men fighting the Japanese. Lieutenant General Bill Slim – who had taken command of the newly-formed Fourteenth Army in August 1943 – was convinced that he could transform the fortunes of his troops, despite the many gainsayers who loudly claimed the Japanese to be unbeatable. His basic prescription – in which he was supported wholeheartedly by a new raft of divisional commanders – was rigorous and realistic training for all troops. Training in simulated battlefield conditions would enable soldiers to cope with the demands of fighting a tenacious enemy in the harsh physical environment of both mountain and jungle. He was certain that if men were adequately prepared to overcome these challenges, if they were helped to do so by better medical care (especially to prevent the mass casualties caused in 1942 and 1943 by malaria) and if the lines of communication that supplied troops in forward areas with food, fuel and ammunition were made more secure – by using air supply rather than relying on tracks and roads – morale would improve, and with it the troops' certainty that they could defeat the Japanese in battle. To focus training on the right things, Slim drafted a set of principles for jungle fighting distilled from his experiences fighting in 1942 and 1943:

1. The individual soldier must learn, by living, moving and exercising in it, that the jungle is neither impenetrable nor unfriendly. When he has once learned to move and live in it, he can use it for concealment, covered movement, and surprise.

2. Patrolling is the master key to jungle fighting. All units, not only infantry battalions, must learn to patrol in the jungle, boldly, widely, cunningly and offensively.

3. All units must get used to having Japanese parties in their rear, and, when this happens, regard not themselves, but the Japanese, as 'surrounded'.

4. In defence, no attempt should be made to hold long continuous lines. Avenues of approach must be covered and enemy penetration between our posts dealt with at once by mobile local reserves who have completely reconnoitred the country.

5. There should rarely be frontal attacks and never frontal attacks on narrow fronts. Attacks should follow hooks and come in from flank or rear, while pressure holds the enemy in front.

6. Tanks can be used in almost any country except swamp. In close country they must always have infantry with them to defend and reconnoitre for them. They should always be used in the maximum numbers available and capable of being deployed. Whenever possible penny [small] packets must be avoided. 'The more you use, the fewer you lose.'

7. There are no non-combatants in jungle warfare. Every unit and sub-unit, including medical ones, is responsible for its own all-round protection, including patrolling, at all times.

8. If the Japanese are allowed to hold the initiative they are formidable. When we have it, they are confused and easy to kill. By mobility away from roads, surprise, and offensive action, we must regain and keep the initiative.

Despite the demands posed by the torrential monsoon rains between May and October physical toughening, weapon training and long cross-country marches – on foot and with mules – carried out over hills, through jungle and across rivers became the order of the day. Live firing with rifles, machine guns and grenades in realistic conditions – often at the end of exhausting marches over huge distances in day and night, and through the dank, sun-parched jungle – was practised constantly. Exercises ranged from patrol actions by sections and platoons, ambushes up to company level, to battalion attacks coordinated with artillery and aircraft. Training was hard and embraced every soldier in every type of unit, including men who in earlier times in the Indian Army would have been regarded as non-combatants. Now, no one was excluded. 'We went through intensive training in jungle warfare,' recalled Jawan Gian Singh, a sepoy in the 1/11th Sikhs:

> Every day we were on manoeuvres of some kind or another. There were patrols day and night, ambushes, water crossings and forced marches. The methods used by the Japanese were by now well-known. We had to outdo them at their own game – road blocks, flank attacks, etc. At the end of the year [we were] fit to meet the Japanese. We had been hard at manoeuvres for weeks.

As Singh acknowledged, robust and realistic training was essential if under the strain of battle exhausted soldiers were to be able to conquer their fear, think clearly and shoot straight in a crisis and inspire maximum physical and mental endeavour. They needed to overcome the tremendous psychological demands entailed in fighting the Japanese who, as a matter of course, ruthlessly exploited mistakes caused by either inexperience or complacency. The Japanese approach to fighting was routinely brutal, shockingly so for green British and Indian troops. In Arakan in early 1944 Gunner Sam Parker of 24th Light Anti-Aircraft/Anti-Tank Regiment looked in horror at the discovery of 'the bodies of some Indian soldiers, a British soldier and two Burmese girls, all of whom had been tied up and used for bayonet practice'. The Japanese believed that this sort of savagery would unsettle their enemy as it had done in the previous two years. Now, however, it was beginning to have the opposite effect, instilling in the troops an implacable hatred of their enemy, many becoming determined on bloody retribution in which no quarter was allowed in any circumstance. The language that the men now began to use was akin to that of exterminating dangerous vermin. Soldiers of 4/14th Punjab came across a Japanese ambush party carrying, of all things, the decapitated body of a Sikh soldier. The discovery induced a shock of rage that led to a furious charge in which every single enemy soldier fell to an Indian bayonet. The 1/11th Sikhs, likewise, discovered the crucified and beheaded bodies of one of their comrades alongside that of a British officer. The vehemence of their hatred for those who had done this guaranteed the absolute annihilation of any Japanese soldiers caught at a disadvantage in the fighting that ensued. Captain Tony Irwin of V Force observed the change of attitude in both British and Indian soldiers following a massacre of hospital patients in Arakan on 7 February. The survivors of the massacre, 'though until the previous day young in war, were now hardened warriors, loathing their enemy before they regretted their friends'.

Had this happened two years before it would have frightened everyone. Now it just made me [as] angry as it was possible for an Englishman to be angry. For now we knew what to give as we knew what to expect.

~

As I stood on the tarmac of what had long ago been Tulihal Airfield, surrounded by the imposing majesty of the green-hued mountains and enveloped in the sticky, pre-monsoon heat, my mind went back sixty-six years to the month, when a widely-separated British and Indian Corps faced the rapidly-approaching forces of the proud, unbeaten Japanese Fifteenth Army. In Arakan, only a month before, the British XV Corps (5th and 7th Indian Divisions) had successfully beaten back an attempt by the Japanese to break through to Chittagong. It now remained to be seen whether this reverse for the Japanese, their first against the British in Asia, was a one-off, or whether the investment that had been made in preparing Fourteenth Army for war would pay its hoped-for and long-awaited dividend. India waited with bated breath the outcome of a struggle that could decide the fate of the empire.

# Chapter 1

# The Offensive Begins

On 27 January 1944 Lieutenant Colonel Geoffrey Mizen, Commanding Officer of 9/12th Frontier Force Regiment (FFR), led a patrol across the Chindwin to investigate rumours that a build-up of Japanese was taking place along the opposite (east) bank. Four weeks earlier, RAF pilots flying low along the river had spotted what they believed to be pontoons hidden along the bank. The patrol crossed the river at night in local dugouts, landing in the dark opposite the village of Settaw. Creeping quietly across country in the moonlight, an ambush was laid on a track leading into the village from the east. At about 10 o'clock the following morning, two Japanese soldiers were observed wandering unconcernedly into the village chatting loudly to each other. They were immediately cut down in a hail of rifle fire. The lax Japanese field discipline came as a surprise to Mizen's hardened Sikhs, and suggested to them that the Japanese were new to the area. The village was now astir, so the patrol made its way back to the British side of the Chindwin, having first harvested a crop of documents from the crumpled bodies. The Sikhs were right: the Japanese were from the newly arrived 15th Division. Other patrols at the time were making similar discoveries, and building up a picture of rapid and sustained Japanese reinforcement, with 15th, 31st and 33rd Divisions – the fighting elements of Lieutenant General Mutaguchi Renya's Fifteenth Army – appearing on the Chindwin's eastern bank. Some weeks later a patrol of the 2nd Battalion, Border Regiment, operating twenty miles south of Tamu, came across a Japanese car parked on the side of a track, its occupants assiduously studying a map, with other soldiers resting by the side of the road. Corporal George, the patrol commander, immediately ran forward with his Sten gun blazing, killing all the Japanese before they could react. Inside the vehicle was a treasure trove of maps and operational plans detailing forthcoming operations up the Kabaw Valley.

This concerted patrol activity by men of Gracey's 20th Indian Division to the south-east of Imphal along the Chindwin River and Cowan's 17th

Indian Division far to the south along the Manipur River, together with aerial reconnaissance over the tracks and villages across the entire border region, proved beyond all doubt by the end of January 1944 that the Japanese had offensive aspirations against India. The work of V Force agents along the Chindwin, together with secret signal intelligence garnered by careful listening to Japanese radio traffic, also pointed unerringly towards this certainty. Indeed, by the end of January a glut of various sources had made it clear to Lieutenant General Slim that his defences in Manipur faced attack by the whole of Fifteenth Army. Loose-tongued Japanese soldiers had boasted to villagers at Mualbem, south of Tiddim on the Manipur River as early as 8 January that a strong Japanese and 'Indian' army would soon be invading India. *Ultra* signals intelligence allowed him even to put a date on the start of the offensive: 15 March 1944. It was also clear that the Japanese attack would be conducted in great strength with at least the three divisions his forward reconnaissance had identified, as well as a division of the renegade Indian National Army (INA), together with a regiment of tanks. What the British High Command did not know in any detail were Mutaguchi's precise intentions. Slim assumed that the Japanese, at the very least, would attempt to isolate and destroy his three frontline divisions in Manipur (17th, 20th and 23rd Indian Divisions, part of Lieutenant General Geoffrey Scoones' IV Corps) and cut the Imphal-Dimapur road at Kohima to prevent reinforcements reaching Imphal, before striking against the strategic British base at Dimapur as the first stage in a deeper penetration of India.

~

That the Japanese were contemplating an offensive against India in early-1944 was a surprise to Allied planners, who had given no thought to its possibility. It was, after all, counter-intuitive. By this time Japan had reached the apogee of its power, having extended the violent reach of its Empire across much of Asia since it launched its first surprise attacks in late 1941. Its initial surge in 1942 into what was briefly to be Japan's 'Greater East Asia Co-Prosperity Sphere' was as dramatic as it was rapid and two years further on several millions of peoples across Asia laboured under its heavy yoke. But, by early-1944, the tide had turned decisively in the Pacific, the American island-hopping advance reaching steadily but surely towards Japan itself, its humiliated enemies fighting back with desperation, and with every ounce of energy they could muster. They were beginning to prevail in the fight although the struggle on the landmass of

Asia was a strategic sideshow in the context of a global conflict: at this time the British and American High Commands were totally occupied with Europe and the Pacific. The British and Americans were preparing for D-Day. The Soviets were advancing in Ukraine. There was a stalemate in Italy along the Gustav Line. The Americans were preparing to land in the Philippines. Germany and Japan were both in retreat, but not defeated. In this global context India and Burma were strategically peripheral, even inconsequential. Yet in this month, at a time when on every other front the Japanese were on the strategic defensive, Japan launched a vast, audacious offensive deep into India in an attack designed to destroy forever Britain's ability to challenge Japan's hegemony in Burma.

The argument for the invasion of India had been presented and won by the dynamic and forceful commander of *Fifteenth Army*, garrisoning northern Burma, Lieutenant General Mutaguchi Renya, who had made his name commanding *18th Division* in the capture of Singapore in February 1942. During 1943 the idea of advancing into India itself began to take shape although a plan to do this by advancing north through the Hukawng Valley (the source of the Chindwin) and then falling on Assam down the Brahmaputra Valley from Ledo – Operation 21 – was rejected at the time as impracticable. North-eastern India (the provinces of Assam and Manipur) was important to the Allies as the American base for the provision of supplies to Nationalist Chinese forces via airlift operations over 'The Hump' (the mountainous region between India, Burma and China) and because it provided the point of departure for any British land offensive into Burma. Indeed, the limited offensive by 3,000 men of Wingate's 'Chindits' in early 1943 had, for three months, caused a nuisance to the Japanese by attacking roads and railway lines, worrying the Japanese that further and more substantial operations might follow to threaten their hegemony in Burma.

In late-1943 the Japanese command in Burma was reorganized, and a new headquarters, Burma Area Army, was created under the command of Lieutenant General Kawabe Masakasu, which included Mutaguchi's *Fifteenth Army*. Initially a strong opponent of Operation 21, he became persuaded of the need to launch an offensive into India. Throughout the latter half of 1943 he lobbied shamelessly across the Burma Area Army for permission to do so. He argued that, at the very least, the occupation of Imphal would prevent the British attempting to launch their own offensive into Burma. In this he was supported from an unlikely source. Following the collapse of British resistance in Malaya and Singapore in 1942 large numbers of Indian soldiers had fallen into Japanese hands, 16,000 being persuaded by a concerted Japanese campaign to change allegiance, eventually forming the Indian National Army. The political leader of this movement – the exiled Bengali nationalist, Subhas Chandra Bose – argued that with the INA in the vanguard of an offensive into India it might even topple the Raj, setting off an unstoppable conflagration of anti-British sentiment among the native population. Mutaguchi eagerly grasped such ideas as further justification for an offensive. After the war he also claimed that he advocated 'the invasion of India' in order to boost Japanese morale at a time when Japan was suffering repeated defeats in the Pacific.

So it was that in March 1944, when on every other front the Japanese were on the strategic defensive, Japan launched an offensive (code named Operation C) deep into India. Mutaguchi had got his way, persuading Kawabe in turn to request permission from Field Marshal Count Terauchi, Commander of the Southern Army in Saigon and ultimately Prime Minister Tōjō in Tokyo for the offensive, comprising the entire 115,000-strong Fifteenth Army. Kawabe gave detailed orders in turn to Mutaguchi on 19 January 1944. The commander of Fifteenth Army was instructed to mount a strong pre-emptive strike against Imphal before the onset of the monsoon in May. To help, a strong diversionary attack was planned for Arakan (Operation Z) a month before. If Lieutenant General Slim was deceived into thinking that this was the focus of an offensive against India, and moved his strategic reserves to deal with it, Operation Z would have done its duty, allowing Mutaguchi the best possible odds in Manipur. At the same time aggressive Japanese operations in the Hukawng Valley would also prevent interference in Operation C by Stilwell's Chinese.

Mutaguchi's evaluation of the British position in north-east India revealed that the three key strategic targets in Assam were Imphal, the mountain town of Kohima, and the huge supply base at Dimapur. If Kohima were captured, Imphal would be cut off from the rest of India by land. From the outset Mutaguchi believed that with a good wind Dimapur, in addition to Kohima, could and should be secured. He reasoned that capturing this massive depot would be a devastating, possibly terminal, blow to the British ability to defend Imphal, supply Stilwell, and mount an offensive into Burma. It would also enable him to feed his own, conquering, army, which would advance across the mountains from the Chindwin on the tightest imaginable supply chain. With Dimapur captured, Bose and his Indian National Army could pour into Bengal, initiating the long-awaited anti-British uprising.

~

The prospect of a Japanese invasion of India placed the British in a quandary. In the first place Slim had been preparing slowly for his own limited offensive into Burma in 1944. Huge efforts had been made during 1943 to improve the rate at which supplies could be transported into Imphal, and then across the hills close to the Chindwin at Tamu, as well as south to Tiddim. The greatest difficulty with trying to conduct such an offensive was the huge logistical challenges provided by the fact that there were only two ways into Manipur from India: the first was by air, the second by means of the single road that ran the 168 miles across the Naga Hills from Dimapur. The annual monsoon washed much of this road, with frustrating regularity, down the hillside. In order to prepare for a two-division offensive by Scoones' IV Corps, a massive upgrading of this road was required, as its peacetime capacity was a mere 600 tons per day. Enormous effort had by November 1943 increased this capacity to 3,070 tons allowing, by early 1944, for the vast dump of stores to be collected at Moreh, ready for a crossing of the Chindwin.

The second difficulty was the fact that, in February, Slim's reserves – as the Japanese had hoped – had been sent to the Arakan coast to shore up British defences against the prospect of a Japanese offensive towards Chittagong. It would take time to reverse these plans, especially as the only means for so doing was either by sea or road to Chittagong. The lack of a land link covering the 400 miles between Arakan and Manipur meant that troops had to be laboriously transported by road and rail back through Chittagong and thence into Manipur through Dimapur. This threat was at the forefront of Slim's mind during February 1944 when Operation Z was launched. The British, however, benefiting from far superior firepower, training and morale were able to withstand this attack which, for several desperate weeks, centred on the divisional administration box for 7th Indian Division, the 'Admin Box' at Sinzweya. With the relief of the 'Admin Box' he wasted no time in ordering Major General Harold Brigg's 5th Indian Division to make its way to Imphal during the period between 13 March and 14 April and for Major General Frank Messervy's 7th Indian Division to be withdrawn from Arakan and placed in Army reserve.

The third difficulty was the question of how to defeat the Japanese offensive when it was launched. This was not a simple proposition as, until the demise of Operation Z in Arakan in late-February 1944, the Japanese had remained unbeaten in battle against the British in south-east Asia. The plan Slim determined upon was one that he hoped would play to British strengths and exploit Japanese weaknesses. Clustered in the hills that surrounded the Imphal Plain, he planned to entice Mutaguchi's Fifteenth

Army into a major battle in India in circumstances favourable to the British. It was nevertheless hugely risky. It was clear to both Slim and Lieutenant General Geoffrey Scoones, commander of IV Corps in Assam, that the two forward divisions ('Punch' Cowan's 17th Indian, south of Imphal at Tiddim, and Douglas Gracey's 20th Indian, south-east at Tamu), unable by dint of geography to provide each other with mutual support, would be easy prey to Japanese encirclement and defeat if they remained in their current locations. Nor would it be possible for them to withdraw into defensive boxes in these forward locations to be sustained by air, as was the case in Arakan, because the Allies simply did not possess at the time the number of aircraft required for such an enormous undertaking. Most of the transport aircraft in South East Asia Command were committed to supporting the 'Hump' airlift.

So, instead of keeping his forces forward and investing in a strong defensive barrier along the Chindwin to the east and south, Slim decided that he would instead withdraw his troops and concentrate them on the hilly outskirts of the Imphal Plain itself. The Japanese would be encouraged to advance deep into Manipur, while the two forward Indian divisions would withdraw from the advanced positions they had been consolidating since late-1943. These two divisions would then occupy positions around the periphery of the Imphal plain where, supported by Major General Ouvry Roberts' 23rd Indian Division (the Corps Reserve), they would hold fast against the Japanese attack. Key points, including Imphal town itself and the six airfields on the plain would be transformed into defensive bastions capable of defending themselves unaided for at least ten days. Allowing them to advance directly onto Imphal would stretch the Japanese supply lines through more than 100 miles of jungle-clad hills from the Chindwin. By contrast, IV Corps would, by withdrawing, enjoy vastly reduced lines of communication and benefit from concentration. 'I was tired of fighting the Japanese when they had a good line of communications behind them and I had an exorable one,' Slim reasoned in 1944. 'This time I would reverse the procedure.'

It would then be possible for the British to take advantage of their growing strength in aircraft, armour and artillery while simultaneously exploiting the enemy's weaknesses in logistics and resupply, problems that would be compounded by the onset of the monsoon at the end of April. However, in attempting such a manoeuvre, Slim risked undermining the still delicate morale of his army. Not only were withdrawals difficult to manage but failure would have a deleterious effect on the morale of his troops, which he and his commanders had built up so painstakingly over the previous months after the disasters of 1942 and 1943, when the exultant Japanese had pushed the British out of Burma and had repelled the advance in Arakan. A withdrawal would also have a correspondingly negative effect politically on friends and Allies. He knew well from his own experience that there was no guarantee that IV Corps would be able successfully to withdraw at the required moment, particularly if the withdrawal was conducted in contact with the enemy. There was no guarantee either that the defences of the Imphal Plain would be sufficient to defeat every attempt by the enemy to break in, or that he could reinforce IV Corps quickly when required. If the Imphal defences were strong enough and if Slim could maintain a steady flow of reinforcements and supplies by some means, the Japanese would merely exhaust their strength in ultimately fruitless attempts to overwhelm the defenders. These were big 'ifs'. To be successful, Slim's plan would require careful planning, a finely-honed assessment of his own troops' capabilities and the ability to juggle limited resources between competing priorities at a moment's notice. What was certain was that the battle would be a long, bloody confrontation where the victor would require perseverance, as well as considerable reserves of both moral and material strength.

There were some indeed, who opposed Slim's plans. It was altogether too sensitive a concept for many at the time. 'I was not surprised,' Slim wrote, 'to find it hard to convince many, especially highly placed civil officials, that it was possible to fight defensively and even to retreat, yet keep the initiative.' By withdrawing he lay open to the charge that he had lost his nerve and lacked the courage to stand and fight the Japanese. Rather than suffer the indignity of retreat, Slim was encouraged by some not to withdraw but to anticipate the enemy by launching his own pre-emptive attack across the Chindwin. Such suggestions were quickly dismissed. 'Had I accepted their advice,' Slim recalled, 'the enemy could easily have concentrated, along good communications, a force greatly in excess of any we could maintain east of the Chindwin. We should have fought superior numbers with the dangerous crossing of a great river behind us and with our communications running back through a hundred and twenty miles of the worst country imaginable.' 'I noted,' remarked Slim rather caustically, 'that the further back these generals came from, the keener they were on my 'flinging' divisions across the Chindwin.' 'It was not ground that mattered,' he argued consistently during 1944, 'but the opportunity to engage, on ground of his own choosing, the might of the Fifteenth Army. 'That done,' he argued, 'territory could easily be reoccupied.'

One factor that worked strongly in Slim's favour was his opposite number's impetuous, emotional and egotistical character. Pulling back from their forward positions to the Imphal plain would be precisely what Mutaguchi expected of the weak and timid British and would reinforce Japanese expectations of an early and easy victory. The Japanese assumed that the British would have no stomach for a fight and would crumble quickly under pressure. The gamble that Slim took, of course, was that his troops would not break and that, once concentrated on the Imphal Plain, with a clear superiority in armour, artillery and air power, IV Corps would prove to be too hard a nut for Mutaguchi to crack. His three divisions would be closely concentrated so they could support each other if necessary. Although he fully expected Mutaguchi to cut the road from Imphal to Dimapur in the area of Kohima, Slim had another card up his sleeve to counter any lack of supply by land, one that had so dramatically helped to bring victory to Messervy's cut-off division in Arakan: air supply.

So far, so good. But the British made a series of misjudgements about Japanese plans. Mutaguchi, for all his personal idiosyncrasies, could not be described as a conventional strategist, and he developed an offensive plan that correctly calculated British defensive moves, and worked around them. Mutaguchi's plan was daring, inventive and aggressive. He intended to seize Imphal by a combination of guile and extreme physical endurance, seeking to achieve the same advantages that *Kirimomi Sakusen* (driving charge) had brought Japanese commanders in their encounters with the British Army in Malaya, Singapore and Burma in 1942. Not unreasonably, Lieutenant General Geoffrey Scoones assumed that the Japanese would attack along the two major routes that led into the plain, the first leading north from Tiddim and the second leading through Tamu from the south-east. He thought that a regiment (three battalions, or no more than 3,000 or 4,000 men) would be tasked with closing the road at Kohima. So he decided that at the first sign of the Japanese offensive Punch Cowan's 17th Indian Division would withdraw unmolested from Tiddim to Imphal, leaving a single brigade to guard the back door at Bishenpur. The second brigade would join 23rd Indian Division and 254 Tank Brigade to form a powerful reserve inside the Imphal Plain itself, able rapidly to counter-attack any ingress as it occurred. In the south-east Douglas Gracey's 20th Indian Division would withdraw to hold positions between Moreh and the Shenam Pass, against which it was expected that the greatest weight of the Japanese offensive would fall, as it provided the fastest route into the plain. The vast swathes of jungle-covered hills that rise protectively from the basin floor to encompass the plain in every direction appeared themselves to deny any invader easy access to Imphal. As he did not have the troops available to guard every stretch of his enormous front, Scoones considered that it was better to place the major part of his forces on these routes while reserving sufficient forces on hand to counter-attack Japanese breakthroughs wherever they appeared. This was a better alternative, he decided, than attempting to defend every part of a huge sector and thus being weak everywhere, leaving only a limited reserve available to deal with crises as and when they arose. Accordingly, huge stretches of territory, much of it apparently impenetrable jungle or impossible hill country, were deprived of real defences. As a result the eighty miles or so of rugged country between Litan and Kohima through the Naga village of Ukhrul came to be defended by only a few weak battalions.

Mutaguchi knew that Scoones would attempt to hold Tiddim and Tamu in strength and decided, therefore, to appear to attack through these areas, while in fact reserving his most dangerous attack to a direction that the British would never expect. His plan entailed three simultaneous thrusts deep into Manipur. In the first place, in the south, the two regiments of Lieutenant General Yanagida Motozo's 33rd (White Tiger) Division were to attack Punch Cowan's 17th (Black Cat) Indian Division at Tiddim and cut the recently-extended dirt track that led up the Manipur River valley north to Imphal. While the main part of 17th Indian Division was to be attacked, 214th Regiment would cut the road behind them at Tongzang, and a further regiment (215th) would bypass the road to the west and cut it at Milestone 100, cutting off the Black Cats from their escape route north. In his vision of victory Mutaguchi had it that, after destroying Cowan, Yanagida would take his victorious division north, along the Tiddim Road and into the now unprotected underbelly of the Imphal Plain. For Mutaguchi this victory would be sweet: the Black Cats had fought the Japanese to a standstill in the mountainous terrain forward of Tiddim in the months since May 1943 and had proven themselves a serious irritant to the Japanese plan of dominating the Chin Hills.

The date set for the start of this advance was in fact 7 March, not the 15th as the British had assumed. Mutaguchi's hope was that this early threat to his southern flank would force the British to send reserves down the Tiddim Road from Imphal, thus denuding their defences elsewhere on the Imphal Plain. The second move, a week later, entailed a strong force of tanks, artillery and infantry from 33rd Division (reinforced by two battalions from 15th Division), under the command of Major General Yamamoto (33rd Division's infantry commander[2]), which was to strike against Douglas Gracey's 20th Indian Division, spread out along the border with Burma in the southern Kabaw Valley. The centre of gravity of Gracey's division was formed by the villages of Witok and Tamu, the latter of which boasted a forward fighter strip. This attack was to be launched on the night of 15 March. Its immediate objective was the Shenam Saddle, the high point in the mountains south-east of the Imphal Plain through which the road from Palel rose and threaded its way down towards Tamu, and from where, at its highest point, Imphal itself could be observed.

These moves would conform to British expectations and, in so doing, Mutaguchi correctly assumed that Scoones would then commit his reserves to his Tiddim and south-eastern sectors as a result. But cunningly, just as Scoones struggled to address the problems in the very two areas where he had always expected an attack to fall, Mutaguchi planned to launch his two most powerful attacks in the east and north. This would take the British by surprise, and at a time when their reserve had been allocated to other threatened areas. Further north along the Chindwin, Lieutenant General Yamauchi Masafumi was to take his 15th Division by raft and pontoon and advance across the mountains of the Somra Tracts to attack Imphal from the north. The division's line of advance was to take them through the village of Humine on the Burmese border and then along tracks and paths to Sangshak, before heading due west, crossing the road to Kohima and falling on Imphal from the north. Still further north, and directed against the mountaintop town of Kohima, the entire 31st Division (three regiments) under Lieutenant General Sato – about 20,000 fighting men – would cross the Chindwin between Homalin and Tamanthi, heading north-west. In the southern prong of this advance, 138th Regiment would make for Ukhrul, cutting the Imphal-Kohima road at Maram: in the middle, 58th Regiment would make for Somra and then Jessami before moving the final thirty miles west to Kohima: and in the far north 124th Regiment would cover the northern flank in the Naga Hills. This triple pincer was calculated to cut Imphal from its external sources of supply and place intolerable demands on Lieutenant General Scoones. Mutaguchi hoped that in facing multiple threats on all but the western side of the compass, Scoones would be unable to cope with the desperate and disparate calls for his limited reserves to fill the inevitable gaps that the Japanese attack would force in his defences. To be successful, Mutaguchi needed to ensure that his troops captured Imphal before the monsoon rains fell and transformed the jungle tracks his men would use into impassable quagmires. He also needed to do it quickly, as the supplies he could promise his three divisional commanders were meagre indeed. The date Mutaguchi set himself for victory at Imphal was 10 April. This would give him plenty of time to achieve victory before the Emperor's birthday on 29 April.

But Imphal and Kohima were not in themselves his ultimate objective. The trap he laid for Generals Slim and Scoones was to make them believe that the main attack was to be placed against Imphal, whereas in fact Mutaguchi's strategic eye lay on Kohima as a route through to Dimapur. If he could capture Dimapur then Imphal would rapidly wither on the vine. The railway to Stilwell's base at Ledo in the north would also be cut, threatening the continuance of American supplies to the Chinese and American forces that threatened Japanese-held Burma from the north. It was a bold plan, and relied on the acceptance of considerable logistical risk, the absolute commitment by his three divisional commanders and of the need, above all else, for speed. So confident was Mutaguchi of capturing Imphal within a month that he ordered his units to carry with them no more than twenty days' supply of supplies, although Sato's division, in the north, took with them 5,000 head of cattle, giving them the equivalent of fifty-nine days of supply. The plan was a disaster, as surviving veterans were to attest. Cattle hated crossing rivers. Private Zenta Makioka described having to persuade them into the water. 'The soldiers got in the boat first then put two animals on the sides. We'd all hold onto the reins and slap their backsides hard to force them into the river. They had no option but to go forward so they'd start pulling the boat. But after a while some would shudder and go wild. When they did that we got turned round and went down with the current, so we'd let go of the rein. Then quickly, down the cattle went, fully loaded. There was nothing we could do.' On the march, the cattle were equally reluctant, forcing the frustrated soldiers to a range of techniques to persuade them to keep moving. For Private Nobuyuki Hata desperation meant that 'We'd set their backsides on fire. They would stand up but once they had gone down they were hopeless. Next we'd tie up their tail and twist it hard, like this, then it would make a snapping sound, and that'd hurt and they'd try to move again only to find it impossible. They couldn't carry anything. Two of us would try, pulling and pushing, but if it's no good, it's no good. They were useless if they couldn't carry anything on their backs. No one was bothered much, though. We couldn't stay there forever. We had to get to the front. We had a job to do.'

Such impediments did little to put Mutaguchi off from his grand design. In an effort to imbue his troops with offensive passion he issued a proclamation on 18 February 1944:

The Army has now reached the stage of invincibility and the day when the Rising Sun shall proclaim our victory in India is not far off.

This operation will engage the attention of the whole world and is eagerly awaited by 100,000,000 of our countrymen. By its very decisive nature, its success will have a profound effect upon the course of the war and may even lead to its conclusion ...

When we strike we must be absolutely ready, reaching our objectives with the speed of wildfire ... we must sweep aside the paltry opposition we encounter and add lustre to the army's tradition of achieving a victory of annihilation.

Not to be outdone Bose, on the same day, encouraged the men of the INA on to 'Liberty or Death!', urging them while so doing to have the slogan 'Chalo Delhi' ('Onward to Delhi') on their lips. On 7 March 1944 Tokyo Radio announced to the world that 'The March on Delhi has begun. Our victorious troops will be in Imphal by 27 March.'

~

The march of Japanese boots accompanied the dulcet tones of 'Tokyo Rose' as Colonel Sakuma's 214th Regiment began to cross the hills from Yazagyo on the Chindwin to cut the all-important road between Imphal and Tiddim where it crossed the Manipur River at Tongzang. The following day the three battalions of Colonel Sasahara's 215th Regiment crossed the Manipur River twelve miles below Tiddim and began moving upstream on the west bank, tasked with capturing the stores depot at Milestone 109 and placing a block at Milestone 100, moves that would complete the outflanking of Cowan's division. Yanagida hoped that he might be able to cut the road to Tiddim before the British knew what was happening but, in the event, Punch Cowan's patrols quickly reported back the fact that strong Japanese forces appeared to be trying to outflank the division's forward positions in the hills around Tiddim. On the night of 8 March Japanese probing attacks were made on British patrol positions in the hills to the east of the Tiddim Road above Tongzang, positioned there by Cowan to keep an eye on any Japanese attempt to block the road. On the same day, Cowan told Scoones that an offensive was imminent and, expecting an order to return north, began carefully to prepare the withdrawal of his two brigades. This was no easy task, as many of his troops occupied positions in the hills high above Tiddim to the east. Engineers demolished bridges over the Manipur river and prepared the destruction of parts of the precipitous mountain road they had spent many months labouring to construct. Stores, equipment and casualties were sent back to Imphal.

But as each day passed no orders were received from Imphal to pull back. Cowan became increasingly nervous about this silence. From his experience of 1942 he was only too aware that the Japanese tactic would be to cut his line of retreat. Once surrounded, his units would then fall prey to a slow defeat in detail. He needed no convincing that he had to make all speed back to the Imphal plain before his exposed division was entirely isolated. On 13 March Cowan accelerated plans to withdraw so that when the order came, and it now seemed that it would only arrive at the very last minute, he would be in a position to respond immediately. In fact, the code word 'Moccasin', instructing Cowan to disengage from Tiddim and to begin the long trek north to Imphal, came at the end of that day through a telephone call from the Corps Commander. 'Good luck, Punch,' added Scoones.

Scoones, convinced that Mutaguchi would not move until the 15th at the earliest, had discounted Cowan's intelligence and delayed giving him the order to withdraw. Now, however, Scoones worked quickly to undo the harm he had created by ignoring Cowan for so long. He ordered the Corps machine-gun battalion (9th Jats) to make all haste down the Tiddim Road from Imphal to Milestone 122, a bottleneck on the road where, just short of Tongzang, it crossed the Manipur River over a Bailey bridge. At the same time Major General Ouvry Roberts, commanding 23rd Indian Division in Imphal, noting with alarm the events at Tiddim, ordered Brigadier Vivian Collingridge's 37 Brigade (3/3rd, 3/5th and 3/10th Gurkha Rifles) to deploy to assist Cowan, clearly suggesting that he thought Scoones was acting too slowly. A day later, Scoones ordered the remainder of his infantry reserve, 49 Brigade, to the Tiddim road as well.

With Cowan's 17th Indian Division about to be embroiled in a fight for its life as it tried to withdraw up the road from Tiddim chased hard by the Japanese, the road itself likely to be blocked at several points, and with a major part of his Corps reserve assisting the extraction of Cowan's troops, Scoones' cupboard was suddenly bare. There existed an urgent imperative for reinforcements to be moved into Imphal at short notice to replace those now moving to positions on the Tiddim road. How was this to be done? Fifth Indian Division was not scheduled to arrive in Imphal from Arakan until mid-April, which would be far too late to alleviate the current crisis. Suddenly, for the British, the situation could not have been worse.

~

From the outset Cowan's withdrawal was a model of discipline and cool planning, despite the desperate lateness of the withdrawal and the fact that

17th Indian Division would now be forced to fight its way out of the trap Mutaguchi was setting for it. Surplus equipment was carefully destroyed, and on the 13th, as 63 Brigade began to march the twenty miles from Tiddim to Tongzang, 48 Brigade guarded the rear, and set extensive booby-traps across the divisional area to catch Japanese troops who might attempt to follow up too hastily. At 7.15 p.m. on 14 March Captain Hume and the Commando Company of 2/5th Royal Gurkha Rifles blew up part of the road to Kalewa, making what was originally a difficult rocky traverse now impossible for vehicles. A large number of anti-tank mines was also distributed liberally along tracks and paths. In Tiddim itself, Major Walker and Captain Eric Yarrow of the Madras Sappers and Miners destroyed the division's fourteen-day reserve of rations and stores, before beginning their own long walk north. Yarrow wrote to his parents:

> I had my work cut out to get everything prepared for demolition in time. Our last troops passed through Tiddim shortly after midnight on 13 March. For the rest of the night, five of us stayed behind and set the place ablaze and blew up what machinery was left. When I left Tiddim the whole area was a mass of flames and smoke. The Japs were still shelling the road further south – a good indication that they hadn't much idea of what was going on.

Instructions had been given that the troops were to carry with them only a day's rations: transport aircraft from Air Commodore Vincent's No. 221 Group RAF would provide for all their needs as they withdrew. Few believed this, however, given their experience of the withdrawal from Burma two years before, although in the end the vast majority obeyed their orders and piled what they could not carry in great heaps to be destroyed. Well before Cowan had given the orders to march, however, twenty miles north at Tongzang the forward elements of 214th Regiment, accompanied by a company of the INA, had begun isolating and attacking the few British platoon positions that lay atop the hills east of the river to give early warning of a Japanese probe from the Chindwin. The approach march from Yazagyo – some ten miles away to the east over the mountains – was, for the heavily-laden Japanese of Major Saito's 1/214th Regiment, exhausting. On the 10th the first British position fell, but only after bitter fighting in which the Japanese brought up mountain artillery guns which they fired point-blank into the British bunkers. In these desperate encounters the Japanese lost eighteen men dead and forty-five wounded, while the British suffered fifty-six killed and missing. In Rangoon the *Greater Asia* declared that 'the vanguard of the Indian National Army in close collaboration with a Nippon unit' had captured Tongzang. This was propaganda, however. In truth the INA was not a success in these actions. Six weeks before, on 29 January 1944, an INA company had attacked the positions held by the 7/10th Baluch in the hills east of Tiddim. The adjutant, Captain John Randle, recorded that the INA received a hostile reception from his sepoys, who were contemptuous of those who had deserted the Indian Army. Compared to the ferocity of a Japanese assault Randle recorded that the INA attack was 'half-hearted. Our chaps jeered at them. We've come here to fight proper soldiers [they called out], not a lot of yellow deserters like you'. But the true intent of many INA soldiers was demonstrated occasionally. On 16 March at Milestone 125 a party of Gurkha 'Jifs' surrendered to men of the 1/7th Gurkhas. It transpired that this was their old battalion, having been captured in Burma in 1942. The men had used their membership of the INA as a means of escape, never having had any inclination to fight with the Japanese and seeking to return to their regiment at the first available opportunity.

Furious with the unexpectedly determined resistance they encountered in the hills above and east of Tongzang, the Japanese summarily executed five prisoners with the sword. Japanese columns now seeped through the peaks and valleys to overlook Tongzang by 14 March. But, despite trying hard, they were not able to overcome any more of the tiny, self-contained British positions. The 1st West Yorkshires, 7/10th Baluch and 1/4th Gurkhas fought successfully to resist every Japanese attempt to overwhelm their positions in the hills above the valley, but they could not defend everywhere and on the night of 13 March troops of 214th Regiment managed to slip into the valley and take possession of the Tuitum saddle, an important piece of scrub-covered ground directly overlooking the road. By now the first troops of 63 Brigade – 1/10th Gurkhas – had arrived at Tongzang along the road from the south, and were immediately pressed into assaults to eject the Japanese from Tuitum.

After pausing for a day to ensure that he could call on both aircraft and artillery support, on 16 March Brigadier Guy Burton launched a violent assault on the saddle which, being rocky and with few trees offered the Japanese little in the way of cover. Hurricanes came in first to strafe the Japanese positions and to drop their 250-pound bombs, accompanied by a bombardment from all the division's artillery – 129th Field Regiment (25-pounders), 29th Light Mountain Regiment (3.7-inch mountain howitzers) and 82nd Light Anti-Aircraft/Anti-Tank Regiment (40mm Bofors firing over open sights and even anti-tank guns) – before 1/4th Gurkhas and a company of 1/10th Gurkhas charged the position. There was little opposition. Major H. H. Croften, a company commander of 1st West Yorkshires, watched the attack, and was impressed both with the bravery of the pilots and of the Japanese defenders:

> My most vivid recollection is the bravery of the pilots of the ... Hurricanes dive bombing and strafing the Japanese. Turning and twisting their planes in the narrow valleys they went in again and again, keeping their sights on the enemy bunkers until the last possible moment before pulling out of their dives. Indeed, one pilot crashed right into the Japanese position.
>
> We were much impressed with the suicidal bravery of the Japanese. Sitting on a ridge we looked down on the battle from about 900 yards. A Japanese officer was standing in a slit trench, his upper half fully exposed, and calmly directing the defence of his sector. Though we turned everything on him, including 2-pounders firing over open sights, he did not flinch or take cover.

Croften had witnessed, in the crashing of the Hurricane, the very real danger that low-level attacks placed on the aircraft. Flight Lieutenant Parry of 11 Squadron flew Mark II variants, armed with four 20mm cannon, which fired in bursts like a machine-gun, as well as two 250-pound bombs:

> It was OK flying over the road with one's canopy open looking over the side for vehicles on the road, but once you closed the canopy to attack, and dived in at low level head-on, the thick bullet proof windscreen reduced visibility considerably. [It was much worse at night.] As soon as you fired your cannon, you were temporarily blinded by the muzzle flashes. There was a grave danger of flying straight into the ground, and we lost a number of pilots on night operations.

By the time of this attack 17th Indian Division was well on its way along the road from Tiddim, leaving the Japanese with no idea that they had gone. Yanagida had expected the British to stand and fight for these positions. It was only as Cowan's Black Cats moved into Tongzang twenty miles north that the Japanese attempted cautiously to probe the now vacated Tiddim defences. It was then that the vast array of mines and booby-traps left by the British came into their own, severely delaying the enemy. Several armoured vehicles were destroyed by mines on the roads around Tiddim and it was not until 23 March that five tanks and two 105mm artillery pieces managed to make their way into the village. By now, of course, the bird had long since flown the coop. During 18 March Cowan moved his two brigades through Tongzang in carefully choreographed leap-frog moves, with his vanguard, rear and flanks constantly protected against attack, ensuring that the support troops and vehicles were safely shepherded to safety. Lieutenant General Yanagida was shocked at the strength and coherence of the resistance by the Black Cats and, weak and short of artillery ammunition, was forced, reluctantly, to let the long columns snake slowly by.

On the road further north, however, at Milestones 110 (Sakawng) and 100 (Singgel) Colonel Sasahara's 215th Regiment, moving fast along the west bank of the Manipur river, had secured positions along the road as early as 12 March, two days before 17th Indian Division had even begun its withdrawal from Tiddim. General Scoones' action in despatching 37 Brigade, a squadron of Stuart light tanks from 7th Light Cavalry and 9th Jats (the Corps' machine-gun battalion, with Vickers medium machine guns) from Imphal came just in time and meant that the Japanese were now caught in a sandwich between Cowan pressing up from the south and Collingridge pressing down from the north.

Sergeant Kazuyoshi Nakahara of 4th Company, 1/215th Regiment had moved secretly with the remainder of his battalion to Mualbem on the Manipur river, crossing in rubber boats on 9 March. Each soldier – some ninety men in his company in all – was equipped with a heavy pack weighing about 100 pounds as they all carried rations and rifle ammunition calculated to last them for twenty days. On 13 March his company, together with a platoon of medium machine guns, captured a hill just south of Milestone 100. Nakahara was responsible in this attack for coordinating the concentrated firepower of the company's mortars. On the following day Collingridge's two battalions arrived short of Milestone 100 after hastily returning from an exercise elsewhere on the Imphal Plain. Ninth Jats had turned up the previous day simultaneously with lead elements of Nakahara's battalion and were immediately and fiercely engaged. Their company position on the road at Singgel was surrounded and attacked, and the Japanese established a road block further north. A company attack by Captain L. C. Martin of 3/5th Royal Gurkhas, supported by the Vickers machine guns of the surrounded 9th Jats further up the road, succeeded in clearing this road block and killing all its defenders, an almost miraculous occurrence against a dug-in enemy, especially when achieved without the support of artillery. Here, along this road, the fighting swayed for five days. With the success of Captain Martin's attack, Lieutenant Colonel Marindin of 3/5th Gurkhas ordered three Stuarts of Lieutenant Morgan's No 1

Troop (A Squadron, 7th Light Cavalry) to try to break through from Milestone 100 to make contact with the vanguard of 17th Indian Division on the other side of Tongzang.

On the morning of 15 March a platoon of Gurkhas was ordered to accompany the tanks on their journey south from Milestone 100. Clambering aboard, they chatted amongst themselves happily as the tanks made their way slowly uphill. The Indian tank crews observed that the young Nepalese warriors always appeared chirpy, no matter the circumstance. The road, however, was blocked by trees. As the tanks slowed down in front of the obstacle, a withering fire from Lieutenant Nagai's company, entrenched on the high ground above them, swept the tanks, killing or wounding many of the Gurkha escort. The tanks immediately swivelled their turrets and returned fire. The Japanese then rushed the British armour. The attack was led personally by Sergeant Nakahara:

> I aimed at the leading tank and had the privates attack the second and third tanks. I threw the mines which stuck to the rear part of the tank … the tank was immobilized but our attack on the other two tanks failed. The second tank went forward and protected the destroyed tank, and the third tank [later] went on north. The second tank fired its tank-gun and machine guns in all directions.

Sowar[3] Jot Ram, the Radio Operator in the middle tank, heard something strike his vehicle with a loud thud. No one inside the middle tank was hurt, but the tank began to fill with smoke. Jot Ram recounted:

> A party of twenty Japs [then] tried to rush our right rear. Our infantry killed some, and then the two tanks caught them in time with canister [ball bearings, akin to a shot gun] and co-ax[ial .50-inch Browning machine gun].

The lead tank could not scale the log obstacle. The tank commander radioed back, 'I think I can climb the barrier, but if I do, my tank will fall nose first into the ditch beyond. There is no way round. I can get off the road, but there is a deep nullah with steep banks across the road.' By now it was dark and raining heavily. Lieutenant Morgan ordered the tanks to open their turrets and to pick up any surviving Gurkhas. They found three, two of whom were wounded. All the others were dead, including the British platoon commander. Morgan then ordered the tanks to make their way back towards Milestone 100 but, soon after setting out, with no lights, his tank slipped into a ditch. Try as they might, they could not recover it. Morgan ordered one vehicle to make its way back, while he remained with the two, defending his two tanks overnight. As dawn broke the next morning the Japanese launched a further attack on the tanks from the forested hillside. Jot Ram recalled the bloody mayhem that ensued:

> There were mortars and bombs, and grenades exploding everywhere. Everyone is shooting. Men are rushing about and falling everywhere. There is shouting, I see a crowd of Japs rushing at us. They come right into the middle of their own bombs. I fire my ack-ack Browning until it stops. The Risaldar Sahib's [Bharat Singh] tank comes up and drives right over them. There are more Japs. Gurkhas charge with the bayonet and shoot at the same time. A Jap falls out of a tree nearly on top of me. His head is a terrible mess.

Quietness descended on the road for a time, and Morgan decided to collect the wounded before taking his one serviceable tank back to Milestone 98. Jot Ram noted that there were at least thirty Japanese bodies littering the ground, cut down in the repeated fusillades from the tank's machine guns. Suddenly, however, a further Japanese attack was launched, this time including men with a pole charge. This was beaten off, but a final Japanese ruse proved to be Morgan's undoing. After what appeared to be several hours of stalemate a man dressed as a Gurkha approached Morgan's tank, waving a message. As Morgan opened the turret Sergeant Nakahara, crouching on the back of the Stuart, threw in a grenade. With the explosion, Nakahara recalled, 'six crewmen, including two British, baled out of the porthole and lay down in the ditch just in front of me, not noticing me. I took my rifle and shot five of them one by one. While I was reloading the rifle after five shots, a Gurkha jumped out with a sub-machine gun but he also was shot dead.' Sowar Jot Ram was the only survivor, throwing himself bodily down the hillside, bullets pursuing him. Thirty-six hours later, he stumbled out of the jungle into the safety of the Squadron's harbour area.

On the 18th, 3/215th under Major Sueki captured the British supply depot at Milestone 109, but not before some 2,700 non-combatants and several hundred soldiers, many from 9th Jats, had been spirited through the hills northward to safety. In the battle to secure the depot the Japanese lost forty killed and seventy wounded, the accompanying INA company also losing heavily. To his surprise, Sueki found that he was now in possession of a vast supply of stores and 1,000 vehicles, although most had been immobilized. The pace of the battle was such, however, that he had no time to enjoy his spoils. The RAF were paying him frequent visits and, a mile or two to the south, 48 Brigade, the vanguard of 17th Indian Division, was pressing against him hard.

To the north Collingridge now concentrated his forces in two boxes near Milestones 98 and 93. The positions secured at great cost by 3/5th Gurkhas and 9th Jats forward of Milestone 100 were evacuated after three days of continuous fighting. Casualties were mounting after fierce hand-to-hand fighting, and food, water and ammunition were exhausted. Late on the evening of 17 March Lieutenant Colonel Marindin of 3/5th Gurkhas ordered the Jats to fire off their remaining ammunition before burying their guns and slipping out of their position with the men of his own battalion and reforming at Milestone 98. By this stage, Marindin's weakened companies had suffered twenty-one dead and seventy-five wounded after three days of relentless fighting and had exhausted both food and water. Their withdrawal route, with forty stretcher cases, took them on a path that dropped 1,000 feet into the valley, before climbing back a further 2,000 feet to the road.

Marindin's withdrawal coincided with the arrival of part of the fresh 49 Brigade (6/5th Mahratta Light Infantry) at Milestone 82, which released the whole of 37 Brigade to clear the road between Milestones 82 and 98. For three days air-to-ground attacks by Vengeance dive-bombers struck against the Japanese positions at Milestones 100 and 99. Efforts to eject them from their deeply-dug positions on the hills above Milestone 98 typified the intensity of the fighting. Lieutenant Colonel Cosens' 3/10th Gurkhas attacked a position known as Fir Tree Hill at Milestone 99. At 5.50 a.m. on 22 March a heavy concentration was fired by the brigade's 25-pounders, followed by a similar bombardment by 3-inch mortars. Unfortunately, the guns dropped close to the waiting infantry, and five Gurkhas were killed. Then, Lieutenant P. P. Dunkley led B Company onto the Japanese position, supported by three Stuarts from 7th Light Cavalry led by Captain Cole, crawling slowly up the steep slopes. As each set of bunker positions was reached the tanks lowered their guns to the lowest possible elevation and pumped their 37mm HE rounds into the aperture. Slow progress was made, although the Japanese fought hard for every inch of ground, and a Japanese suicide bomber managed to throw himself onto Cole's tank. Cole shot the man dead, but the bomb ignited and set the tank ablaze. A 75mm armour-piercing shell penetrated Jemadar Ram Gopal's tank, killing the gunner but without immobilizing the vehicle, which continued fighting. Despite this work the extensive Japanese position remained unbroken, and the men of B Company were forced to dig in where they could, Japanese artillery and mortar fire making their exposed positions extremely dangerous. The next morning, just as the Japanese were preparing to counter-attack the tenuous 3/10th Gurkha positions, a Hurribomber strike broke up the Japanese assault party, and a 20mm round tore through Lieutenant Colonel Irie, the dynamic commander of 1/215th, killing him instantly. Without his presence to direct and animate the attack, it was postponed. The following morning, 24 March, attacking from the south, C and D companies of 3/10th Gurkhas managed to penetrate but not entirely secure the Japanese position.

The British continued to be supplied by air, an urgent request for 750 gallons of water, mortar bombs, ammunition and barbed wire being dropped accurately on the defensive box at Milestone 98 on the 23rd. No such support was afforded to the Japanese. Sergeant Nakahara's position, he recorded, was 'attacked constantly and casualties increased' which meant that they could not be resupplied with food or water, although ammunition was plentiful. As a result, they 'could not go down to the river to get water and boil rice. So we ate uncooked rice for four days.' The ability of the USAAF and the RAF to supply their necessities from the air gave tremendous hope to the British, Indian and Gurkha troops of 17th Indian Division, and a tangible sign of the resources that lay behind the entire Fourteenth Army. 'Throughout the whole withdrawal from Tiddim,' wrote Eric Yarrow to his parents, 'we enjoyed complete air supremacy – a very different story from the Burma evacuation of 1942.' The result, recalled Major Ian Lyall Grant, was that the Dakotas 'gave a daily service which was so efficient that units were scarcely aware of any difference from the normal system.'

While 37 Brigade fought bitter battles to break through the blocks in the north, Cowan replenished his force at Tongzang. With great skill Dakotas flew at low level down the valley over the next few days, dropping food and ammunition to the troops and the defensive positions built around the Tuitum Saddle. A major attack developed against positions held by 1/10th Gurkhas and 1st West Yorkshires on the night of 24 March, in which Japanese tanks attempted to bypass the position. Mines placed on the road by the Royal Engineers destroyed all four tanks, however, and the West Yorkshires' machine guns, firing on fixed lines in the dark to cover the minefield, killed the crews. Major Ian Lyall Grant, who commanded 70 Light Field Company of the Bengal Sapper and Miners attached to 17th Indian Division, noted that the Japanese troop commander, alive as dawn rose, blew himself up with a grenade as men of the West Yorkshires approached warily to try to take him prisoner.

The vanguard of 17th Indian Division, Brigadier Ronnie Cameron's 48

Indian Brigade, which he had commanded ever since the disaster at the Sittang Bridge in February 1942, now began to infiltrate into the hills south of Milestone 109 from 20 March, sandwiching Sueki's force between them and the troops and tanks of 37 Brigade just to the north of Milestone 98. Seeking to outflank Sueki's defences, Cameron successfully attacked each Japanese position in turn in a series of fierce engagements across the hilltops in which the Gurkhas and British infantry demonstrated determined courage in the assault – together with well coordinated artillery and air strikes – and the Japanese showed once more their penchant for fighting to the death. Ian Lyall Grant described the methodical professionalism of Lieutenant Colonel Robert ('Deadly') Hedley's 2/5th Royal Gurkha Rifles attacking the ridge above Sakawng Village, overlooking the supply depot at Milestone 109, at first light on 23 March. A first 'blitz' attack by A Company on Japanese positions along the crest of the hill was bought to a halt at thirty yards' range and a cost of twenty casualties. Two further attacks by A Company fared no better but a fourth attack by men of B Company with six Bren guns and eight tommy guns in the leading line succeeded in penetrating the Japanese weapon pits:

> Brilliantly led by Captain Tannock and Jemadar Jangbahadur Thapa this attack was unstoppable and swept over the first Japanese position killing everyone in it.

A second Japanese position was dealt with in the same way, following a mortar barrage, at 11 a.m. Lyall Grant was impressed with the extraordinarily high standard of soldiering demonstrated by the Gurkhas in these attacks, noting with some relief that they 'were now more of a match for the best Japanese troops'.

> A subsequent investigation of this position disclosed two circles of foxholes, each circle about the size of a tennis court. The two circles were only about forty yards apart and seem to have been the headquarters and one platoon of 215/12 Company. There were some twenty dead Japanese in each circle, including four officers. Two soldiers appeared to have committed suicide by blowing their chests open with grenades. Two wounded men, however, were taken prisoner.

Once the Sakawng positions had been taken (in which casualties on both sides were high, 2/5th Royal Gurkha Rifles alone losing twelve killed and sixty-six wounded), C and D Companies moved round the eastern flank of the supply depot to attack high ground astride the road at Milestone 105. D Company was commanded by Lieutenant M. J. G. Martin:

I set off at 0230, ahead of me was the reconnaissance platoon commanded by Jemedar Netrabahadur Thapa, who was . . . awarded a posthumous VC later in the Imphal battle. C Company and Battalion HQ followed. The terrain was abominable. There was no track. We heaved ourselves up the steep slopes tree by tree.

Eventually we hit the unmetalled road to Imphal. On the other side was an earth cliff about 15 foot high, and above that the Japanese position. We and the recce platoon dumped packs and shovels, and got ready to attack. The only way up this earth cliff was to make a ladder with bayonets and kukris. To our utmost astonishment we took the Japanese by surprise. Our attack roared in and the Japanese fled, leaving five dead and lots of equipment.

Although the Japanese later counter-attacked with mortars and machine guns, causing many casualties among the exposed Gurkhas, and subsequent attacks by C Company failed to make any further ground, these were the last gasps of Sueki's exhausted battalion. With no ammunition remaining, having had no food for several days, and after suffering very heavy casualties, Sueki on the early morning of 26 March was forced to vacate his positions overlooking the supply depot at Milestone 109. Virtually surrounded, he admitted that he could not have resisted another attack. Sergeant Nakahara's position at Milestone 100 had been evacuated the previous night:

> We had been attacked persistently by enemy infantry and artillery, so our casualties increased, creating a lot of gaps in our position. We were in a critical situation and could be destroyed easily if the enemy were to attack our positions. On 25 March we received the awaited order to retreat and moved in darkness to regimental headquarters. The number of fighting men in our company was reduced to little more than twenty out of the ninety that had crossed the Manipur River two weeks earlier.

The message that got back to Lieutenant General Yanagida's HQ on the night of 25 March from Colonel Sasahara suggested to the divisional commander that the entire 3/215th had been destroyed, which meant that at least half of his force advancing on Imphal had not managed to progress any further up the Tiddim Road than Milestone 109. This, of course, was an exaggeration but Yanagida, who had never been convinced by Mutaguchi's plan, panicked. His private fears about the risks he was being asked to undertake flooded to the surface, and he sent a signal to Mutaguchi in which he expressed his disquiet about the operation. The original does not exist but an eyewitness report suggests the following signal:

The combat situation of 214th Regiment is not developing satisfactorily and discouraging reports are coming in from 215th Regiment. The capture of Imphal within three weeks is now impossible. The wet weather and lack of supplies will only lead to disaster. The strategic importance of Imphal has in any case been exaggerated. Accordingly, the 33rd Division is unable to comply with the orders of 15th Army. I suggest that you give alternative orders so that some failure does not occur elsewhere.

This extraordinary act of insubordination, in which Yanagida suggested that Operation C be terminated, came as a thunderbolt to Mutaguchi, who furiously demanded that Yanagida comply with his instructions. The commander of 33rd Division was in no mood to compromise, however, and refused to be bullied. Yanagida proceeded to advance on Imphal in a slow and deliberate fashion, eschewing the taking of risk and the opportunity for dash, allowing Cowan and Scoones to deal with the threat from Tiddim in an equally controlled and methodical manner. Unfortunately for Yanagida, his own headquarters was divided against him. Some supported their divisional commander while others supported the chief staff officer, Colonel Tanaka Tetsujiro.

Tanaka had a poor opinion of Yanagida and regarded his superior's reaction to the fighting at Tongzang to be tantamount to moral failure. The two engaged in bitter argument that verged on insubordination by Tanaka, but Yanagida was too weak to discipline or dismiss him. Mutaguchi, enraged at what he regarded to be Yanagida's defeatism, began now to deliver instructions directly to Tanaka – a man of his own ilk – and to ignore Yanagida altogether. This disintegration of the senior command relationships augured badly for the mutual trust and confidence that are indispensable to the exercise of high command and which were essential to the achievement of Mutaguchi's plans.

Yanagida's 'go slow' prompted Mutaguchi to send one of his trusted staff officers, Major Fujiwara Iwaichi, to Tiddim to remonstrate with Yanagida and to order 33rd Division to make all haste for Imphal, where the great prize of capturing the capital of Manipur would make up for all current deficiencies. Yet Yanagida ignored these instructions and continued to advance at a snail's pace, determined above all to preserve the integrity of his force. His caution was a boon to the British, however, allowing Cowan to withdraw in good order to the relative safety of the Imphal Plain, and for Slim to reinforce Imphal.

With the road now open through to Milestone 105 Cowan ordered the demolition of the Manipur Bridge, further south at Milestone 126, and the withdrawing convoys of 17th Indian Division pressed up to the recaptured supply depot at Milestone 109. Hurricanes flew low and dropped sandbags full of rotor arms for the disabled trucks, allowing many to be driven out. Captain Peter Longmore of 129th (Lowland) Field Regiment told David Atkins that he 'liberated' an abandoned lorry full of tinned peaches at Milestone 109. On informing Lieutenant Colonel Younger, his Commanding Officer, of this news he received the reply, 'Peter, your main job is to get that lorry through and, by the way, try and match it with a load of Carnation milk.' A less amusing sight was that of two dead Indian soldiers, hung by their hands from a tree, stripped naked, and punctured by multiple wounds. They had been used by Sueki's men for bayonet practice.

Most of the troops marched out of the broken Japanese trap, reaching the forward positions of 37 Brigade at Milestone 82 on 30 March, both 37 and 49 Brigades coming under Lieutenant General Cowan's direct command for the first time. The Japanese were known to have constructed a final block on the road in the vicinity of Milestone 72. This comprised the bulk of 2/213th Regiment, which had descended on this part of the Tiddim Road after marching directly across the hills from the Chindwin in the east over the Mombi track. The men of 48 Brigade did not know it at the time, but this was the battalion that had decisively bettered the British at Rathedaung in Arakan the previous year. On this occasion, however, they proved no match for the determined troops of 9th Borders, 1/7th Gurkha Rifles and Hedley's 2/5th Gurkha Rifles. After severe fighting, in which Hedley's battalion lost another thirteen killed and forty-six wounded, the road was cleared and the long convoys of ambulances and support vehicles began to flow directly into Imphal. Then, in a carefully managed leapfrog manoeuvre, Cowan guided his division to safety south of Imphal over the period between 2 and 4 April, with one brigade holding the rearguard while the others (the division now temporarily comprised 37, 48, 49 and 63 Brigades) moved methodically from each position towards the safety of the Imphal outskirts.

The rearguards did effective work. Believing that the British had departed from Milestone 87 the Japanese confidently marched in columns down the road, to be caught in a well-sited machine-gun ambush mounted by 3/3rd Gurkhas. As Lyall Grant recalls, at least twelve Japanese were killed and some curious items of booty captured, including a full-dress uniform. Covering the bridge at Milestone 85 the twenty-three-year-old Lieutenant John Hudson of 91 (Royal Bombay) Field Company (part of 23rd Indian Division) had been lying in the grass when the Japanese advanced across the *padi* towards his sixty-strong Number 3 (Sikh)

Platoon, spread out in a defensive ring forming the rearguard to the bridge. With a Japanese officer brandishing his sword at the front of his men in his sights, Hudson gently squeezed his trigger and his .303 Lee Enfield barked out its deadly report. The Japanese officer collapsed in a muddy heap in the rice *padi*, and Hudson's well-trained platoon responded to the signal to fire by opening up a devastating rifle barrage against the advancing enemy. The well-oiled rifle bolts worked back and forth as the highly accurate Short-Magazine Lee Enfields played over the open ground to their front into the ranks of the ochre-clad Japanese. The Japanese were certainly brave, Hudson thought, but he and his men were also determined, and extremely skilful. They had prepared for many months for this moment. 'Sapper!' shouted an officer from 3/3rd Gurkhas, 'Have you got any explosives with you? I think we'll have to get out of here before we're overrun!' Hudson and his men moved quickly to demolish the wooden bridge over the nullah across which the remainder of the division had already crossed, along with a number of trucks now surplus to requirements:

> I organized my men into parties to destroy the line of stationary vehicles. The first team removed all the sump plugs and drained the black engine oil out into the dust; the second party started each motor and jammed open the throttles until the engines screamed to a seize up; the rotor arm man followed; the carburettor man with a sledge hammer; the tyre slasher, and finally an arsonist to fire the fuel tanks.

His last remaining truck, containing three tons of explosive, was driven under the bridge and detonated with a roar that was heard in Imphal eighty-five miles away. It was far more than was necessary, but on Hudson's admission he loved blowing things up, and was determined to leave the Japanese only a deep, smoking crater. He succeeded.

In this sort of fighting there was rarely a discernible front line, and support and rear echelon troops often found themselves involved in terrifying combat. Private Len Thornton, drafted into the Royal Army Medical Corps in 1940, found himself posted as an Operating Assistant (Class 1) to 41st Indian General Hospital (IGH) at Kanglatongbi in 1943. On 16 March panic set in with the news that the Japanese were close, and the recently arrived 14th British General Hospital was evacuated by road to Dimapur, whilst the 41st Indian General Hospital was ordered to move into a secure 'box' at Imphal. All the existing patients had to be evacuated, the walking wounded sent by truck to Kohima, and stretcher cases evacuated by air:

Every plane – bombers, fighters, cargo transport, anything that flew – was filled with the wounded and then they were flown over the mountains to Comilla. It was only a small airstrip, so we had to load the wounded onto the planes quickly as other aircraft were arriving and we didn't have much time. It took about twenty minutes to load each one. We couldn't have taken longer. Inside it was so hot, the aircraft was like a sauna while stationary. As soon as they were full, they took off to their destination. They didn't hang around.

With the evacuation under way Thornton was rushed to the Tiddim Road to set up a First Aid dressing station for troops of 17th Indian Division, and soon found himself unwittingly in the thick of the fighting:

> A Jap patrol broke into our first aid area and a hell of a battle raged. It was the first action I had seen. I had a Sten sub-machine gun and a revolver with me at the time. Suddenly, a Jap officer came charging at me with his sword waving above his head. It seemed so unreal, almost as if in slow motion. I stood there frozen. It was as though I was watching it all from the outside. Fortunately, it only lasted a few seconds then reaction set in. I squeezed the trigger on my Sten gun and fired at him. He just came on. I couldn't understand it: I thought I must be missing him or firing blanks. His face had a terrifying look on it and he came closer and closer. I couldn't move, I was riveted to the spot. I suppose it was fear. Then, he gradually fell to the ground and his sword came to rest on the toe of my boot.

By 5 April, with no further casualties, Cowan's entire division had arrived safely on the outskirts of Imphal, and 37 and 49 Brigades were able to rejoin Ouvry Roberts' 23rd Indian Division. General Scoones now had his reserve again, and 17th Indian Division's 1,200 wounded were flown out to India. During these three weeks Cowan's 16,000 troops, 2,500 vehicles and 3,500 mules had travelled slowly northwards, fighting their way through four major Japanese roadblocks, while elements of 37 and 49 Brigades, together with 9th Jats and a squadron of 7th Cavalry, had fought southwards from Imphal. The British had found themselves interspersed along the road with the Japanese, who attempted constantly to encircle and cut off the retreating British columns. 'The situation on the Tiddim road was now for a time as it had once been on the Arakan coast,' explained Slim, 'a Neapolitan ice of layers of our troops alternating with Japanese ... But in both training and morale our men were much better fitted to deal with such a confused and harassing business than they had been in 1943.' Air support, both in terms of air supply in the closing days of the withdrawal, and of ground attack throughout it by Air Commodore Stanley Vincent's No. 221 Group RAF proved to be of considerable value to 17th Indian Division. Despite the confusion evident at the start of the battle and the casualties suffered by the division, Cowan's fighting withdrawal from Tiddim, under constant pressure from the Japanese, was highly successful. Vincent recalled a meeting with Scoones on the morning of 15 March, in which the Corps commander was depressed by the prospects facing him on the Tiddim Road. Two weeks later, however, the gloom had lifted somewhat. Yanagida had been unable to isolate or outfight Cowan's Gurkha and British battalions and both brigades managed to reach the safety of the Imphal Plain.

In so doing substantial delay had been imposed upon 33rd Division, and the heavy casualties it suffered (probably 2,000) severely reduced its ability thereafter to break through to Imphal. Certainly, the morale of its commander was seriously compromised. Astonished at the unexpected ferocity of the resistance by the confident Black Cats, as Cowan carefully and methodically shepherded his division back to Imphal, Yanagida did not throw his troops into the aggressive and unrestrained headlong charge that Mutaguchi demanded. Apoplectic with fury at Yanagida's persistent refusal to recognize the need for haste, Mutaguchi finally made his way by air to Yanagida's headquarters north of Tiddim on 22 April. The resulting confrontation with Yanagida left him physically shaking with rage. Yanagida's explanation to Mutaguchi's angry demand as to why his division was not yet in Imphal, namely that he was not strong enough to break through Cowan's defences, was instantly dismissed. Instructing Tanaka to ignore his divisional commander, as from henceforth orders would come to him instead, Yanagida was thereafter forced to look on helplessly as Mutaguchi commanded his division from afar. His agony lasted a month, until a replacement commander was found. In the southeast, with Lieutenant General Yamauchi (15th Division), and in the east and north, with Lieutenant General Sato (31st Division), Mutaguchi had more reason to be hopeful.

# Chapter 2

# Crossing the Chindwin

Lieutenant Colonel Jim Williams commanded Fourteenth Army's Elephant Companies, based in Moreh (at the appropriately named 'Elephant Camp'), where the road over the mountains from Imphal debouches into the Kabaw Valley. Williams, known to all as 'Elephant Bill', had been an employee of the Bombay Burma Trading Corporation since 1920, managing the elephants used in the lucrative teak industry. 'I well remember,' he later recalled, 'wondering how many people who had waltzed on the teak deck of a luxury liner had ever realized that the boards of which it was built had been hauled as logs from the stump by an elephant in the Burma jungles.' He had been in Moreh with his beloved charges and their Burmese handlers ('Oozies') since the withdrawal from Burma in 1942. His seventy-nine elephants had proven indispensable in the work since then to extend and maintain the Imphal-Tamu road, especially the construction of log bridges over the many culverts, chaungs and rivers, as well as on the development of roads leading south from Tamu into the southern Kabaw Valley (towards Htinzin), and north (towards Mintha). But rumours had been sweeping the Burmese villages for months that the Japanese were planning at least a raid into the British-held central Kabaw Valley. One evening in early-March 1944 the telephone bell rang:

> I had just calculated that the elephants had delivered two thousand three hundred tons of timber at the road in three months. It was the divisional commander [Gracey] speaking, not with his usual cheerful personal touch, but giving me a grave invitation to lunch next day, to meet the Corps Commander [Scoones]. I could tell that the invitation meant something very serious …
>
> At luncheon next day there was a tension, as though something very serious were the matter. After lunch the Corps Commander and the Divisional Commander took me alone into a tent and said to me, 'This is Top Secret. How many days' warning would you need

to get all your elephants collected together, and how would you get them out of the Kabaw Valley?'

It was clear to Scoones and Gracey that, in the warm, sticky pre-monsoon heat, a massive Japanese offensive, instead of merely the strong raid that some had originally expected, was imminent, and required the switching on of defensive preparations. Along the Chindwin and in the mountain barrier that lay between this mighty river and the Imphal Plain the scattered outposts of V Force forward of both Kohima and Imphal reported by radio on growing evidence of Japanese activity on both sides of the river. Even further into Burma a secret organization (Z Force), comprised of small parties of Britons and Anglo-Burmese, including former employees of British firms in the teak trade, was reporting directly to Slim's Fourteenth Army HQ in Comilla and describing the large-scale movements of Japanese troops towards the frontier with India.

Moreh and Tamu sit to the east and south-east of Manipur where the jungle-clad mountains drop steeply first into the wide Kabaw Valley (through which flows the Yu river) before rising slightly and then falling again to meet the wide, muddy Chindwin river. It was here that Gracey's three brigades watched and waited in the days that followed news of the Japanese attacks on the Tiddim Road. They did not do so passively, however. Patrolling had ever been a feature of this stretch of the front, as it separated British India from Japanese-held Burma, since 1942. This activity had been stepped up in late-1943, including long-range patrols across the Chindwin, as a precursor to the offensive Scoones intended to launch in 1944. The 9/12th Frontier Force Regiment (part of 32 Brigade) provided a forward screen in the northern sector. Patrols were soon at home on either bank of the Chindwin, watching and observing Japanese preparations for what was clearly soon to be an offensive of their own.

Behind this thin screen lay Gracey's expectant brigades. Two battalions of 100 Brigade (2nd Border and 4/10th Gurkha) were deployed forward in the Kabaw Valley, dispersed on the tracks and high grounds that centred on the village of Witok, while the third battalion (14/13th Frontier Force Rifles) guarded the track over the steep Kuki-occupied hills to Mombi, which provided access to the Imphal Plain. These tough frontiersmen from the Punjab and the North West Frontier patrolled the Kabaw Valley as far south as Yazagyo, where the Japanese were building up their forces ready for their advance across the hills to Tuitum in the west, and Witok in the north. Further forward, and closer to the Chindwin, lay the three battalions of 32 Brigade, while 80 Brigade, based in Sibong, was responsible for defending the road from Moreh to Tamu along the main track that led from the Chindwin and over the Shenam Pass into Imphal.

Gracey's division was supported in its positions between the Kabaw Valley and the Chindwin by the 25-pounders of 9th Field Regiment and the 5.5-inch medium guns of 8th Medium Regiment. In addition, sixteen of the heavy Lee Grant tanks of A Squadron, 3rd Carabiniers under the command of Major Teddy Pettit travelled over the hills from Imphal in early-March (camouflaged on tank transporters), where they operated in troops of three tanks each to strengthen the dispersed infantry positions dotted across the network of tracks, hamlets, *padi* fields and clumps of trees that characterized the country on either side of the Yu river.

Scoones' initial plan to deny the Japanese access to the Imphal Plain was to create three brigade-sized defensive positions in depth along the road between Moreh in the east, leading back to the rear brigade box on the Shenam heights, the point at which the road dropped dramatically into the plain. Scoones concluded, in an appreciation of the operational situation on 29 February, that, in the event of an overwhelming Japanese offensive, his worst case option would be not to fight 'forward', i.e., in the central Kabaw Valley where 20th Indian Division was currently situated, but instead would be to concentrate the division 'around Moreh, the site of his divisional administrative base, and to fight a delaying action back to Shenam after covering the withdrawal of other units on the road. Shenam will be held to the last.' This way, Scoones argued logically and in accordance with Slim's overall strategic intent, the 'disadvantages of [a] long L of C [Line of Communication] will then fall on the Japanese'. On receipt of the code word 'Wellington', the division would withdraw into these three 'boxes', the first in the foothills of the mountains in the area of Moreh (100 Brigade), the second around the crucial Lokchao Bridge at Sibong fifteen miles behind on the road to Imphal (80 Brigade), and a third providing a backstop on the Shenam Heights (32 Brigade). It is apparent, given subsequent developments, that while Scoones informed Gracey fully about these immediate plans, he did not divulge to him his plans for the 'doomsday scenario' (i.e., the entire withdrawal of 20th Indian Division to the Shenam Heights). Perhaps he did not believe that it would ever lead to this.

Scoones certainly didn't think that it was going to happen as quickly as it did, for 1 Brigade (part of Roberts' 23rd Indian Division) was at the time in the Upper Kabaw Valley simulating a crossing of the Chindwin, attempting to take Japanese attention away from the launching of Orde Wingate's second Chindit adventure – Operation THURSDAY – which had just got underway. Likewise, 37 Brigade was involved in an infantry/tank cooperation exercise twenty miles south of Imphal. It would take at least a week to recover the brigade back into the Imphal Plain. In any case, Gracey judged that, concentrated and with the prospects of many months' supply to hand, his well-trained and highly-motivated division, which he had raised in Ceylon in 1942 and trained himself, could fight in its three boxes every bit as well as Messervy's 7th Indian had done at Sinzweya in February, if not better. The tangled, knotty jungle hills, riven with deep rocky gorges, were considered impassable to large numbers of invaders, and were deemed, therefore, to strengthen the power of the defenders. From 9 March the back loading began from the forward area to Imphal of the engineers, logisticians and non-combatants, including Williams' elephants, who had been preparing for the anticipated advance across the Chindwin.

The rapidly developing intelligence picture suggested that the Japanese blow against the belly of the 20th Division defences in the Kabaw Valley would begin on 10 March, which happened to be, in Japan, National Army Day. Major Henton-Wright of 9th Field Regiment, along with many others, waited expectantly all day for the attack, and especially for any intimation of the code word 'Wellington', at which point they were to withdraw to the base at Moreh, which Henton-Wright had been instructed was to be defended to the 'last man and the last round'. But the day went by with no action, the troops waiting in their slit trenches behind their mined and wired defensive positions, sweltering in the pre-monsoon heat, the wind rustling the teak leaves in the undergrowth in a noisy symphony. The weather had been gradually warming up and the vegetation drying out, leaves shrivelling and dropping from the trees of the vast forests that carpeted the valley floor. The only activity on this day took place near Htinzin, where a jemadar of 14/13th Frontier Force Rifles watching the road stepped out of the verge to welcome a patrol of Bren-gun carriers clattering along the track, only to be fired on by the vehicle's INA occupants, men of Colonel Kiani's 2nd (Gandhi) Regiment. Captured in numbers in both Malaya and Burma in 1942, these lightly-armoured vehicles were ideal elements of the Japanese deception plans. The jemadar escaped, with the information that not all British-built armoured vehicles in the area could be assumed to be friendly, but that their occupants were poor shots.

Instead, it took a further three days before the first signs of Japanese movement could be heard along the tracks running south down the Kabaw Valley, as Major General Yamamoto's striking force moved north along the Yu river from their crossing point over the Chindwin at Kalewa forty miles to the south. This force comprised nearly four battalions of infantry (3/213th Regiment; two companies from 215th Regiment; 2/51st Regiment and 3/60th Regiment) supported by the sixty Type-95 Tanks of 14th Tank Regiment, as well as sizeable numbers of artillery and combat engineers. The British could hear the noise of tanks for two days before the first major attack fell against positions around Witok held by 2nd Borders and 4/10th Gurkhas (supported by gunners of 114th Jungle Field Regiment, acting as infantry) on the night of 14 March. Henton-Wright's 25-pounder battery fired on pre-planned target areas around the positions, and the Japanese attack failed. To the surprise of the waiting British, the Japanese tactics at Witok were of the less than subtle type, charges by large groups of infantrymen behind officers waving swords falling easy prey to the rifles, machine guns and artillery fire of the defenders. Determined to destroy the feared British 25-pounders, the Japanese also attacked the positions held by 20 Battery, 9th Field Regiment at Puttha, north-east of Witok. Fortuitously a company of 4/10th Gurkhas occupied the defences that night and assisted with the defence. Two 25-pounders were soon firing over open sights against massed Japanese infantry attempting in vain to get through the barbed wire to the front of the gun positions. A 40mm Bofors anti-aircraft gun soon joined in, pumping its explosive shells into the enemy ranks. Over the radio, Henton-Wright could hear the artillery Forward Observation Officer (FOO) reporting, 'The shells are falling right in amongst them. They are milling around, trying to move away.'

Undeterred by failure during the days that followed, the Japanese attempted to penetrate the stubborn British defences across a wide front, seeking those decisive points at which a successful infiltration could be transformed into an expanding torrent, and the irresistible force of the offensive overwhelm the British all the way across the hills into Imphal. Small groups of 3rd Carabiniers' tanks co-located with infantry in prepared positions during 15 March, pre-arranged artillery barrages on road junctions and potential forming-up points, together with carefully-sited ambushes, all exacted their toll on the men of Yamamoto's force attempting to find a way through to Tamu. The machine guns of the six Lee Grants attached to 2nd Borders on 16 March caused great slaughter against a foolhardy Japanese infantry assault over open ground at Milestone 16 and, two days later, another troop helped push the Japanese out of a 2nd Borders' defensive perimeter into which they had managed to break.

The British task was made all the more difficult because the dry atmospheric conditions made radio communication, difficult in any case in the hills, almost impossible. The fallback – field telephones – had their wires cut regularly by both the Japanese and by artillery fire. Companies operating independently were forced to rely on runners and despatch riders and, with the area swarming with Japanese patrols, these were especially dangerous jobs.

Evidence of large-scale crossings of the Chindwin further north came on 14 March. As part of his eyes and ears along the Chindwin, Slim deployed two specialist groups of militiamen recruited from the Naga and Kuki tribes. In each of six separate areas from Ledo in the north, through Kohima, Imphal, the Chin Hills and the Lushai Hills in the far south, to the Naga Hills due west of Imphal, through which ran the track to Silchar, troops of the paramilitary Assam Rifles formed the regular component (usually four dispersed platoons), supported in each area by a further thousand or so irregulars from local villages, each equipped with a rifle or shotgun and basic equipment; their task was to report any hostile activity or intelligence back to each area commander, whose HQ boasted a heavy radio transmitter to send messages in turn back to IV Corps HQ in Imphal. The V Force base in the hills above Homalin, commanded by Lieutenant Colonel Dymoke ('Moke') Murray of the Assam Rifles, was attacked by a company commanded by the man who had conducted deep reconnaissance patrols into the hills the previous year, Captain Nishida Susumu of 58th Regiment.[4] Murray managed to escape and to get a message back to Imphal that the Japanese were over the river in force, but the rest of his unit was destroyed. Lieutenant Walton commanded a 9/12th FFR patrol that watched the Japanese noisily launching themselves across the Chindwin south of Tonhe, on the eastern (Japanese) side of the river, on the evening of 16 March 1944. His detailed patrol report was the first to confirm unequivocally that the Japanese were crossing the river in considerable strength. The day before the men of Lieutenant Colonel Geoffrey Mizen's 9/12th FFR had watched and reported Japanese crossings north of Thaungdut, and a number of sharp engagements had taken place in which some two hundred casualties (killed, wounded and missing) were sustained. By the 17th the Japanese were in full occupation of Myothit, twenty-five miles north of Tamu and the battalion pulled back to rejoin 80 Brigade at Sita on the Tamu road on 20 March.

Mutaguchi's northern columns were now on the march, Yamauchi's 15th Division crossing at Thaungdut and Sittaung and Sato's 31st Division further north at Homalin, Kawya and Tamanthi. At least 45,000 fighting troops, accompanied by many thousands of porters, made their way into the jungle-covered hills along the carefully-reconnoitred paths towards Sangshak and Kohima.

It was now clear that a considerable Japanese operation was in play as both 15th and 31st Divisions made multiple crossings of the Chindwin along a very wide frontage. It was time, Scoones decided, to withdraw 20th Indian Division into its three prepared defensive boxes. Accordingly, 'Wellington' was issued on 16 March. Withdrawals in contact with the enemy are never easy. Major Tony Bickersteth was a company commander with 4/10th Gurkhas. The plan was that, on receipt of the codeword, both 2nd Borders and 4/10th Gurkhas would move along jungle tracks to Milestone 16 after first destroying unwanted baggage to prevent it falling into Japanese hands. This all took time, and by the time (midday on the 17th) that the withdrawal got underway, Japanese snipers had already winkled their way into Witok and begun a harassing fire. In fact, the Japanese were all round them:

> The Jeeps with the Mortars were escorted back ... by the tanks and got clear away up the road save that one jeep trailer blew up on a mine and a mortar was lost. The Carrier party also left that night, had a battle, then closed on Moreh the following day.

Soon after the two battalions set off down the path, with a large number of mules of both battalions, the Japanese ambushed the track. Before counter-action could be taken the mules stampeded in all directions; and for a short while there was much confusion:

> The Border Regiment had the brunt of the attack, but the situation would have been OK and the enemy ambush liquidated, if it had not been that a grenade landed slap among the mules. These panicked and everyone scattered ... That night the battalion in its various bits was attacked five times, and the enemy's tanks on the road came into play, though they didn't actually open fire.

Order was restored by one of the 2nd Borders' buglers, Private Lennon, who sounded the Regimental Call followed by the 'Charge'. On hearing this, the men of the battalion cheered, and a number of bayonet charges were launched and the enemy was driven off. Lieutenant Colonel Godfrey Proctor, Commanding Officer of the 4/10th, was caught up in the stampede caused by the ambush. He was thrown bodily into a chaung by panicked mules and injured by a Japanese grenade. Adding insult to injury a toppling mule fell on him as well, only Proctor's pack, which had found its way above his head, shielding him from danger. Half-stunned, bleeding from shrapnel wounds and lying on his back in a pool of water, he was rescued by a Borders' corporal. This was one of a series of opportunistic ambushes of British parties during the afternoon, resulting in the carefully-planned withdrawal breaking into confusion. Most soldiers nevertheless made their way back in independent parties the thirty miles to Moreh by 19 March. Confused its end may have been, but the stand of 100 Brigade had denied Yamamoto's penetration of the southern Kabaw Valley for a week and caused him extensive casualties, not least in scarce armour.

On the early morning of 20 March 3rd Carabiniers found themselves pitched against the tanks of Colonel Ueda Nobuo's 14th Armoured Regiment for the first time. The Japanese, worried by the presence of the British Lee Grants, compared with their own thinly-armoured Type-95s (light tanks very similar in size and armament to the British Stuart) had prepared an anti-tank ambush on the Nanmunta Chaung, five miles north of Witok. British deception plans had worked: the Japanese had entirely ruled out the presence of armour in Manipur. Earlier that morning Major Teddy Pettit had been tasked to lead a force to assist the recovery of a Punjab platoon surrounded by the Japanese. The rescue column comprised six Lee Grants, the Bren-gun carrier platoon from the Northamptonshire Regiment and a truck-borne company of 9/14th Punjab. Moving along the road leading south from Tamu, the column encountered the Japanese ambush at 7.30 a.m., enemy tanks on one side of the road and Japanese infantry on the other. The Japanese tanks were heavily camouflaged and well back in the jungle verge. However, the ambush contained one significant flaw: there was no means of preventing the ambushed vehicles from simply driving through it, which is what Pettit ordered when he realized that the way was clear. One Lee Grant, hit in its petrol tank by a 37mm armour-piercing round, was soon on fire but the remaining five tanks cleared the ambush area, turned in a patch of clear ground and brought their own guns to bear on the now trapped Japanese. Foolishly, the Japanese tank commander, seeing that the tables had turned, now squandered the last remaining advantage he had by driving forward out of his jungle cover onto the road to engage the British tanks head on, instead of withdrawing back into the forest to get away. It was an unequal contest, the 75mm British tank guns slicing through the thin armour of the Japanese tanks. Five were soon burning fiercely, and a sixth was captured intact. In the face of this fire the Japanese infantry melted away into the bush.

While the withdrawal to Moreh was underway, a temporary defensive position nicknamed Charing Cross was prepared covering the main track south of Tamu by 9/14th Punjab and 3/8th Gurkhas of 32 Brigade (which had been withdrawn from the Chindwin at Sittaung). Helping to defend the box were the 25-pounder guns of 9th Field Regiment, in Moreh, and Pettit's triumphant Lee Grants. Brigadier David Mackenzie of 32 Brigade (a large, burly man, at 6 feet 5 inches his nickname of 'Long Mac' was particularly apt) confidently told Henton-Wright on 20 March, 'I expect to be attacked tonight and I hope I am, for the Japs will get a bloody nose'. He was right. Henton-Wright arranged a series of 'defensive fire' areas prepared in front of the brigade's positions, so that at night a simple codeword would be sufficient to identify a target allowing the guns, several miles away, to fire accurately on the pre-registered targets. In addition to the 5.5-inch guns and the 25-pounders, Henton-Wright recalled, 'We also had some 6-pounder anti-tank guns together with some mortars and many automatics.' Sometime after dark fell the clank and grind of approaching tanks grew ever closer. Suddenly, the roar of a 6-pounder anti-tank gun shattered the silence, the resulting explosion from the brewed up Type-95 at almost point-blank range illuminating the night, signalling the start of a fierce, largely one-sided battle:

> The battle raged all night. The 20 Battery fired all their first-line ammunition and some of the dumped ammo. The mortars illuminated the hostile troops and tanks with their excellent parachute flares and the 6-pounders had a field day with the target clearly silhouetted ... Our losses that night amounted to a dozen or so killed but those of the enemy mounted into the hundreds.

As dawn rose an exhausted but jubilant Henton-Wright could see from his battery position that 'many Jap bodies were lying about', the enemy clearly having taken a hard knock, leaving twenty-eight 'stiff Japs ...' to the front of the British positions. Japanese tactical carelessness cost them many unnecessary lives during these early skirmishes, as they attempted to use speed to overcome the British defences. Earlier in the day an ambush by 3/8th Gurkha Rifles some miles down the track from Tamu caught a long column of Japanese soldiers marching to the front in threes, who were cut down in large numbers by the concentrated fire of the battalions' Bren guns, which had been brought together for the purpose. After the successful action at Charing Cross, 32 Brigade were pulled back into Moreh the following morning, allowing 100 Brigade to withdraw further back to Shenam. Twentieth Indian Division was thus ready in its prepared positions, confident that they could take on whatever the Japanese were to throw at them.

~

In the days that followed the Japanese fought increasingly desperately to squeeze Moreh dry. Attacks took place by day and night, the Japanese employing infiltration raids by infantry and armour as well as 'jitter' raids by INA soldiers designed to unnerve the defenders and reveal their positions. The Japanese were very expert with their 'jitter' parties, recalled Henton-Wright, their sole job being 'to worry the occupants of a defended position by making much noise, firing their discharger cap grenades, rifles and automatics thus making the defenders 'Stand To' to repel an attack and incidentally preventing them getting any sleep'. Fire crackers were also widely used by the Japanese. A nervous fusillade of shots in response to these provocations would reveal a defender's positions, and enable the Japanese to locate them precisely in preparation for a subsequent attack. It sometimes worked, even in 1944 when the Japanese practice was well understood. Gracey had what he described as one 'dud' battalion – 4/3rd Madras – about which he complained to Scoones in late-March. These ill-trained and nervous troops helped provide some of the perimeter defences at Moreh, against which the jitter raids, recalled Major Henton-Wright, were, on at least one occasion, very successful. 'Twenty thousand rounds of small-arms ammunition was fired that night.'

Nevertheless 32 Brigade withstood these attacks, and a feeling of superiority developed, although the Japanese had considerable artillery support (including huge 155mm guns) against Moreh, employing it very accurately. At Moreh, Major Henton-Wright noted 'that the enemy guns always remained quiet while we had aircraft overhead and full use was made of this fact although it was not possible to have a couple of Hurricanes flying around during the whole of the day'. Japanese communications were also working well as many guns fired simultaneously from many different positions whenever they started a bombardment. Generally their harassing fire was not spread over a long period but would be confined to about thirty or forty minutes' continuous shelling, usually in the evening. However, on one occasion aerial bombardment caught Henton-Wright's gun battery napping:

> We had become so used to our aircraft dominating the sky that little notice was taken of some high flying machines, although it was unusual to see fighters as escort. I was in the Regimental Command Post and suspecting they were hostile I told Gunner White to watch them from the trench outside. He'd just announced that they were directly overhead when the old man, moving quicker than I had ever thought possible, dived into the dugout head first to the

accompaniment of screaming bombs, which were well on the mark and killed several Gurkhas nearby.

~

The operations to withdraw 20th Indian Division to its three brigade boxes went largely according to plan. But the orderliness of Gracey's withdrawal to the Tamu road positions hid a fundamental problem for Scoones, whose preparations in the south-east and east were deficient in ways that Mutaguchi had never hoped possible. Scoones was a competent though conservative strategist, who assumed that a Japanese offensive would require the use of roads, principally those that led to Imphal from both Tamu and Tiddim. By concentrating his defensive effort around these routes he risked leaving open significant gaps in IV Corps' defences in areas of steep hills and deep jungle, gaps that were ruthlessly exploited by Mutaguchi. In the south-east the Japanese Army Commander placed Yamamoto and his armour on the Tamu front in an attempt to punch through 20th Indian Division and use the road to gain access to Imphal. This front, however, was also the focus of an operational deception that succeeded completely in reinforcing Scoones' perceptions of Japanese intentions. To the north of the Imphal–Tamu road, through horrendous terrain regarded by Scoones as impassable to large bodies of troops, Mutaguchi was going to thrust a strong column of 15th Division, to attack Imphal from the north.

Unlike Scoones, Mutaguchi had done his homework, and knew that this terrain was far from impassable. His spies had told him that the British were close to completing the construction of a jeep track through the hills between Humine and Imphal. In fact, this was opened formally by Major General Ouvry Roberts on 4 March, only days before the Japanese offensive began. It seems that no one in Scoones' headquarters ever considered this track to be a potential invasion route. Mutaguchi had a contrary view, informed by a series of very effective long-range patrols that, for at least six months, had been scouring the hills for tracks, measuring bridges and fords and identifying ways in which a division, together with its supporting arms and services, could make their way across the hills to Imphal and Kohima. Mutaguchi's plan was to cut the Imphal–Kohima road fifteen miles north of the vast British supply depot at Kanglatongbi, and then to drive down on the Imphal Plain along the route Kamjong, Sangshak and Litan, the latter of which was the site of the HQ of 23rd Indian Division. Mutaguchi hoped that the British, distracted by the battles for the Tamu road, would not even notice his feint to the north. He was right. What Mutaguchi had not counted on, however, was that Yamauchi's force would be seriously weakened before the offensive began, by British air raids on 15th Division's concentration areas, the result of successful intelligence gathered by IV Corps' intelligence chief, Lieutenant Colonel Derek Holbrook. Yamauchi was further hampered by the slowness in getting his third regiment (67th Regiment) to the Chindwin in time for the start, because of British bombing of the railway lines up through Burma from Thailand. He was forced to begin his crossing on 15 March with only 51st and 60th Regiments – totalling perhaps 20,000 troops – themselves both sorely depleted by attacks from the air.

To compound British failings, the territory through which this track ran (centring on Ukhrul), had only the lightest of garrisons, and no real defences. Until 16 March it was home to 49 Brigade, now despatched to the Tiddim Road. Forty-nine Brigade had considered itself to be in a rear area and, extraordinarily, no dug-in and wired defensive positions had been prepared. It was one of the most serious planning failures of the campaign. The gap left by the brigade's departure had been filled in part by the arrival of the first of the two battalions of the newly-raised and part-trained 50 Indian Parachute Brigade (comprising the Indian 152nd Battalion and the Gurkha 153rd Battalion) whose young and professional commander, 31-year old Brigadier M. R. J ('Tim') Hope-Thomson, had persuaded the powers-that-be in New Delhi to allow him to complete the training of his brigade in territory close to the enemy. The area north-east of Imphal was regarded as suitable merely for support troops and training. At the start of March the brigade HQ and one battalion had arrived in Imphal, and began the leisurely process of shaking itself out in the safety of the hills north-east of the town. To the brigade was added 4/5th Mahrattas under Lieutenant Colonel Trim, left behind when 49 Brigade was sent down to the Tiddim Road. To Scoones and his HQ, the area to which Hope-Thomson and his men were sent represented the lowest of all combat priorities. Sent into the jungle almost to fend for themselves, it was not expected that they would have to fight, let alone be on the receiving end of an entire Japanese divisional attack. They had little equipment, no barbed wire, little or no experience or knowledge of the territory. No one considered it worthwhile to keep them briefed on the developing situation. To all intents and purposes, 50 Indian Parachute Brigade were irrelevant appendages, attached to Roberts' 23rd Indian Division for administrative purposes but otherwise left to their own devices.

Before long information began to reach Imphal that Japanese troops were advancing in force on Ukhrul and Sangshak. Inexplicably, however, this information appeared not to ring any warning bells in HQ IV Corps, which was pre-occupied with the developing threat in the Tamu area where the main Japanese thrust was confidently predicted. It was, perhaps understandably, unwilling to consider information that appeared to tell a story different to its own preconceived notions.

~

On the night of 16 March the single battalion of 50 Parachute Brigade took over responsibility for the Ukhrul area from 49 Brigade, which was hastily departing for the Tiddim Road. The news that Moke Murray had sent to Imphal on the 14th, that the Japanese were landing in strength opposite Homalin, a short march from the terminus of the jeep track at Humine, never reached Hope-Thomson, headquartered at Milestone 36 on the track between Litan and Ukhrul and blissfully ignorant of the onslaught that was about to engulf his tiny force. Warned only to be on their guard against long-range Japanese patrols, the idea that they might soon be the target for an entire Japanese division of 20,000 men was unthinkable. Captain 'Dicky' Richards of 50 Indian Parachute Brigade recalled being briefed by Major General Ouvry Roberts to the effect that

> it was thought that the expected main Japanese thrust against India could only develop from well south of Imphal, since it seemed highly improbable that a major attack could be mounted from the east. There were several jungle-clad mountain ridges, rising up to 3,000 or 4,000 feet, which ran north to south, and also the Chindwin river, which an attacker would have to cross. Certainly the terrain looked almost impenetrable by a force of any size. He then gave us a vast area of this mountainous jungle, on the east side of Kohima and Imphal, measuring about eighty by fifty miles, which we were to patrol on foot with animal transport only. Our orders were to keep the area clear of Japanese patrols and infiltrating agents.

On 19 March Richards recalled that HQ 23rd Division had put out a signal to all brigade and 'box' commanders, telling them that 'the Japs have embarked on a foolhardy ambitious plan for the capture of Imphal, and may be expected to "infiltrate" any day'. In the first light of dawn that day Hope-Thomson received anxious calls from the commanders of both his

152nd Battalion and 4/5th Mahrattas to say that they could see heavy columns of Japanese clearly marching on their undefended encampment at Sheldon's Corner, a few short miles to the east. The most forward position, based on high ground overlooking the road that led to the east, was occupied by C Company, 152nd Battalion. Surrounded at 2 p.m. that day, its 170 men refused to be intimidated by the 900 soldiers of the Japanese 3/58th Regiment, who launched repeated, fierce attacks on the young Indian paras and their seven British officers that afternoon and throughout the night that followed. By first light the next morning a radio report revealed that the British company commander and three other officers had been killed, along with forty men, that there were many wounded and ammunition was short. The account of the end of C Company on 20 March comes from the Japanese regimental history:

> By mid-morning the enemy's fire slackened considerably. Suddenly, from the top of the hill, a small group of about twenty men charged down towards us, firing and shouting in a counter-attack ... At the very top of the position an officer appeared in sight, put a pistol to his head and shot himself in full view of everyone below. Our men fell silent, deeply impressed by such a brave act ... the 3rd Battalion suffered 160 casualties in the action, with one company and two platoon commanders killed and another four officers wounded ... The enemy had resisted with courage and skill.

There were, in fact, twenty British survivors, the lone remaining officer withdrawing his men back to Sheldon's Corner. In the swirling confusion and terror of the next thirty-six hours Hope-Thomson and his staff kept their heads, attempting to concentrate what remained of the dispersed companies of 152nd Battalion and 4/5th Mahrattas back to a common position at the heart of the old perimeter, at a place called Badger's Hill. On the 20th the second battalion of the brigade began to arrive at Litan after its journey over the hills from Dimapur, but in the confusion that gripped HQ IV Corps during these early days of Mutaguchi's onslaught, only 390 men of 153rd Battalion had arrived at the seat of the battle, Sangshak, by the 22nd. Realizing that his dispersed positions could easily be bypassed and destroyed by the Japanese at their leisure, Hope-Thomson ordered his three weak battalions (152nd, 153rd and 4/5th Mahrattas, together with two poorly-trained companies of the Nepalese Kali Bahadur Regiment now, after battle casualties, reduced to no more than 1,850 men) to concentrate at Sangshak, which dominated the tracks south-west to Imphal. It was at this now deserted Naga village that Hope-

Thomson, on 21 March, decided to group his brigade for its last stand, his staff desperately attempting to alert HQ IV Corps in Imphal to the enormity of what was happening to the north-east. No one seemed to be listening. Urgent pleas for rations and, above all, for barbed wire fell on deaf ears as the Japanese columns infiltrated quickly around and through the British positions, heading in the direction of Litan. The 153rd arrived at Sangshak late on the 21st, and Colonel Trim's Mahrattas by noon on 22 March, just as the Japanese began to launch one of their many assaults against the position. Fortunately, four Indian mountain guns also arrived and began work immediately. Just as happily, as the day drew on, and as the Japanese began to attack from the north and the west, 152nd Battalion and the remainder of the Mahrattas arrived from the east, and quickly settled into their allotted positions on the perimeter. However, as the troops dug in they discovered to their discomfort that they were atop an ancient volcano, and the rock was impervious to their picks. All they could dig were shallow trenches, which provided ineffective protection from Japanese artillery. Like all Naga villages that at Sangshak was perched on the hill, and had no water: anything the men required had to be brought up from the valley floor, through the rapidly-tightening Japanese encirclement.

While men of the Japanese 3/58th Regiment (Major Shimanoe), part of Sato's 31st Division – troops whose objective was Kohima, and not Imphal – had first engaged the troops of C Company, 152nd Battalion at Sheldon's Corner, Major General Miyazaki decided that he needed to eliminate these elements, probably because they posed a threat to his long lines of supply and communication to Kohima, despite the fact that he knew Sangshak to lie not in his, but in 15th Division's area of responsibility. Accordingly he despatched both the Second Battalion (2/58th, commanded by Major Nogoya) as well as 3/58th to Sangshak where they arrived late on 22 March. Hoping to overwhelm the defenders, the Japanese attacked immediately, throwing infantry forward into the assault without undertaking a detailed reconnaissance, or waiting for the arrival of supporting artillery. It was a serious error. The 400 waiting Gurkhas of 153rd Battalion could not believe the sight before them as, facing north-west across the valley to West Hill in the failing light of early evening, a swarming mass of enemy rushed to overwhelm what they had imagined to be weak and puny defences. Wave after wave of enemy were cut down as they ran down the slopes of the hill, into the precision fire of 153rd's Lee Enfields and the chattering Vickers firing above and behind them. In addition to the four mountain guns, Hope-Thomson's brigade was also blessed with 3-inch mortars. The battalion's medical officer, Captain Eric Neild, described the scene as something akin to 'a gory Hollywood epic'. It was Neild's first experience of battle:

> We had the 15th Battery of the 9th Indian Mountain Regiment with us, commanded by Major Lock – a typical mountain gunner if ever there was one. He was a large burly fellow, with the appearance of a rugger player, wearing the most ridiculous little fore-and-aft forage cap and puffing contentedly at a pipe. He was in no hurry and waited until the whole length of the road was full of Japs before he let them have it. We saw the little white puffs bursting all along that road. Lock beamed – his only regret was that the guns had no shrapnel. He said that it was the best day's shoot of his life.[5]
>
> All night long the attacks came in and all night long the wounded passed through the regimental post where I was medical officer. There was little that we could do except stop any bleeding, give morphia and then evacuate them during lulls to the 80th Parachute Field Ambulance in a little dip about 200 yards away in the centre of the perimeter.
>
> During the day we began to realize the seriousness of our position as the reports of the casualties came in. The machine-gun company had suffered very heavily – all shot through the head while sitting up firing from their exposed positions. We were only partially heartened by finding a large number of Japanese dead in front of our positions.

Lieutenant Shosaku Kameyama, adjutant of 2/58th Regiment, who wearily tramped west through the Angousham Hills after crossing the Chindwin on 15 March, recalled being thrown into battle that night. Japanese morale was high:

> We climbed up and then went down the steep mountains, undisturbed by British troops or planes. After six days hard march we poured into Ukhrul, a small village on the road from Kohima to Sangshak. British troops seemed to have evacuated it only a few hours before and the village was burning. We then realized that the enemy had destroyed all their food and supplies, to our great disappointment, but a sergeant brought a bottle of whisky he found and wanted me to give it to Major General Miyazaki, commander of the Infantry Group accompanying us. He seemed pleased to receive the bottle. We were very tired because of the long march ... but to

my disappointment when I went to General Miyazaki, he ordered our battalion to pursue the retreating British and to occupy Sangshak.

On the evening of 21 March, we occupied the village of Sangshak and found that it was not the main position of the enemy, so we then attacked a hill north-west of the village and occupied the enemy's south front position. The enemy mounted a heavy counter-attack on us after sunrise. This was the first time that we had fought with the British-Indian forces, which was very different from our experience of fighting the Chinese army which had inferior weapons to ours. Our battalion commander observed the enemy positions and ordered an attack during the coming night: 8th Company to lead the attack, followed by 5th and 6th Companies. From our experience in China we were confident of the success of the night attack. But when 8th Company broke through the enemy front line, 5th and 6th tried to advance, but very fierce enemy firing made their progress impossible. Under a strong counter-attack the commander and most soldiers of 8th Company were killed or wounded. Though we wanted to advance we could not even lift our heads because of the heavy fire which we had never before experienced.

In fact the Japanese 8th Company of 2/58th lost ninety men from 120, including Captain Ban, its company commander, in the space of fifteen minutes. They learned their lesson, however, and the defenders of Sangshak never again faced such ripe targets. Instead, as the days drew out they were subjected to increasingly frantic Japanese efforts to break into Hope-Thomson's position. Gallant attempts to drop precious water to the beleaguered troops, as well as ammunition for the mortars and mountains guns, largely failed, about three-quarters of these valuable cargoes floating down to the Japanese. Although the weight of Japanese attacks tended to be on the north and west of the perimeter facing 152nd and 153rd Battalions, as the days went by increasingly strong probes were made against the Mahrattas on the eastern edge.

Hope-Thomson's men found themselves alone and faced by heavy odds. Fortunately, however, and at long last, Imphal had now awoken to the enormity of the threat on its north-eastern perimeter, Ouvry Roberts signalling to Hope-Thomson on the 24th, five days after the first appearance of the Japanese, 'Well done indeed. You are meeting the main Jap northern thrust. Of greatest importance you hold your position. Will give you maximum air support.' Unfortunately, with no barbed wire, no water and rapidly diminishing reserves of ammunition, the long-term prognosis for the hugely outnumbered 50 Indian Parachute Brigade was never in doubt if Miyazaki decided to delay his advance to Kohima in order to crush the defenders.

During the early hours of the 25th the Japanese launched a ferocious attack on the north-west perimeter of the Sangshak position, but were again repelled with heavy loss. Japanese shelling and sniping, however, had turned the entire position into a bullet-swept and shell-torn hell, the defenders crouching in their shallow shell-scrapes awaiting the next attack. Major Harry Butchard, of 153rd Battalion, recalled the plateau to be extremely dangerous:

> By day, conditions on the plateau soon became pretty grim – bodies lying about, human and animal, decomposing rapidly. Snipers were a constant nightmare – one morning I was speaking to two officers of 152 Battalion, and when I returned that way a few minutes later, I found them both lying dead, in exactly the same place — shot through the head.

Exhaustion was now a serious problem, as many men – especially 4/5th Mahrattas and 152nd Battalion – had had little sleep for seven days. Captain 'Dicky' Richards:

> We continued to fight by day and night. The position became utterly gruesome and macabre. The perimeter was littered with corpses which could not be buried and there were mule carcasses everywhere. Some went into the cooking pot, but others very quickly rotted in that climate – and there were Japanese bodies, our own bodies, and excreta everywhere. It was impossible to construct properly dug-down trenches, dysentery became rife and the situation was almost intolerable. We were getting weaker by the hour – our men were getting killed off one after the other, we were running out of ammunition and food and some men were almost delirious after many days without sleep. Some of us would drop off for a few minutes in mid-conversation. The situation was desperate, and by 25 March, none of us expected to get out alive. But somehow that didn't seem to mean anything, either – we just went on, relentlessly. I never heard a single man complain.

The final day came on Saturday 26 March. With the sun beating down mercilessly on the parched defenders, the Japanese closed in from all sides, with bullet, bayonet and grenade, desperate to break the hold that the defenders had placed on *31st Division's* advance. In a day of fierce attack and counter-attack across the Sangshak plateau the brigade lost more men than in the fighting so far. In the hand-to-hand struggle to regain possession of the Baptist Church, which sat at the height of the position, the counter-attacking troops of 152nd battalion lost heavily. The centre platoon lost thirty-two of the thirty-six who had begun the assault, but the Japanese also lost heavily: all but eight of the 120 men who had begun the assault that morning were killed. It was a difficult, bloody and hard fought day. 'Dicky' Richards:

> Shortly before dawn on the 26th, the Japanese actually penetrated our position in the Church area, and set up machine guns in the trenches which had been occupied by the brave men of 152 and 153 Battalions. Things got incredibly intense – they were now only 100 yards from Brigade Headquarters and we'd run out of grenades. But our men became even more ferocious and daring. Every man was fighting for his life and there seemed no limit to their endurance – everyone, everywhere, was pleading for more ammunition and grenades. By 0730 hours the situation was desperate, but the brigadier was determined to regain complete control of the Church area. He sent a party from the Brigade Defence Platoon on a frontal counter-attack. This was led by young Lieutenant Robin de la Haye ... Robin and his men made a spirited attack but were cut to pieces by enemy fire from West Hill. Again and again we counter-attacked, now led by Lieutenant Colonel Hopkinson, later by Colonel Abbott – but each time we were beaten back. At last, at 0930 hours, Major Jimmy Roberts with his A Company of 153 Battalion was successful and restored the situation, accompanied by deafening blasts from our own howitzers firing over open sights.

That night HQ IV Corps recognized the inevitable and ordered the survivors to break out and make their way as best they could – over the hills crawling with Japanese – to Imphal. The immovable wounded, some 150 men, had to be left behind, and the remaining 300 wounded had to walk out with the rest. Fortunately, the Japanese were equally exhausted. Captain 'Dicky' Richards:

> As the 2230 hours start-time approached, tension mounted. That evening Japanese fire had been limited to sporadic shots and a few bursts, but we wondered whether they would strike. If they did, our chances for survival would have been slim – but they didn't. Colonel

Abbott ordered me to channel the few remaining exhausted men of 152 Indian Para Battalion through the 4/5th Mahratta Light Infantry position, which was the safest of the lot. The former had taken a terrible hammering with over 350 killed. Few had properly eaten or rested for well over a week and they were now practically without ammunition or grenades, or senior ranks to guide them, with a tortuous journey facing them through the Jap-infested jungle to Imphal.

As the break-out got under way, I felt surprised at the quietness and orderliness as parties with makeshift bamboo stretchers and walking wounded vanished from sight into the jungle below. It was a painful and heart-rending experience, particularly for the medical men, whom I saw patching up and attending to anyone showing any signs of life.

It was a heartrending decision to leave their wounded comrades behind, particularly in the light of the knowledge of what often happened to them at the hands of the vengeful victors. In this case, following the successful extraction of Hope-Thomson's force that night, a remarkable feat only achieved through the sheer exhaustion of their Japanese enemy, the wounded were well treated. After occupying the vacated British positions the following day, Kameyama discovered the shallow grave the British had dug for Lieutenant Ban:

I was very much impressed to see that the corpse and sword of Lieutenant Ban had been buried and neatly packed in a blanket. Our men were all moved by this. As the enemy had treated our company commander respectfully, our regimental commander ordered that enemy wounded should be treated and prisoners of war should not be killed.

While 50 Parachute Brigade was virtually destroyed in the four days of the Sangshak battle (152nd Indian Battalion lost 350 men – 80 per cent of its strength – and 153rd Gurkha Battalion lost 35 per cent), considerable benefit fell to IV Corps by their sacrifice. The battle cost Miyazaki probably 1,000 casualties and his advance was held up for a week, causing serious delay to Sato's plans. From both 2/58th and 3/58th Miyazaki had lost six of his eight company commanders, as well as most of the platoon commanders. Kameyama recalled, 'Eight hundred and fifty men of our battalion crossed the River Chindwin [on 15 March], but now after twelve days, active men were reduced to half, 425 men.' Even Major Shimanoe,

Commanding Officer of 3/58th, was badly wounded. Miyazaki's speculative attack on Sangshak drew him into an unnecessary battle of attrition that delayed the journey of his column to Kohima and proved in time to be a serious setback to Mutaguchi's hopes of capturing all of his objectives within three weeks. It was the first sign on this front that Mutaguchi's plan was turning awry: the British at first seemed intent on flight, but here was stubborn – even fanatical – resistance, and it took the Japanese by surprise. The battle also gave Slim and Scoones valuable breathing space to reorganize and reinforce the Imphal positions, although it seems clear that a significant intelligence coup at Sangshak was not exploited by the British. A map taken from the dead body of a Japanese captain describing Sato's entire strategy in the north and his plans to surround Kohima and to make for Dimapur, was copied and smuggled out of encirclement to HQ IV Corps in Imphal. The officer concerned – Captain Lester Allen – then made the journey back to his comrades at Sangshak. Unfortunately the map, and its extraordinary information, disappeared and was never seen again. Slim received no benefit from this extraordinary stroke of intelligence.

'Dicky' Richards reached Imphal a week after the escape of the brigade from Sangshak:

> We had survived walking into an armed Japanese supply column heading for Sangshak by throwing ourselves or rolling into the thick elephant grass and lying 'doggo', whilst they passed within feet of some of us – we had no grenades and hardly a round between us. Days later whilst intelligence officers were debriefing us, I had a quiet cup of tea with Ouvry Roberts, whom I knew well. He left me in no doubt about the value of the stand which we had made. He said that the brigade, with its attached units, fighting under the most appalling conditions, had undoubtedly saved both Kohima and Imphal from the danger of being immediately overrun by the Japanese spearhead troops.

~

The bitter struggle at Sangshak led Scoones belatedly to an awareness of the danger posed to Imphal from the north-east. On 25 March Brigadier Bayley, Scoones' Chief of Staff, sent an urgent signal to Gracey warning him that he might have to relinquish one of his brigades in order to bolster the weak sector to the north, through which, if 50 Indian Parachute

Brigade gave way at Sangshak, the whole approach to Imphal lay open. This would mean that Gracey would have to withdraw further back towards Shenam, and relinquish the defence of the foothills around Moreh. Gracey, taken unawares by the proposition, did not receive it warmly. His division had successfully completed a difficult withdrawal to its new positions between Moreh and Shenam, and he did not view kindly the prospect of another, particularly one that appeared to be the result of poor forward planning, and he complained bitterly to Scoones by letter on 26 March.

'This division has fought magnificently so far,' he wrote, 'and all the troops have been fully aware of the necessity of withdrawing to their present position, with the Army Commander's [Slim's] assurance that behind them is a pile-up of reserves rapidly being reinforced to deal with the situation behind them. Our morale is sky high, as we have beaten the enemy and given him a real bloody nose everywhere. Everyone is prepared to hang on where they are now like grim death. It is their Verdun. It will be most shattering to morale if they are now asked to assist in the Imphal Plain and they will feel that someone has let them down.'

Gracey was particularly reluctant to abandon Moreh, but the Sangshak battle left Scoones with little choice as 20th Indian Division was in danger of being outflanked by 15th Division's assault on Imphal from the northeast. If Yamauchi were successful in penetrating the Imphal plain the whole defence of Imphal would unravel and Gracey's defences at Shenam would become irrelevant. Scoones undoubtedly made the right decision. If he is to be criticized it is for failing to keep Gracey informed about the overall situation from the outset. Gracey had no option but to withdraw further west towards Shenam. After destroying virtually everything that remained, 32 Brigade withdrew from Moreh, with the Japanese at their heels, at the end of the month. Major 'Ted' Kelly of the Northamptons recalled in his diary for 20 March,

> We are pulling out today, all kit not wanted is being sent back to Palel. Stood-to most of the day. Shells in the area in afternoon. One gun must be very close. Whizz-bang less than a second. 3-inch mortar ammo dumped in latrines exploded. The stink cannot be described. Crap everywhere. Got all the new clothing we wanted, and tinned milk and rum. Plenty of socks.

Eighty and 100 Brigades occupied positions between Shenam and Tengnoupal, about nine miles from Palel, while 32 Brigade was withdrawn into Corps Reserve. Twentieth Indian Division now held a twenty-five-mile front from Tengnoupal through Shenam to Shuganu, fifteen miles south-west of Palel. Gracey's new plan was to defend a number of fortified boxes on the high ground on Shenam Ridge and keep the road to Shenam and thence Palel open, rather than to hold the whole of his twenty-five-mile front in its entirety. Intensive patrolling covered the gaps.

~

Slim's fears for the security of Imphal were magnified suddenly by Cowan's unexpected withdrawal from Tiddim in contact with the enemy on 13 March, and the loss to Scoones over the following days of the major part of his Corps reserve. With 17th Indian Division potentially no longer available to defend Imphal, Scoones' reserve already engaged on the Tiddim Road and Gracey's division about to be fully occupied in the Kabaw Valley, Slim knew that the only way he could prevent Imphal from being overwhelmed was by the rapid and substantial reinforcement of IV Corps. In this sudden, dramatic and entirely unexpected turn of events Mutaguchi came close to achieving all his objectives well in advance of his own timetable. Had he been successful it would undoubtedly have resulted in one of the most serious reverses of British arms in the war. That Slim was conscious of the need to reinforce Imphal is demonstrated by the orders he had already given to fly in 5th Indian Division from Arakan when the situation on that front had stabilized. He had also approached General Sir George Giffard, his immediate superior and commander of 11 Army Group, for extra reinforcements to protect the base area at Dimapur from any long-range Japanese penetration through the Naga Hills. But the urgency of the new situation meant that speed was now vital. The only way that troops could be delivered to the threatened areas in Assam in days rather than weeks and months was by aircraft. Slim, however, had no transport aircraft at all, although in SEAC considerable numbers of American aircraft were involved in the Hump airlift over the Himalayas from India to China. By September 1943 the USA had provided fifteen squadrons (amounting to 230 Dakota and Commando aircraft) for the airlift, flying from airfields in north-east Assam, as part of Air Marshal John Baldwin's 3rd Tactical Air Force. These aircraft became the solution to Slim's sudden predicament. On the morning of 14 March Slim and Baldwin met Mountbatten at Comilla airport, explained the grave and unexpected situation facing IV Corps, and asked that some of these aircraft be diverted to reinforce Imphal. 'If we lost the Imphal-Kohima battle,' Slim reasoned, 'the Hump route would be closed. It seemed obvious therefore that it would be madness not to divert some of the China airlift to the vital needs of the Fourteenth Army.'

Realizing the critical nature of the sudden emergency, Mountbatten immediately and on his own initiative agreed to do what Slim had requested. He had, in fact, no authority to do anything of the kind, responsibility for tasking these aircraft sitting very firmly with the US Chiefs of Staff in Washington. Indeed, he had previously been instructed by Roosevelt not to divert these aircraft to any other use. But with no time to lose he decided to divert the aircraft first and ask permission later. On the same day – 14 March – Mountbatten instructed Giffard to waste no time in reinforcing Fourteenth Army with elements of the Army Group reserve when Slim requested them – Lieutenant General Montagu Stopford's XXXIII Corps, the major part of which was the well-equipped and experienced British 2nd Division (4, 5 and 6 Brigades), then in training on the other side of India near Bombay. This formidable division was home to a roll call of battalions from some of Britain's most famous county regiments: Royal Scots, Royal Norfolk Regiment, Lancashire Fusiliers, Royal Welch Fusiliers, Worcestershire Regiment, Dorsetshire Regiment, Royal Berkshire Regiment, Durham Light Infantry and Queen's Own Cameron Highlanders.

That evening Slim quantified his requirement for aircraft, sending Mountbatten a request for no fewer than 260 Dakota sorties to get each of the three brigades (9, 123 and 161) of Briggs' 5th Indian Division to Imphal in time to prevent a possible disaster. When, on the next day – 15 March – Slim discovered during a visit to Imphal that Scoones had been forced to send Collingridge's 49 Brigade to the Tiddim Road in addition to 37 Brigade, the urgency of the situation was reinforced. Slim therefore sent another message to Mountbatten asking urgently for twenty-five to thirty aircraft for the period 18 March to 20 April. Mountbatten immediately agreed. Slim then proceeded on 17 March to give orders for the air move of the whole of 5th Indian Division. A day later, from Dohazari airfield near Chittagong, the battalions of 123 Brigade began the fly-in. Flying two sorties a day, the division was flown into Imphal and Dimapur in the period through to 29 March.

Fortunately HQ Fourteenth Army had, months previously, prepared detailed loading tables to transport the whole of a division by Dakota in an emergency. Suddenly this foresight paid off (even though movement by air had never been practised), and the first operation of its kind in history seamlessly to transport by air a whole division from one battlefield to another was completed without a hitch. For the vast majority of the soldiers involved it was their first-ever flight in an aircraft.

Mountbatten's courage in unilaterally taking aircraft from the Hump to meet the needs of the current emergency when he had no authority to do so was a critical factor in the successful defence of Manipur. Washington could do little but retrospectively agree Mountbatten's fait accompli on 17 April, authorizing the diversion as a temporary measure to overcome the crisis of the moment. Retaining these aircraft to maintain the airlift into Imphal in order to sustain IV Corps, in addition to the fly-in of 5th and 7th Indian Divisions as rapid reinforcements, was an altogether different problem. On 23 March Slim wrote to Giffard stressing the need to increase the air supply to Fourteenth Army in the event of Imphal being cut off. With land routes cut, an air bridge was the only way in which IV Corps could be supplied. Slim warned Giffard that if the aircraft supporting IV Corps were withdrawn he could not be responsible for the consequences. Mountbatten needed no second urging, appealing immediately to Washington for another seventy aircraft to supply IV Corps while it lay besieged. This was no easy thing for the Chiefs of Staff to agree, as there was intense pressure on the limited number of transport aircraft across all theatres of war at the time. But Mountbatten refused to budge. Churchill signalled Mountbatten giving his support, 'Chiefs of Staff and I are backing you to the full, I have telegraphed the President [that] in my view nothing matters but the battle – be sure you win'. Mountbatten won the argument and the return of the aircraft was deferred until 15 June.

Even before Slim had come to him on 14 March with his urgent request for air transport, Mountbatten had been exercised by the need to increase the flow of reinforcements to Imphal. Privately he believed that Giffard was not doing enough to ensure that Slim had the resources he required to fight the forthcoming battle. On 5 March Slim had asked Giffard for a division to defend Dimapur and to provide rapid reinforcement for Kohima and Imphal should it be required. The obvious solution was to send forward the bulk of Stopford's XXXIII Corps from India to relieve an experienced Indian division in Arakan, and to transfer that division to the Naga Hills. Giffard was concerned, however, that moving an additional division from India would place intolerable burden on the Assam railway. A compromise was reached. Slim was given the two battalions of 50 Indian Parachute Brigade and Giffard promised him Major General Grover's 2nd British Division should it become necessary. Slim admitted later that this 'was by no means what I asked for', although he recognized Giffard's concerns about exacerbating the already significant supply problem on the Imphal plain.

Shortly afterwards Giffard agreed also to give Slim 23 Long-Range Penetration Brigade, commanded by Brigadier Lancelot Perowne, which was still in India. 'He agreed to rail it to Jorhat,' Slim recalled, 'where I could place it as a mobile force to cover the railway to Ledo, and, if necessary, use it against the flank of an attack on Dimapur.' On 18 March Slim decided to ask for HQ XXXIII Corps and confirmed his request for 2nd British Division to go to Chittagong to replace 5th Indian Division, even then flying into the Imphal Plain. Giffard at once agreed. Giffard also accepted Slim's request for 23 LRP Brigade and decided that, once the airlift of 5th Indian Division was complete, 7th Indian Division would then also be airlifted to Manipur.

However, with the rapid deterioration of the situation on the Imphal Plain, Slim requested on 27 March that Grover's 2nd British Division be sent not to Arakan, but to Dimapur instead. This brought its own problems, as the earliest it could arrive was the first week of April, although the division was already on the move, travelling by train across India in the direction of Calcutta.

The aircraft secured by Mountbatten to support IV Corps in Imphal were unable to begin their airlift into Manipur until mid-April. Scoones therefore took the precaution of cutting the ration scale by a third and flying out 43,000 non-combatants and 13,000 casualties to India by returning aircraft. Baldwin's 3rd Tactical Air Force began Operation STAMINA on 18 April but it took some time to build up to the daily requirement of 540 tons. By contrast, as Slim had predicted, the Japanese supply situation became increasingly precarious. In his assessments of possible British reactions to Operation C, Mutaguchi could have had no inkling of the dramatic power air transport would give to them to move troops around the battlefield. Certainly he could not have expected the rapid transfer of two whole divisions from Arakan to Imphal and Kohima to meet the threat posed by the sudden onset of Mutaguchi's offensive.

~

The RAF and IAF were engaged in the battle from the outset, fighting from the six airfields on the Imphal Plain. The primary strip was Imphal Main, a handful of miles north of Imphal town, overlooked by the extraordinary Nunshigum hill, a sharp pointed ridge jutting spectacularly 4,000 feet above the valley floor and providing a clear view over Imphal town below. Tulihal⁶ was just to the south and Kangla sat on the town's eastern outskirts. Sapam and Palel lay in the south-east, where the Shenam hills debouched onto the Plain, and Wangjing was halfway between these two and Imphal. Only Imphal Main, Palel and Tulihal, however, were all-weather, the latter being covered with 'bithess', a product made from soaking strips of hessian in bitumen and laying them across the dirt strip, a process also used extensively on many of the otherwise fair-weather tracks in the region to improve mobility during the monsoon season. They were all rough and ready. Sergeant Frank Thomas of the radio direction finding team based at Imphal described Kangla 'as the most awful place which I can recall'. It was built on a *padi* field, and during the rainy season was populated with 'gruesome fish' which seemed to emerge from the parched earth when the rains arrived.

There were few comforts, outside of some ramshackle buildings and tents at Imphal Main. At Sagam, the pilots and ground crew lived in windowless huts borrowed from the villagers a mile from the airfield, but at night at all airfields men retired into a defensive 'box' on the strip itself surrounded by barbed wire (if they had it) and trip wires, close to the aircraft, sleeping in trenches. Aircrew and ground crew alike contributed to sentry duty. Where it was available corrugated iron was placed over the trenches to keep out the rain, but more often canvas was stretched over the roofs, and sandbag ramparts provided some degree of protection from shrapnel. The accommodation was primitive, being damp and uncomfortable. Being forced to live like infantrymen beneath the ground with few home comforts came as a particular shock to those RAF personnel used to sleeping in a warm, dry bed at night between operations. For Flight Lieutenant Wilfred Goold, an Australian flying in the RAF this 'was not the type of living and work we were brought up to expect. We considered it highly dangerous…' It was. It took at least one Japanese strafing or bombing attack to force the otherwise reluctant airmen and ground crew to dig with any sense of purpose, as Flying Officer John Hopkins, a Canadian with 42 Squadron (Hurricanes), found at Imphal. They had only paid lip service to the instruction to dig, scratching holes a mere two-feet deep in the ground, until three Japanese fighters came in low soon after and strafed the airfield:

> Most of us were having breakfast at the time and when the strafing began we headed for the trenches all at once and all in the same trench! The strafing was quite accurate and we were all quite concerned.

The trenches were dug immediately, energetically and deeply.

When the Japanese offensive began, the Imphal-based aircrews spent time hunting along the river, attacking boats and pontoon bridges where they could find them, although Japanese camouflage was superb. Flying Officer Ken Lister recalled that this was often a difficult task as 'the river craft were more or less impossible to sink as they were small, made of wood, which were not badly affected by the odd hole made by a 20mm shell'. Oliver Moxon's pseudonymous Hurricane pilot, Stefan James, recalled how, on 22 February, he and Flying Officer 'Smokey' Boyes spotted camouflaged motor transport on the Chindwin during a low-level sortie along the river:

> The heat was suffocating, and the Burmese sun beat through the Perspex making a sort of haze in the cockpit, but where the river takes an easterly sweep at Yuwa, it was I who noticed an irregular pile of brushwood and scrub tucked well into the left bank. I gave Smokey a buzz and shot some cannon into the middle of the bush. Next second the sky was filled with heavy black smoke and licks of orange flame. Smokey had a shot, then we circled for a bit and took camera shots at the bonfire. As the foliage burnt away we saw the target was a largish motor boat, obviously carrying petrol or Diesel oil for transport.[7]

Mutaguchi's use of every possible means of transport made the pilots' task extremely distasteful on occasions, when cannon-firing Hurricanes were detailed to attack herds of Japanese elephants. Navigation was also difficult. Squadron Leader 'Buck' Courtney of 113 Squadron:

> Since one jungle-covered valley or mountainside looks very much like another, map reading was difficult in any case, and navigational aids non-existent.

Many fighter sorties were at very low levels, often fifty feet, especially cannon-strafing missions against Japanese positions or transport. The pilots did not enjoy these. 'Buck' Courtney led twelve aircraft to attack a Japanese-held village on 22 March, diving onto the target with cannon blazing before pulling out of their dive to release the two wing-mounted 250-pound bombs. Unfortunately, Courtney flew so low that his Hurricane was damaged by the blast from his own explosions, although he was able to coax his damaged aircraft safely home. At low level the aircraft were especially vulnerable to ground fire. Flying Officer Perry was killed on 27 March when he took his Hurricane in low to strafe a Japanese truck convoy on the Tiddim road. Hit by Japanese fire, Perry's aircraft exploded in mid air and spun into the ground. Likewise, if things went wrong when the aircraft was at low level, the pilot was lucky to escape. During a ground attack mission at Merema, north of Kohima, in April, Flight Lieutenant 'Shag' Shannon, a New Zealand pilot with 34 Squadron suffered an explosion in one of his 20mm cannon – a not irregular peril – forcing him to bale out at very low level. He survived the ordeal, landing safely within British lines.

~

In early March Imphal boasted six fighter squadrons for its defence, a total of around forty-eight aircraft. Two Hurricane Squadrons were based at Imphal Main and two were at Palel. Two further squadrons, one of Hurricanes and one of Spitfires, were on the fair-weather strip at Sapam. A third Spitfire Mk V squadron – 615 – joined 81 (Kangla) and 135 (Wangjing) on 19 March, being based at Silchar, in Assam. The Japanese had long kept Imphal under high-level aerial surveillance and, as March began, Air Vice Marshal Vincent's 221 Group RAF began moving extra fighter squadrons into the plain to protect against the expected onslaught. Within days of arrival, Spitfires of 81 Squadron had shot down three twin-engined Mitsubishi 'Dinah' Ki-46 reconnaissance aircraft. These had, until now, been flying with impunity at 30,000 feet, but the arrival of the Spitfires came as a rude shock to the pilots of the Japanese *sentai* of 5th Air Division. Flying Officer Larry Cronin, an Australian, scrambled with two other Spitfires of 81 Squadron at 7.40 a.m. on the morning of 4 March to chase intruders reported by the early-warning radar in the hills. Climbing rapidly under his unsuspecting victim he poured a burst of cannon fire into its belly. The Japanese aircraft, shocked at the sudden loss of its immunity, immediately slipped to the left and dived steeply in an attempt to escape its attacker. Cronin dived after it and although his cannon then jammed, he could see bullets from his four .303-inch machine guns scoring repeatedly on the enemy's fuselage. The Dinah was doomed, crashing five miles south of Palel. British soldiers investigating the crash discovered that the pilot had been killed by one of Cronin's bullets which had gone through the back of his head.

The men of 221 Group RAF had by this time been in almost constant combat over Burma in support of the Chindit operations, which had dropped the troops of Orde Wingate's Special Force deep behind Japanese lines. As the RAF was heavily committed to these operations the Japanese stepped up their attacks on the Imphal Plain, although the high-level reconnaissance flights all but ceased. The Japanese also tried hard to destroy the airbases outside the Imphal Plain in Assam, such as Silchar. On

12 March an attack was launched by sixty fighters escorting a small force of bombers. In the Imphal Plain itself early morning mist and the mountainous country made the embryonic radar even less effective than it would have been in flat country. It was not possible to prepare for every raid. In the darkness of the early morning of 17 March two Japanese bombers managed to drop their bombs directly on HQ IV Corps, a testament either to extraordinary luck or to high quality Japanese intelligence about British locations. The attack caused thirty-two casualties. As the darkness lifted, a clutch of Ki 43 'Oscar' fighters swept at low level over both Tulihal and Palel, damaging a Dakota transport, a B-25 bomber and a Hurricane fighter, all on the ground.

The loss of Tamu on 22 March cost Imphal its early warning airfield, where radar had warned of incoming raids into the Imphal Plain, giving fighters in the Plain an eight-minute warning to scramble. Not knowing that the airfield had fallen, three Hurricanes landed on the strip on 22 March. The pilots were taken prisoner and executed instantly.

Occasionally dramatic successes were achieved against Japanese infantry. On Wednesday 29 March an entire Japanese battalion was spotted in the open, ten miles north-east of Imphal, by a lone Hurricane flown by Squadron Leader Arjan Singh, commanding No 1 Squadron, Indian Air Force. In response to his calls for assistance, thirty-three Hurricanes were scrambled from four squadrons around the Imphal Plain to attack this rare target, and a heavy strafing attack was put in, resulting (according to Japanese reports) in the death or wounding of 241 men. It was unusual to be able to engage the elusive Japanese from the air with such success, as the jungle canopy rarely provided anything but fleeting glimpses of activity beneath.

By the start of April 1944, the Japanese had pressed up in the south to the outskirts of the Imphal Plain. In the north, Kohima was about to be invested and the road to Dimapur severed, forcing supplies for Imphal to be flown in by air. It was a nerve-racking moment. Could Imphal hold out? Not everyone within the plain was confident that Imphal would survive. Following his squadron's withdrawal from the dirt strip at Kangla out of the Imphal Plain to the relative safety of Kumbhirgram, west of the Chin Hills and home to four squadrons of Vultee Vengeance twin-seat dive-bombers, Larry Cronin noted pessimistically in his diary on 31 March:

> All quiet at the moment. The Japs are closing in on Imphal from north and south. The army here have occasional brushes with them but seem content to withdraw and 'defend' the valley itself. All 'dromes in the valley are on the box defence system. I reckon we'll lose this valley before long, despite the army's confidence.

# Chapter 3

# Kohima Besieged

Kohima is the capital town of Nagaland.[8] It straddles the single road that runs from the Brahmaputra Valley across the mountains east and south-east into Manipur. This road enters the Naga Hills on the plain at Dimapur and then immediately rises into the hills, twisting its way up through mountain gorges till it reaches the apex of its climb forty-six miles later, at Kohima. For the traveller going further into the hills, eastward towards Manipur and the Imphal Plain a hundred miles further on, the journey follows the rough road hewn from the hillside that snakes around the mountain, high above the valley floor, to Mao Songsang, the first village in Manipur. After leaving Mao the road drops down into the Imphal Plain to Imphal (Palel is at Milestone 164) before climbing over the Angousham Hills to its terminus at Tamu, just inside the Burmese border, at Milestone 200.

Leaving the heat of Dimapur, the road into the mountains takes the traveller up steep, sharply angled and thickly forested hills. The road in 1944 was newly metalled for most of the way, only degenerating into a riot of ruts and potholes the closer one got to Imphal. The greatest danger to unwary drivers was the sharp bends, many jutting out above precipitous slopes. Captain Eric Neild of 153rd Gurkha Parachute Battalion feared for his life when he first travelled this route, visiting Kohima from Imphal on 18 March 1944. 'Going back we nearly slid over the precipitous khudside several times – it was no place for a two-wheel-driven vehicle on that narrow slippery surface and we soon gave it up and decided to walk the rest of the way.' Lieutenant John Henslow, newly posted to 59 Independent Field Company (part of 23rd Indian Division) on the Imphal-Tamu Road, had travelled through these hills several months before:

> The ascent is through bamboo vegetation, its delicate tracery arched over the small tortuous track that wound its way up one hillside to the other. In places cascades of water fell down the mountain side

raising water vapour that sparkled in the sunlight, but for much of the way you drove through a green tunnel of bamboo but always conscious of the precipitous drop on one side and the hanging hillside above you on the other.

The final stretch of the road into Kohima climbs steeply up the western edge of the Kohima Ridge, curving tightly across a deep, two-mile-wide valley separating the Pulebadze Ridge that dominates the right (southern) side and Kohima Hill, atop which lies Naga Village, on the northern. Possession of Naga Hill and the ridge that runs due west to Merema (i.e., parallel to the road from Dimapur on the northern side of the valley), allows observation of the northern edge of Kohima Ridge (comprising 'Summerhouse' or Garrison Hill, and the High Spur or Indian General Hospital (IGH) Spur), as well as a considerable portion of the road that snakes back in the direction of Jotsoma and Zubza. At Zubza (Milestone 36), one can stand and look up the valley towards the Kohima Ridge towering in the distance ten miles further in terms of distance and 2,000 feet higher in altitude. Between Zubza and Kohima the valley narrows rapidly, the ridge on the left running from Merema all the way to Naga Village, both sides ending in a bottleneck at the Kohima Ridge. Ejecting an opponent from the Kohima Ridge was aptly likened by Lieutenant General Montague Stopford, commander of XXXIII Corps, 'to forcing a cork out of a bottle'. On the ridge itself, after passing the IGH on the right-hand side, the road bends around the ridge and bifurcates at a junction known as the Traffic Control Point (TCP), filtering the road left and up the hill to Naga Village, while the main road continues around the eastern side of the ridge and on to Imphal. The slopes leading up to the ridge from the valley floor at this point are savagely abrupt and covered in thick jungle. On the northern side of the Kohima Ridge, across a thin saddle connecting the two, Naga Village sits atop a vast rounded hill, as broad and as wide again as Kohima Ridge, and standing much higher. From the top of Naga Village one can look directly across the valley well over a mile to the Deputy Commissioner's bungalow on Garrison Hill.

The Kohima Ridge is an enormous physical barrier, especially so to an army intent on moving further west towards Dimapur; consequently, its defence and retention is critical if this route is to be barred to an invader. In 1944 the thickly forested Kohima Ridge was home to the scattered support depots and stores necessary to sustain a small peacetime garrison swollen since 1942 by the pressures of war in Burma. Charles Pawsey MC, the Deputy Commissioner for Nagaland since 1935, veteran of the

Western Front and one of the few honorary civilian members of V Force, lived in a bungalow on the northernmost slopes, the driveway to his house slipping down the hill to touch the main Imphal-Dimapur road at the TCP. To provide some leisure facilities a tennis court had been built below his bungalow. It was a source of polite amusement to those Naga *Gaonburas* (tribal and village chiefs) who visited the bungalow on official business; their idea of sport for centuries past had mainly been raiding neighbouring villages to relieve the inhabitants of their heads. The contrast presented by Kohima to the dusty plains of Bengal certainly appealed to Henslow:

> The giant bamboo that curtained the steep ascent to Kohima gave way suddenly ... to neat white bungalows, grass and delphiniums that were in full bloom around the tennis court by the District [sic] Commissioner's bungalow. Tall spruce and very English looking trees lined some of the roads. Plum and pear trees could be seen in most of the gardens together with all the cultivated flowers from roses to hydrangeas that were so reminiscent of English country gardens.

The remainder of the ridge boasted 53rd Indian General Hospital (IGH) on the north-western slopes overlooking the road from Dimapur, a Field Supply Depot (FSD), and the Detail Issue Stores (DIS). Overlooking the entire ridge from the southern end was a distinctive pimple known as Jail Hill, named after the local prison that lay at its base. The highest point of the ridge was Kuki Picquet. Dominating all these features from a greater distance, however, are the 9,000-foot-high mountains of the Japfü range on the southern side of the valley, projecting their shadow over the whole of the Kohima area. These hills run parallel to the valley which rises into Kohima from Dimapur. As one approaches from Dimapur the first point of high ground is Jotsoma, two miles from Kohima and enjoying a clear view of the ridge. Leaving the road and heading up the hillside to the right a stiff three-hour climb carries one to the top of Mount Pulebadze (7,522 feet). Behind Pulebadze a track crosses the saddle over to the top of Aradura, and spurs flow down northwards into the eastern side of Kohima. In the foothills of these spurs sit, among others, the deeply-forested Congress Hill and General Purpose Transport (GPT) Ridge, all of which offer sight of, and dominate, Kohima Ridge from the south. If an enemy could control the whole of Kohima Ridge it would be in command of the route into Dimapur, the gatehouse of India. If they could simultaneously occupy Naga Village, the ridge could be observed from two sides. There was virtually no part of the ridge that was not dominated in some way by another feature, or could not be fired at or observed from elsewhere. It could easily be surrounded (although the western slope was extremely steep), and without water could not hold out for long. In fact, it was, in conventional terms, indefensible. Because of this no thought had been given to its protection.

The Naga people in 1944 largely remained loyal to the Raj, as did the Kukis in the Charchar Hills south-west of Kohima unlike the Kukis in the Somra Tracts and Angousham Hills, most of whom favoured the Japanese. American missionaries had been instrumental in converting large numbers of Nagas to a robust Christianity, beginning as early as the 1830s. The Nagas are enthusiastic and gifted singers. Lieutenant John Henslow, driving through Kohima for the second time in late 1943, stopped his vehicle to rest. He was immediately mesmerized by a sound that floated towards him on the breeze:

> It sounded like a mass choir singing – 'Abide With Me'. The effect was dramatic in the extreme. Thousands of miles from Britain in the remote Naga Hills to hear a mass of voices singing 'Abide With Me' was both unforgettable and inexplicable. Slowly it grew louder until round the bend of the road the choir appeared. Not a contingent of Welsh miners but several hundred Naga tribesmen who had been working on the road. They passed us in full throat and wound their way down the road until the hymn hung on the air like a fading dream.

The war brought many changes to life in the Naga Hills, not the least of which was the arrival of many new and uncommon races of people as well as extraordinary innovations, such as the appearance of aircraft in the sky. Few villagers had ever seen such things before. Noumvüo Khruomo was twenty when he saw his first aircraft. He was working with his family in the fields when he saw the aeroplane, exclaiming in astonishment how amazing it was that they were to witness something so spectacular in their lifetime. Neilao, a young man of the same age, first saw a plane flying above Khonoma village. He stared at it in wonder:

> The others with me shouted "*Lei,Lei,Lei,kepruo lei*" (look, look, look, a plane, look). We were so filled with awe at seeing that flying object in the sky. I thought to myself, so that is what a *kepruo* is. The second time we saw aircraft was when four-five planes flew over Khonoma. The British set off a loud alarm telling people to hide. Later, we heard that those planes had bombed Silchar.

On first seeing an aircraft the villagers of Chakhesang ran outside to watch, the elders calling out: 'Come, come out and see, there is a strange bird in the sky!' The 'bird' then proceeded to open its belly and drop bombs into the valley below. The villagers were shocked, some calling out in surprise, 'Look out! It's defecating!' before the bombs exploded deafeningly, sending the villagers running back in terror to their huts. The next day was declared a taboo day, a no-work day to purify the village of any ill consequences from the sighting of the strange bird and its terrifying excrement.

~

It was at Kohima that the British came close to losing the Battle for India. In 1944 the importance of Kohima – obvious to all who had visited the ridge and seen its dominating position on the single mountainous road between Manipur and the Brahmaputra Valley – was not appreciated by those responsible for the defence of India. The mountain town lay 120 miles beyond the Chindwin, across formidably mountainous terrain far beyond where anyone expected the Japanese might be able to reach in strength. If they did advance into the Naga Hills the British assumed that the most the Japanese could infiltrate was a regiment (i.e., the equivalent of a British brigade). The ridge guards the only route between Dimapur and Imphal: if Kohima fell, Imphal would be without access to succour or supplies, and with the further prize of India beyond. In any case Lieutenant General Slim believed that the real prize, were the Japanese to penetrate this far, was at Dimapur, where vast depots and stores had been assembled to support the growing forces in Manipur, together with the entire structure supporting the Chinese/American forces under Lieutenant General 'Vinegar Joe' Stilwell in the north. What would the Japanese gain by securing Kohima if they failed to seize the British supplies in Dimapur? It made no sense to Slim for the Japanese to attack Kohima without pressing on to threaten Dimapur.

Giffard, Slim and Scoones met together in Imphal on 20 March to consider the impending crisis. As yet, they did not know the true scale of the imminent threat to Kohima. The severity of the threat facing Kohima was not realized by the British until it was nearly too late. Slim claims that he had realized within a week of the start of the offensive (i.e., by 22 March) that the situation at Kohima was likely to be more dangerous than he had anticipated. It seems clear, however, that even by early-April Slim had still not realized that the bulk of Sato's 31st Division was pushing on to the town. If he had known that this was the case he would undoubtedly have defended the ridge robustly to prevent its capture. As has been seen there is no evidence that the copy of Miyazaki's battle plans, which had fallen into the hands of 50 Parachute Brigade during the Sangshak battle, pointing to Kohima as the objective for the whole of 31st Division, ever reached him. Even without this knowledge the situation was grave. Cowan's 17th Indian Division and the major part of Roberts' 23rd Indian Division were fully engaged on the Tiddim road, Gracey's 20th Indian Division was withdrawing in contact with the enemy to Moreh, and Hope-Thomson's unprepared and weakened 50 Parachute Brigade had suddenly and unexpectedly been confronted by large numbers of enemy in the Ukhrul area the day before. In addition, enemy forces were known to be moving on Kohima and it was assumed that the Japanese were likewise closing in on Silchar to the south-west.

Certain that Scoones now had enough on his plate with the defence of Imphal, Slim gave temporary responsibility for the defence of Dimapur and Kohima to Major General Ranking, commander of 202nd Line of Communication Area. Ranking was to transfer responsibility to Stopford when the latter arrived with his XXXIII Corps in early April. When fully constituted the corps was to consist of 5th and 7th Indian Divisions and 2nd British Division. On 22 March Slim ordered a scratch garrison under Colonel Hugh Richards to move to Kohima to act as a forward defence for Dimapur. Richards was a fighting soldier with a fine reputation who had recently been released from the Chindits because Wingate believed anyone over forty to be too old for his Special Force operations (Richards was fifty and Wingate was forty). On the same day Slim briefed Stopford at Comilla. When, exactly a week later, 'Daddy' Warren's experienced 161 Brigade arrived from Arakan Slim sent it directly to Kohima to assist in the defence of the ridge.[9] Slim told Warren that he expected the Japanese to arrive at Kohima by 3 April and to reach Dimapur by 10 April, by which time only one brigade of 2nd British Division would have arrived to support the defence of this strategically vital base area.

Stopford's plan was to concentrate his corps as it arrived at Jorhat, sixty-five miles north-east of Dimapur, ready to launch a counter-stroke against Dimapur if, in the meantime, the base had been occupied or was under attack by the Japanese. One brigade would be despatched as soon as it arrived to hold the Nichugard Pass, eight miles south-east of Kohima on the road to Dimapur, in order to support 161 Brigade already defending the village. Finally, Perowne's 23 Chindit Brigade would be diverted to the defence of Kohima. This brigade, which was expected to arrive on 12 April, would be used to strike south of Kohima and to the east of it to disrupt and cut the Japanese line of communication back to the Chindwin.

~

On 29 March Sato's 31st Division cut the Imphal-Kohima road at Milestone 72. The race to feed units into Dimapur before the arrival of the Japanese was now one of dramatic urgency. With Stopford's troops still several days away, following their diversion from Chittagong, the question of how to defend Kohima and Dimapur became critical. There was no simple solution, as the sum total of experienced combat troops available before Grover's 2nd British Division arrived was Warren's 161 Brigade (1/1st Punjab, 4/7th Rajputs and 4th Royal West Kents, known colloquially in the British Army as 'The Dirty Half Hundred'). On 29 March Slim met to discuss the issue, first in Imphal with Scoones and Stopford and then later in the day, after a short flight from Imphal, with Ranking at Dimapur. Stopford, as incoming corps commander, was concerned that if 161 Brigade was surrounded and isolated at Kohima before Grover's division arrived there would be nothing with which to defend Dimapur. Slim agreed that this was a serious risk but argued that a well-defended Kohima would certainly force Sato to deal with it prior to proceeding to Dimapur, thus giving valuable breathing space to Stopford to move the remainder of 2nd Division into position. A compromise of sorts was reached, but, as with most compromises, some clarity as to the main intention was lost.

Following these two meetings Slim issued his orders to Ranking in writing. Ranking was to prepare Dimapur for defence and hold it when attacked; to reinforce Kohima and hold it to the last; and to prepare for the reception of the reinforcements from XXXIII Corps that were on their way from elsewhere in India. Ranking interpreted in these orders no instruction to evacuate 161 Brigade from Kohima. Indeed, Warren's troops, on Slim's orders, were arriving that very day after having flown directly into Dimapur from Arakan. Private Raymond Street thought the flight from Dohazari into Dimapur in American transport aircraft (Curtis Commandos) was an execrable experience:

> It wasn't very comfortable. There weren't any seats. We had to sit on our packs. The crew were American. The navigator kept poking his head out telling us that if we saw any Japs to put the Bren guns out of the windows and shoot them ...
> [Lieutenant] Tom Hogg went with the mules in British Dakotas. As soon as the engines roared into action they urinated everywhere.

> In the heat the stench was awful. The aircrew went mad. The urine collected beneath the floor of the fuselage amongst the electrics. I don't know how they got rid of it. It must have stunk for ages.

But the airlift worked and, in a matter of hours, the entire brigade had been safely deposited in Dimapur. Meanwhile Stopford concentrated on moving his Corps HQ to Jorhat, where it was established on 3 April. That night, the day before Ranking formally transferred command, Stopford made what proved to be a serious error of judgement. Still firmly of the belief that the Japanese objective was Dimapur, and in response to erroneous intelligence that Japanese units were at that very moment in the process of out-flanking Kohima, Stopford ordered Ranking to withdraw 161 Brigade from Kohima immediately. All involved in the defence of Kohima – Warren, Colonel Hugh Richards, and the civilian Deputy Commissioner, Charles Pawsey – were aghast at, and protested against – the decision. When told that the Japanese were out-flanking Kohima to the north, Pawsey scoffed, retorting that if true, 'my Nagas would have told me'.

Despite this, that evening the two battalions had fallen back several miles along the road to Nichugard, leaving in Kohima a weak garrison comprising two companies of the Nepalese Shere Regiment and about 260 men of the Assam Rifles under the command of Major 'Buster' Keene, together with odds and sods recovering in the hospital and manning the depots. Ranking, sure that Stopford was making a mistake, went over the head of his new superior officer and called Slim directly by telephone to petition him to leave Warren at Kohima. Slim, perhaps unwilling to overrule Stopford, and in any case as convinced as Stopford that Dimapur was the Japanese objective, confirmed Stopford's original order. The compromise reached on 30 March had not led to a clear understanding of whether, with the limited troops available, it was better to defend Kohima or Dimapur. Warren's 161 Brigade, which had been in the process of organizing the desperately needed defence of the ridge, left Kohima virtually undefended only one day before Japanese attacks began. Had Warren's men been allowed to remain where they were the trauma of the siege that followed would have been much reduced and the stranglehold which Sato was able to maintain on the vital road to Imphal for two long months would have been significantly weaker than it turned out to be.

~

During this week of embarrassing confusions Sato was rapidly and skilfully pushing his columns through the mountainous terrain from the Chindwin.

The only British defences in the Naga Hills comprised V Force watching posts in the mountaintop villages, a company of the Assam Regiment at Jessami and another at Kharasom, several days' march forward of Kohima. In the weeks before they first arrived in these villages in force, Japanese and INA reconnaissance patrols had moved extensively across the Naga Hills, identifying tracks and sources of food. There were many signs from mid-March – and even earlier in villages along the Chindwin – that Japanese troops were deep in the region. Around the village of Phek, Viketu Kiso saw many of their footprints – the Japanese wore distinctive rubber cloven-soled boots with a separate toe – in the fields, on the tracks and around the streams. But the Japanese took care otherwise to keep themselves from view, operating in small numbers and at night with the effect that their presence was likened to that of ghosts, and some of the more superstitious were frightened by the appearance of the invisible cloven-footed spirits. It was only on the morning of 3 April 1944 that Viketu Kiso saw the Japanese arrive in large numbers. He heard some of the villagers shouting, 'The whole forest is moving! So many of them have come.'

> We ran to watch this phenomenon and indeed it was as they said. The whole forest came alive and there was not one spot that was still. Men poured out of the trees, from behind every rock and green plant, the Japanese soldiers with guns out-thrust, they made a terrifying sight, our hearts froze within us. They surged forward and even as we stood there transfixed, they had reached the village ... But as they came closer, there were no signs of animosity. Indian Officers led the Japanese into our village and when they spoke to our elders, they did not sound threatening. The Indian officers told us, 'Don't be afraid of the Japanese. They are here to chase the British forces out of India and the Naga Hills. Once they have done that, they will go back directly to Japan. Don't be afraid of them at all. After they have driven the British away, we shall be independent and we shall rule ourselves. We shall no longer be under the white man.' That sounded reasonable enough to the elders.

On news that the *Japani* were coming many of the Phek villagers fled to hide in the fields. Twelve-year-old Neikahi Keyho and his family followed many others to the huts that they had constructed alongside their fields to provide shelter from the elements and wild animals when they had to stay in the fields overnight. Most were sturdy and weatherproof. 'We stayed at our hut in the field for about a month. As we knew in advance what was to happen we hid our stock of rice here and there in the field. Some people even went to the village at night and retrieved food from their houses.' The more inquisitive, like Vesusa Huire, were co-opted by the Japanese to help guide the Japanese to their camps around the village. 'We were sent on long distances to bring back those who had been left behind.'

Twenty-seven-year-old Sovehü Nienu was a soldier in the newly raised 1st Battalion, Assam Regiment, based at Jessami, when the Japanese arrived:

> At Jessami, we heard that the Japanese were coming closer toward us, so we readied ourselves by digging trenches, storing our food and even storing water in bamboos and these supplies were all spread across the trenches as it would be impossible for us to move around if the war began.
>
> On the day of the invasion, the Japanese marched toward us rapidly. We started to fire at them. I saw three or four of them fall down dead. The Japanese surrounded our camp and during the day casualties were light but when night fell the casualties became heavy. Our war went on for five days and we did not know night from day sometimes. We were unable to cook or eat, so we had our stored rations like biscuits, jam, chapattis, tinned meat etc and we went on fighting our war eating our ration food. On the sixth day of battle we retreated from the camp and we fled in different directions. I reached Wokha on 31 March 1944. I had shrapnel injuries from a mortar shell explosion and so I went to hospital at Wokha.

The young and inexperienced soldiers of the Assam Regiment had, like their compatriots at Sangshak, fought like veterans, astounding the Japanese of Colonel Torikai's 138th Regiment by the ferocity – and determination – of their response, even when they knew themselves to be surrounded by an overwhelming enemy force. Captain Peter Steyn, an officer in the regiment and later its historian, described the cool panache of these teenage soldiers, Naga, Kuki and Assamese, under their young Glaswegian commander, Captain John ('Jock') Young, who now lies in the Kohima cemetery:

> Young and inexperienced sepoys were fighting like veterans; red-hot machine-gun barrels would be ripped off, regardless of burns suffered in the process; Japanese grenades and cracker-bombs were picked up and thrown clear of the trenches with all the calmness in the world and there did not seem to be a man in the garrison afraid to carry out any task given to him.

When ordered to withdraw back to Kohima, Young instructed his sepoys to leave, remaining at his post on the night of 31 March while his men slipped out through gaps in the perimeter until his position was swamped the next morning by men of at least one Japanese battalion, this extraordinarily brave young officer firing his Bren gun and throwing grenades to the last.

~

On the morning of 4 April Japanese troops from 1/58th Regiment attacked the southern edge of Kohima at GPT Ridge after a march of some 160 miles in twenty days over terrain which both Scoones and Slim had considered impassable to large bodies of troops and following the bloody battle at Sangshak. It was a remarkable feat. Yoshihiro Yamada recalled that the exhausted troops threw away anything they felt was not necessary to the coming battle. 'We chucked our blankets away.' Even on the march to Kohima men fell by the wayside, dying of exhaustion. Where there were no jungle paths the troops advanced along the riverbed. Private Zenshiro Tsukada recollected occasionally hearing men calling out from behind, 'So-and-so from such-and-such squad has fallen in the river'. They carried on regardless. For Private Nobuyuki Hata,

> It was all just so agonizing. For a whole week, I hardly recall sleeping at all. We could only take brief naps when we stopped for a long halt, which was dangerous up in those mountains, as it was mountain warfare at a height of 2,000 metres or so. So in order to get through that, we had to carry on for a week or ten days without sleeping or eating.

But in its execution Ranking and Warren's worst fears were realized, the Japanese arriving, albeit in small numbers, only hours after Warren had withdrawn his brigade from Kohima. Troops of 2/58th and 3/58th quickly fed through the hills and valleys leading into Kohima from the east. They were surprised to find that they were not expected. Captain Tsuneo Sanukawae of 11 Company 3/58th Regiment was astonished to find that Naga Village, on the northern side of the Kohima area, was undefended and asleep when his troops arrived during the early hours of 4 April. The men were exhausted but were urged on by their commanders. Lieutenant Kobayashi Naoji, one of Tsuneo's platoon commanders, appeared at the outskirts of Kohima village as the light dawned that morning, and pushed on aggressively with his platoon in the unsuspecting village. On top of Church Knoll two sleepy sentries of the Shere Regiment were bayoneted, their crumpled bodies lying in the open space for the next several days, until removed by villagers. Down the hill, in the area of the barracks, just short of Kohima town itself, the Japanese arrival came as a complete surprise as Captain Tsuneo recalled that 'The enemy had not noticed our advance and at 9 a.m. came to the depots to draw their rations. We got them and made them prisoner'.

Twelve-year-old Khriezotuo Sachü was astonished the next morning to see the Japanese soldiers rebind their blistered feet with dirty, bloodstained bandages, the result of their extraordinarily punishing march. They were kind and conciliatory towards the Naga villagers, and even attempted to play football with the youngsters who, lacking the fear and inhibitions of their parents, crowded around to have a closer look at the newcomers. On the southern side of the Kohima area the previous night a patrol sent out by Colonel Richards into the densely-forested foothills of the Aradura Spur had encountered a group of Japanese soldiers digging. A quick determined rush with the bayonet quickly disposed of these interlopers, but the news that the Japanese were so close to Kohima came as a profound shock to Richards, who knew just how poorly the area was defended. When the message got back to Stopford in Dimapur the folly of the previous instructions that Warren's brigade withdraw from Kohima were suddenly apparent. In desperation, 161 Brigade immediately began to retrace its steps. By the following morning – 5 April 1944 – the leading battalion of the brigade (446 men of 4th Battalion Royal West Kents, commanded by Lieutenant Colonel John Laverty, a ramrod backed Irishman originally from the Essex Regiment whom the men nick-named 'Colonel Lavatory' or 'Texas Dan' depending on the circumstance) had managed to rejoin the Kohima garrison on the ridge that stretched from the DIS to the IGH as Sato launched further attacks on the ill-prepared defenders, the remainder of the brigade unable to get in before the Japanese tentacles enclosed the garrison.

Private Raymond Street of the Royal West Kents sat in the back of a truck with his comrades, bumping their way towards the sound of the fighting from Nichugard, hearing shell bursts 'and mortar bombs and hearing the crack-pop sound of the Japanese rifles'. Petrified Indians were running in confusion and terror down the road towards Zubza. When the vehicle convoy reached the road alongside the IGH Spur, gunfire from across the ridge from the area of Naga Village hit some of the trucks, brewing up an ambulance. The men dismounted quickly, moving up through the pines, oaks and alder trees of the ridge to begin digging their defences: Major Tom Kenyon's A Company on top of Summerhouse Hill, B Company under Major John Winstanley on Kuki Picquet, C Company under Major P. E. M. Shaw on DIS Spur and D Company under Major Donald Easten, who had led the convoy back into Kohima, on the IGH Spur. At this stage the close-range shelling from four Japanese mountain guns firing from the area of Naga Village was intermittent, but sufficient to hasten the men's digging efforts. Fortunately Sato's initial attacks were weak and disparate as he was unable fully to concentrate his forces for several days. No serious attack on the frantically digging garrison took place that day, although the initial Japanese tactics of rushing the British positions was undertaken at high cost. By nightfall on 5 April a shocked Lieutenant Kameyama observed that 3/58th Regiment had already suffered 110 casualties.

The fact that the British had never considered Kohima to have been at serious risk was made obvious to a horrified Warren when he had first arrived on 29 March, no systematic defence of the ridge having been prepared. Colonel Hugh Richards had been as equally shocked when, days earlier, he had been given responsibility for its defence. Consequently the motley garrison was forced to dig in and defend itself where it could – without barbed wire, because it was prohibited in the Naga Hills – hoping that even without the detailed planning for the resupply of food, water and ammunition necessary in a defensive position, they might nevertheless be able to 'muddle by'. By a stroke of misfortune, Laverty had mistakenly assumed when he had arrived on 5 April that Richards was one of the indolent staff types whose lack of foresight and preparation had doomed Kohima to desperate siege. This could not be further from the truth, but the damage was done, and Laverty barely spoke a civil word to Richards during the fifteen days that followed.

Unable to get the remainder of his brigade back into the confined space provided by the Kohima Ridge, Warren decided to position his two remaining battalions (1/1st Punjab and 4/7th Rajputs, together with the eight remaining guns of his mountain artillery, from Lieutenant Colonel Humphrey Hill's 24th Indian Mountain Regiment) two miles to the rear on Jotsoma ridge, one of the Pulebadze spurs, where Kohima could easily be observed and where the mountain guns could be sited to fire in support of the Kohima defenders. This was actually a stroke of luck, particularly for the artillery, as it meant that when the battle began these guns were outside the perimeter, and hence the danger area, and were able, with the help of Forward Observation Officers on the ridge, to bring down accurate and unimpeded fire in support of the defenders. Ammunition resupply was relatively easy from Dimapur, with vehicles able to drive up the road to the gun positions at Jotsoma. Protected from Japanese attacks by 1/1st Punjab and 4/7th Rajput, Hill's guns proved to be decisive instruments in the defence of Kohima. This would not have been the case if they had not been safely in Jotsoma. 'There were nights when the guns were never silent,' wrote the divisional historian, 'one or more firing defensive fire targets that ringed Kohima. On one target alone the Regiment fired some 3,500 rounds in five hours.' These bombardments were fearsome for those on the receiving end. Private Sakae Sekiguchi remembered that 'The bombardments were unbelievable. They'd find a jungle and mount a concentrated attack. The jungles were so dense, yet after a bombardment, only one or two trees would be left standing. The enemy's guns drastically outnumbered ours, so however hard we tried, we stood no chance. Everyday, we'd pull along the damaged guns, and it was madness, but that was all we did.' For Private Yoshihiro Yamada the guns didn't make a '"boom boom' but more of a droning sound, because there were tens and hundreds being fired at the same time. It just never stopped.'"

On the ridge itself the puny garrison now consisted of some 2,500 men of whom 1,000 were non-combatants unable to make their escape along the road to Zubza and Nichugard before the Japanese net closed in on Kohima. Spread across the ridge (1,100 by 950 yards at most) the garrison included, in addition to the Royal West Kents, a group of disparate units that the Kents quickly but affectionately called 'the odds and sods'. These included 20 Battery (Major Dick Yeo) of 24th Indian Mountain Regiment, a troop of Indian engineers from John Wright's 2 Field Company, about two companies worth (260 men) of 3rd and 4th Assam Rifles, many of whom had made their way back after fighting at Jessami, and a large number of bewildered support personnel who in peacetime had manned the various depots scattered across the hills and who had not managed to make good their escape.

Japanese pressure on the perimeter increased on the morning of 6 April: repeated attacks by Colonel Fukunaga's 58th Regiment on Jail Hill and GPT Ridge (to its rear left) overwhelmed the defenders, a mixed force of men from 1/3rd Gurkhas and Burma Rifles. Heavy artillery and mortar fire quickly denuded trees of their foliage, snapping branches and scattering jagged splinters to accompany the whine and hiss of exploding shrapnel. By 11 o'clock the surviving defenders were forced off Jail Hill and down into the steep valley through which ran the road, and then up into the relative safety of the trees on DIS, where Major Shaw's C Company were desperately digging in. The Japanese attack was relentless and although securing Jail Hill, dominating the south-eastern edge of the Kohima Ridge, they suffered extensive casualties, including Captain

Nagaya, the commander of 3/58th Regiment. 'When I ran to him,' recalled Kameyama,

> he was dead, lying on a makeshift stretcher, a tent sheet tied between two poles. A small bundle of white wild chamomile was laid near his nose, which was the only offering to him. As we were to charge the enemy that evening, I could do nothing for him as my duty came first. I asked someone to take care of the corpse; to bury him in earth and cut off his finger and cremate it. The finger bone would be sent to his home.

The many British casualties were crowding the IGH spur where the energetic and inspiring Lieutenant Colonel John Young of 75th Indian Field Ambulance was organizing an Advanced Dressing Station and tarpaulin-covered pits where surgery could be carried out. Major Donald Easten was ordered to retake Jail Hill with D Company, 4th Royal West Kents but, by now, the Japanese had already dug deeply into the hillside and could not be ejected without considerable expenditure of life. Easten took his company and dug them in around the FSD. Since Jail Hill dominated the southern edge of the ridge defences, the disappearing tree cover became a problem for the defenders who became visible to the Japanese and consequently could only move at night. Even then it wasn't safe, as repeated night attacks and infiltration patrols, not to mention artillery and mortar fire as well as machine guns firing on fixed lines, were to demonstrate.

Despite Japanese pressure from the south (on GPT and Jail Hill) and the north (Naga Hill), welcome reinforcements on 6 April made their way inside the perimeter up the steep valley to the west. They included a company of 4/7th Rajputs commanded by Captain Mitchell. Six hours later the telephone cable back to Jotsoma and Warren's HQ was cut. Except for Laverty's and Yeo's radios (Richards' soon ran out of batteries and he was forced to rely on Laverty) the Kohima Ridge was now cut off. Its 1,000 defenders (together with the 1,500 non-combatants milling around in confusion and impeding the defenders) squeezed inside the perimeter and were soon surrounded by up to 15,000 eager Japanese. That night, when the sun was replaced by a resplendent shining moon, a company of Japanese came down the steep slopes of Jail Hill, crossed the road and climbed up DIS Hill to a cacophony of war cries and blaring bugles. The attack was frontal, entirely without subtlety. The defenders believed the Japanese were 'psyching themselves up' into a fever of martial emotion to brave the British bullets. The fire from the waiting Royal West Kents scythed into the attackers as did bombs from Sergeant Victor King's mortars, landing within yards of the West Kent positions. Raymond Street, in his trench, held his fire till he could see the enemy advancing through the trees about thirty yards away. The mortars were

> very accurate and had a devastating effect, killing and maiming many of the enemy as they charged. But they kept coming, wave after wave of them, rushing towards our trenches. We used rifles and grenades plus the Bren guns. We cut them to ribbons but they still got through. There was so many of them.

Corporal Roy Wellings of 13 Platoon had crawled forward down the slope to be able to provide accurate fire control orders to King's mortars, and now found himself alone. He just couldn't fire quickly enough, Street recording:

> Despite hitting many as possible, he was overrun. They ran past him towards the trenches beyond. He thought they might shoot him in the back but he couldn't look round. He didn't have time. He just continued firing and hoped those behind would deal with the others.

Private Nobuyuki Hata of 58th Regiment described the ferocious intensity of these attacks in terms of a sort of combat madness that took over the men.

> We attacked close-range. When we mounted these close-range attacks, we'd take three, four, or five hand grenades and pull the pin out. We'd pull the safety pin out. And we'd put them in our pockets or somewhere. When we charged the enemy, we'd carry our guns and have the grenades in one hand. You usually pull out the safety pin with your mouth but we didn't have time for that. The pin would already be out so we'd bounce the grenades against the soles of our shoes. (With the safety pin already pulled out, the firing pin was struck against the boot, to ignite it, before the grenade was thrown.) So we went out there, knowing full well we could self-detonate. When you're charging the enemy, you're driven into this state of madness. Of course it's terrifying. But however terrifying it is, you can't just hang back and not do anything. When you charge the enemy, you just become this crazed being. As soon as it's over, you go back to being a normal human being, but when you're in that situation, you go completely mad.

Apparently not disheartened by their casualties, the Japanese persisted doggedly and soon, in the noisy, moonlit darkness, the situation was looking grave for the West Kents, the hand-to-hand fighting carrying on through the night, flashes of light here and there across the position denoting the points where defender and attacker fired at each other in the darkness. By the early light of the reluctant dawn on 7 April – Good Friday – Major Shaw was one of many wounded, both his legs broken by a tree burst, and ammunition was running low. When visibility had improved, Donald Easten led a counter attack onto DIS from neighbouring FSD but, as the day flooded into light, a further menace arose: the Japanese could fire without hindrance onto the southern and south-western slopes of DIS, and machine-gun fire swept across the hill, as well as the low trajectory fire from a 75mm gun, the shells of which arrived without warning. In the centre of DIS a number of Japanese had inveigled themselves at the onset of dawn into a series of ammunition storage huts and the bakery, hoping to avoid detection in the daylight, including Lieutenant Kameyama and Battalion headquarters:

> As dawn came shelling ... became more and more intense and under its cover enemy soldiers came crawling up from the valley and threw grenades at us; a strong counter-attack. If they took this position and climbed up the hill, our men on the hill as well as the regimental commander and the battalion commander would be wiped out. So we had to prevent them getting up the hill at any cost ... The Machine Gun platoon, with two guns, fought very calmly. They waited until the enemy soldiers came very close and fired accurately at them, followed by grenades, and several attacks were repulsed while enemy corpses were heaped up in front of us. Corporal Kawase was shot through his head and another section leader fell down as his right thigh was cut through by a shell fragment. But all men remained bravely in position. Our men near the hilltop were fighting with grenades, but were also shot from behind and the sides from FSD and were in a critical battle. By 9 a.m. on 7 April, 6th Company was decimated after its desperate 'Banzai' charge.

Sergeant Major Haines led a spirited attack against these positions, dashing forty yards up the hill with a mixed group of West Kents and Gurkhas, bayonets fixed and lobbing grenades amongst the bashas. Those Japanese who ran were cut down by waiting Bren guns: those who stayed put were burned alive as the thin structures caught fire. The bakery, whose large brick ovens in peacetime produced several thousand loaves of bread each day, were more impervious to these tactics, but Lieutenant John Wright's engineers destroyed the doors with the help of large quantities of gun cotton. Instead of merely blowing in the doors, the ensuing explosion destroyed the entire building, only the brick ovens inside withstanding the blast. Escaping Japanese were brought down by rifle fire, while Raymond Street watched one commit suicide by holding a grenade to his chest. Donald Easten shot dead a fleeing Japanese at point-blank range with his revolver. Unusually, two Japanese soldiers were taken prisoner, and although one died later of his wounds the other, in the parlance of the time 'sang like a canary', providing details about the strength and dispositions of the attacking forces. Captain Shiro Sato, Nagaya's successor in 3/58th Regiment, was killed. Over sixty Japanese were killed in this struggle alone, leading the men to mutter among themselves that this was a worse ordeal than Sangshak. Private Hidehiro Shingai mused on the best way to die.

> If it's the head, it's instant death. But if it's the stomach, there's nothing more terrible. If you're hit in the stomach, it's torn apart, and then your guts spill out. In those cases, the person remains conscious but dies within two or three hours. I saw comrades die like that. When the guts burst out like that, there's nothing you can do to treat the wound. If it's the stomach, or a leg or an arm that gets torn off, it's not instant death.

Before the battle Kameyama used humour to rouse his men, explaining to them that when they felt afraid they should put their hands down their trousers and feel the state of their penis. If it was hanging down, he said, they were not afraid:

> I tested mine, but it was shrunk up so hard I could hardly grasp it. More than thirty soldiers did the same thing, then looked at me curiously, but I kept a poker-face. I said, 'Well mine's down all right. If yours is shrunk up, it's because you're scared.'
>   Then a young soldier said to me: 'Sir, I can't find mine at all. What's happened to it?' With this everyone burst out laughing and I knew I had got the confidence of the men.

One of the problems now encountered by the men of C and D Companies of the Royal West Kents was the fact that hundreds of bodies lay littered across the position, some of friends but mostly of Japanese, attracting clouds of slow-moving bluebottles, feasting on the carpet of corpses covering the ground. Attempts were made to remove bodies where it was possible, but snipers and the sheer number meant that it was not possible to dispose of them all. As the days went by, the effects of artillery bombardment dispersed some of the remains, with the result that the DIS became an unpleasant place to defend at best, and injurious to health at worst. The West Kents attempted to burn the bodies at night, but this had a poor effect on morale as the appalling smell of burning flesh drifted across the position. Where they could the Japanese cremated their dead.

For the defenders the days began to assume a monotony of intermittent terror and constant discomfort. The men knew that they were cut off from help, but they also knew that they had so far managed to withstand the swamping attacks of Sato's men. When not faced by the threat of direct attack the men crouched in their trenches, alive to the danger of the intermittent machine-gun fire that played over their heads both from Jail Hill and GPT Ridge, and from the sporadic mortar fire that would drop almost vertically from the sky with no warning. 'We were always thirsty,' recalled Raymond Street, 'We used an old fruit tin for urine and threw the contents over the parapet. We used our old redundant shell holed trench for a toilet whenever we could. The whole area began to stink.'

Some men were able to dig trenches for use as latrines, but many could not. Tom Greatley would 'do his business' in an old SEAC newspaper while his mate in the trench would turn politely the other way. He would then wrap the contents up and throw it in the direction of the Japanese. During that night the Japanese launched both real and 'jitter' attacks against the southern perimeter, and the next morning – 8 April – it was discovered that Japanese soldiers had infiltrated back onto DIS Hill during the confusion of the night, placing themselves and a machine gun in a bunker on the top of the hill. It was here that the fearless twenty-nine-year-old Lance Corporal John Harman demonstrated the type of behaviour that was to lead within days to the award of a Victoria Cross, and his death. Realizing that the Japanese machine gun could cause untold damage if unchecked he crawled alone up the hill, standing up at the last minute to charge the Japanese-held bunker. Miraculously, the enemy fire tore into the empty air above his head, and Harman reached the bunker door, coolly extracted the pin from a grenade, released the firing lever, counted to three (on a four-second) fuse and lobbed it inside. The occupants were killed instantly and Harman returned triumphant with the captured machine gun down the hill to the cheers of his comrades. But nothing the defenders could do seemed to slow down the relentless Japanese assaults. That night a fearsome bombardment fell on Summerhouse Hill, Raymond Street observing that 'the shells seemed to be directed at my trench':

> At the same time the Japs attacked C Company from Jail Hill. Again it was with wave after wave of fanatical, screaming troops. It was the

heaviest attack so far. We cut them to ribbons but they kept coming. They lost hundreds but it didn't deter them.

Street and his comrades were fighting the remnants of 3/58th. By this stage, notes Lieutenant Kameyama, the battalion (fighting with two companies, the 5th and 6th) had lost most of its men and could not mount a sustained attack on its own,

> So the regimental commander [Colonel Fukunaga] ordered [the regimental] Signal Company to attack the hill with us. It was a critical decision; if the soldiers of Signal Company died, the regiment, without communication, would not be able to continue fighting as a systematic unit, which was like burning our own boats.
>
> From the bitter experience of the last attack, we realized that we could not win against the strong enemy, who had many automatic weapons, by surprise night attack as we had done successfully in China. So we laid out all available anti-tank guns, medium machine guns, light machine guns and grenade launchers [2-inch mortars], and assigned each gun a specified target. I commanded these support weapons on Jail Hill, while the battalion commander went to attack DIS with the Signal Company and the remnant of our battalion (mostly 5th Company). After breaking through several defence lines we finally captured the hilltop by noon of 9 April. But our strength had been exhausted.

On the same night that the remnants of 3/58th attacked the southern edge of the ridge, the Japanese attacked the north-east sector of the perimeter for the first time, attempting to strike through the dense rhododendron bushes forty feet above the TCP against the positions dug around the Deputy Commissioner's bungalow, and the asphalt tennis court that lay behind it, forty feet higher up the hill. This end of the ridge was terraced, with the north and eastern edges falling sharply down to the road. Gradually, pressure of overwhelming numbers pushed the men of A Company, Royal West Kents back, up the hill to the Tennis Court where they dug in only twenty yards from the closest Japanese. In the south, and amidst heavy driving rain, the men on DIS fought desperately against yet another Japanese infantry attack preceded by the worst mortaring to date. Bombs landed in such profusion that several scored direct hits on trenches, destroying their occupants. Crouched in his trench, throwing grenades and thrusting his bayonet at figures scuttling by, the exhausted Raymond Street was fuelled by an uncontrollable mixture of terror and adrenalin, 'some hideous hand-to-hand fighting' characterizing the seemingly relentless advance of the Japanese infantry up the slopes. As day dawned on 9 April the relief at the onset of daybreak was offset by the power exerted over the battlefield by Japanese snipers, who tied themselves to the topmost branches of trees on GPT ridge to terrorize the slopes on DIS and FSD that were rapidly being denuded of their foliage and exposing the defenders to this new danger: 'They were in the trees, hidden amongst the leaves. You couldn't see them. They picked people off at will.'

During the 8th Warren's base at Jotsoma had been cut off by troops of 138th Regiment who had crossed the deep Zubza nullah from the area of Merema to the north, with the aim of cutting the road to Kohima. Sato had now managed to concentrate the bulk of his division against Kohima, and the pressure exerted by his troops was sustained and inexorable. The result was that, over the ensuing twelve days, the British positions along the Kohima Ridge would shrink to a single hill. For over two weeks fierce hand-to-hand fighting raged, the shrinking battlefield a ghastly combination of exhausted men, mud, corpses and trees denuded of their leaves by constant shellfire. But even as 31st Division dug its claws into Kohima, Mutaguchi reminded Sato that the real objective, the one that would make the strategic difference for Operation C, was Dimapur. Accordingly, on 8 April, Mutaguchi ordered Sato to continue on beyond Kohima to Dimapur. Sato obeyed, if somewhat reluctantly, sending a battalion of 138th Regiment along the track that led from Merema to Bokajan. However, Mutaguchi's order to Sato had been copied to the Burma Area Army HQ in Rangoon and Kawabe, who had anticipated such a move by his army commander, lost no time in countermanding the instructions. Sato's battalion, five hours into its march on Dimapur, was recalled.

What might have happened if Sato had turned a Nelsonian blind-eye to Kimura's order, or if he had delayed its official receipt for another twenty-four hours? Sato was apparently happy to obey Kawabe and withdraw to Kohima partly because his deep-seated animosity to Mutaguchi led him to assume the Army Commander's demands were motivated solely by visions of military glory. Sato's hatred of Mutaguchi blinded him to the strategic possibilities offered by continuing his offensive through to Dimapur, and lost for the Japanese a crucial opportunity for victory in 1944. Slim was astonished when he realized that Dimapur was safe. The failure to secure Dimapur while the British were reeling in confusion at the speed and scale of Mutaguchi's 'March on Delhi' was indeed, as Slim recognized, one of the great missed opportunities of the war: it led directly to the failure of the Kohima thrust, and contributed to the collapse of Operation C. It was the consequence of Sato's lack of strategic imagination, framed by Kawabe's rejection of what he regarded as an attempt by Mutaguchi to secure for himself undying glory. What he – and Sato for that matter – failed entirely to see was that Mutaguchi was right. The capture of Dimapur might have been the decisive strategic movement of the campaign leading to a dramatic worsting of the British reminiscent of Malaya and Burma in 1942.

When he heard that Sato had turned back Mutaguchi was furious at what he regarded as Kawabe's timidity. 'The worst crime of a soldier is irresolution,' he exploded. 'Kawabe ... [did] not let me advance on Dimapur, even when the national fate depended on it ... I blame his timid character.' Whilst this is patently unfair – Kawabe provided Mutaguchi with all the support he needed to get Operation C off the ground – it is true that Kawabe refused to endorse Mutaguchi's vision for the capture of Dimapur. What Kawabe lacked was not courage as Mutaguchi suggested, but strategic vision. The capture of Dimapur was not, as he surmised, a product of Mutaguchi's fierce egotism but, in actuality, a profound realization that it was the key to British vulnerabilities in eastern India. There is no evidence that Kawabe ever recognized this truth for what it was. It is impossible to conceive of an effective British riposte to a move against Dimapur. Its capture would certainly have denied Slim the opportunity to launch his own offensive into Burma in 1944 or 1945. As Slim saw clearly, Sato's lack of strategic sense in understanding the wider context and broader possibilities of Operation C in favour of the strict interpretation of his orders removed the chance for decisive success in 1944. 'It was always a wonder to me why Sato did not attempt a bold stroke of this kind,' recalled Slim. 'It would have been typically Japanese ...'. Slim clearly knew nothing of the hatred that Sato harboured for Mutaguchi, nor indeed of the deep-rooted failings of the Japanese command system that allowed such self-destructive antagonisms to flourish so openly. The truth is that Sato could have taken Dimapur had he wished. Stopford later acknowledged this.

> ... if 31 Division had left a small unit behind to control Kohima and had continued to advance, he [Stopford] would have been placed in the gravest difficulties. It would have become very difficult to deploy 2nd Division, and if fighting had broken out around Dimapur, Kohima would have fallen like a ripe fruit.

~

There was little to celebrate among the defenders of the Kohima Ridge on Easter Sunday, 9 April 1944, even if they did have knowledge (and they did not) that Sato's application of Mutaguchi's plan was strategically flawed and doomed to eventual failure. Indeed, issues of higher strategy and leadership interested them not one jot, as they fought for their lives amidst the mud, blood and fly-blown, blackening corpses. The numbers of wounded lying in shallow trenches around the Indian General Hospital Spur where John Young had established his Advanced Dressing Station were daily increasing, the crowded area offering little protection from either the elements or incoming artillery, men being wounded for the second and sometimes third time. As the days passed the ADS became a veritable hell, men lying and dying in their blood and excrement, over 600 wounded crowded into a tiny area by 20 April.

As dawn broke on DIS Donald Easten noticed that the determined Japanese had once again managed to infiltrate onto the hill and were developing an old weapon pit, from where they could fire against the remainder of the position. Once more, John Harman decided to mount a solo attack to remove this threat and, covered by two Bren guns firing from his left and his right, dashed up the hill. Frantically the Japanese returned fire but in their excitement fired wide. Harman reached the trench and, standing four yards to its front, firing his Lee Enfield from the hip, shot four Japanese dead, before jumping into the trench and bayoneting the fifth. He then stood up, triumphantly holding the captured enemy machine gun above his head, before throwing it to the ground. The cheers of his comrades reverberated around the hill. Harman then nonchalantly began to walk back down the slope. Unfortunately, he had forgotten that with the denuded foliage he was in full view of the Japanese positions on Jail Hill. Unheeding of the shouted cries of his comrades to run, he leisurely made his way back down to his weapon pit, only to be struck by a burst of machine-gun fire in his back just as he reached safety. Donald Easten ran out into the Japanese fire, and dragged Harman into a trench. Within a few minutes, however, this extraordinarily brave man was dead.

Japanese fire continued heavily throughout the day. Corporal Trevor 'Taffy' Rees was hit and fell into a dip outside his trench. He lay paralyzed in the open, calling out in agony but unable, because of the weight of Japanese fire, to be reached by his friends. He took eight horrible hours to die, Street recalling that it was an awful way to go, their impotence in the face of Rees' despair upsetting everyone dreadfully. More men fell that day to the ubiquitous snipers. 'You couldn't do much about it,' Street observed. 'You didn't know where the enemy were and just kept your head down.' The Japanese attacked again in force that night, amidst a wild rainstorm that reduced visibility to nil:

We didn't see them forming up but as they charged, they used grenade launchers again, showering our positions with high explosives forcing us to keep our heads down as long as possible. They didn't get past the rifle and machine-gun fire from four weapon pits some ten yards from the road.

Warren was doing what he could to protect his precious guns at Jotsoma, and to help relieve the pressure on Richards and Laverty on the ridge. From his vantage point, only two miles away, he needed no reminding of the desperate straits in which they lay, especially as his mountain guns were pumping out shells almost endlessly. On most days the Indian mountain gunners fired 400 rounds. But when, on 9 April, 1/1st Punjab tried to clear Picquet Hill between Jotsoma and the ridge they encountered a number of log-covered bunkers out of which spewed automatic fire, causing twenty-five casualties in the day's fighting. It was clear that any attempt to break the siege by force was going to be long and difficult: it took until 15 April for these bunkers to be sufficiently subdued to allow 1/1st Punjab to occupy Picquet Hill, the final piece of ground needing to be secured before the road itself could be opened up into the garrison's perimeter.

On the ridge itself the killing continued. Large numbers of fiercely brave Japanese from 58th Regiment were killed by the remorseless chatter of the British Bren guns, as during the night three successive assaults were made on C and D Companies of the Royal West Kents, the Japanese being denied success by the interlocking fire of eight Bren guns, the red-hot barrels having to be changed repeatedly. Casualties on both sides were high, the Japanese attempting to gain access to the hill from the road by use of ladders, seemingly unperturbed by their losses. On the northern side of Garrison Hill, 138th Regiment again launched attacks against A Company. 'You couldn't see much from A Company's position because of steep slopes,' remarked Street, 'so we didn't see them forming up on the lower terrace. We could hear them though, with their screeching and yelling, so knew they were coming.' The attack was held, Bren guns, bayonets and grenades in the darkness bloodily halting Japanese ambitions. Victor King's mortars fired in support, the bombs landing with superb accuracy in front of Major Tom Kenyon's positions. It had seemed for a while that sheer weight of numbers would overwhelm the much reduced A Company, but the reliable Brens, considerable reserves of grenades, the accuracy of King's mortars and the determined courage of the Royal West Kents denied the penetration so desperately desired by the Japanese.

The next morning, 10 April, allowed Laverty an opportunity to consider his options. Casualties had been heavy in those five nights and six days of fighting. C Company had suffered 50 per cent casualties and was ordered to abandon the DIS that night to withdraw onto FSD through a screen provided by 4/7th Rajputs. Supplies were destroyed and Lance Corporal Hankinson and his section crawled to within ten yards of the Japanese, holding their position for six hours, thus allowing C and D Companies to withdraw to FSD, before crawling back all the way themselves. That night snipers continued to pick out their victims, and artillery and mortar fire continued their deadly harassment. Lieutenant Phythian was wounded as was Lieutenant Gordon Inglis of B Company. Phythian survived, but Inglis died of his wounds some weeks later. A mortar bomb killed Sergeant Boxwell and severely wounded Donald Easten, dislocating his back and injuring his arm. By this stage C Company had been so reduced that on FSD it was merged with D Company, and Tom Coath (who had replaced the wounded Shaw a few days before) took command. On the northern side of the hill, A Company still managed to resist the Japanese assaults over the Tennis Court, the strength and depth of their trenches with its overhead cover providing critical protection time and again as Japanese mortars and artillery crashed around them. The explosions kicked up dirt and dust, blinding and choking the defenders who could never relax their vigilance with the enemy barely twenty yards distant. Showers of grenades preceded a Japanese assault, but even the fiercest and most determined of attacks always ended in failure, although each resulted in more dead and wounded among the defenders. Ammunition and grenades were dragged down the slopes each night to the exhausted occupants in the forward positions.

To cap it all, the monsoon rains had come early, and heavily; driving rain on 10 April, together with the effects of battle and of sleep deprivation, had pushed men to the edge of exhaustion. Tea was rationed to half a mug per man. Fortunately, the rain made up something for the acute lack of water within the perimeter, men lying back in their weapon pits and trenches to allow the rain to fall directly into parched, open mouths. It was found that a trickle of water was available from a pipe leading onto the road behind the ADS, behind the Japanese positions. Dangerous nightly journeys were made, through hundreds of wounded lying in the open, down the slope to the road. Private Raymond Street described one of these patrols:

> The NCO held the pipe while another man took my bottles and filled them. A Bren gunner lay flat behind his gun a couple of yards away, the barrel pointing along the empty road towards the enemy. It seemed to take forever before the bottles were filled and handed back

to me. This was a very tense time, four of us alone on the road under the noses of the Japs but it was the only way to replenish our water supply.

On the night of 11 April Major John Winstanley's B Company relieved the exhausted men of A Company, who were withdrawn up the hill to Kuki Picquet. Within minutes of their arrival the Japanese attacked, the first of three heavy assaults that night, the screaming attacks petering out in the face of almost continuous Bren-gun fire, returning showers of grenades and the accuracy of Victor King's mortars. Winstanley believed that the Tennis Court was held against desperate attacks for five days

> because I had instant contact by radio with the guns, and the Japs never seemed to learn how to surprise us. They used to shout in English as they formed up, 'Give up!' which gave us warning each time an attack was coming in. One would judge just the right moment to call down gun and mortar-fire to catch them as they were launching the attack, and every time they approached us they were decimated. They were not acting intelligently and did the same old stupid thing again and again.

The Japanese now held the area to the east of the Tennis Court (to the right of their position as the Royal West Kents viewed it) and the Deputy Commissioner's bungalow, or what remained of it, although the Royal West Kents still held the high ground. Snipers remained a pestilence, and Winstanley's company suffered a handful of casualties. Lieutenant Tom Hogg's platoon now numbered eight men (it should have been thirty, and by the end of the siege would number only three), and guarded a corner of the Tennis Court. In the early hours of the morning, the Japanese tried another tactic: a silent attack, a dozen men rushing the position wearing plimsolls and carrying bayonets. Raymond Street recounts the story:

> One Jap charged at Hogg. Hogg tried to shoot him but couldn't get his shot off in time. The Jap drove his bayonet at him but fortunately for Hogg, it got caught in his belt webbing, hardly injuring him at all. Hogg didn't mess about. He wasn't going to give him a second charge and emptied the twenty-five round magazine into him.

For the defenders, the new enemy inside the perimeter was exhaustion, the tidal waves of fatigue that rushed in without warning to swamp men's consciousness in oblivion. But surrendering to this meant certain death. By catching precious doses of sleep, measured in minutes rather than hours, men seemed just about able to go on. Their waking hours were filled with preparing grenades, reinforcing and repairing damaged trenches, completing ablutions in the disgusting conditions and making sure that weapons were clean so they didn't malfunction when most needed. The whole position now smelt of faeces and the putrid, sickly-sweet odour of bodily decay from the many hundreds of blackening corpses and body parts that lay mingled on the ground amid the shattered remains of the once luxuriant forest. By now, however, most men were inured to the awful smell that hung over Kohima Ridge like a thick blanket: it was something that was encountered with horror only by those at the end of the siege who entered for the first time. The new fear was that a moment of inattention could lead to the Japanese seizing their chance to leap into one's trench, especially at night when the darkness was replete with dancing shadows that were, at one moment, Japanese soldiers and, the next, figments of one's fearsome dreams. Often only a split second stood between dream and reality. On a mound of earth just above the Tennis Court, where for days Bren-gun teams had battled savagely against the rising hordes surging only yards beneath them, Private Williams and Corporal Veall now occupied the weapon pit in which many of the previous occupants had died. Suddenly a group of Japanese loomed out of the gloom and when the Bren gun jammed, Veall was stabbed through with a bayonet. Williams jumped up and grabbed the first weapon he could find. It was a shovel. Swinging wildly he struck and killed the first man before turning to the remainder who, to his surprise, now fled in terror.

The position, both on the Tennis Court to the north and on FSD to the south, remained firm. But each day made the situation grimmer with 13 April generally regarded as the 'Black Thirteenth'. Heavy Japanese artillery fire killed many in the ADS, including two irreplaceable doctors, adding to the misery of that bloody place. Much priceless equipment and medicines were also destroyed. Of the 446 men of the 'Dirty Half Hundred' who had moved back into Kohima on 5 April, 150 were now dead or wounded. The thought on everyone's minds was 'when, if ever, is all this going to stop? Are we ever going to be relieved?' Officers attempted to maintain morale, as did Charles Pawsey (he had refused to leave for the relative safety of Jotsoma), who defied the snipers each day to walk around his diminishing fiefdom, pausing to say comforting words to the bearded, black-eyed scarecrows in their trenches. Raymond Street was struck by Pawsey's apparent nonchalance:

> He was a kind chap and moved around the hill lifting our spirits as
> he moved between our trenches and Battalion HQ. He stopped and

talked to us saying that relief would get through and told us not to worry too much … He seemed without fear of bullets and shells as he strolled along in the open as if defying the enemy.

~

Attempts were also made to drop supplies during the siege to the defenders from the ubiquitous Dakotas, although, given the tiny, postage-stamp size of the dropping area, most of these failed, with precious food, water and ammunition floating down into the eager hands of the hungry Japanese. Flight Sergeant Jim Bell, a Canadian Dakota pilot with 31 Squadron RAF, was shocked to see the battlefield from his vantage point 300 feet in the air:

> Kohima was a battle that we could see plainly from the sky. It was pitiful – like World War One – slit trenches, no-man's-land etc. DZs were often not coordinated. At our low level drops we could see each side of the staggered and small pockets of our troops cut off from the main force. There were torn bits of parachutes of our previous drops torn to read a message on the ground, such as 'H20' for water, or 'AMMO', 'MED' and 'FOOD'.

On 13 April three entire planeloads, including 3-inch mortar ammunition, were dropped on the enemy (which the Japanese promptly used in captured British mortars against their erstwhile owners), the men on Kohima Ridge watching miserably as the swaying parachutes floated down over the valley to the east. Supply dropping was a hazardous task. Flying Officer 'Chick' Delaney flew his Dakota that day over Kohima, his aircraft being holed several times by Japanese ground fire. 'Our Drop Zones were very small,' he recalled, 'and it was very difficult for the Army to leave their trenches to recover the food and ammunition which we dropped. During the next three weeks we did fifteen trips to Kohima and each one was exciting as there was always plenty of ground activity.' Some pilots in the lumbering transport planes supplying the troops on the ground took on the Japanese themselves. Two weeks later, on 1 May, Flight Sergeant Vallance was about to drop his load on the DZ when he saw the flashes from a Japanese mortar position about a quarter of a mile to the south-east, the shells landing on the DZ. Turning his aircraft towards the enemy position, the Dakota's two door gunners strafed the area with machine-gun fire, after which Vallance returned to his fly-in and completed the drop.

The Japanese and the difficult terrain combined to make each flight extremely dangerous. On Monday 19 June Warrant Officer Christie, a

Canadian pilot flying with 194 Squadron was dropping 600 pounds of supplies onto the Kohima area in appalling weather. Lining up for his final approach, he flew into a cloud without realizing that behind it a hill lay hidden, the Dakota exploding on impact. Flight Lieutenant Peter Bray, of 31 Squadron, flew nine supply sorties above Kohima in April and a further four in May, each flight taking a round trip of three hours and forty-five minutes to and from Agartala airfield in Assam. Dropping on the area of the Deputy Commissioner's Bungalow was extremely difficult, 'and any inaccuracy in dropping resulted in irretrievably lost supplies. On one occasion RAF Hurricanes were dive-bombing the adjacent hill only a few hundred yards away from the supply dropping Dakotas.' Supply dropping had become an art form, and the pilots became so knowledgeable about the battlefield that they followed its every turn. Pilot Officer Simpson recalled one occasion when he 'dropped live anti-tank mines in front of the Japs'. The Japanese did everything they could do to bring down a Dakota and, unusually, for the Japanese generally remained hidden under the jungle canopy, the crews could clearly make out the Japanese positions and the faces of the Japanese soldiers firing up at the passing aircraft. In preparation for the supply drops, recalled Flight Sergeant John Bell, the planes 'would end up about 250 feet over the hills, with the Japs shooting at us. All I could see was a mass of faces looking up at us'. Even the ground attack role, when fighter aircraft such as Hurricanes, fitted with 20mm and 40mm cannon, and carrying two 250-pound underwing bombs, was a dangerous business, although a decided morale booster for the sweat-stained infantrymen in their holes, who called in the Air Force to attack enemy tanks and bunkers, the latter of which were largely impervious to anything but direct sniping by tanks or a direct hit by a 'Hurribomber' carrying two 250-pound bombs equipped with eleven-second delay fuses. Early on the morning of Tuesday 18 April, Flight Lieutenant Jimmy Whalen, a Canadian Hurricane pilot who had experience in North Africa, was shot down over Kohima Ridge by ground fire while strafing a Japanese bunker. His aircraft was only twenty feet above the ground when it was hit, rolling over and diving into the ground, exploding on impact.

~

Desperate to squeeze the British from the ridge and to prevent them from using the supplies raining from the sky, Japanese pressure against FSD remained unrelenting. Captain Mitchell of the Rajputs was killed on the morning of 12 April, and furious counter-attacks against the Japanese who had infiltrated amongst C/D Company (which now comprised a mere fifteen men) of the Royal West Kents failed to remove the intruders. A Company, after their short rest on Kuki, now moved to support C/D Company. That night the Japanese attempted to rush the FSD. The defenders were ordered to wait until they could see the whites of the Japanese eyes before opening fire. They did so, recalled Street:

> This was very difficult as the area was saturated with Japs and their shadows were everywhere as they moved amongst the remaining tree and leaf cover. When the order to fire was given the whole platoon joined in and parachute flares lit up the area. A chap in D Company shot three Japs one by one as they jumped into his trench.

During a lull in the fighting Private Peacock from A Company dropped off, exhausted with fatigue. When he came round he discovered that he was sharing his trench with a Japanese officer who had assumed that Peacock was dead. Unable to find his rifle Peacock leapt at the officer and strangled him after a fierce struggle with his bare hands. Then, to make sure, he ran him through with the man's own sword.

Winstanley's weakened B Company were replaced on the Tennis Court positions during the darkness by 'Buster' Keene's Assam Rifles. All the while the Japanese were attempting to get on to FSD but on the night of 14 April the news zoomed around the position that a patrol of 4/7th Rajputs had made their way up the western valley and through the encircling Japanese. Laverty told the patrol commander that although morale was high he judged that the position could only hold for a further forty-eight hours. Unfortunately, the message, when the patrol returned, stressed the fact that the men's spirit was high, and Warren judged that relief could wait a few more days. Colonel Hugh Richards, the Garrison Commander, issued an Order of the Day to the defenders on 14 April from the bunker he shared with Pawsey on Summerhouse Hill. 'By your efforts you have prevented the Japanese from attaining this objective. All attempts to overrun the garrison have been frustrated by your determination and devotion to duty ... '. It was, as Street remembered, a hugely important uplift to morale, but still the shells fell, and still the Japanese continued to attack. Fourteen of the West Kents were killed that day.

The Rajput patrol had the unfortunate result of raising some expectations of relief on the ridge. To the fighting men still desperately resisting every Japanese encroachment this made little difference to their lives. 'We were told that relief was on its way but didn't take much notice,' commented Street:

That was old news that never seemed to materialize. We hoped it would, before it was too late. Apparently Laverty was told that relief would come the next day and made arrangements for some of the wounded to be evacuated. I never heard anything. It was just as well because it didn't come.

Instead, life and death continued their seemingly arbitrary, parallel journeys. The shattered hillside was now almost bare of foliage, the remaining trees standing forlornly, others leaning drunkenly where shells had smashed the trunk or branches. The ground was a churned morass of mud, which the defenders shared with rotting corpses, excrement and the inevitable detritus of war: scattered equipment, discarded helmets, broken weapons, and unexploded shells. Yet Laverty was right: across the British positions morale remained high, despite the wet discomfort of his men's mole-like existence and the uncertainty as to when their ordeal would end. Street likened it 'to being put into a firing squad and being reprieved each time. This happened twice a day, every day'. But the troops knew that they had achieved a remarkable feat of endurance, and resistance. On the evening of 16 April Street was passed a bottle of rum, from which he took a swig and passed it on to his mates. Warming inwardly, he began to sing 'Onward Christian Soldiers': before long the hymn was picked up lustily by soldiers across the hillside. 'I don't know what the Japs made of it,' he commented, but noted that when the next Japanese barrage arrived it seemed heavier than expected.

The Japanese continued to press hard and on the 17th managed to force the remnants of A and C Companies right to the top of FSD, the Royal West Kents then being relieved in their positions by a mixed group of soldiers from the Assam Rifles and the Assam Regiment before retiring to new positions on top of Summerhouse Hill. Above the Tennis Court the men of the Assam Rifles and Assam Regiment continued to defy the odds, turning back repeated attacks, but on the night of 17 April the Japanese finally took FSD and successfully rushed Kuki Picquet, overcoming the sorely-depleted defenders by sheer weight of numbers, Kameyama writing that '7th Company with a platoon from regimental headquarters charged towards the top of FSD shouting *Wasshoi! Wasshoi!*' (rush forward). The enemy was startled by this dashing cry and fled towards Kuki Picquet along the ridge. We chased them and captured FSD as well as Kuki Picquet.'

The garrison was now crammed into an area extending not much more than 350 by 350 yards. In the view of Donald Easten, some of the wounded, many of whom had lain in the open for two weeks, now gave way to despair.

Unable to fight, some kept a revolver or a grenade close by for the moment when the Japanese finally broke through:

> Many of the wounded I feel sure died in the last few days because they had given up hope. Yet they were incredibly cheerful, outwardly, up till the end. Those who were not wounded were too busy to think much, except perhaps at night, just before the time due for the evening hate, when they wondered whether their turn would come tonight.

But by now the dirty, scruffy, exhausted defenders could see elements of the relieving force advancing up the valley to the west, through the trees below the road, and the first shells of 2nd British Division began to fall thickly on the Japanese positions, guided by radio from Dick Yeo. By the following morning, with the Royal West Kents on Summerhouse Hill the men could see, through the damp grey mist, the distinctive turbans of the men of 1/1st Punjab on Picquet Hill. Later that day the men of Major Ware's B Company 1/1st Punjab made contact with the defenders, bringing with them Lee Grant tanks which were able to make their way along the road to the side of the IGH spur, although they remained in full view of the enemy across in Naga Village.

This was not to be the sort of relief, however, occasioned by the defeat of the enemy. Rather, it was a relief-in-place, where troops from both 2nd Division (and 161 Brigade) moved in under Japanese sniper and artillery fire to take over the positions eagerly given up by their erstwhile defenders. The Japanese pressed the Kohima Ridge vigorously, even frantically, knowing that this was their final opportunity to seize the ridge before fresh British troops arrived but, on 19 April, the day before the first of the relieving troops made their way onto the position, Hurribombers strafed the Japanese positions, Dakotas dropped ammunition, water and food accurately on the ridge and the 25-pounders of 2nd Division pounded away relentlessly, firing from Zubza. The relief took place in the nick of time. On 17 April the garrison didn't know whether they could carry on but, as Raymond Street asserted, they also knew that they couldn't give up. Two days later, as casualties mounted and as the Japanese continued to press their attacks, to snipe onto the position, and fire their mortars and artillery, Street considered that if the relieving force did not arrive that day 'it would be all over for us'.

But relief arrived. The men of the 1st Battalion, Royal Berkshire Regiment could not believe their eyes or noses as they climbed up onto Summerhouse Hill on the morning of 20 April. 'We climbed very cautiously until we reached the top,' recalled Corporal Roy Welland, 'but we lost three men on our way up. When we finally made contact with these gallant defenders we got a few "low gear" cheers from these unshaven, smelly chaps who you could see had had a very rough time. One chap, with a bloodied bandage around his head, seeing me and my section approaching his trench, said "It's good to see yer, Corp. Give them bloody hell. Black your faces first, otherwise they will think you are a bloody bunch of virgins.' Watching the Berkshires arrive on the position Donald Easten mused,

> We must have presented a strange spectacle. Bearded, filthy men with glazed eyes, who had not slept for fourteen days – we all slept a little I suppose, but mainly standing up. Wounded, with filthy bandages and pale, grey faces, and weak but cheerful grins. The entire hillside was pockmarked with trenches, the trees shattered by shell fire and festooned with parachutes.

Warned by anxious defenders to keep their heads down, many gagged at the repulsive smell of death and excrement that hung like a repressive fog over the position, weighing the hill down with the stench of horror. As Japanese bullets and shells continued to fall the weary veterans of the siege made their way down the gullies adjacent to the IGH spur, strewn with Japanese corpses, to waiting trucks, guarded by the Lee Grants. The fresh relief troops on the road were astonished by what they saw when the red-eyed, unshaven survivors make their way quietly out of the trees, but were in no doubt that they were witnessing the end of the first phase in one of the grimmest struggles of the entire war, and the gallant defenders of a modern-day Rorke's Drift. '*Shabash*, Royal West Kents!' called the Indian troops in warm acknowledgement of what all the defenders of the Kohima Ridge had achieved, congratulating the tired, bearded scarecrows even as shells fells among the convoy, injuring some of the wounded again and killing some even as they were being lifted into the trucks, including Captain John Topham of the Royal West Kents, who had been wounded earlier in the battle. As the trucks crawled down the pitted road towards Jotsoma, and then Zubza before making their slow way down through the green mountains into hot, steamy Dimapur, the exhausted survivors had long collapsed into deep, delicious sleep. Their ordeal was over.

Of the 446 Royal West Kents who had made their way onto Kohima Ridge on the morning of 5 April, only 168 remained unharmed. Two hundred and seventy eight had been killed or wounded during the sixteen days of siege in a stand which, although neither they nor the Japanese knew it at the time, would prove to be the turning point in each side's respective fortunes in the war. For the British it was also a story of extraordinary fortitude in the face of overwhelming odds. For the Japanese, driven on in desperation to overcome the last resistance before the Brahmaputra could be reached, it was an epic of dogged perseverance, a determination to overcome or to die in the attempt. At Kohima the Royal West Kents were the inadvertent sacrificial lambs for the defence of India. Without their extraordinary stand, likened without any charge of hyperbole by many contemporary observers and later commentators to that of the Spartans at Thermopylae, Kohima would undoubtedly have fallen, allowing the Japanese to flood – if they so desired – into the Brahmaputra Valley through the unguarded Naga Hills.

The ferocity of the battle that had taken place was clear to the relieving force. 'If Garrison Hill was indescribable for its filth and horror and smell,' recalled Major David Wilson, 6 Brigade's (2nd Division) Brigade Major, 'the sight of its defenders was almost worse. They looked like aged bloodstained scarecrows dropping with fatigue, the only thing clean about them was their weapons and they smelt of blood, sweat and death.' Lieutenant General Slim recounted, 'Kohima had been changed beyond recognition. Most of its buildings were in ruins, walls still standing were pockmarked with shell bursts or bullet holes, the trees were stripped of leaves and parachutes hung limply from the few branches that remained. It was the nearest thing to a battlefield of the First World War in the whole Burma campaign.' The truest record of what the garrison had achieved came from one who had survived, Donald Easten[10], who averred that 'the greatest honours are due to Tommy Atkins'.

> He had fought for six months in Arakan, they had flown him to Dimapur, marched him up to Kohima, marched him back again. Then back once more to Kohima, where he was shot at as he got out of his trucks. He fought hand-to-hand battles practically every night, and his pals were shot down all round him. If he was wounded, he had no hope of evacuation. Day after day he was promised relief which never came; and his platoon, or section, or just 'gang' got smaller and smaller. My own company finished up twenty-five strong; one platoon consisted of a single grinning private, who asked if he could put a pip up. And Tommy Atkins did all that on half a mug of liquid every twenty-four hours.

~

Lieutenant General Slim admits that, as a consequence of these three series of near-disasters, the first week of April was 'an anxious one. Thanks to my mistakes the battle had not started well; at any time crisis might have slipped into disaster-and still might'. Even though the Japanese were doing what he expected them to do, this knowledge was cold comfort, as they clearly retained the tactical advantage on three different sectors of the front during this time. Indeed, to Mutaguchi everything appeared to be going his way. By early April Fifteenth Army had successfully pushed IV Corps onto its heels, and had cut all land links to the rest of India. It seemed only a matter of time before Scoones would be starved into submission, unless of course the demoralized British and Indian troops capitulated first. However, by the second week of April Slim had cause to relax somewhat. The successful concentration of IV Corps on the Imphal plain by 4 April, the rapid insertion of 5th Indian Division and the arrival of XXXIII Corps by the end of the first week of April meant that the immediate danger was over. Despite the poor start to the battle in the Tiddim, Ukhrul and Kohima areas, IV Corps had not been defeated and the makeshift defences at Sangshak, Kohima, Tamu and the fighting withdrawal up the Tiddim road had inflicted grievous and irreplaceable casualties on the enemy. Slim's cautious optimism at the beginning of April grew stronger as the month progressed. By mid-April his command of the situation had been unequivocally reasserted.

Nevertheless, the stabilization of the front heralded merely the beginning of the end of British difficulties. While the immediate crisis was over, Stopford now had to prevent Sato capturing Kohima and Dimapur; Scoones to prevent Yamauchi from penetrating Imphal from the north, Yamamoto from penetrating Gracey's defences at Shenam, and Yanagida from breaking through at Bishenpur in the south. Slim also had to ensure that IV Corps, cut off in the Imphal Plain, was resupplied. While the first signs of panic and chaos were now behind them, a long hard fight lay ahead for the British if they were to guarantee victory.

## Chapter 4

# War Comes to the Nagas

Aviü (pronounced 'Ah-vee'), is the daughter of Apuo, who worked for Charles Pawsey. She was nineteen in 1944. A Christian, she lived with her family in the Mission Compound on the slopes of Naga Hill, above Kohima Town, in a house surrounded by flowers and orchards. It was an idyllic childhood. The previous year she had fallen in love with a young British Royal Engineer – Staff Sergeant Victor Hewitt – and was now carrying his child. The first signs of war had come in 1942, with the straggling and suffering humanity trundling up the road from Imphal on their way to safety after escaping the Japanese invasion of Burma. Many Nagas joined the Indian Army or supporting services, while others helped the British to extend and improve the Dimapur-Imphal road, and Aviü was no different. She worked as a supervisor of contracted labour on the road improvement programme overseen by the Royal Engineers, an activity that allowed her to see much of Victor Hewitt. He called her 'Mari', after the profusion of wild marigolds that covered the orchard floor. The war still seemed far off.

But when March [1944] came, the situation was very different. News reached us that the Japanese were just days away from Kohima. Father, who was a Treasury Officer in the Deputy Commissioner's office, had to leave quickly for Shillong carrying important documents and money ... The traders at Kohima, who were largely Indian, had fled to Dimapur and beyond, having sold their shops or closing down their shutters when they could not sell. The local people escaped to the villages in the north, to Tsiesema, Rükhroma and other northern villages.

With the shops closed, there was no movement at all in the town's streets. No people loitered around and the vegetable market was bereft of the sellers and thronging buyers. A few stray dogs were on the streets. Quite frequently, the army jeeps would come by and go back in a tearing hurry. Apart from that, there was no sign of life at all in Kohima. The few people who remained behind were surprised when they met their relatives or friends. Every family was in the process of either leaving or packing to leave Kohima. Vic was very worried for our safety. With Father away in Shillong he took charge of our family. On 30 March 1944, he took my younger sisters to Chieswema, seven miles from Kohima. They stayed there with an uncle of ours.

On the night of 2 April, Victor did not show up. I felt increasingly lonely to be in the house alone with my mother … There were so many rumours of the Japanese. Some of the men said they were short and ugly and some others said they were like us and would treat us well. But there were so many reports and it was difficult to decide what to believe. I hoped we would not fall into Japanese hands and be dealt with cruelly. The mental picture of the refugees who were fleeing the Japanese advance [in 1942] flashed into my mind. I prayed we would not be reduced to that.

That night, after dinner, everyone slept. My brother and his wife who lived on the other side of the house and my mother … were fast asleep. Vic failed to come and I was both anxious and fearful … After some time, the sirens wailed and we quickly ran to take shelter in the trenches. These were trenches that had been built in 1942 when the Japanese suddenly bombed Burma. The sirens were instantly followed by the sound of bursting grenades and the roar of big guns. I feared for Vic, where was he? Was he in the midst of those bursting shells? When the firing died down, we returned to the house and the others slept but I stayed awake. Then I heard my name being called and the sound of frantic knocking, 'Aviü, open the door, do you hear the shots? They're coming closer and closer, we are so frightened!' It was our two neighbours, a boy called Jimmy and his younger brother. I let them in. My brother and his wife came and joined us too and we all sat huddled together, listening to the sounds of battle … We had never heard the sound of gunfire in such intensity before. Though we were well drilled at what to do if the sirens sounded, it was terrifying to be actually putting what we had learnt into practice. In the weeks before, we had grown used to gunshots in the distance or the shelling of places at a great distance from Kohima. Now, it seemed that those sounds had come closer, magnified and multiplied a hundred times. The boys said that their parents had forbidden them to leave the house till they returned to get them. But they were too frightened to stay on their own.

Towards dawn, the noises died down. The silence was eerie. The long night had accustomed us to the intermittent sound of rifle shots and exploding hand grenades, and we braced ourselves at every gunshot sound for more. With the sounds of gunfire completely subdued, we went outside the house to get a closer look at the valley below us. It was a strange sight. There were no jeeps or trucks in sight. The busy sub-area of Mission Compound, which used to be a hubbub of activity at all times, seemed to have suddenly dissolved. Not a soul was around. While we were watching this in amazement, Vic's jeep tore up the road and he clambered down from the vehicle. 'Marigold,' he said, 'Get ready quickly, there's no time. I'm taking you and the whole family to Chieswema where you will be safe. You have to be there for a few days until this madness is over. Don't worry, I'll come and see you when I can. Come on, you have to get ready.' I was numb and speechless. I was not prepared for this parting from Vic. Nor had the seriousness of the war fully dawned on me until the frightening experience of the night before.

Gently leading me into the house, he began to pack a suitcase for me. He stuffed it with tinned food to last us for months, some of my clothes and toiletries, whatever he felt I might need while away from Kohima. But Mother refused to leave. No amount of persuasion would make her change her mind. 'I cannot leave my parents behind. Don't worry about me, God will take care of me. But you must all go and care for the younger ones as well.' Mother's aged parents had stubbornly refused to leave Kohima. So Mother was determined to stay and look after them. Vic spent a long time talking to my mother but she would not leave so he gave up trying. Five of us, my brother, his wife and a woman called Vikieü and her baby got into the jeep and Vic drove toward Chieswema. It was 3 April when we left Kohima. None of us ever thought that we would be away for more than a few days.

I think it never entered anyone's head then, that Kohima would become a battlefield where so many British, Indian and Gurkha forces would fall. We had such faith in the British Government that we could not believe it could be defeated by any other nation. They had always protected us and our lands. So I did not think that Vic was in any great danger from the war … The whole morning Vic stayed with us, helping us to settle in and unpacking our things. It got later than he thought so he hurriedly got into the jeep and drove off, waving back to us. I stood and watched the jeep till it disappeared in the distance and all I could see was the trail of dust it left behind. We were safe now.

The next day, we went down to the main road and waited for Vic. We waited for a long time but there was no sign of his jeep. Out on the road opposite the village, we could see vehicles moving on the Kohima-Dimapur road. But as it got quite late, we gave up hope of him coming that day and we returned to the village. When we reached the wooden gate of the village, we heard the loud roar of guns and exploding grenades and bombs. Anxiously we looked toward Kohima. The village of Chieswema faced Kohima directly and from the high point where we stood we had a good view of the township. How shocked we were to see the whole of Kohima ablaze and covered with thick black smoke. We could not believe our eyes. The peaceful and charming little town which had been our home all these years was going up in smoke! Tears streaming down our faces, we stood there transfixed and sobbed aloud at the sight before us. Other thoughts crowded in. How was Mother? How was Vic? Was this the reason why he could not come today? Were they both alive? The thought that they might have been killed did not bear thinking about. We stood there for many minutes. It was dark when we made our way to the house, choked with our emotions and dazed from the sight of that beloved place burning and enveloped in black smoke.

We were not the only anxious ones. By night, the *gaonburas* and elders of the village were meeting to discuss what was to be done next. Chieswema was seven miles from Kohima; it would be just a matter of a few hours before the enemy was upon us. Seeing Kohima fall was a great shock for all, and showed the vulnerability of the British forces. Now the villagers of Chieswema were consulting among themselves about where they could go to seek refuge. So it was paradoxical that a village that had offered refuge to others should now be worrying about seeking refuge for itself after the bombing of Kohima. That night, many Indian sepoys and soldiers of the Assam Regiment came to shelter at the village. They were those who had escaped from Jessami and Kharasom. The villagers supplied them with food and provided guides to them, to lead them to the next village, Keruma, so they could join their unit at Dimapur.

The next day was 5 April. The village was a flurry of activity. Quite early in the morning people had begun to kill their cattle. We bought some meat from them and cooked it. My brother and his in-laws were being given Naga haircuts when we went across to their house. The men had cropped their hair with a dao[11], straight across the back and sides, so that they would look like the other men of the village. Sam and the young men who had been to school wore their hair in the western fashion and this made them easy targets for the Japanese. They could be picked out and forced to work as spies.

One man was posted at the top of the village so they could tell if anyone was approaching. Suddenly the man shouted, 'Many soldiers are coming this way, but they are not wearing British uniforms and helmets. They are marching towards our village!' We were alerted in an instant. As we ran out to get more news, we found our brother with a Naga haircut and dressed in an old torn shirt. He had removed his trousers and around his waist was the black kilt worn by the village men. All his in-laws were dressed in the same manner. Sam was unusually fair and so ash had been rubbed on his neck where his fair skin was exposed. We sat outside among the villagers and waited for the approach of the Japanese. Everyone seemed too petrified to try to run away. Our neighbour, young Jimmy, couldn't trace his parents and was still with us. While Sam's brother-in-law was getting his hair cut, the guard shouted again that the soldiers were approaching the village very fast, 'They're coming up like ants, there are so many of them,' he shouted again. The man cutting Sam's brother-in-law's hair was only halfway through his job when this second shout came. The barber hurriedly finished the job. With his unevenly cut hair, the man tried to blend in with the rest of the village menfolk.

The rest of us changed out of our western clothing and wore the old, faded woven waist-cloths of the Angamis hurriedly given to us by our relatives in the village. A woman came and smeared ash and charcoal on my face saying, 'My dear, I have to disguise your fairness or else the Japanese will know that you are not a village-dweller.' I looked around and saw that two other women were doing the same to my younger sisters. The coal stung my flesh but I gritted my teeth and waited for her to finish. Sitting among the sunburnt villagers, we stood out because our limbs were more fair than theirs. So, we rubbed coal and ash on the exposed parts of our legs and arms. We tried to sit unobtrusively among the others so that we would not draw the attention of the Japanese.

As the Japanese marched into the village, people stopped what they were doing and stood still. We were separated from my brother's family. Jimmy sat with us with his hair half-cropped. As we sat thus, we saw the Japanese enter our house and begin to take away our belongings. First, they took our clothes out of the house, our nice dresses, shoes, coats and then they began to take our carefully stored rations. Tears stung at my eyes as I looked on and saw the soldiers taking away the coat which Vic had given me. But I was helpless, I dared not protest. I fought back my tears and tried to sit very still. They took Jimmy's new coat which he had been given when he went to Tiddim to work with the civilian labourers for the British troops. Vic had stocked a good amount of tinned food for us when he brought us to the village. But now, those tins of food had fallen into Japanese hands. The soldiers laughed and talked loudly to one another as they walked off with their hands full of what they had plundered from us. We sat on, looking at one another, tears glistening in our eyes. Before they came, my cousin had had the foresight to hide my small suitcase in their garden and that was undiscovered. There was a little food in it, some clothes and toiletries.

In moments, the village of Chieswema was swarming with Japanese soldiers. They quickly set up their radios. Then some of them came to the village people and demanded chickens, eggs, water and rice. One of them waved and signalled to Jimmy to get up. Jimmy got up and went closer to him. The soldier ordered him to go into the house and fetch eggs. Jimmy smiled and made gestures with his hands to show that there were none. Then they pushed an earthen jar into his hands and told him to fetch water. Jimmy picked up the jar and in the next moment, he pretended to lose his grip on it and the jar fell to the ground and was smashed, all the water inside it pouring out onto the ground. The soldier was very angry with Jimmy. He slapped him roundly on his cheek. Poor Jimmy turned red from the insult but he had to swallow his pride as the soldiers were heavily armed and any retaliation might bring a bullet. These first encounters with the Japanese were unpleasant and it grew worse. We both feared and hated them.

~

'At first' said Zhovire, who was eleven at the time and lived in the Angami village of Jakhama south of Kohima, 'the sight of so many hundreds of soldiers marching upon them filled our hearts with fear. We had never seen the Japanese before but had heard so much about them and the whole of the month of March the dreaded phrase, "The Japanese are coming" was repeated in the southern villages even as the British forces made preparations at Kohima to meet the invasion. But the Japanese, when they came, did not at the start show any hostility to the villagers. Women soldiers probably from the INA's Jhansi Regiment accompanied the large body of soldiers who came.'

Hearing of the imminent arrival of the Japanese many Nagas hid their stocks of rice. A few weeks before the Japanese came, Ami Toukhrie and Neiselie (aged twelve) from Kohima Village took about twenty basketfuls of rice to Biaku and stored it at Sievilie's cowshed. 'So, when our houses were burnt and the village was overrun by the Japanese we camped at Biaku and ate the rice we had hidden earlier.'

When the Japanese arrived in the Naga Hills they came ostensibly as friends. Sipohu Venuh had never seen an Indian before he saw some members of the INA at Phek. 'The next day I saw men of the black race [Indians] with the Japanese. They were friendly to us and when we went close to them, we saw that they were sitting and playing cards and smoking pine leaves. They did not behave badly toward us.'

> The Japanese opened a school as soon as they settled into our village. They provided school books and other materials to the people and I too was enrolled in this school. Till today I can remember how to count and read 1 to 20 in their language.
>
> The friendly Japanese troops would always eat and drink and do what we did. Once, Vesosa invited all of us to his field for the initiation of field work, which we call *tekhudu*. General Sato came along with some of his soldiers and he worked and feasted with us. He said, 'I eat and drink what you eat and drink, we are brothers and sisters.'

Sato first established his headquarters on Phek, living himself in the teacher's house, before he moved to a new headquarters in Naga Village. He became a common sight in the village, which at that time numbered probably 1,000 dwellings. 'General Sato was plump-faced, more well built than the others,' recalled Viketu Kiso. 'He must have been around forty years of age. He displayed great courage, at the same time he was very steadfast. The General often said this: "Don't be fearful, lots of Japanese forces are coming bringing in plenty of rations from Burma and Imphal, don't fear for anything".' Japanese propaganda had a blatantly racist theme, recalled the sixteen-year-old Phek resident Sipohu Venuh, who listened to one of Sato's early lectures to the populace:

General Sato said to us, 'Our skin colour is the same, the colour of our hair and eyes are same, our food is same but the British are different from us. Their skin is white, their eyes and hair are differently coloured and their food is different from us, so we Nagas and the Japanese must unite together as one and work together since we are brothers and sisters.' The General said this at the gathering of the village.

Lhoutuo Shüya recalled the Japanese arriving at his village, Merema, marching and singing. Oxen and horses carried their supplies:

The majority of the Japanese spoke English. Many of us had hidden our belongings in the woods. They were not unfriendly and they told us, 'We are brothers and sisters, we belong to the race of small bodied people, the British are well built, they are not our brothers and so we need to help one another.' They promised to build a school in the next two days and provide rations for the poor and needy, and they said they always did what they said they would do. People shouted happily at the end of this speech. But they said their rations had not arrived yet and so they could not start working on what they had promised and asked the villagers to help them with rations. At first, the villagers came forward and helped them with rice, pumpkins, tomatoes and other vegetables. They would buy our goods with their currency.

~

But as they began to starve the pretence of Japanese friendship wore thin. Subsistence farmers, the Naga people lived close to the breadline. The carefully-harvested rice crop was stored in village silos, and the best kept back to be used for seed, each family having enough to get them through to the next harvest, and no more. Within a week or two, however, these precious stocks were being raided by the Japanese. 'Apart from the soldiers, the horses had to be fed regularly and women watched with tears in their eyes as their granaries were emptied for horse feed.' At Jakhama the eleven-year-old Zhovire watched in astonishment as, even in the early days of the offensive, the Japanese were so hungry that they ate the gruel meant for pigs which was being cooked on large pots in some houses. It was apparent from the outset that they brought little food with them. Nusacho Vero recalled that at Phek the Japanese immediately 'searched for the leftovers of the British, such as cigarettes, condensed milk cans, etc'. When the

Japanese didn't get what they wanted, recalled Neikahi Keyho, they would threaten him, 'We can skin off your skin, burn you alive,' they taunted. His friend, Zavesho, tried to hide one of his last hens in a basket, but that too was stolen by a Japanese soldier. It didn't take long for the food to run out: there was simply insufficient to feed the Nagas and their increasingly desperate and unwelcome hosts.

Rape was the result of indiscipline rather than of official policy, but it was widely recounted among the Nagas. Neiputhie Rutsa (aged about twenty-five) lived at Chienuogaphe with his wife and mother when an INA soldier attempted to rape his wife. She ran to escape, his mother following the soldier, screaming, who promptly turned around and shot her dead. Defenceless, Neiputhie Rutsa could do nothing. However, he plotted his revenge:

> My brother ... persuaded me to accompany him to town where he would try and get me some arms and ammunition. I agreed to that plan and we reached Jotsoma where the British Government provided me with a rifle. After that I did not return to our shelter in the fields for six days. In those six days I killed five or six of the Japanese and I chopped off the head of one of the Japanese as proof. When I came back to the British authorities at Kohima and showed them the head of the Japanese, the Britishers were so happy that they lifted me up in the air. My feet did not touch the ground then and they carried me from one place to another place.

Consequently, it didn't take long for the Nagas to fall out of love with the Japanese. They 'were very cruel to us,' Neilhou Dzüvichü recalled, 'They killed our pigs and chickens and they ate our grain. They killed people and they frequently took men away to carry their loads.' He ended up working voluntarily for the British and involuntarily for the Japanese. Within days of their arrival the Japanese were pressing able-bodied men into working as porters and bearers. The villagers had no choice and although the Japanese sometimes paid for the goods and labour they demanded it was in worthless currency notes stamped 'Japanese Government'. By contrast, the British scrupulously paid for the goods they bought, and the services of Naga men as porters, with silver rupees. The Japanese squandered the opportunity to attract local people to their cause, by treating them fairly. Instead, British treatment worked as a powerful comparator to Japanese propaganda, the fine words of which rarely matched the realities of Japanese behaviour. Although the Naga Hills registered no accounts of wanton slaughter akin to that suffered on Guam, in the Philippines, or Malaya, for instance,

Japanese treatment of the Nagas grew increasingly brutal, turning many who were at worst indifferent neutrals into active enemies. According to Zhovire, those in Jakhama and elsewhere who appeared strong enough, and who were over twelve years of age, were forced to carry ammunition for the Japanese across to Lierie where the battle was raging:

> Women and old men were sent to gather edible herbs or pound grain. Each clan was assigned a specific number of gunny bags of herbs to gather each day. Labour was paid in the beginning with Japanese money but as the war became grimmer, forced labour and forced extraction of rations became the order of the day. When they were paid for their labour in the beginning, the villagers would take the Japanese currency and joke, 'Well we've been paid, but what a pity that we can't buy anything with this money.'
>
> Every day, in the village of Jakhama, people pounded grain for the Japanese and steadily grew rebellious at the loss of their food and at their forced labour.

~

Japanese brutality to British prisoners of war in contravention of the Genera Convention (to which Japan was not a signatory) was a common occurrence. During the fighting for Kohima Lieutenant Philip Brownless of 1st Essex was forced to leave twelve wounded men alone in the bush while he went to get help. When he returned he discovered a scene of profound and indescribable horror: the Japanese had got to them first. 'All were found bayoneted to death, a corporal tortured and beheaded.' Even the Nagas, with generations of head-hunting in their blood, were surprised at the cold-bloodedness of the samurai's *bushido* code, and wondered whether punishing prisoners was in actuality a sign of weakness. Was it not more praiseworthy for a victor to be magnanimous after battle, instead of vindictive? Certainly, the manner in which murders of prisoners were carried out by Japanese (and possibly INA) troops removed from the battlefield any hope of magnanimity in return, either by the British or by the Nagas. In the heat of battle one could understand such things, but not, if soldiers had any compassion or concept of shared humanity, afterwards. Zhovire recalled the execution of a dazed young British soldier by the Japanese.

> In May, there was great commotion in the village one day. I heard people shouting, 'There's a prisoner, a British soldier.' I ran out to

look at this strange phenomenon. A tall young British soldier, heavily guarded by Japanese soldiers, was being led around the village. A few days later the village crier shouted the news, 'The Japanese are preparing to behead the British soldier today. All are ordered to come and see.' This message was carried all over the village.

My friends and I excitedly ran to the spot to watch the event. We had never seen a beheading in all of our young lives. The Britisher's hands were tied behind his back, there was a black cloth tied over his eyes as a blindfold. The air seemed pregnant with tension and no one spoke as the strange spectacle took place. The Japanese officer took out his sword and it glinted as it momentarily caught rays of the sun. I felt distracted by the light on the sword. It looked very sharp and I was quite convinced it would do the job in no time. Soon, the Japanese officer barked out a sharp order and the Japanese soldiers prepared the prisoner for beheading. The Japanese officer raised his sword high and brought it down in one stroke. At that vital moment when steel touched flesh, I shut my eyes and put my hand over my eyes, too scared to watch further. When I opened my eyes again, I saw blood spurt out in a wide jet from the prisoner's neck and land in a messy splotch on the Japanese officer's shirt. 'Esh,' said the Japanese with an expression clearly showing his disgust.

Frequently, the Japanese displayed indiscriminate cruelty to the villagers. Neilhou recalled one of his fellow villagers, Vilelhou, being shot dead by the Japanese and regretted that he had no weapon with which to avenge his killing. Refusing to work for the Japanese risked receiving a bullet in return. 'The Japanese would come and write down names of the men and boys who were to carry loads for them,' remembered Neiselie. 'I was twelve but said I was ten years because I knew that they did not take boys below twelve. So they didn't take me. But my friend Kocha, who was the same age as I, refused and ran off when they called him to carry their loads. Then they shot at him but he ran very fast, and he was not hit by the bullet.'

Ten-year-old Neichieo was carrying supplies for the British with some of his friends to Jotsoma when they were fired at by the Japanese:

There were five of us, Toulhou, Lelhou, Khrielie, Lhousalie and myself. Lhousalie and I went ahead and we quickly threw off our packs but we heard shots very close to us. It was Lelhou and Toulhou they were shooting at and Toulhou was shot dead. Lelhou was also wounded. It happened in seconds and when the shooting started, Lhousalie turned his neck and he saw the soldiers very close by. He shot off into the woods but not before they emptied a machine gun at him. We were very worried for Toulhou so Khrielie went back to look and had his ear shot through. We didn't stay much longer after that. I jumped into the woods and climbed along the slopes till I got back onto the track. I ran like a madman, I never felt my feet touch the earth as I ran. All of us ran in different directions, thinking the others to be killed. When I met up with Khrielie later, I exclaimed, 'Hou, I thought you were dead, are you alive still?' We couldn't go back to look for Toulhou, not until after many months and when we did we also found many empty shells too.

The Nagas noted also the savagery with which the Japanese treated their own men. It was not only towards their enemies (the British and Indians), and their ostensible friends (the Nagas) that the Japanese could demonstrate remarkable cruelty, but to their own kind. Lhoutuo Shüya spoke of a soldier who had been badly wounded in the legs. 'His friends tried to help him and they put him on a horse but he fell from it so his friends left him behind. He was crying bitterly as they left and after a while one of them returned and shot him dead with three bullets.'

The terror the Japanese brought with them to the Naga Hills had its reward. As the tide turned against them, small groups of Japanese were hunted down by Nagas and killed without mercy. Kiezotuo, who lived in Rüsoma, remembered a Japanese soldier who tried to hide in the village. 'On a hot afternoon many of the villagers went to bathe at Khrusa's pond. Zepuzhü led the soldier who was hiding from the British and came to the pond whilst others were bathing. There, two men took him down below the pond and killed him there.'

~

Many Nagas fled into the jungle to escape this oppression, and especially to avoid the chance of being caught up in the fighting. Aviü was one such, scrabbling to survive in the jungle until the end of April, in spite of the threat of man-eating tigers, starvation and the ever present danger of the Japanese, themselves desperate for food and prepared to take it from the jungle-dwelling refugees by force if necessary. On 17 April her small party received instructions to make their way to safety at Khonoma. It mean having to travel due south, over the ridge near the Japanese-held village of Merema and across Dzüdza river to Zubza. 'The path we used was a small footpath which led towards the woods near Kohima,' she recalled.

It was a steep downhill climb in places. We had been walking for five miles when we had our first sight of British troops.[12] They were heavily armed, rifles readied for firing and they held grenades in their hands. They had stuck leaves in their helmets and on their clothes and we were frightened to see all of them looking very stern and hard-faced. But when they saw us they smiled and waved to us and waved us on. As for them, they walked silently in a long line toward Merema village and that was the last we saw of them. But the relief all of us felt at the sight of British uniforms was immense. It meant that the area had not wholly fallen into Japanese hands, that the British still held some areas in Kohima and beyond. Perhaps then, our loved ones were also safe somewhere.

The next morning they could see Garrison Hill in the distance, garlanded with parachutes and denuded of vegetation. Bullets whistled by and the ground shuddered with the reverberations caused by the relentless pounding of mortars and artillery. Aviü prayed for Vic and his friends to be safe especially when, walking along jungle paths, the refugees

> often came across wounded soldiers being carried on stretchers by our men. Those who could walk, did so, slowly stumbling along after their comrades, with the help of bamboo staffs. It broke our spirits to see the wounded soldiers ... The wounded soldiers looked helpless and vulnerable, many of them not much older than us.

Moving slowly, the exhausted Nagas reached Jotsoma finally on 24 April. 'Mother's uncle was there, as well as another family from Kohima related to us,' she recalled. 'They welcomed us warmly and gave us chicken broth and hot rice to eat. How wonderful the food tasted, it was the best food we had eaten having fed on half rations or rice and herbs for many days. Jotsoma was full of British, Indian and Gurkha troops.' Although the battle continued to rage on Kohima Ridge nearby, Aviü felt 'wonderful to be in Jotsoma, far from the threat of the Japanese and in the vicinity of a well-armed and friendly army'.

Her relief was to be short-lived, however. Some days after her party had managed to reach Jotsoma, Jimmy managed to make his way down to Dimapur, in search of Aviü's father. 'By evening he was back in the village,' she recalled.

> We spotted him immediately and we waved and called out to him. But he looked tired and sad. Strangely, he did not respond to our smiles and waving which was so uncharacteristic for Jimmy. In all

the years I had known him, he had been a cheerful lad and in the ordeal we shared in the jungle, Jimmy had always kept our spirits up. I thought he was playing a joke on us. But he drew near and said heavily, 'I have sad news ... Vic was killed on the 18th by a sniper's bullet'. My world collapsed around me at his words. I couldn't react at first and Jimmy's words echoed in my mind. Vic killed, on 18 April – the news slowly sank in – I wanted to scream – but a choked cry was all that came out of my throat. Then we were all in one another's arms sobbing at this unbelievable loss ... Oh God, how difficult to bear was this last blow. After all we'd been through, we had hoped to find each other again and be granted happiness. This was so unexpected, none of us could accept it. I think I finally fell asleep from exhaustion though I don't remember sleeping at all. I lay in bed staring at the roof, the walls, my eyes filling with tears and my body feeling spent with all the crying I had done. The next morning we packed and left. I did not want to stay a day more at that place, which had first given so much relief and promise of happiness, only to snatch it away without any warning.

Sergeant Victor Hewitt lies there still, but not forgotten, on Garrison Hill.

# Chapter 5

# The Defence of Imphal

On the evening of 20 March 1944 Warrant Officer Pat Bowen, navigator in a twin-engined Bristol Beaufighter nightfighter based at Kangla airfield on the outskirts of Imphal town, watched in astonishment as a seemingly endless stack of Dakota transport aircraft dropped slowly from the sky into the airfield. This was the arrival, direct from the battlefield in Arakan 250 miles away, of two experienced brigades of 5th Indian Division, most of whom had never flown before.[13] It was just like a train service:

> These Daks were stacked up one behind the other, quarter of a mile apart, touching down and those with troops were simply taxiing along and the soldiers rolling out and then the Dak was straight off again. Then the others came in on the other side of the runway with mules, guns etc. A half hour before dawn the larger part of the division was in Imphal. It was the most magnificent piece of air transport I'd ever seen. The logistics were unbelievable. They were literally coming in, rolling along and then taking off again back to Chittagong.

Lieutenant John Hudson of the Bengal Sappers and Miners also watched the scene with incredulity. The entire fly-in of the 'Ball of Fire' division between 18 and 29 March (the divisional sign was known more colloquially as the 'flaming arsehole') was, he considered, nothing short of a miracle, and it helped revitalize morale within the pocket. Only two days before, Lieutenant Basil French, a Gun Position Officer of 4th Field Regiment, a 25-pounder regiment supporting 5th Indian Division in the hills of northern Arakan, was astounded to hear that 'a serious situation was developing in Manipur' and that as a consequence the *whole* of 5th Division was to fly up to Imphal within the next two days. It seemed a task that was too large to be possible, as it had never even been practised before.

Well, it was such a flap, but quite a well organized flap; we were issued with 'Loading Tables' which listed what was to be carried in each transport aircraft. I was to be in charge of one aircraft and would have to load into it two Jeeps, one motor cycle, a certain weight of stores, so much 25-pounder ammunition and ten men … I was aware that the aircraft was bumping a lot as it taxied along and all of a sudden it stopped. A crew member in a baseball cap (American, of course) appeared at the flight deck door and shouted to us 'Sorry guys we've got a flat, we'll have to unload'.

And that was it. They couldn't change the wheel with the load on board so all the work of the night before was to no purpose and off it all came. Loading was, of course, not such a problem on the second attempt as we knew what snags to avoid and by lunchtime we were airborne at last. [When we arrived in Imphal] transport was loaned to us by 23rd Indian Division and at last we moved off to quite a respectable camp which had been built for the Chindits who spent some time there before flying into Burma.

Brigadier Geoffrey Evans, now commanding 123 Brigade, provided an example of the process by which 4th Field Regiment's 25-pounders were moved from action in Arakan by air to begin operations in the Imphal pocket:

Monday, 1400 hours: Guns taken out of action.
Tuesday: Unit moved to Dohazari airstrip, arriving at 1630 hours.
Tuesday/Wednesday night: Guns dismantled for loading into aircraft.
Wednesday: Flight to Imphal and guns re-assembled on the airfield.
Thursday: Guns in action on the Imphal front.

Lieutenant Peter Toole of the Royal Bombay Sappers and Miners observed that the American pilots 'had a disturbing method of judging their load for take-off … They would cast an eye at the tail wheel and, when it seemed sufficiently squashed, were ready to take off'. The news that they were being taken from one battlefield to shore up another, did not go down well with all the troops. Major Kenneth Ingham, a company commander in Lieutenant Colonel Gerald 'Munshi'[14] Cree's, 2nd Battalion, West Yorkshire Regiment, recalled that after losing all twelve platoon commanders in the Arakan fighting (six killed and six wounded) the men felt that they deserved a rest, not to be thrown in the deep end at Imphal.

~

Scoones' original plan for the physical protection of the Imphal Plain was to create two complementary layers of defence. The outer layer comprised a defensive ring where his Indian infantry divisions, supported by armour, artillery and ground attack aircraft defended against potential Japanese entry at the four major points of danger, in the north, north-east, south-east and south. With the attacks on Sangshak, the arrival of 5th Indian Division by air from Arakan and the withdrawal of 20th Indian Division from Moreh, in practical terms this meant the concentration of his forces:

> on the road northwards to Kohima, which the Japanese had cut in late March following the battle of Sangshak;
>
> on the Iril river valley which ran parallel to the Kohima road, both of which were separated by the Mapao-Molvom plateau (both areas the responsibility of 5th Indian Division);
>
> on the track to Ukhrul running to the north-east (23rd Indian Division);
>
> on the hills of Shenam in the south-east across which ran the main road between Palel and Tamu (20th Indian Division);
>
> and at Bishenpur on the road to Tiddim in the south (17th Indian Division).

Within this outer ring he constructed a number of self-contained, self-defending 'boxes' on the Arakan model, designed to protect strategic facilities such as the airfields as well as providing a local focus for defence against the threat of Japanese infiltration. Most of the troops in these boxes were support and administrative personnel, including some 6,000 RAF ground troops, supporting the expanding resupply and reinforcement requirements of Operation STAMINA. Troops withdrew into the boxes at night (even aircraft from some of the airstrips were pushed as close to the defended positions as possible), and with the exception of known patrols all other activity was regarded as hostile. The boxes also contained the heavy guns of the field artillery, although the 25-pounders serving the fighting divisions were located close to the troops they served, dug into positions in the *padi* fields or hidden among re-entrants in the hills.

Briggs' division arrived in the midst of a confusing and fast-moving battlefield. The Japanese were advancing in force from what seemed to be every side, attempting to seize the high ground overlooking the plain as a precursor to pouring into it. When Field Marshal Sir Archibald Wavell, the Viceroy of India, visited HQ Fourteenth Army in August 1944 he was perplexed by the nature of the fighting, describing it in a letter to London as taking place, strangely, in 'penny packets'. He was right. The battle did not involve massed brigades and divisions fighting in carefully choreographed coherence on a perhaps traditional model (if a normally chaotic battlefield could ever be described thus) but was instead a confused and disparate section and platoon – sometimes company level – struggle fought at many different points of the compass in the jungle-matted hills and valleys encircling the Imphal Plain, and the swampy terrain around Bishenpur. None of the land battles were directly interconnected, the struggles for the north and north-east (Sangshak, Nunshigum, Mapao and Ukhrul), the south-east (Tamu to Shenam) and the south (Tiddim to Bishenpur) being conducted largely independently by both attacker and defender.

With the cutting by Lieutenant General Yamauchi's 15th Division of the road between Imphal and Kohima on 30 March, Imphal was cut off from its lifeline to the north through Kohima. The siege had begun and until the road was open again the only way in and out was by air. Erroneously imagining the British everywhere to be in panicked flight, Yamauchi urged his regiments to exploit this opportunity (*'senki'*), attacking without hesitation, pushing forward where they could, independently and on their own initiative, taking advantage of the fact that no defender could possibly hold every hilltop, every jungle track, moraine and re-entrant that led onto the plain.

On the news that the Japanese had reached Kanglatongbi and were now bearing down from the north, Scoones rushed 63 Brigade (just back from 17th Indian Division's withdrawal from Tiddim and hoping in vain for something of a rest) forward to Sengmai, ten miles north of Imphal on the Kohima road, to plug the gap. The two brigades of Briggs' newly flown-in 5th Indian Division were also rushed north as soon as their planes touched down on the vast airfield of 'Imphal Main'. In fact, the first troops of 123 Brigade (2/1st Punjab and 2nd Suffolks) were despatched to support Brigadier Hope-Thomson's weak 50 Indian Parachute Brigade clinging to their hilltop position at Sangshak on the track to Ukhrul. Unable to break through to Sangshak, the two battalions took responsibility for providing the defensive screen through which 50 Parachute Brigade's gallant survivors withdrew on 26 March. The Japanese attempted to brush past the newly-arrived veterans of 123 Brigade in the days that followed. Half a mile to the west of Litan the men of Lieutenant Colonel W. G. Smith's 2/1st Punjab held a bare peak on the night of 24/25 March against the expected Japanese onslaught. The divisional historian described the following night as 'one of the most nerve-racking nights in the battalion's history'.

> C Company, on a small hill ... was attacked by a battalion of Japanese troops. Without a break the battle raged through the night. Part of the company was overrun. Hand-to-hand fighting was of the most ferocious. But the enemy was repulsed.

The 2/1st Punjab held, although only six of the fifty men who had started the fight remained unwounded the next morning. During the next two weeks the three battalions of 123 Brigade, based in the foothills at Kameng, where the Ukhrul road debouched into the Imphal Plain, patrolled the hills, tracks and villages east and north-east of Imphal to engage the groups of enemy troops attempting to break into the plain. Pressed hard by Yamauchi to advance quickly and without reconnoitring, it was at Kameng that the Japanese of 3/67th Regiment, sent to carry out a *coup de main* assault on Kangla airfield, received an unexpected bloody nose at the hands of 2/1st Punjab on 4 April. After a night march of nine miles through the hills from Litan the eighty Japanese of No. 10 Company came down from the hills onto the flat ground of the plain just as dawn began to break. They had, unfortunately for them, arrived directly in front of the Punjab positions as the order 'Stand To' was given. Rifles and machine guns began to cut into the unprepared Japanese ranks, exposed in the cleared scrubland to the front of the Punjab positions. The *banzai* assault was a standard response to such situations and, bravely though recklessly, the Japanese charged into the mouths of the waiting machine guns. Second Lieutenant Nakamura was wounded by grenade fragments as his company was decimated around him:

> The shelling and firing grew more intense as the sky lightened, and when I ran up to the company commander, the men in the front were trapped at the enemy positions. We were very close by now. The company commander ordered us to attack at once, but our men began to fall, the lead platoon commander was severely wounded, and we could make no headway against the enemy positions. The attack failed, and we lost half our strength.

British artillery then opened up and during a pause the Punjabis rushed out of their trenches with bayonets fixed, driving the attackers back into the bush. Then, at 10 a.m., British tanks arrived on the road from Imphal, and began firing their machine guns and heavy guns into the patches of scrubland where the Japanese had sought cover. They had no entrenching tools and so could not dig. In any case the ground was shale and digging under fire without explosive aids was impossible. The result was slaughter. Captain Nakanshi, commanding 10 Company was killed and by the end of the day, when darkness finally fell, only eight exhausted survivors managed to escape back into the hills whence they had come.

That night, 3 April, further west, the Japanese fell in force against the large administrative base at Kanglatongbi, some fifteen miles north of Imphal. A mile further south lay 'Lion' Box in which resided some 12,000 support staff, including 41st IGH, with only a few fighting troops to defend them. A mile further south at Sengmai lay Brigadier 'Sally' Salomon's 9 Brigade, comprising 3/9th Jats, 3/14th Punjab and Lieutenant Colonel 'Munshi' Cree's 2nd West Yorkshires, supported by Major Dinsdale's squadron of 3rd Dragoon Guards with its Lee Grant tanks, in reserve. Unperturbed by the news from Kanglatongbi, the battle-toughened brigade created a strong defensive position with responsibility for ensuring that the Japanese did not penetrate any further south onto the Imphal Plain. However, with Japanese pressure from the north increasing inexorably, and his defences severely stretched, Scoones decided on 7 April that Lion Box was too exposed, and ordered its evacuation (including 41st IGH), as well as the abandonment of Kanglatongbi, which was impossible to defend as it was low lying with no natural defences. Vast quantities of stores had to be left to the enemy.

Within an hour of the last patients from the hospital being evacuated from Kanglatongbi, Private Len Thornton was told by his CO that the Japanese were now a quarter of a mile away: the sound of machine-gun, rifle and mortar fire provided a noisy backdrop as darkness fell. Making their way through the night on Naga tracks, the following day, along with sixteen colleagues, the men reconstructed their tented hospital, a task they managed to achieve in two days. Thornton:

> Stretchers were put on the floor in between the beds, anywhere really, where the men could be treated. They were impossible working conditions.
>
> It was hard labour … it was raining all the time … No one slept much … We slept on the ground when we could, but that was out of sheer exhaustion most of the time.
>
> We used a medium-sized tent for the operating theatre such as it was. It was very basic, all we had were three antique operating tables, paraffin lamps and one very small Tilley lamp. We used Primus stoves for sterilizing the instruments. For sterilizing gowns and

gloves (when we had them) we used a small autoclave, converted from a flame thrower.

In a few days 41st IGH had received 2,000 casualties.

> First of all it was panic, then chaos. There was no time to stand there wringing hands in despair. We didn't have time for that. We just got stuck in. People were dying. After a while, we could see a glimmer of light as things started to get into some sort of order.
>
> The hospital was situated in the middle of the box to give maximum protection. It was also near the airstrip, which was not necessarily a good thing because we were getting daily air raids and the airstrip was a prime target. The drill at the hospital was put into order of priority and as soon as the casualties arrived they were sorted out. We dealt with the surgical cases. Two of my mates would put them on plasma drips and look after them before bringing them into the operating theatre.

Yamauchi meanwhile was making every effort to infiltrate through the mass of jungle-covered hills that swept in a wide crescent across the northern part of the Imphal Plain, seeping troops southward through the hills despite the reverse at Kameng on 4 April. It was not physically possible for Briggs to defend every possible point of entry on the northern front, so the solution was extensive patrolling to identify and disrupt Japanese routes through the hills. The one quite obvious physical feature the Japanese made for was Nunshigum. Towering dramatically over Imphal town and the vast airstrip of Imphal Main, Nunshigum's vast 3,833-foot bulk thrusts sharply upwards and forms a spectacular backdrop to the flat plain which sweeps south before it. It is the final, jagged piece of high ground reached by a traveller from the north before arriving at Imphal, sitting a mere four miles from Kangla airfield and six miles from Scoones' HQ. Standing atop its lofty grandeur one feels that a thrown stone would reach the scattered atap-roofed dwellings that skirt Imphal town itself. If held by the Japanese it would pose a danger of immense magnitude to the defenders, because for the first time it would allow them to *see* the object of their desire, and fortify their determination to break into the plain that stretched invitingly before them.

A standing patrol of Lieutenant Colonel Bernard Gerty's 3/9th Jats held part of a steep feature that overlooked the road that ran up the left-hand side of the Nunshigum massif. The Imphal Plain is often obscured at this time of year in a thick heat haze that rises high over the surrounding hills, substantially reducing long distance visibility. This was a problem more for pilots than it was for the Poor Bloody Infantry, for whom close encounters of the violent sort tended to take place at very close range indeed, often the distance of a grenade throw or a bayonet thrust. But the dawn of 6 April was unusually haze-free when 51st Regiment advanced on the mountain, driving the tiny Jat patrol from its position. A weak Jat platoon, commanded by Jemadar Abdul Hafiz, immediately counter-attacked, supported by a bombardment by the 25-pounder guns from Lieutenant Colonel Bastin's 4th Field Regiment firing from the valley below. Captain Anthony Brett-James described the action that led to the award of the Victoria Cross to Abdul Hafiz, the first to a Muslim soldier in the Second World War:

> Abdul Hafiz led his Jats in to the attack. They charged up the hillside that was bare of cover, shouting their war-cry as they neared the top. Then the waiting Japanese opened fire with machine guns. On the approaching Jats they threw down grenades. Jemadar Abdul Hafiz was wounded at the outset. A bullet struck him in the leg. Yet he dashed forward and seized the enemy machine gun by the barrel, while another Jat killed the Japanese gunner.
>
> The jemadar then took up a Bren gun dropped by one of his men who had fallen wounded, and notwithstanding the heavy fire from the enemy positions on this hill and on a feature to the flank, he shot a number of the Japanese soldiers. And so fiercely did he lead his men that the enemy ran away: hence the name Runaway Hill. But Jemadar Abdul Hafiz was mortally wounded in the chest, still grasping his Bren gun. To his men he shouted in his own language, 'Reorganize! I will give you covering fire.' But he died, without having been able to pull the trigger.

During the hours of darkness on the morning of 7 April two Japanese companies scaled the peak and in fierce fighting seized the high ground from the sixty men of B Company, 3/9th Jats, who suffered twenty-four casualties in the struggle. Unwilling to accede such an important advantage to the Japanese, the Jats immediately counter-attacked and threw the Japanese off the highest ridge. But Nunshigum stretched laterally for 7,000 yards, and the Jats would struggle to hold it indefinitely against determined opposition. Repeated attacks over 8 and 9 April by an entire Japanese battalion failed to break the Jats' hold on the mountain until, on 10 April, Japanese artillery managed to subdue three of the Jat Bren guns, and a fierce attack overran the forward platoons. For a second time Nunshigum lay in enemy hands. A Jat counter-attack that day failed to shift the Japanese, at considerable loss to the Jats.

A full brigade attack was now ordered, with Lieutenant Colonel 'Lakri' Woods'[15] 1/17th Dogras for 13 April. In what was to prove to be an inspired decision from his experience in Arakan, Evans asked that, whatever the physical difficulties encountered, the assault be supported by tanks, to provide intimate support to the infantry in the final assaults against the formidable bunkers that he knew the enemy would even then be feverishly sinking into the summit.

The day began warm and grew rapidly hotter, the sun high in the sky by mid-morning burning off the early-morning mists, leaving a high degree of visibility for both attacker and defender unusual in this pre-monsoon season. As the Dogras sweated their way up the two main spurs (one to the south-west, and the other to the south-east) towards the top of the ridge (one company on each spur) up which crawled the Lee Grants of B Squadron, 3rd Carabiniers, the entire divisional artillery fired concentrations on known Japanese positions, while Hurribombers and Vengeance dive-bombers (twenty four aircraft in all, a prodigious number) swooped from above, strafing with cannon fire and dropping their wing-mounted 250-pound bombs. Far below, on the southern edge of the mountain, Major General Harold Briggs, together with Brigadier Geoffrey Evans of 123 Brigade and Lieutenant Colonel 'Lakri' Woods sat on the Ukhrul Road next to 123 Brigade HQ at Sawombung, watching the Dogras and tanks climb slowly above the tree line.

After a climb taking an hour and a half the troops and the Lee Grants reached the summit of the ridge and closed in on the Japanese from both directions, gainsaying the few pessimists on the *padi* far below who had suggested that putting tanks on top of Nunshigum was a fool's errand. Intense and hand-to-hand fighting erupted at once, the arrival of the tanks a considerable shock to the Japanese. Colonel Omoto, observing from a nearby peak, felt hopeless with anger when he was told that the British had managed to get heavy tanks onto the top of what the Japanese referred to as Point 3833. Grabbing the binoculars from one of his staff officers to see for himself, he yelled in rage, 'We're done for! That's it!' Omoto had earlier been dismayed to hear Yamauchi recklessly (so it seemed) urging him to attack everywhere because the British were weak and undoubtedly fleeing, and now he had firm evidence that this simply was not true. He had thought that Yamauchi was a far more intelligent and reasonable man than Mutaguchi, who was well known to argue the 'cowardly British' line but these nonsensical orders from his divisional commander made him doubt Yamauchi's mental stability for the first time. Nevertheless, on Nunshigum the men of Major Morikawa's 3/215th Regiment fought desperately, firing rifles and throwing grenades at the slowly advancing leviathans. Men rushed forward in suicide attacks to try to thrust mines under the tracks of the tanks. Each Japanese position had to be destroyed individually, the tanks inching their way along the knife-edged ridge protected by the Dogras. Private Yamamoto Yutaka waited behind a small pile of soil, his face crammed into the dirt, as a tank track stopped a foot from his head. 'I am going to die,' he thought. Amazingly, he wasn't killed. With his head still firmly pressed into the ground his body slid slowly down the hill and off the ridge, where he withdrew to safety. Corporal Arthur Freer, the radio operator in Major Sanford's tank, the B Squadron Leader, described the battle:

> As we got closer some of them ran out of the bunkers, and ran up to the sides of the tanks carrying sticky bombs attached to a bamboo rod, they stuck the bomb on the side of the tank and as they ran off they pulled the pin and the theory was it would blow the tank to pieces. We managed to deter them from sticking them on by firing machine guns along the side of the [other] tank[s]. I fired the front Browning which could not traverse but only elevate or depress. If I could have traversed it I could have killed a lot more Japanese.

Infantry casualties among the Dogras were high, every single officer being killed or wounded. Likewise, all of the six Carabinier officers were also killed or wounded, having to stick their heads out of their turrets to see where they were going (a mistake of a few feet might easily cause a tank to topple over the edge of the ridge: one Lee Grant did so, falling 100 feet, but both crew and tank survived unscathed). Tank commanders also needed to direct their gunners' fire, making them vulnerable to the cascade of bullets that the otherwise impotent Japanese sent in torrents towards each vehicle. The hammering rounds were a daunting challenge to the men who had to place their heads out of the turret, yet they did so repeatedly. Arthur Freer:

> We started hearing [over the radio] of people being killed, usually 'Number 9 hit in head'. These were the tank commanders with their heads out of the turret looking for the way forward. As they instructed the drivers, they were firing their pistols and throwing grenades at the Japanese … I heard a thump at the side of me, called up to 'Sherley' Holmes, 'what's happened'. He said, 'Dizzy's been hit in the head.' That was the nickname for our Squadron Leader, and I looked into the turret, because my head was on the level of the feet of anyone standing in the turret, and I could see the Squadron Leader lying on the floor.

A bullet had entered under Major Sanford's chin, exiting through his helmet. Lieutenant Basil French, on the gun position in the valley below listened to the sounds of the fierce battle over the radio set from the Forward Observation Officer, Captain John Bellman, who accompanied 1/17th Dogras onto the position:

> Over the radio I could hear his voice against a background of machine-gun, rifle fire and grenades exploding as he calmly gave his order for us to fire in support of the infantry.

The combination of infantry, artillery and armour proved irresistible on Nunshigum, the non-commissioned officers of both Carabiniers and Dogras taking command of their respective troops (led by CSM Craddock of 3rd Carabiniers and Subadars Ranbir Singh and Tiru of the Dogras) in the absence of their dead and wounded officers.[16] Holding the top of the ridge the survivors of the attack repelled Japanese counter-attacks that night with the help of heavy concentrations of artillery support from 4th Field Regiment. Corporal Arthur Freer again:

> That night Colonel [Ralph] Younger came round to our tank, bubbling with the success ... The next day we had a lot of work oiling guns, replenishing ammo and cleaning up the tanks. The tracks were clogged with bits of Japanese uniforms, bones and bits of flesh.

Lance Bombardier Ron Bunnett, an anti-tank gunner in 5th Indian Division, saw a large number of Japanese corpses littering the foothills of the mountain the next morning, and was struck by the fact that they were 'not the common conception of Japanese, but big, well-fed men'. Evidence taken from the few prisoners and from a search of the dead (many Japanese kept diaries and gave little thought to the possibility they might fall into the hands of the enemy; the British, in contrast, forbade the men to keep diaries, as it potentially endangered so many lives) began to show that the massive casualties sustained by the Japanese in their relentless aggressive rush to seize Imphal was leading to a crisis of morale in their ranks. The diary of one of the few prisoners captured on Nunshigum, a badly-wounded Japanese NCO, revealed the pressures faced by the Japanese:

> April 1/2. I think the men are getting browned off. If this keeps up the operations are bound to be a failure.
> April 7. The enemy are bombing us again. What the hell are our planes doing?
> April 9/10. The attack on the airfield by 10 Company [this was the

company of 3/67th Regiment destroyed at Kameng on 4 April] has been stopped and they have come back ... I wonder how important this present operation is: I cannot readily understand how pressed we are. I wonder when the independence of India will come into effect. I cannot see how it can be done. At this rate the war will go on forever. In the end the only results are loss of men by each side and there is no end to this bloody affair.

Unfortunately for the British, poor Japanese morale rarely evidenced itself in a refusal to fight or an enhanced willingness to surrender. In four months of fighting around Imphal only slightly more than 100 prisoners were taken. Japanese losses at Nunshigum – the result of their desperate *banzai* assaults and an unwillingness to abandon their posts except as corpses – were extremely heavy, no less than 250 bodies being counted. Major Morikawa was killed, and all officers were either killed or wounded. Likewise British casualties – especially in terms of officers – were also high, but this action expelled the Japanese from the closest point to Imphal they ever managed to reach. For the Japanese it was a shocking repulse. Mutaguchi certainly recognized it for what it was. Realizing that Yamauchi would now struggle to penetrate Briggs' defences without reinforcement, Mutaguchi instructed Sato – further north at Kohima – to send a regiment south to assist 15th Division.

These instructions also coincided with orders Slim gave to Scoones on 10 April to turn Briggs' troops on to the offensive, the key task being the opening of the Kohima road. Scoones' plan was for 5th Indian Division to advance north on either side of the road to Kohima beyond Kanglatongbi and for Roberts' 23rd Indian Division to push 15th Division back in the direction of Litan and Ukhrul, through the range of hills now infested by Yamauchi's men. Defeated at Nunshigum, they were far from being beaten, however, although exhaustion and sickness were taking their toll. Elsewhere, Scoones planned to continue to hold the Bishenpur front with Cowan's 17th Indian Division (now rejoined by 63 Brigade) and to launch a limited counter-attack against 33rd Division's line of communication on the Tiddim road. Gracey's 20th Indian Division would continue to absorb Yamamoto's punches against the Shenam defences. These were clear, practical and aggressive plans. The further back from the immediate battlefield one went, however, the less confident men were about the ultimate outcome of the battle. On the evening of 14 April Wavell had dinner with Mountbatten in New Delhi, having met his Chief of Staff, Lieutenant General Sir Henry Pownall in the morning. Both were pessimistic, Wavell noted in his diary, about the state of the Assam battle: 'Mountbatten thinks that at best it will take them 5 or 6 weeks to clear the Japanese out'.

In the wild, tempestuous country in an arc running north-west, north and north-east of Nunshigum between the road to Kohima and the Iril river valley lies a vast inverted triangle of jungle-matted hills (the southern point of which touched Imphal) stretching from the village of Mapao in the south, distinguished amidst the dark jungle foliage by its white-painted American Baptist Mission church, three and a half miles north as the crow flies to Molvom. These few miles became a Japanese defensive arena par excellence, the individual peaks and ridges – Hump, Twin Peaks, Foston, Penhill, and Buttertubs – occupying 5th Indian Division expensively for the next six weeks as they struggled in the teeming monsoon to push their way north and to remove, through battle, the tentacles Yamauchi's troops had wrapped around this rugged terrain.

Briggs began his offensive by attempting to defeat each position in turn. On 23 April Salomon's 9 Brigade launched a deliberate attack on Japanese positions in the hills around Mapao. To the west, 3/9th Jats and 3/4th Punjab, supported by the guns of 4th Field Regiment and following strikes by Hurribombers, captured the high ground north of Mapao, although to the east Cree's West Yorkshires were unable to wrench free the Japanese hold on Foston and Penhill. As was their wont, the Japanese simply refused to budge and in time forced Briggs to consider an alternative stratagem for clearing the hills, other than one employing the expensive use of scarce and difficult-to-replace infantry.

At least, with 5th and 23rd Indian Divisions going on the offensive, the direct threat to Imphal from the north appeared to have reduced, although Slim and Scoones, during April and May, were not complacent. The Japanese were still fighting desperately, refusing to consider anything but the prospect of victory. However, it seemed clear to Slim that Mutaguchi was now playing into his hands. By over-extending himself on three separate fronts, each of Mutaguchi's three divisions was now doing what he had expected, namely fighting tenaciously to hold positions they had secured regardless of their strategic value, unwilling to relinquish ground because of their fear of losing 'face' by withdrawing from the high-water mark of their advance. Mutaguchi, of course, gave repeated sanction to the urge to continue onwards, whatever the cost.

~

In the south-east during early April Yamamoto's three battalion columns, together with mountain artillery and light tanks, pushed aggressively against the new positions hurriedly occupied by two of Gracey's brigades, following the withdrawal from Tamu and Moreh. This initiated a bloody, ten-week-long struggle for the vital Shenam position. The long 5,000-foot-high Shenam Ridge in fact comprised a range of jungled peaks jutting high into the clouds through which ran the road[17] between Palel and Tamu. Both sides named these Brigade Hill, Recce, Sita, Gibraltar, Malta, Scraggy (Ito[18]), Lynch, Crete East (Ikkenya), Crete West (Kawamichi), Cyprus and Nippon (Maejima). Whoever controlled these peaks controlled the road over the Shenam position into Imphal.

The monsoon rains that had arrived in late March 1944 brought not just huge volumes of rain that clattered down in torrential sheets and attempted to wash away the hillsides, but thick mists and cold temperatures – especially at night – that shocked British soldiers new to service in 'hot' India. At night the temperature often fell below freezing and was achingly miserable. Hunched sodden, in the bottom of a slit trench for day after day and cold night after night with no means of keeping dry, short of drinking water and without warm food or drink while fighting the most formidable foe imaginable, tested the men's mental and physical stamina to the limit. Occasionally during the day the sun would burst through the rain-sodden purple clouds to bring some momentary comfort. With the difficulties posed by the climate came a stark reminder to any British Commonwealth troops who had not yet experienced the toughness of their adversary of just how extraordinarily fit and physically hardy were the Japanese, how committed they were to achieving their objectives, how apparently unconcerned they were with regard to human comforts and how determined they were to do what the Emperor (through their officers) demanded, or die in the attempt. Repeated, fanatical and suicidal attacks were thrown at the British, Indian and Gurkha defenders and counter-attacks had to face the toughest defensive positions imaginable, prepared by men whom Slim was to describe as 'warrior ants'. As the days went by the battlefield became one large charnel house, littered with bodies in various states of decomposition as it was rarely easy to recover and bury the dead.

Private 'Ray' Dunn of the Devons was not the only one to admit openly that he 'was ill prepared for the ferocity of the Jap attacks'. Training was extremely important to inculcate in the men a knowledge of their enemy, but nothing could quite prepare them for the type of experience, for example, of the men of 4th Mahrattas who, when guarding Palel Bridge in the teeming rain on the night of 29 June were suddenly and fiercely attacked out of the darkness by a body of Japanese armed only with swords. It was only with difficulty that the men succeeded in repelling their assailants, each of whom was stopped by the desperate parrying of bayonets. This type of fighting – thrusting, slashing in panting, adrenalin-fuelled and terrified exhilaration – was, averred Private Jack Clifford of the Northamptons, horrifying 'beyond human endurance'.

When the Japanese turned to the defensive in mid-April in the north and the south-east, jungle-topped hills became bare from the shell fire and the monsoon turned positions, often only yards apart, into a muddy morass of indescribable horror and ugliness. Once dug in, the Japanese had to be grenaded out, one by one, bunker by bunker. Otherwise they were immovable. His platoon sergeant told Lieutenant Ken Cooper of the Borders when he arrived on the Ukhrul Road in May, 'By Christ, them little bastards can dig. They're underground before our blokes have stopped spitting on their bloody 'ands.' On rare occasions bunkers were destroyed by shellfire or by a direct hit from a Hurribomber strike although the only real guarantee of success was direct sniping by tanks. As the Devons were to discover, failure to ensure that each bunker was completely clear, or that every stiffening corpse was indeed dead, meant that the next attack often came from within one's own perimeter, from positions that were assumed to be clear and bodies thought to be lifeless.

Harrying the withdrawing 20th Division from Moreh, Lieutenant Maejima of 3/213th Regiment managed, on 2 April, to capture from a company of 2nd Borders the commanding heights of a peak guarding the eastern entrance to the Shenam Pass, at the northern end of the Tengnoupal Ridge, which the British immediately named 'Nippon Hill'. Guarding the northern side of the entrance on the other side of the 'Upper Road' lay 'Crete' ridge, its western edge overlooking the two roads as they crossed, with Crete East and Crete West at either end. Repeated attacks by two of the battalions of Brigadier Sam Greeves' 80 Brigade (9/12th Frontier Force Regiment and 3/1st Gurkha Rifles) failed to eject the deeply-ensconced Japanese from the bunkers they had feverishly and skilfully dug across the tree-covered Nippon Hill. These attacks seemed to do nothing more than denude the trees of their vegetation, even direct strikes by 25-pounders, and those of Hurribombers dropping their twin 250-pound bombs, failing to make any impact on the thickly-roofed bunkers, some of the tunnels of which went as deep as twenty feet.

The sixth attack was launched by the men of 1st Devons, commanded by Lieutenant Colonel G. A. Harvest, a man whom one of his soldiers remembered as physically indistinguishable from the rest of his men, with a rifle under his arm and bush hat on his head, calm, approachable and professional. The Devons were on the appropriately named 'Devon Hill' in the centre of the Patiala Ridge, alongside and to the west of Nippon Hill. The start of the attack was signalled by the regimental mortars marking the position with smoke, prior to a strike by three Hurribombers dropping their 250-pound bombs and then raking the hill with cannon fire, after which the 25-pounders from the valley far below pulverized the ridge. At least one bunker was seen to take a direct hit and its shattered remnants heaved lifelessly into the air. During the bombardment the Devons climbed down into the valley separating the two hills before climbing the enemy-held ridge from two sides, reaching the top without firing a shot as the artillery fire lifted. When they emerged from their bunkers to find the Devons among them the Japanese reacted with angry fury. But in the stabbing, thrusting melee that followed they were unable to prevent the Devons taking the position after a four-hour slog, despite the West Countrymen suffering eighty-seven casualties, including three company commanders wounded, one of whom (Major Phythian) died the following day. Corporal May, a Medical Orderly at the Regimental Aid Post positioned in a gulley behind Nippon Hill, watched the regiment's twenty-four stretcher-bearers bring in the wounded, some beyond hope:

> I remember Sergeant Major Jimmy Garvey of D Company. They brought him into us dying. He charged, leading the men with the bayonet. He said, 'Don't waste time on me.'

Digging themselves in and wiring the position, A Company of the Devons settled down to await the inevitable counter-attack. Almost immediately an incautious ten-man Japanese reconnaissance patrol was wiped out, but this proved the precursor of a long and fear-filled night. In the morning the men counted sixty-eight bodies in front of the position before they were relieved by troops of 9/12th FFR. Relentless Japanese pressure proved too much for the 'Piffers', however, and after several days of fighting, which included attacks by tanks, they relinquished control of the crest to a Japanese assault commanded by Major Ito on 16 April. The hill was not retaken until July. Meanwhile, the fighting for the surrounding hills had not diminished in its intensity, B Company of the Devons holding on to 'Crete' against heavy and repeated attacks while the remainder of the battalion dug in on Cyprus and Scraggy. A characteristic of the fighting at this early stage in the campaign was that of the mass, suicidal attack, the Japanese military code (*bushido*) insisting that the moral power of the offensive would overcome any material superiority enjoyed by the enemy.

Japanese experience against weak-willed opponents in 1942 had persuaded them of the correctness of this approach to warfare, but it had taught them some false lessons. As time was to show on the Shenam heights and elsewhere around the Imphal Plain, it was an entirely inappropriate tactic in the face of well-trained and well-equipped opponents determined to resist the psychological and physical impact of a massed *banzai* attack.

As an example of these tactics, at 3 a.m. on 14 April, a few miles to the north of the Tamu road on a hill nicknamed 'Sita', 213th Regiment launched a mass assault on the waiting men of 3/1st Gurkhas. The Gurkhas had prepared their position well, with liberal quantities of barbed wire and anti-personnel mines, Bren guns covering all the obvious approaches and boxes of primed grenades lying in each trench. In the ensuing fight the Japanese lost an irreplaceable 500 casualties. It was a shocking loss of life for any army determined to preserve its most precious resource, its manpower. But even at this stage Japanese commanders persisted in the belief that the cowardly British would be swept away by the force of Japanese *samurai* willpower alone, as had been done in Malaya, Singapore and Burma two years before, and these costly mass attacks continued. The exercise of command by the Japanese was thus profoundly flawed and, in the face of an enemy better able to care for its wounded, with a more humane attitude to the lives of its men and an immeasurably superior logistics system, the end result of Mutaguchi's stratagem should have been clearly observed in the early stages of the fighting, and his tactics adjusted accordingly. It wasn't and they weren't. The struggle in the darkness of Sita Hill cost 3/1st Gurkhas fifty casualties in return. Japanese arrogance and inflexibility could be shocking to those who were forced to observe the lack of subtlety in their techniques. On a memorable occasion on the evening of 17 April the Japanese launched what they considered to be such a devastating artillery bombardment on Crete that no one could have survived. As the bombardment lifted, the waiting and largely untouched Devons were astonished to see the Japanese marching along the road towards their position in column of threes, a ripe and unexpected target that was quickly and efficiently engaged by machine guns and artillery. At a personal level, however, the Japanese soldier gave meaning, time and again, to the power of *bushido*. Sergeant Leech and Corporal Venner went forward one morning to attempt to recover a wounded Japanese officer from the wire to the front of their position, and take the man prisoner. When Sergeant Leech tried to pick the wounded man off the wire the Japanese bit him in the hand and refused to let go. Corporal Venner hit him hard on the head with a steel helmet but this only made the man bite more deeply. It became clear that the only way to separate teeth from arm was to kill the Japanese officer, which Corporal Venner duly proceeded to do with the man's own sword.

The senior Japanese commander behind the relentless attacks in this sector, Lieutenant General Yamamoto, 15th Division's Infantry Commander, was a bully who was hated by his officers (a characteristic shared by many Japanese generals). He harassed his unit commanders to continue advancing whatever the impediment, and abused them roundly as cowards if they failed to achieve battlefield success. On 20 April, Major Ito struck with infantry and tanks at Crete East, Cyprus and a small hill between them called Umbrella Tree Hill. Because the Upper Road circled the south of Crete and the Lower Road cut between Crete and Cyprus, the Japanese were able to make use of their light tanks in these attacks and, although one was knocked out, the Japanese proved to be too strong for the lightly-defended Umbrella Tree Hill. With Japanese tanks on this position Crete East was suddenly vulnerable: if Crete East fell then Cyprus would be cut off. A Devon company withdrew prematurely and without orders from Crete East on 22 April: Brigadier Greeves immediately sanctioned the arrest of the Company Commander for dereliction of duty. But Japanese pressure was intense nevertheless and, to forestall having his forward defences cut off, Gracey gave the order to withdraw from Crete East and Cyprus completely, occupying positions on Crete West and Scraggy Hill on 25 April. It was here that the front stabilized somewhat to become the focal point for the bitter Somme-like struggle that developed between May and July. But Yamamoto's insistence on attacking at any cost had in fact cost him dearly: by this time Ito's battalion, for example, was down to a mere eighty men.

~

Moving with his battalion across the Chindwin to reinforce Yamamoto in mid-April, Major Takemura saw men of the INA's 2nd Gandhi Regiment on the road from Tamu marching to the chant *'Jai Hind! Chalo Delhi!'*[19] The HQ of 1st INA Division, together with the 2nd (Gandhi) and 3rd (Azad) Regiments, the men still dressed in the British khaki uniforms they had worn when first captured (the British Indian Army had long since converted to wearing jungle green) had made their way to Rangoon from Malaya. In March Colonel Mohammed Zaman Kiani, the divisional commander, had rushed north to meet Mutaguchi at Maymyo to plead for a role in what he fancied would be the beginning of the end of British India. Mutaguchi, his optimism as yet unchecked, hastened Kiani on to Tamu, there to join Yamamoto's northern thrust over the Shenam Saddle, from where it would debouch like a flood onto the Imphal Plain at Palel, sweeping the detritus of a corrupt Empire before it. But, to Kiani's disappointment, Yamamoto made no offer to put the Indians in the vanguard of the offensive, placing them instead to guard the Mombi track, which crossed the hills from Witok in the Chindwin Valley into the Imphal Plain to the south of Palel. The hype surrounding the INA's despatch to the front, however, left the troops with the expectation that they would not need their heavy weapons and equipment. These – machine guns, mortars and even grenades – were left on the Chindwin at Kalewa and the troops climbed into the hills from the Chindwin valley with what they wore, together with a blanket, their personal weapon and fifty rounds of ammunition. By 28 April they were established ten miles west of Witok, from where their first foray into the plain was to be launched.

This was to be an attack on the British airfield at Palel designed to coincide with an advance by Yamamoto from the east on 1 May. In the event the Indian attacking force, 300 men under the command of Major Pritam Singh, took two exhausting night marches to reach their start point, and launched their attack on the night of 2 May, without a Japanese supporting offensive. For months the INA had been awash with the self-delusional propaganda that when confronted by their kith and kin the Indian troops of the British Army would refuse to fire, and joyfully join in the revolution. For the men of B Company, 4/10th Gurkha Rifles, however, nothing could have been further from the truth. Five miles south of Palel, dug in along a ridge, the Gurkhas watched the Indians approaching in an extraordinarily lackadaisical manner in the bright moonlight, talking amongst themselves and smoking. The sustained and disciplined firepower of the waiting Gurkhas, unmoved by the thought that they might be firing on their erstwhile colleagues, scattered the startled Indians and slaughtered those who had the courageous temerity to attempt, in the confusion and noise of the moment, to assault the Gurkha position. For the loss of two Gurkha dead the INA lost two officers killed and many soldiers, together with the surrender of thirty-five. A few miles to the rear the INA Regimental HQ was attacked by a company of 9/12th Frontier Force Regiment, and the following morning was hit by a strike by RAF Hurricanes coordinated with an artillery bombardment. The attacking force was largely decimated by these actions, about a hundred casualties being suffered. The greatest effect of these disasters, however, was on INA morale which, combined with repeated Japanese failure to supply the division with either food or ammunition and with the ravages of disease – especially malaria – precipitated a series of crises in INA ranks. Many men deserted, while

The principal actors in Operation C. Sitting in the front row (left to right) are Yanagida, Tanaka (as GOC 18 Division, he was not involved with the invasion of India), Mutaguchi, Matsuyame and Sato. (Topfoto)

Sergeant Victor Hewitt, Aviü's common-law husband, who was shot dead by a sniper on 18 April 1944. (Grace Savino)

Lieutenant John M Young, Argyll & Sutherland Highlanders. A granite street plaque unveiled in Glasgow in March 2011 describes how the 24 year old 'Jock' Young, attached to the Assam Regiment 'at Kharasom near Kohima, gave his life in a heroic stand to protect India from invasion having first saved the lives of the brave men he led.' (Roy McCallum)

Aviü before the war arrived in the Naga hills. A Naga road-gang provides the backdrop to the photograph, taken in Kohima. (Grace Savino)

Lieutenant General William ('Bill') Slim walking purposefully in a still from cinematography taken at the height of the Imphal/Kohima battles. Lieutenant General Montague Stopford, of XXXIII Corps, follows. (IWM)

The well-loved Deputy Commissioner Charles Pawsey (second from right) introducing the Supremo (Admiral Mountbatten) to Naga gaonburas after the battle for Kohima, in August 1944. (IWM)

Stopford's IV Corps in the Imphal pocket was sustained throughout the siege by Operation Stamina, the largest air supply operation of the Second World War. These C-47s are about to fly out of Imphal from Tulihal airfield, bound for airfields in the Brahmaputra Valley. (IWM)

Spitfires operating from one of the Imphal airfields, close to the jungle fringe, during the siege. (IWM)

Brigadier Lancelot Perowne, commander of 23 Long Range Penetration (Chindit) Brigade, which operated successfully to disrupt Japanese efforts to dominate the Naga hills. (IWM)

The point at which armour from Imphal joined up with the 2nd British Division advancing south from Kohima on 22 June 1944. The soldier in the helmet shaking hands with the Indian cavalryman is Major General John ('Black Jack') Grover, the highly respected GOC of 2nd Division. Much to the anger of his men he was sacked by Stopford at his moment of glory. (IWM)

Looking up Garrison Hill, the brick remains of Charles Pawsey's bungalow can be clearly seen. (IWM)

An aerial shot of the Kohima Ridge taken looking south-east on 15 April 1944, ten days into the siege. The large scar in the landscape is the site of the Indian General Hospital, and the site of today's hospital. Smoke from the fighting can be seen above Kuki Piquet. The point at which the road exits the picture on the left hand side is the TCP (Traffic Control Point). (IWM)

An ingenious though nerve-racking attempt to cross a destroyed bridge in the Naga hills: a wire suspension bridge. (IWM)

The railway station at Dimapur (often called Manipur Road) was the terminus of rail-borne supplies across the Brahmaputra. Dimapur was a massive supply depot serving not just 14 Army to the east, but Stilwell's forces far to the north east. (IWM)

General Sato's formal surrender late in 1945. (IWM)

A C-47 drops supplies to the Chindits of 23 LRP Brigade over the Naga village of Ukhrul. (IWM)

A wounded British soldier is evacuated from the fighting at Kohima. Many of the ambulance men were pacifist volunteers of the American Field Service. (IWM)

Gaunt members of 23 LRP Brigade recovering in Dimapur at the end of operations in July 1944. (IWM)

The standard means of supply in the mountains was the mule. (IWM)

A Japanese light tank being put through its paces after being captured by the British at Imphal. (IWM)

An Indian Army mortar crew firing very high elevation from their firing pits at Jotsoma, in support of their colleagues besieged on the nearby Kohima Ridge.

The British would have found it almost impossible to fight in the Naga hills without the almost universal support of the indigenous population. Here, a Naga labour gang works to build a road.

A photograph of the Shenam Ridge following heavy fighting along the hilltop road running from Palel to Tamu. (IWM)

Major General 'Punch' Cowan, GOC 17th Indian Light Division, controlling operations that successfully extracted his division from forward positions in Tiddim, back to the Imphal plain, in the first weeks of the battle.

Men of Sato's 31st Infantry Division advancing on Kohima. (Topfoto)

Indian soldiers operating in the swampy country around Bishenpur. (IWM)

Men of the Queen's Regiment resting after their capture of Jail Hill, Kohima, 13 May 1944. (IWM)

Men of a British infantry battalion, possibly the 7th Worcesters, preparing to 'go over the top' with fixed bayonets on Naga Hill, Kohima. (IWM)

A British Lee Grant tank sitting atop the tennis court on Kohima Ridge. It was the use of these leviathans which finally tipped the battle against the Japanese on the tennis court. (IWM)

British troops were forced methodically to eliminate every Japanese position. This Japanese bunker on Kohima Ridge was destroyed by pole charges. (IWM)

These men, possibly of the Dorsets, take no chances as they clear up Kohima Ridge at the end of the battle in the second week of May 1944. (IWM)

British infantry prepare to assault Kohima Ridge, early May 1944. (IWM)

British 25 pounders firing high elevation against Japanese positions at Kohima from their fire base at Zubza on the Dimapur road. (IWM)

Naga warriors took the war to the Japanese in their traditional way. The British supplied them with rifles.

Other Nagas acted as porters and stretcher bearers. This photograph was taken at the base of Aradura Spur during the final battles for the Kohima position. Notice the .303 bandolier. The black umbrella was, and remains, ubiquitous in the Naga hills. (John Burkmar)

The tension of battle is palpable as these British troops, possibly of the 7th Worcesters, look out towards Japanese positions on Naga Hill, Kohima. (IWM)

others shot themselves through the foot or hand in an attempt to escape the battlefield. Of the 3,000 men of the 2nd (Gandhi) Regiment who marched into the hills at the end of March only 1,000 remained by 15 June, and then only 750 two weeks later.

~

Meanwhile, in the south on the Tiddim Road Gracey's third brigade (Mackenzie's 32 Brigade, comprising 1st Northamptons, 9/14th Punjab and 3/8th Gurkhas) was sent by Scoones on 13 April to block the advance of Yanagida's columns towards Imphal while Cowan's two exhausted brigades refitted (although 63 Brigade was thrown temporarily into the gap on the Kohima road north of Imphal). Mackenzie's brigade relieved 49 Brigade, which rejoined 23rd Indian Division on the Ukhrul road. Mackenzie's chosen position was seventeen miles behind the original 49 Brigade defences at Milestone 33, because he judged that these could be easily bypassed and the mountains to the west of Bishenpur offered a far more substantial obstacle to Japanese plans. He was right, although withdrawing enabled the Japanese to move eighteen miles closer to Imphal. With Cowan and Scoones' permission, Mackenzie placed his three battalions on defended locations on either side of the Silchar Track, as it entered the deep valley west of Bishenpur. On the southern side lay Wooded Hill (Point 5250, on the British right) and Wireless Hill (Point 5350 on the British left). Towering over both positions on the northern side of the valley was Point 5846, a craggy outcrop covered in thick bamboo with a 1,000-foot sheer drop on the northern side. Strategically the 32 Brigade position acted as the door to Imphal, with Logtak Lake on the left, and the high ground of Point 5846 on the right. Yanagida's plan was to push one column (2/213th Regiment less two companies, together with 14th Independent Engineer Regiment) directly against Bishenpur; 215th Regiment was to block the Silchar Track between Bishenpur and Tairenpokpi, through which, a day later, 2/214th Regiment would cut the road behind Bishenpur at Nungang, and make for Imphal through the expanding breech.

On the night of 15 April a Japanese patrol under command of Second Lieutenant Abe Toshio destroyed the suspension bridge on the Silchar track, west of Bishenpur, removing the final land link between IV Corps and Assam. On the same night the first of a flood of assaults fell against the rudimentary British positions on Wooded Hill. These continued on 16 and 17 April. Sergeant Kelly, a sniper in 1st Northamptons (nicknamed 'Killer

Kelly' for his sniping exploits by a Japanese historian), was attached to No. 1 Company (Captain Cubey), dug in on Wooded Ridge. Private Jack Clifford remembered the 'carpets of orchid like flowers growing wild. We soon churned them up digging in and building bunkers.' Kelly's diary for 18 April captures the terrifying intensity of the hand-to-hand fighting that characterized all combat against the Japanese:

> No. 1 Company have got one strand of wire 12 inches high in front of their positions. Better than nothing I suppose. Saw [a] Jap on top of Wireless Hill and shot him ...
>
> Stood-to all last night. Can't rest in half a hole. Sharing the slit with Private Storer. Topper Brown is on my right with another chap of 1 Company. There is a line of trenches in rear with overhead cover – don't like them. A shell would do a lot of damage – cover isn't thick enough! Two tanks [Lee Grants from Y Squadron 150th Regiment RAC[20]] come up in afternoon – one positioned between 1 Company and [3/8th] Gurkhas, one in middle of No. 1 Company trenches – 20 yards in rear. The Gurkhas are on our left. [Kelly did not know that one of the Lee Grants, climbing up the hill to support his position had toppled over and rolled to the bottom, the troop commander being killed.]
>
> 1900 hours. Japs shell the ridge and most of No. 1 Company dive into covered trenches. They soon dive out again – they are not splinter-proof.
>
> 1950 hrs. A green flare from Japs who attack immediately. Reckon there must be about 50 of them. Driven off with bayonets and grenades. Most of the [British] grenades had seven second fuses and some were not primed. Private Storer had collapsed in a corner of the trench – terrified. I got him on his feet and he said it wouldn't happen again. More grenades – unprimed. Seconds later another attack came in – no warning this time. This attack was in greater strength – possibly 80–100 of them. They jumped over the forward trenches and got into the Company HQ area. Storer collapsed again and there was a huge bastard going at him with his sword. Damn near cut his arse off. I'd got an old rifle with a long bayonet but I couldn't reach him over Storer's body. Shot him in the guts and again, in the head. Never want to get this close to the bastards again! This attack petered out and the only Company NCO on his feet was Sergeant Bishop, whose platoon was on our right and hadn't been shelled or attacked. Lance Corporal Davies was in a hole – firing flares and HE from a 2-inch

mortar. A Jap had gone for him with his bayonet. Davies hung on to the bayonet and somehow managed to get his .38 pistol out and shoot the sod. Hands cut to ribbons, he had to go back. Half an hour later the Japs came in again – between us and the Gurkhas. The tanks switched on their headlights and caught the Japs in the open. The Japs had occupied two of our trenches but died when the platoon of Gurkhas counter-attacked. The rest of the night was quiet.

On the 19th Lieutenant Colonel Ted Taunton led the major part of the Northamptons to the top of Point 5846, there to dig in to repel attack, reinforcing a company of 7/10th Baluch already on the position. The Northamptons arrived on the hill only hours before the Japanese. Private Jack Clifford had newly joined No 2 Company of the Northamptons after arriving from recruit training in Britain. He found it hard to believe that he was now on a battlefield, finding it especially disconcerting, despite Colonel Taunton's warm words of welcome, to realize that he was a battle casualty replacement. 'Now I am about to face my enemy,' he mused, 'my feelings are of loneliness and emptiness.' As the battalion climbed up Point 5846 he came under fire for the first time. 'My reaction was to take cover, which is what everyone else did. The enemy were spraying the jungle with machine-gun bullets, probably to panic us off.' His first night was not auspicious, being bitten by a snake. It was the following night that the full *banzai* fury of the Japanese assaults began to fall on the position. Private Ken Darlaston of the Northamptons waited nervously inside the position:

It was silent, even the birds and chirping insects were quiet. We peered into the black, tree trunks seemed to move. Fingers itched on triggers and hellish doubts of whether to fire or not gripped many of us. To give way to one's fear and fire may bring a deadly return shot from a nasty little man waiting to see where you were and not to shoot at a shadow may mean a grenade in your lap. This waiting before a show I always found to be the worst. When it all started, there was usually too much going on to feel afraid.

This hiatus went on until 7 p.m. when the silence was shattered by a machine gun on the right flank opening up with a long chattering blast that echoed again and again through the hills. It had barely ended when guns on each side, his and ours, split the air, to which was quickly added the harsh detonations of bursting grenades ...

The first attack developed by the Jap breaking into the cleared area and blindly charging our forward positions. They were repulsed but they came on again and again, at times almost face to face. It was suicide. They were led by officers waving swords and screaming 'Banzai' and were simply mown down. All one could do was to point a rifle and fire until it was too hot to hold. The damage was done by the machine guns. We suffered many casualties including two pals of mine, Percy Whitear and Sammy Yates who were killed in the first hour.

After about 3 hours they gave up and at dawn we surveyed the wreck, buried the dead, tended the wounded and dug our holes deeper.

Held off the Silchar Track the Japanese did, however, manage to seize the village of Ningthoukhong on 22 April. This village lay on the Tiddim road bordering the low-lying area between the road and the Logtak Lake, and as such presented a serious threat to Mackenzie's left flank. An immediate counter-attack on Ningthoukhong by two companies of 9/14th Punjab supported by C Squadron, 150th Regiment RAC, failed to eject the new occupants on 22 April, and suffered a severe repulse, a Lee Grant being struck by a mortar bomb and burnt out, the Punjabis suffering eighty-five casualties. Each village in this low-lying area was surrounded by a thick earth 'bund', designed to keep out floodwaters but ideal also for use as a defensive bulwark against attack, even that by tanks. A further attack on 25 April by troops of 1/4th Gurkhas suffered similar ignominy: the long approach over the *padi* fields (800 yards) allowed a hidden 47mm anti-tank gun to pick off the approaching Lee Grants one by one, the accompanying 1/4th Gurkhas being unable to locate or destroy the gun. By the time the attack was called off two Lee Grants lay burning in the *padi* and six were damaged, withdrawing whence they came. The accompanying FOO and his precious radio was in one of the destroyed tanks, with the result that artillery could not come to their rescue. In any case artillery ammunition was in desperately short supply by this time. Every round, once the link to Dimapur was closed on 28 March, had to be flown in by aircraft. Lieutenant Basil French of 4th Field Regiment recalled that 'it was not unusual to be rationed to five or even three rounds per gun per day which made it tough for the infantry who we were there to support'. In a further attempt three days later 1/4th Gurkhas gained a lodgement in the village and further tank attacks took place on the 29th, a Lee Grant finally clambering over the bund. The anti-tank fire was too intense, however, and the attack was called off, the Japanese exploiting their success by seeping through to the nearby village of Potsangbam (nicknamed 'Pots and Pans' by British soldiers) and securing the village on 29 April.

~

The offensive by Major General Ouvry Roberts' 23rd Division (1 and 37 Brigades) to open the Ukhrul road as far as Kasom following the victory at Nunshigum succeeded by 20 April in ejecting 15th Division from the area. With the road open, 1 Brigade (1st Seaforth Highlanders, 1/16th Punjabis and 1st Patialas) then continued its pursuit and harassment of Yamauchi's HQ. By early May Ouvry Roberts had driven 15th Division twenty miles east to Litan, scattering its units through the remote jungle vastness and persuading Scoones that no further serious offensive could be expected from this direction. He was right and although no further threat to Imphal emanated from Ukhrul the Japanese caught in these mountains continued to fight with the life-or-death desperation of a cornered animal. Lieutenant Ken Cooper joined 2nd Borders at Milestone 16 at the height of the fighting in May shortly after the battalion had been transferred from the Shenam fighting. At 4,241 feet he noted that his company positions lay 1,000 feet higher than Snowdon. Thunder clouds dark with rain sat ominously above the mountain peaks, pouring out their contents in heavy torrents, filling the trenches with water and turning the ground into a muddy morass:

> My first night near Battalion HQ was startling. There were distant flashes, followed by dull reports, and every now and then a hastening whirr … which seemed only feet overhead, almost immediately followed the deafening slap and crash of exploding shells. The impersonal whine and crunch of the howling missiles coming out of nowhere, left me trembling and in a cold sweat, although the night air was clammy and hot.

The Japanese stubbornly refused to relinquish their hold on the hills. A Company, 2nd Borders occupied a position on a hill astride the track the troops called 'Sausage', cut off by the Japanese, being forced to rely on air supply, parachuted supplies landing outside of the tiny perimeters being fought over savagely by both sides. It took five hours of exhausting toil to climb from Battalion HQ to each of the company positions. Cooper's recollection of the fighting forms a deep sear in his memory:

> I was left with vivid nightmare pictures of walking wounded – ragged men, carrying their weapons and little else, hobbling and sliding and cursing towards the Regimental Aid Post; of the half light dawn, beneath dripping trees, with the wounded huddled in groups under sodden blankets or lying, heads in the mud, torn and gashed with appalling injuries, some already turning gangrenous in the festering conditions.

The Japanese sought every opportunity to attack, even when they were on the defensive. Pushed relentlessly by the 100 Brigade advance, the Japanese reacted by furiously counter-attacking, outflanking 2nd Borders and throwing themselves at Brigade HQ itself:

> Utter chaos ensued, and the wounded were hit again and again. Everyone – cooks, mule-drivers, staff officers and anyone who could – took up the weapons of the dead and fought where they stood. Dug-in tanks blasted the ferocious enemy attacks over open sights with high explosives and smashed their quickly constructed bunkers with solid shot. Extreme fatigue assailed everyone. There were some men going mad with fever and the strain of the hellish conditions.

Yamauchi's offensive capability had been severely blunted in the first few weeks of fighting, partly because of his excessive optimism about the ability of his tired troops to defeat the cowardly British and their pathetic Indian lackeys. Yamauchi's strength now lay in his ability to defend terrain that was key to Scoones' ability to open up the Kohima road. These efforts were undermined by the fact that in common with Yanagida and Sato, his relationship with Mutaguchi was deteriorating. The three Japanese divisional commanders had only ever given the venture into India lukewarm support. From the beginning the idea for the offensive had been Mutaguchi's: he had given it life and now was its most passionate protagonist. None of his subordinates shared this degree of commitment, a fact that was made worse because Mutaguchi enjoyed extremely poor relations with his three divisional commanders. In fact, Sato and Mutaguchi loathed each other. Sato had long been a political enemy of the Army Commander and this underlying belligerence made him a difficult, if not impossible, subordinate. For his part Yamauchi, something of an intellectual, hated the Army Commander for his lack of intellectual sophistication, considering him to be a 'blockhead' and 'unfit to be in command of an army'. Yanagida likewise had an equally poor opinion of the Army Commander, considering him to be a womanizing bore and a bully. He had little confidence in the plan for Operation C, and was overheard on one occasion to lament, 'What's going to become of us with a moron like Mutaguchi as our Commander-in-Chief?' The loathing was reciprocated. Mutaguchi described Yanagida on one occasion as 'a gutless bastard' and had little time either for him or Yamauchi, believing both to be too soft and western in outlook (both having served abroad as military attachés), and even referring to them sarcastically as 'my American generals'. There was a further problem with Yamauchi. He was slowly dying of tuberculosis. Mutaguchi removed him on 10 June and he died in Maymyo on 6 August.

~

Meanwhile Briggs' 5th Indian Division, reinforced by Crowther's 89 Brigade (2nd King's Own Scottish Borderers, 4/8th Gurkhas and 1/11th Sikhs), flown in from Arakan on 7 May, began moving gradually against the enemy up the Iril valley from Nunshigum on to the heavily-defended Mapao Ridge. It was here that the three battalions of Salomon's 9 Brigade battled bloodily for six weeks to expel the ever tenacious Japanese from the positions into which they had dug themselves, determined not to be moved. The most stubbornly defended position at 'Hump' resisted seven separate assaults by Lieutenant Colonel Furney's 3/14th Punjab during May. 'Every wisp of greenery was churned and burnt away by the shells and bombs that landed on that small piece of hillside day after day, and often at night,' recalled Captain Anthony Brett James, 'when our Gunners were shooting harassing fire at the stubborn enemy.'

Further to the east, up the Iril river valley, British troops had attempted to push hard against the Japanese who turned every hilltop over a wide area into a fortified position. It proved virtually impossible to eject the Japanese from their positions, despite repeated and gallant attacks by infantry, supported by tanks and Hurribombers. Infantry battalions, including Cree's 2nd West Yorkshires and Gerty's 3/9th Jats, were rapidly worn down by repeated attacks on immovable Japanese positions, delivering little more than an alarming number of casualties. A strategy evolved in coming weeks, therefore, to isolate the main Japanese positions by means of heavy patrolling, denying the defenders food, water and ammunition by aggressive attacks on the Japanese supply routes through the jungle. With 123 Brigade now switched to support 89 Brigade on the Kohima road between Sengmai and Kanglatongbi, 9 Brigade began its task of denying the jungle-covered terrain to the enemy, and to contain and starve their opponents rather than launching unnecessary and costly assaults against his defended positions.

It was a strategy that was to bring decisive if not rapid results. On the left flank of the division's advance the Japanese were slowly inched back along the road. They had constructed three road blocks at Sengmai, supported by defensive positions in the adjacent hills. Crowther secretly infiltrated a whole battalion through the Japanese front lines on 15 May to form a block to their rear. The main attacks by his brigade on the surrounding heights made little headway, but the block worked superbly and the Japanese launched furious though unavailing assaults upon it. Briggs was able to reinforce the block and, by 20 May, the enemy were forced to give up the struggle and evacuate their forward positions while 123 Brigade applied pressure along the road. By 21 May the vast dump at Kanglatongbi that had fallen into Japanese hands on 3 April was recovered. Just short of Kanglatongbi Jawan Gian Singh's 1/11th Sikhs came across an almost destroyed village which they occupied moments before a screaming rush of Japanese, led by an officer waving a sword, nearly overwhelmed them. But cool, steady rifle fire soon resulted in all the Japanese lying crumpled on the ground in front of them:

> We went forward to inspect the dead. The officer with the sword was furthest from us. His men had rushed forward; he had been our first target. I got to him and as I approached I saw him lying on his back a pistol in his left hand and a sword in his right. The pistol was one we all admired so I took it and had my back to the dead Japanese. Something made me look round to show the others what I had got. I had pulled the lever to check if the pistol was loaded, it was. Out of the corner of my eye I saw the Japanese officer pulling himself up with a half-raised sword. It happened in a flash as I took one step back the sword came down. I felt nothing not even a tug. As the blade fell so did he as he lost his balance. It came automatically to me to raise the pistol – his pistol – and shot him in the head. We examined him and found he had bullet wounds in his stomach and thigh. He was paralyzed yet he tried to kill me.

~

The Japanese placed unrelenting pressure on the Shenam Ridge during May. British and Japanese positions snaked through the hills, devoid of vegetation after many weeks of shelling. Only yards apart in places, the ground lay littered with the decomposing corpses of British, Indian and Japanese alike. The smell of putrefaction was often overwhelming, although the monsoon rains did much to wash away the most noxious smells, and the heat aided decomposition. What was unbearable were the clouds of heavy bluebottles feasting on the rotting bodies and then attempting to lunch off the men's bully beef and biscuits, and drink the sweat running from the men's lean frames. The Japanese, desperate to break through the hills to reach the promised land beyond, launched repeated assaults on the British positions. Some hilltops changed ownership several times as the battle raged across the mountains.

Apart from one company on Crete West, following the earlier fighting the Devons were concentrated on Scraggy Hill, with a platoon on a small hill called Lynche's Pimple (just to the north-west of Umbrella Tree Hill), named after the Devon subaltern, Lieutenant Lynche, whose platoon first held it. Still very much on the offensive, Yamamoto attacked again on the morning of 7 May, with light tanks and artillery, attempting to force the defenders from Crete West. Continuous bombardments by the Devons' mortar platoon on Scraggy during the day held them off, but the next morning they also stormed the weakly-held Lynche's Pimple, forcing off the survivors (twelve men) and threatening Scraggy from the north-east. An attempt by the Devons, supported by air attack, to throw back the Japanese failed, the enemy withdrawing into the jungle during the air attack and then reappearing in time to receive the British infantry assault as the men clambered onto the position. It was not long before the British learned to counter these tactics by their own ploy: they would agree with the RAF a number of 'attack' sorties into the enemy position, with a 'false' sortie at the end during which the infantry rushed the final position. The Japanese would then remerge or reappear, to find enemy troops already on the location. This tactic was used very successfully by Briggs' 5th Indian Division as it progressed slowly northwards up the Kohima road.

The Japanese launched another overwhelming *banzai* attack on Crete West at 4 a.m. on 9 May, supported by heavy artillery bombardments. The regimental historian records the relentless waves of attacks being beaten back each time by men of D Company, 1st Devons. Ammunition was now extremely low – the Japanese had virtually surrounded the hill and resupply was impossible in daylight. Early the following morning Lieutenant Colonel Wingfield's 3/1st Gurkhas again attempted to retake Crete West, relying in their final assault only on their kukris, but the Japanese refused to budge. Later that day the survivors of D Company, together with their wounded, managed to slip back through the Japanese cordon to the relative safety of Scraggy. That night continuous waves of Japanese infantry fell against the well-dug forward defences on Scraggy, held by Wingfield's Gurkhas, troops clambering over their dead comrades on the perimeter barbed wire in their desperation to capture the position. Sheer weight of numbers threatened to overwhelm the Gurkhas so Wingfield used his FOO to call in a Final Protective Fire (FPF) attack on his own trenches using the divisional artillery, a last ditch and highly dangerous stratagem to destroy an attacker in the open when all else had failed. Fortunately the well-drilled Gurkhas recognized the FPF signal, and crouched low in their slit trenches as the thunder of twenty-four guns firing repeated salvoes fell amongst them, shredding the leading Japanese assault troops in a ground-shaking paroxysm of smoke and fire. In the morning the shocked 2nd Borders, a company of which came up to relieve the men of the 3/1st, estimated that 800 Japanese corpses lay across the shell-shattered hillside. Gracey's casualties paled into insignificance compared to the extraordinary numbers of experienced fighting men being lost every day to these reckless Japanese assaults. In the course of ten days of fighting the Devons lost nearly 200 killed and wounded. With the change of tactics by Briggs' division in the north and no let up of pressure on the Shenam ridge, Scoones decided to replace Gracey's two exhausted brigades with 23rd Indian Division, released from the Ukhrul advance, the exchange taking place between 13 and 16 May. Thirty-seven Brigade, reinforced with two extra battalions (1st Seaforth Highlanders and 1/16th Punjab), now moved into the Shenam positions, the remainder of 1 Brigade (1st Patiala) going into Corps reserve while 49 Brigade (4/5th Mahratta Light Infantry, 6/5th Mahratta Light Infantry and 5/6th Rajputana Rifles) guarded the Palel airfield at the point where the hills ended and the Imphal Plain began.

~

During the first two weeks of May the attritional fighting between Yanagida and Mackenzie continued unabated for the positions on the high ground dominating the Silchar Track west of Bishenpur, as well as for the village of Potsangbam. By this time 3/8th Gurkhas had been defending the area of Wireless Hill for nearly two weeks, resisting all attempts by the Japanese to eject them, when Cowan decided to replace them with the rested 1/4th Gurkhas. The route between Bishenpur and the hills guarding the Silchar Track, however, was now a labyrinth of Japanese positions, and on 27 April an attack on a Japanese block outside the village of Toulang resulted in twenty-nine casualties. The Japanese came out that night on three occasions to try to beat down the temporary defensive position the Gurkhas had thrown up preparatory to another attack the following day, but failed to put off Lieutenant Colonel Oldham's Gurkhas from their purpose. Joined on 28 April by three Lee Grants, the Gurkhas managed to destroy the block on the 29th, but at the heavy cost of fifty-six casualties. Without being able to relieve 3/8th Gurkhas on Wireless Hill, 1/4th had, in the meantime, suffered eighty-five casualties. It was going to be a long and difficult business to wrest this critical reinforcement route from the

Japanese, and to prevent them from returning once the position had been cleared. The way that Cowan sought to achieve this was by reverting to the tactics of the North West Frontier, where picquets were established at regular intervals along the cleared route.

On 30 April, 1/4th duly set off on its approach march towards Wireless Hill, joined from the west by a company of Northamptons from Point 5486 converging on the same objective. Each part of the route needed to be cleared of small pockets of determined Japanese. Lieutenant James Evans of 1/4th described attempts by his platoon to overcome one enemy-occupied knoll:

> I was sent with a platoon of C Company (equivalent to two sections in strength) to attack a knoll where the Japanese were sited in reverse slope positions. I did not like this at all, you had to get over the crest before you could attack the position. I decided to outflank the enemy with one party, while distracting them with another. I could see the outflanking party move round, so we crawled forward gradually until we could see the enemy trenches. I could see my Jemadar popping up, aiming his rifle, firing, ducking down. I got out a grenade and raised myself on my elbow, he came up on aim, I threw the grenade, and at that moment I was hit.
>
> A Gurkha piper came up and put a first field dressing on me, saying 'it's a small hole Sahib. You'll be all right'. He turned me and his face fell. He must have seen the exit wound. He gave me morphia. I felt light headed as I walked back to the ambulance.[21]

The position was finally taken, by seven Gurkhas supported by tanks of 3rd Carabiniers. Twenty-eight Japanese dead were found on the position. But by now it was apparent that the full-time task of 1/4th would be to keep the Silchar Track open by defending their line of picquets stretching into the hills from Bishenpur: 3/8th would have to stay where they were, unrelieved, although with hopefully less pressure on them now that 1/4th had joined the fray. Lieutenant Colonel Oldham[22] wrote a citation for Jemadar Gajbir Pun that highlights the intensity of the infantry fighting that took place for the Silchar Track:

> On 8 May 1944, Jemadar Gajbir took over command of the platoon picquet 200 yards north of the water point at MS 21.6 on the Silchar Track. That night the Japs made a heavy and sustained infantry attack on the picquet preceded by a twenty-minute bombardment from two 75-mm guns. Although the barbed wire round his perimeter was shattered by the weight of shells which fell in the area and several of

his bunkers received hits which restricted their fields of fire, Jemadar Gajbir successfully repulsed a very heavy attack made by about 200 Jap infantry on his isolated platoon. The enemy assault began shortly after dusk and continued till 0300 hours and was directly supported by MMGs as well as by a high-velocity gun firing at less than one hundred yards range from the jungle edge. When dawn broke, no less than twenty-five enemy dead as well as a considerable quantity of arms and equipment were found outside the picquet's perimeter.

This type of fighting was expensive in blood, subsequent attacks by Oldham's battalion resulting in forty-eight casualties. In a matter of days the fighting had cost 1/4th Gurkhas 212 dead, wounded and missing. The close-quarter nature of the fighting was captured by Captain John Randle of 7/10th Baluch, who described conditions in the monsoon as being akin to the Western Front:

We were dug in, the positions were wired and the Japs were only about 50-60 yards away. Everyone was mixed up. For about three weeks there was very intensive fighting. The scrub was thicker than in the Chin Hills and very wet. It was a very hard infantry slog. The Japs attacked, then we counter-attacked. Positions changed hands several times. It was the most close fighting I ever saw in Burma. Japanese attacks tended to come up and close the last few yards with bayonets. In a counter-attack we gave enemy positions a really good pasting, then fought our way in, clearing enemy positions with grenades, Tommy guns – Gurkhas with kukris, and our chaps used a bayonet. Casualties were high in this period but we had no morale problems. We felt we were winning. We had far more artillery than the Japs, and the RAF were in evidence all the time. Rations came up. The wounded were taken out by the American Field Service.

Despite the huge losses being inflicted on the Japanese, Cowan's precious infantry strength was also being whittled away by the fighting. It clearly couldn't go on for ever, and a decisive offensive was required to clear the weakening 33rd Division from Bishenpur. Potsangbam remained in enemy hands, defended by a ring of powerful anti-tank guns and defying every attempt to broach the defences until 9/14th Punjab managed to capture four of these guns, one of them a new 47mm, on 6 May. But the Japanese held on to the bulk of the village still. At first light on the following day the Punjab, together with Major Teddy Pettit's A Squadron, 3rd Carabiniers and a troop of Stuart light tanks, closed in on the village following an attack by American Liberator bombers dropping 1,000-pound bombs and dive-bombing by Vengeances. A small breech was made in the bund, but fierce resistance followed. Lieutenant Freddie Shepherd, a troop commander in 3rd Carabiniers recorded the battle as he saw it from the commander's seat in his Lee Grant:

> Through the periscope I was watching my machine gun fire spraying the wood, when about ten yards from me I saw three bashas and through the smoke the outline of an anti-tank gun. The coax[ial machine gun] was almost on so I put him on and saw spots of daylight appearing all over the gun shield. I got very excited and loaded and fired the 37mm [secondary armament] myself three times ... 1 AP, 2 HE and 2 x 75-mm HE [main armament] which completely decked it and set the ammunition on fire.

Conditions inside the Carabinier (and 7th Cavalry) tanks were appalling, remembered Freer, whose B Squadron, 3rd Carabiniers were diverted to the Bishenpur front in May:

> At this time we all got the 'runs' ... There were three of us with the runs at the time and I was the worst. To sleep in the tank you sit in your seat. To crap you got the 75mm gunner, who was standing on the escape hatch on the other side of the tank, to move to your seat, and you lifted the hatch and crapped on the ground a few feet below. You then got the driver to move the tank a bit away from the stench. Put the lid back again. Nobody slept. We all stank to high heaven, we were all unwashed. There was always a revolting stench in the tank. At dawn you stood to, the tank guard would move away, and we would go into action again. It could go on for three days and nights at a time.

~

Yanagida's inability (or unwillingness, in Mutaguchi's view) to break into Imphal from the south resulted in his Chief of Staff, Colonel Tanaka, taking effective command of 33rd Division in early May while awaiting the arrival of a permanent replacement. Yanagida's sidelining took place at a critical time for operations on the Tiddim Road, as Cowan turned his troops onto the offensive in order to try to break the Japanese grip on the road. Cowan's plan took time to prepare, and it was not until mid-May that this counter-offensive got underway. The two battalions of Brigadier Cameron's 48 Brigade, then in IV Corps reserve at Wangjing (2/5th Royal Gurkhas and 1/7th Gurkhas) were secretly inserted, after an eleven-day march, on the road near Torbung far to the rear of the forward Japanese troops in the region of Bishenpur, and Milestone 32, after approaching unseen and unsuspected from the east, across the southern edge of Logtak Lake. The intention was that once this anvil had been formed, Burton's 63 Brigade (at this time comprising 1st West Yorkshires, 9th Border, and 1/3rd Gurkha Rifles) would then smash through Ninthoukhong and Potsangbam from the north, destroying Yanagida's battalions caught between. Unknown to him, Cowan's offensive in fact coincided with a major effort by Mutaguchi to achieve a successful breakthrough at Bishenpur, using all of Fifteenth Army's artillery and all of its tanks, transferred from the Shenam sector and laboriously moved up the road from Tiddim, reinforced by four additional infantry battalions.

The Japanese response to the discovery of Cameron's block at Torbung on the morning of 17 May was hornet-like. The men of 48 Brigade had not reckoned with having to fight tanks but fortuitously they had brought with them a handful of the awkward, short-range, spring-loaded PIAT[22] anti-tank weapons. The Japanese, surprised, swarmed around the block furiously from both north and south, but in an action which was to lead to his being awarded the Military Medal, Rifleman Ganju Lama crept forward with a PIAT and managed to destroy two Type-95s, forcing a further two to withdraw. The Gurkhas meanwhile attempted with what few resources they had to prepare a defensive position ready to receive further attack. Cameron's block held, supported by air attacks by Hurribombers and with supplies dropped by C-47s flying at tree-top height down the valley.

However, Burton's 63 Brigade was unable to break through from the north, although not for want of trying. The brigade fought furiously for possession of the villages and the hills that lay to the east of Potsangbam, capturing the Japanese-held Kha Aimol and Three Pimple Hill and drawing off Japanese pressure from the Silchar Road. At this time – 19 May – 33rd Division made a further attempt to break through the 17th Indian Division defences, by inserting a block (400 men of 2/214th Regiment) on the road at Maram, north of Bishenpur, and perilously close (although they did not know it) to Cowan's HQ. Red Hill (Point 2926) nearby was also captured. The 500 men of 1/214th Battalion meanwhile attempted to attack Bishenpur from the north-east. The desperate battles during late-May to eject the Japanese from these positions – the closest they had come to Imphal – meant that Cameron was forced to remove his block on 24 May and fight his way back in stages to the British positions at Bishenpur. This he did, holding on the first night, 25 May, a position at Moirang, eight miles to the north. The retreating brigade was given no respite by the Japanese who attacked repeatedly, by day and night, with both infantry and tanks.

Giving the Japanese defended localities at Ninthoukhong a wide berth the brigade arrived, with its wounded, at Potsangbam on 30 May, where ambulances – most of whom were manned by the magnificent volunteers of the American Field Service – recovered the wounded back to Imphal. The operation had been expensive in terms of manpower and Cowan failed to achieve his objective in shattering Yanagida's division.

He had, however, arguably disrupted Mutaguchi's plans for a final, decisive offensive into Imphal. In the process of the fighting against Cameron's brigade the Japanese lost over 1,150 men, a large number of vehicles and six tanks while 48 Brigade lost 421 men. The butcher's bill for 33rd Division was horrendous, and yet they fought on. By the end of April Colonel Sakuma of 214th Regiment had only 1,000 fit men remaining from the 4,000 available at the start of the month. Likewise Colonel Sasahara's 215th Regiment had only 400 men available from a starting strength of nearly 5,000. A month later the situation looked even more desperate. In the fighting for Maram and Red Hill, which ended on 30 May, 214th Regiment had been decimated: 1/214th was reduced to thirty-seven men and 2/214th had entirely ceased to exist. British casualties, however, had access to a luxury that the Japanese could not afford: rapid evacuation to 41st IGH in Imphal and, if necessary, transport by air out of the pocket. British medical care was incomparably better than anything the Japanese could offer. Conditions were primitive in the extreme, considered Private Len Thornton but in spite of this the success rate was very good.

> We did really save a lot of lives although we were desperately short of supplies. We used to crush sulphanilamide tablets into powder and put it in and on the wounds and we rarely had to stitch abscesses. I used to do a lot of the stitching up myself as the surgeon was sizing up the next case and during that time he would leave me to finish off … After treatment, the worst cases would stay with us for a few days, but where possible, we flew the others out as soon as we could; we needed the beds and the bandages for new cases.

~

By now Japanese command relationships had broken down irreparably, a consequence of Mutaguchi's repeated insistence on advancing whatever the cost. The men were also starving, 17th Division having destroyed rice stocks in the villages around Bishenpur at the start of the fighting. Yet Mutaguchi had refused to listen to Yanagida's explanation in April that the task was too difficult for the resources he had to hand, that the British had placed a wall of steel around the approaches to Bishenpur that he had inadequate strength to break. The fact that Japanese tactics had proven to be entirely inadequate against the determined professionalism of Fourteenth Army, far better supplied, equipped and trained than Yanagida had ever anticipated, was entirely lost on Mutaguchi. It was left to the weary *samurai* of his rapidly depleting army to make this reality clear on the soggy battlefields around Mapao, Shenam and Bishenpur as they struggled, and failed, to get any closer to the tantalizing prize of Imphal.

# Chapter 6

# The Chindits

Major General Orde Wingate's great Chindit expedition (Operation THURSDAY), launched deep into Burma between March and August 1944, was largely incidental to Operation C. Nor, too, was it ever part of Slim's master plan, being wished on him as a result of Wingate's political clout with Wavell. The strategic effectiveness of Operation THURSDAY remains disputed among veterans and historians. Nevertheless, it is a matter of no dispute that many Japanese were very worried about the effect of a large enemy force operating behind their lines. Likewise, the eventual capture of Myitkyina by Stilwell's American/Chinese forces from the north in August 1944 certainly diverted the Japanese 18th Division which might otherwise have been used to reinforce Mutaguchi's army. But there was one Chindit brigade which was deeply involved in combating the Japanese invasion forces in the Naga Hills. The imminent threat to Kohima and Dimapur had persuaded Lieutenant General Slim on 8 March 1944 to allocate one of Wingate's formations –23 Long Range Penetration (LRP) Brigade – to the defence of the vast, remote swathe of the Naga Hills which lie to the north and east of Kohima. This would interrupt Japanese efforts to resupply their forward troops should they launch an offensive against Kohima and Dimapur, and restrict their opportunity to use the mountains to break through into the Brahmaputra Valley while presenting a tangible demonstration to the Naga people of Britain's intent to expel the invader. Evidence that this was indeed what the Japanese planned prompted Slim to authorize the despatch of the brigade in early April, where it was moved by road, rail, river steamer, and narrow-gauge railway to Bokajan, ten miles beyond Dimapur in the Brahmaputra Valley, from where it could make its ascent eastwards into the Naga Hills.

The diversion of the brigade, under the command of the tall, gaunt, monocled Brigadier Lancelot Perowne, to help defend Kohima was inspired by Slim's grasp of what the Japanese would need to do to sustain their operations over incredibly difficult terrain more than 120 miles from their sources of supply east of the Chindwin. The RAF would fly interdiction missions against the Chindwin by day and night to harry the Japanese supply boats, convoys, tracks, bridges, rest camps and depots, but this would do little but jab pinpricks into the Japanese operation from the air. What was needed was a complementary force on the ground, which would maximize the effectiveness of air power by giving the RAF eyes on the jungle floor, denied to them by the thick green canopy, and which could also occupy ground. Such operations were ideally suited to the troops of 23 Brigade, who had been brought by dint of hard training to an unmatched level of physical toughness and battlefield preparation.

Indeed, Wingate's training programme was exhaustive, even brutal, building on the bitter lessons learned during his first expedition in May 1943. Accordingly, any man who now failed to rise to the physical and mental strictures demanded of him would receive a curt and humiliating 'RTU' letter, instructing him to 'Return to Unit'. Lieutenant Paul Haskins of 1st Battalion, Essex Regiment spoke of marching 'until the packs on our backs brought tears of agony to our eyes, and the soles of our feet felt like red-hot irons'. For Captain Harry Good, Regimental Medical Officer to 4th Battalion, Border Regiment, the training was severe 'and, apart from the tactical training, consisted, quite frequently, of marching up to forty miles a day with full equipment'.

> As the training took place from October to April, it was not in the heat of summer, nor during the monsoon period, so we did not suffer those discomforts … At the end of the training period, the battalion was not only highly trained in jungle and Chindit operations but, with the constant exercise and increased rations, was very fit.

For Corporal Stanley Hutson, a twenty-three-year-old gunner from 60th Field Regiment, the training had been tough, but at that stage no one expected that they would soon be marching through the Naga Hills: the expectation was that they would be landed by Dakota deep behind enemy lines in Burma with the remainder of Wingate's force, where the terrain was, for the most part, flat:

> For the survival part we were force marched all day until we were ready to drop, then made to carry on through the night with a possible river crossing, so that we were wet through, cold, hungry and tired out, before making a mock bayonet charge as dawn broke. We practised receiving air drops of food and ammunition until we

and the RAF were perfect. We were made to go without food for two or three days at a time and made to cover extra distance just to prove that we could do it. Wingate brought out all the mistakes that were made on the first [Chindit] expedition [in May 1943] so that they would never be made again. We always had a perimeter guard out at night so that the Japs would never catch us unawares. We were taught to read signs like Red Indians and to hide our tracks so that if the Japs did cross them, they would be unable to follow us to our destination. Everything we had was green or brown and the idea was to be able to merge into the jungle with no sound and to see but not be seen.

Lieutenant Philip Brownless of 1st Essex found himself in charge of his unit's mules. The brigade was to be entirely dependent upon these animals for its transport:

The need for silence on the march meant that our mules and ponies had to be de-voiced. Mules have keen hearing and if one detected the presence of mules in another column, even a mile away, a deep bray would have evoked an instant response, developing into a 'conversation' and betraying the presence of both columns to the Japanese. A team of veterinary surgeons arrived one morning in our training camp, set up their tables and each mule was led forward by his muleteer. With rope through his shackles to bring his feet together, he was gently 'cast' (capsized) and with a chloroform pad held to his muzzle, he quickly became muzzy and unconscious while the vet made a small nick in his neck to sever his vocal chords. It was skilfully done and a few minutes later the mule got to his feet and was soon back in his place munching happily.

Hard training helped prove to the Chindits that they were tough enough to cope with the challenges posed by the extraordinary terrain of the Naga Hills, and the ruthless tenacity of their enemy. For while they could laugh about 'Tōjō's Boys' as they called them (they would sing '*My mother said, I never should, Play with the Japsies, In the Wood*'), they held the Japanese in the highest regard as hardy and determined soldiers. The intensity of the Chindit training did have the desired effect, however, on the British soldiers' belief in their ability to take on the Japanese on their own terms, and win. Hutson felt confident that he and his fellows were as prepared as they ever could be for fighting the Japanese, whose reputation for extreme hardiness and endurance, and their determination on the battlefield had allowed a widespread canker of hopelessness to sweep the *old* Army in 1942 and 1943. Now, thanks to Wingate's bible-quoting, onion-chewing but highly-effective training methods, the Chindits – ordinary British infantry battalions and artillery regiments transformed into jungle-living fighting columns – marched into the mountains unafraid of the Japanese, even relishing the prospect of the coming confrontation. The old bogey of the enemy superman had been banished by the emergence of these tough, hard-hitting, hard-swearing 'jungle-weaned Spartans'.

On 12 April the first six of the nine LRP columns of Perowne's 23 LRP Brigade – each column was between 300 and 400 strong – set out into the northern Naga Hills in their eastward march to attack and disrupt 31st Division's supply routes between Kohima and the Chindwin and, where possible, to protect the Naga people from the depredations of a ruthless enemy. Two columns (33 and 76 Columns) were made up from 2nd Battalion, Duke of Wellington's Regiment, two (34 and 55 Columns) from 4th Battalion, Border Regiment, two (44 and 56 Columns) from 1st Battalion, Essex Regiment, two (60 and 68 Columns) from the gunners of 60th Field Regiment and one (32) from the Royal Engineers. The two Essex Regiment columns were despatched to watch the Bokajan-Phekekrima track, one Border Regiment column was despatched to Wokha and the second Border Regiment column was sent to Mokokchung, sixty-seven miles due north of Kohima, to guard the tracks that led west from the border village of Jessami. For the first week the frustrated men of 32, 60 and 68 Columns remained in the Brahmaputra Valley to protect the railway to Ledo, which, it was believed, was threatened by long-range Japanese patrols. By 22 April the remainder of Perowne's columns were making their way into the mountains. Operating as independent columns they managed to present to the Japanese a picture of strength and geographical coverage that was far outweighed by the reality that 23 Brigade comprised a mere 3,000 men. Supported by the Hurricane fighter-bombers based on the Imphal Plain for ground attack and by American and RAF Dakota transports for their weekly airdrops of supplies, the brigade was entirely independent of ground-based lines of communication.

Life as a Chindit in the Naga Hills entailed 95 percent perspiration interspersed with five percent heart-thumping action. The very act of marching into the Naga Hills through what Flight Lieutenant Wilcox, attached to 76 Column, described as 'a topographical riot' of hills, mountains and jungle, was itself an extraordinary feat of endurance. The seemingly endless range of hills swept into the distance until they touched the cloud-mottled spring sky. The sweeping hills were covered like a thick blanket with the blue-black rain forest, dark, wet and gloomy in the valleys and lower slopes, and across the higher reaches by an assortment of pines, eucalyptus and oak. Lieutenant Paul Haskins viewed the 'grey silhouette of the 6,000-foot Naga Hills' ten miles to the east of Bokajan with no little trepidation, his heart failing him at the sight of what he was later to call 'those monstrous mountains'. He had reason to be fearful, as the physical demands of the adventure that awaited the men of Perowne's brigade would drive them to the very limits as they battled mountain, disease and torrential monsoon rains as well as their implacable foe. 'How we kept going, I honestly don't know,' recalled Private Ken Keen of 1st Essex. 'I think it was the fear of being wounded and the Japs catching you, if you got wounded. There was no chance of evacuating you.' On reflection, he added, 'It's unbelievable what the human body and flesh can stand, but, at the back of your mind, that knowledge was there, that you WOULD win and would be going home.' This widespread self-belief was largely Wingate's doing, and his death in an air crash on 24 March was a devastating blow to the men whom he had trained, and inspired.

Leaving Merepani and the Brahmaputra plain below them on 12 April, 76 Column toiled laboriously into the hills. The path from Bokajan was steep. The packs on their backs seemed to grow increasingly heavy, the sun beat down and sweat soon soaked men's shirts, turning them white with salt. 'Moving across hundreds of miles of this mountainous, thickly jungle covered country, with our mules, and carrying packs weighing more than 60 lbs in addition to our rifles, grenades, ammunition and machine guns was an exhausting business,' attested Lieutenant Philip Brownless. The tracks were so precipitous that in 'places the mules had to be unloaded and they and their loads hauled up separately by the ropes used to tie on their loads. Several mules were lost falling down mountain sides.' It was hard, said Wilcox, speaking for all the Chindits sweating their way into the mountains,

> Up and up we toiled, thankful for every brief rest when, after unloading the mules, we could stretch out in the shade of the overhanging rock and smoke the cigarette for which we had been longing.

At the hilltop village of Bandheri, Wilcox came across people of the Lotah Naga tribe for the first time:

> The inhabitants came out to greet us and we got our first real glimpse of village life in the Hills. They were an incredibly happy people, simple and unaffected, basking in the seclusion of their hill-top home. Short, muscular and of sturdy build, they wore the merest scrap of loin-cloth, their hind-quarters being uncovered. They wore necklaces and bracelets of coloured beads and animal's

teeth, and their heads were shaven below the scalp, leaving a bush of hair on top.

The Japanese, he quickly learned, were already feared and hated in the hills, even though most of the villagers this far north had not yet met any. Stories of atrocities and pillaging had swept the hills like wildfire, and young Naga men were enlisting with the help of the Deputy Commissioner in the 'Scouts' and bands of porters to help the British soldiers to push the invader out of their ancestral homelands. Wilcox watched one morning in June 1944, near Phezachedama, close to the Kohima-Imphal road, a party of four solemn, unsmiling Naga men walking into the Chindit camp, two carrying a bamboo pole between them. Underneath, tied with rope and swaying like a trussed pig, was the dead body of a Japanese, his head cloven. 'This is a man who robbed their village a week ago,' the Chindits' interpreter explained. 'He came with a party of soldiers and took their rice and pigs, and now they have killed him. They found him alone in the jungle last night; he was sick with dysentery and malaria.'

More than a few pilots had cause to thank the Naga people for rescuing them from the wrecks of their downed aircraft, and protecting them from the Japanese. Both Naga villagers and 23 Brigade were involved in the dramatic rescue of Flying Officer Ray Jackson. On the afternoon of 22 March 1944 Jackson took off from Palel in a 34 Squadron Hurricane IIC on a bombing and strafing mission against the village of Kuki, over the border in Burma. During the attack, however, he was hit by ground fire and rapidly began losing oil. Knowing that he would have to bale out he pulled back the stick to gain height. At 1,500 feet his engine stopped and caught fire. Flipping his aircraft onto its back Jackson fell, but knocked himself out in the process and lost most of his precious emergency rations, which had been stored in a pocket that ripped as he fell. Fortunately, when he came to he found himself floating under his parachute, watching his aircraft far below hit the ground. He landed on a scrubby hillside, but his descent had been observed and within minutes he could hear the sounds of men making their way in his direction. Hastily scrambling up the hill towards denser jungle Jackson managed to elude his pursuers, even after they had started a series of bush fires on the slopes below in an attempt to flush him out. Hiding in a patch of jungle he could, at one stage, have reached out and touched two of his Japanese hunters.

With him he had a .38 revolver, knife, machete, map and a few survival rations including a canvas water chargul. Calculating his position and determining his direction of march by the sun he decided to make his way across the hills north-west to Jessami, thinking that he would reach it in two or three days. But the terrain was far more difficult to cross than he had expected and after twelve days of struggling up the steep jungle-covered hills and down again into deep valleys, crossing the streams that ran through them, he had not yet reached safety. Growing progressively weaker he narrowly avoided capture after stumbling into a Naga village occupied by Japanese soldiers. All about him were signs of considerable Japanese activity, the paths covered in their distinctive cloven footprints. He survived on a dried melon and some grains of corn that he picked up after coming across abandoned fields, together with salt tablets from his emergency rations. Exhausted, attacked by mosquitoes, leeches and ticks he was on one occasion charged in failing light by a panther, which at the last moment veered off into the jungle, leaving him alone, and surprised at his escape. Looking down, he was astonished to find that he had his revolver in his right hand. 'I had no recollection of doing it,' he said later, 'but it must have been one of the fastest draws ever made in the RAF.'

On the twelfth day of these exertions Jackson came across a Naga village unoccupied by Japanese. Dazed with exhaustion, he collapsed on a path leading up to the village:

> I had lain there a short time when I heard a scream and saw a Naga woman running down the path to the nullah. After a few minutes two Nagas with spears came up the path. They were followed by four women bearing baskets on their backs. I smiled and tried to look friendly and saw signs of relief pass over their faces. A young woman smiled at me. I then made signs that I needed food and drink. They all smiled and produced a calabash full of a liquid that tasted like a sour white wine with a sherbet added. I managed to swallow some of this and it seemed to pull me round a little. They then gave me some rice containing some berries that looked like blackcurrants.

Fed and sheltered by the villagers, Jackson then learned that he was still two days' walk from Jessami. Leaving the next day, he made his way along the tracks towards the village, which he skirted to the east because of sounds of gunfire around the town. Coming across a further village to the north of Jessami – equipped ominously with skulls on bamboo poles at its entrance – he was well treated and fed. On the following day, attempting to travel west, he rounded a bend on a track and encountered two young men, each one carrying half a bleeding pig on his back. He had stumbled into the outskirts of the village of Phekakedzumi, thirty miles east of Kohima. 'You British?' one of them enquired quickly. A nod from Jackson had them hustling him quickly back in the direction he had come, away from the village, which housed a substantial Japanese garrison. One of the men – Vepopa – recalled the moment he first saw the tired Jackson:

> One evening as I was coming back from the Japanese camp, I met a person but as soon as I saw him, I knew he was not a local person. I could not speak English or Nagamese[24] or Hindi so through sign gestures, I asked, 'What happened to you?' He replied in signs that his aeroplane had crashed and he pointed toward Jessami. I realized that he had been saved by God's grace and took him away because he was very close to the Japanese camp. I took him to Phek Basa [huts in the fields to where the villagers had decamped when the Japanese occupied the village]. He was so weak that I could almost see his bones. He also had dysentery and had bruises on his face. I knew that he would not gain strength if he did not eat good food so I fed him with chicken, pork and fish as well as sugar and milk which were difficult to procure at that time.

The other man – Susai Hoshi (25) – was a local Christian pastor. He and his wife bathed Jackson's feet and treated his wounds. When they found out that he was a Christian too, they sang hymns for him. 'I was reminded of the Bible story of Jesus having his feet bathed. The tenderness and care with which they treated me moved me very deeply.' Hoshi and Vepopa now had the problem of how to guide Jackson to safety. Vepopa recalled,

> As I spoke no Hindustani or English, we talked through sign language and later, my brother, Vechotsu acted as my interpreter. Because the Japanese were at the old Phek village so close to us, I sent him on his way with some escorts, on toward Sohomi. A brother of mine who was settled there took care of him and took him to Vesoba village.

Disguised as a Naga, clothed in a blanket and carrying a spear, Jackson made his way westward through the hills accompanied by a phalanx of six Naga guides, similarly dressed. They looked like a typical Naga foraging party and successfully evaded the ubiquitous Japanese patrols in the area. Several days later the little group finally met with a patrol first from V Force and then from a Chindit column. The V Force group was commanded by a British Army major, and all 'bristled with grenades, sten guns and knives'. On 22 April, exactly a month to the day since he had baled out, a gaunt and heavily-bearded Jackson arrived unannounced at his squadron. The surprised greeting he received by the first man he met, after long being presumed dead, was '**** me, it's Mr Jackson!'

Ray Jackson's adventures were paralleled by Flying Officer McPherson who, a month later, on Wednesday 19 April crashed his Hurricane into the jungle north of Tetzami during a reconnaissance flight between Kohima and Jessami. Knocked unconscious in the crash, he came to some six hours later when he was hauled out of the cockpit by tribesmen, who hid him in a lean-to shelter a short distance away to recover. After three days of hiding, McPherson was helped across the mountainous jungle tracks on a trek to the village of Kuzani, a journey which took ten days and into the hands of one of the Border Regiment columns. After these adventures he arrived back at his Squadron, exhausted, emaciated, but safe, on 5 May.

~

After resting for a day at Bandheri, 76 Column moved off, and the regular routine of marching was re-established. It was now that their punishing training regime paid off (the mantra employed by their instructors was 'The harder you train, the easier you fight'): the men were fit and well-prepared for their exertions, but this didn't make the task any easier. Day after day, impossible hills were scaled, men often having to pull themselves up by roots, only to struggle down the other side, into steep, jungle-matted valleys where they were torn and scratched, slashing through head-high vegetation to make a way for the heavily-laden men and mules. In the valley bottoms huge, swaying forests of giant bamboo and matted vegetation prohibited passage. In such locations it would take hours of hard hacking with a *dao* to clear a hundred yards. Lieutenant Haskins observed his men at the top of one hill lying in a state of utter exhaustion, and yet they had to go on. In the deep nullahs they would often lose sight of the sun – but not the heat, and the lack of air underneath the jungle canopy was stifling. They would either tramp through black ooze in lifeless streams or wade waist deep through mountain streams, to climb upwards again in an agony of tortured muscles and aching limbs, all the while stinging sweat pouring into their eyes. 'We cursed every foot of it,' Wilcox admitted. 'Marching up a mountain with a heavy pack on your back is like beating yourself on the head with a hammer – it's so pleasant when you stop … We threw off our packs and sank to the ground, exhausted but grateful.'

The Dakotas of 216, 117 and 194 Squadrons RAF kept the columns resupplied. Each column had a small RAF team to guide in the aircraft and even, on occasions, to arrange for messages to be snatched from the ground by hooks trailing from light aircraft. A supply drop was a laborious affair, though a triumphant demonstration of British logistical supremacy and a dramatic contrast to the lamentable Japanese supply arrangements. Where possible bonfires were lit at either end of the L-shaped flight path, green foliage placed ready to provide smoke at the appropriate moment. The supply planes for 76 Column were called in by Flight Lieutenant Wilcox:

> I scanned the sky through borrowed binoculars. The weather was far from being good [but] … I hoped the low cloud, which was about eight-tenths in the west, would not discourage the supply-fliers.
>
> My binoculars picked up a few tiny dots in the sky. I counted three, four, five – five aircraft. They came nearer and I recognized them as [C–47s] so, picking up my Very pistol, I called 'Smoke!' and went down the hill to my [radio] set, as the thick smoke billowed up from the flare-path fires.

The aircraft flew in over the position, recognition signals flashed between the lead pilot and Wilcox's signalling lamp, and the Dakotas then turned in a wide circle to come in again to drop the supplies from a height of 400 feet. The Japanese were not unknown to imitate British soldiers on the ground and persuade the planes to drop supplies to them, so security procedures were as tight as could be managed. Soldiers in the aircraft, known as 'kickers', manhandled the supplies and pushed them out of the rear cargo door, which in the Dakotas operating on the Imphal supply run were left permanently open. Ammunition, water and other stores received the benefit of a small parachute which, when opened, had only a few seconds in the air to slow its descent before hitting the ground. On one occasion a kicker fell out of the doorway and plummeted to earth, but was miraculously saved by grasping at and holding onto some stores as they came down under its parachute. Equipment that didn't require a parachute was simply pushed out the door, free-falling to the ground, such as rice for Naga villagers who had been left starving by prowling Japanese. The general shortage of silk parachutes forced Slim's headquarters to devise alternatives, and a type employing jute was widely deployed. Philip Brownless recalled that these were not without danger:

> Bags of grain for the mules fell as 'free drops' – without parachutes – sometimes hazardous. Often the wind took the chutes away from the steep hillside and we could only watch as our stores sailed out of reach. My batman, addressing the sky, was telling everyone what he thought of the wind, the weather and the Japanese when half a

dozen shovels, tied together, landed at his feet with a smack which silenced him for a whole minute.

Desmond Whyte, the Senior Medical Officer of 111 Brigade, operating behind Japanese lines in Burma, recalled the use of the term 'death by flying fruit' to describe those killed by free drops, some of whom had been hit by tins of fruit. The monsoon clouds made navigation all but impossible for the pilots and, combined with the mountainous terrain, made the task of flying over the Naga Hills extremely hazardous. Warrant Officer Deryck Groocock, a young pilot in 194 Squadron, describes one such flight, dropping to 34 Column (4th Border) north of Kohima in mid-May 1944,

> We were to drop at a DZ near Chipoketama, and twelve Dakotas had been briefed for the job. We were loaded (grimly overloaded, I reckon) with bags of rice for free-fall dropping. We were flying from Agartala, but when we got a little way north we found ourselves flying above eight/eighths layer of cloud, and could see nothing of the ground.
>
> However, we passed on in the clear blue sky above, hoping that somewhere in the vicinity of the DZ we would find a break in the cloud which would enable us to make a visual let down through it. When we got somewhere near where we thought the DZ should be, we were flying at 8,500 ft which gave us clearance of 1,500 ft above the mountains which rose to 7,000 ft. Still hoping to find a hole in the cloud, I told my wireless operator to prepare the loads for dropping. This entailed opening the rear door and piling the bags of rice ready for pushing out by the two-air despatch men aboard.
>
> A few minutes later, to my great consternation, the aircraft's airspeed, (normally about 125 mph) started to drop off for no apparent reason. I put on more power to no avail, it just dropped off faster, and I had to put more and more forward pressure on the stick to keep the nose level. When I could hold the nose down no longer, it reared up, and the aircraft flicked over into a right hand spin with a rate of descent of about 2,000 ft per minute. This gave us about 45 seconds before we hit the mountains, which were still invisible.
>
> I took the normal spin recovery action – full opposite rudder, stick forward, and thought, 'This is the end'. I saw the altimeter go down to 6,000 ft, 5,500 ft, and 5,000 ft and still we had not hit. The next second we came out below the cloud at 4,500 ft under control and in a valley with great peaks vanishing into the clouds on either side of us.

Trembling like a leaf, I flew down the valley, and we considered what had happened. Fortunately, all the crew were still with me. They had not been wearing parachute harness and were still struggling into them when we emerged from the cloud. We realized that the aircraft must have been very badly loaded, and putting extra sacks near the door ready for ejection must have put the centre of gravity right outside the limits, causing the aircraft to become uncontrollable. Once in the spin, the sacks near the door fell forward putting the centre of gravity back within limits and enabling us to get out of the spin.

Suddenly, ahead, we saw a column of smoke coming up from the ground, and flew towards it. To our amazement, it was the DZ, displaying the correct recognition letters, we flew round and round it, waving like mad to the chaps on the ground, and pushing out the rice which had so nearly been our downfall.

We were now faced with getting home. We realized that there was no way of flying out of that particular valley at low level, and that we would have to climb out of it to do so. Selecting the widest part we could find, I put the aircraft into a steep climbing turn into the cloud, praying that we would not drift into either of the ridges on each side of us. After what seemed like an age, but was actually about 1½ minutes, we emerged out of the cloud into bright sunshine, and headed back for Agartala.

Out of twelve aircraft, which were sent out, we were, of course, the only one which had dropped. The others had all wisely brought their loads back. The next day we received a signal from Rear Brigade HQ congratulating us on achieving the drop. Little did they know how the drop had been accomplished.

Captain Harry Good of 55 Column asserted that because of this effectiveness of aerial resupply during 'the whole period of operation from May to August, we missed only one meal, despite most difficult flying conditions due to mountainous terrain, and frequent early morning mists common in this area'. From a total of 782 sorties allotted to supply 23 Brigade, 560 were successful and only three aircraft were lost. The sight of the British supply planes flying overhead was a devastating message to the Japanese, many of whom had run out of food as early as mid-April. His commanders had told Private Manabu Wada of 3/138th Regiment that when they entered the Naga Hills they would capture a cornucopia of British supplies as they had done in Malaya and Burma, feasting their way to victory. At Kohima, this did not happen, however:

The British had burned their food and supply depots so that not even a grain of rice or a round of ammunition was left for us in the captured enemy positions. The best my comrades and I could do was to find three tins of corned beef in the enemy positions. How could we be expected to fight on in these circumstances? As April entered its third week, we had to stave off the pangs of hunger by eating meagre supplies of biscuits and the corned beef ...

Throughout our long siege of Kohima enemy fighter aircraft flew along the face of the valley in front of us and cargo planes dropped arms and water to their leading troops. Without meat, rice, rifle and machine-gun ammunition we could only watch.

One day a rather mangy, flea-bitten dog wandered into Private Masaoki Okoshi's camp. Within weeks of arriving in the Naga Hills he and his mates were starving. They were eating anything available, from wild grass to the trunks of banana trees, and small lizards. In fact, anything that moved was fair game, literally. Private Tomohiro Sato recalled that killing the dog was easy.

We put some oil in a pan, fried it and then ate it. But I'd never had dog so it didn't taste very nice. It was just a case of eating and easing our empty stomachs a little, that was all. It wasn't a question of whether it tasted good or not. We didn't care what it was as long as we could put something in our stomachs. With the bananas, we'd peel the outside and get to the core, which smelt a bit like cucumber, and we'd eat that. Eating that stuff gave us diarrhoea. We knew that, but when there's nothing to eat, you just eat anything. It wasn't just one or two of us, we were all thinking the same thing, so everyone ended up getting diarrhoea.

One of the motives for attacking British and Indian positions was, for the half-starved Japanese, the opportunity to rob enemy dead of whatever meagre rations they themselves might be carrying. Private Hidehiro Shingai recalled the feeling they all had when an attack was announced, 'We'll get to have something nice for dinner today.'

~

The advancing columns, slowly but surely seeping into the hills like an ink stain moving through blotting paper, came across the Japanese only occasionally during the first week. During this time, aided by Naga guides, the Chindit columns encountered mainly parties of Japanese sent to forage amongst the hill tribes and to steal their chickens, eggs and rice. In the hills rudimentary psychological warfare by the British had an effect even on the Japanese. Brigadier Perowne established a number of false radio nets that made out that his force was much larger than it was, and stories sent through the Naga villages talked of a large British army bearing down on the Japanese from the north-west. When Major Simmonds' company from 76 Column approached the village of Wokha, three days' march north-west of Kohima, the Japanese had evacuated their otherwise impregnable positions on the slopes around the village and fled into the jungle. 'Evidence of their haste was soon forthcoming,' reported Wilcox, 'in the shape of helmets, pieces of equipment, maps, documents, and a jar of hair-brilliantine which stank to high heaven.' The area was littered with the discarded feathers and bones of misappropriated chickens, broken eggshells and still-warm camp fires. It was rare for the Japanese not to stand and fight but even they, occasionally, fell prey to their fears.

~

The Chindits arrived at some villages, especially those in the northern Naga Hills, well before the Japanese. Sergeant Alf Simpson of 1st Essex found himself responsible for supervising the construction of an airstrip for light aeroplanes at one such, Mokokchung. The strip was being carved out of the side of a hill and to pay the Naga labourers Simpson flew low in an American Sentinel light plane on 23 April – his first-ever flight in an aircraft – to drop two heavy bags of silver rupees. Unfortunately the bags broke on impact, Simpson observing the labourers scuttling round like a swarm of ants picking up the coins. A week later Simpson made it to the village by jeep, carefully negotiating a heart-stopping, winding track boasting a sheer drop down the mountain for most of its route. He then watched, along with the entire population of the village, the first aircraft – another Stinson – land on the new airstrip:

> At one end of the air strip was a sheer drop of about two thousand feet, a plane taking off would shoot over the edge and disappear from sight. We all held our breath until it reappeared again safely airborne.

The aircraft each had a metal frame welded to the outside and a stretcher with a casualty strapped to it. Until Kohima was relieved in late-June this was the only way to get casualties out of the mountains, the only alternative for the wounded being the laborious and often painful trek, carried by Naga bearers, down into the Brahmaputra Valley, a journey that could take many days.

In the valleys north and east of Kohima, however, the Chindits arrived after the Japanese, and had to fight for dominance. At the village of Tseminyu, two days' march due north of Kohima, a Japanese foraging party had taken up residence in the village within a few days of the attack beginning on Kohima. The village, perched 4,600 feet up on the top of a steeply-sided mountain peak, served as the local store for the rice the Japanese were filching from villages in the area. The approach of 76 Column, on 14 April, came as an unexpected surprise to them. In the dead of night, guided by a local Rengma Naga, a party of men under the command of the giant, bearded Major Henchman – whose daytime attire extended to a bush hat, shorts, boots and a webbing belt holding a .38 revolver (he never seemed to wear a shirt) – climbed quietly to the summit. Unforgivably, the Japanese sentry was fast asleep. Quietly removing the man's rifle, the Japanese was knocked unconscious with a rifle butt and taken prisoner. Henchman then ascertained that the remainder of the Japanese were asleep in the hut normally reserved in the village for visiting government officials. Grenades and the rapid staccato fire of Sten sub-machine guns surprised the sleeping tenants and in a short while the very one-sided battle was over.

Despite their fitness and the regularity of the food drops, disease took a rapid hold on many of the Chindits, men quickly succumbing to various ailments such as diarrhoea, malaria, fever, stomach cramps, jaundice, tick bites, exhaustion and a general loss of appetite, a condition seemingly exacerbated by the full onset of the monsoon in May. Wilcox went for seven days drinking only tea. Everything he tried to eat was vomited back. At first the medical officers were unable to pinpoint the exact cause of this common complaint. Undoubtedly the extreme physical demands made by the terrain, the monotony of the rations (the men were on American K rations – according to one report the 'mere sight of some of its items – the tin of corned pork loaf, especially, was enough to create feelings of nausea') – and the constant wetness all played their part. It was only discovered subsequently that the water from the springs in the Naga Hills has a high magnesium sulphate content, which is a powerful laxative.

In at least one column an outbreak of typhus spread by lice was threatened. The Column Medical Officer immediately ordered a supply drop of new clothing for the entire force, and all existing clothing, including boots, was burned, an action that staved off the threat of an epidemic. The difficulties for the Column Medical Officers, such as Captain Harry Good, were considerable:

> As casualties were left for my attention, I and my orderly marched at the rear of the column and, rather than be left behind, we carried the casualty's pack ourselves as well as our own, and it sometimes happened that I arrived at the midday or evening rendezvous with two 80-pound packs on my back. The casualties were mainly exhaustion with malaria. Even though suppressive Mepacrine tablets were regularly taken, malaria was not entirely suppressed. Usually relief of the pack enabled the casualty to finish the day's march to the rest area, but we had a small number of ponies in the column on which we transported the more serious casualties. Evacuation of casualties was a further problem. We had a difficult, but frail, Line of Communication back to Brigade HQ where they had an airstrip. So, into the breech stepped the Naga Hillmen. They were small, around 5 feet in height, but wiry and capable of running up and down hills with heavy loads. Stretchers and litters were constructed of bamboo and casualties were evacuated with Nagas acting as stretcher-bearers. No escort could be provided but all casualties evacuated by these means arrived safely at Brigade HQ. The Nagas were completely loyal to us and never let us down.

At Tseminyu the men of 76 Column came across members of the INA – 'Jifs' as they called them – for the first time. It was difficult for the British to judge whether these men were genuine supporters of the INA or men who merely used it as an expedient way of making their own way back to India. The men who were brought into the village at Tseminyu had their pockets full of INA propaganda and the orange, green and white INA badge. They had no weapons. In this case it transpired that they had been captured only recently at Kohima. There, an INA recruiting officer by the name of Captain Anjur Singh had urged them to join the INA, the alternative being the dubious pleasure of becoming a Japanese prisoner of war. The new INA 'converts' duly joined foraging parties. Given INA badges to provide unrestricted access through the Japanese-controlled area, the men were only too happy to acquiesce, before slinking into the jungle at the first available opportunity in search of the British lines. When troops did come across genuine 'Jifs' still in possession of their weapons they were shown little sympathy. They were shown little mercy if they fell into the hands of an Indian unit: Major Hornsby of 3rd Gurkhas had some difficulty in stopping his subedar major from shooting a whole batch of them, 'They are evil men, sahib.'

On 15 April after three days of marching, the Essex men of 44 Column surprised a large Japanese patrol from 124th Regiment near the village of Phekekrima, dispersing it with gunfire. The Japanese, confident that the siege of the Kohima garrison a few miles to the south would soon end in their favour, were comprehensively emptying the Naga villages of foodstuffs. In the distance the deep and constant booming of the guns at Kohima, in which lay the tiny besieged garrison almost at the limit of its endurance, provided a noisy though haunting backdrop to the scene and a reminder to the Chindits of the urgency and gravity of their task. The village of Phekekrima, however, was well defended by the Japanese, Lieutenant Philip Brownless noting that these 300 Japanese 'were dug into beautifully prepared positions' on top of a mountain one thousand feet higher than Snowdon'. Resembling a medieval fortress, Phekekrima boasted sheer and unscaleable cliffs on three sides, only a single footpath along an exposed ridge allowing access from the north. Over the next sixteen days a number of attacks were made against the village, before the Japanese, concerned about running out of food, slipped away:

> We attacked this position twice unsuccessfully [on 22 April], and then one column [55] led by Major Alec Lovelace moved round behind them and the Japanese withdrew. Meanwhile a patrol, sent further east with a wireless to report enemy movement, was attacked by a party of two or three Japanese platoons and having inflicted quite a few casualties on the Japanese and suffered one man killed, withdrew.

The Essex attack was supported by the Hurribombers of 11 Squadron RAF flying from Lanka airfield in Assam, forty miles west of Dimapur. The wanton brutality of the Japanese was made painfully apparent when the position was finally captured. 'When we occupied the village,' Brownless recalled, 'we found the bodies of the five wounded whom we had been unable to get out had been bayoneted to death and a sixth, bayoneted five times, who was still alive.' The Essex sustained thirty casualties, but they left behind the noxious smell of what Haskins described as 'fifty putrefying Japanese corpses'.

> The stout wooden Naga homes were a mass of crumbled wreckage, mutely eloquent of the hideous destruction of war. Silent villagers sat staring wretchedly ... at the ruination of their possessions.

After the Phekekrima battle the two Essex columns moved east of Kohima to the village of Chechama, four miles south of Tseminyu. The column had suffered several officer casualties at Phekekrima and Brownless was given command of a platoon in C Company, as well as continuing his responsibilities for the column's mules. As the column entered the village from the north it came under fire from the lower part of the village:

> We were on higher ground, returned their fire, and were mortared. After a while they appeared to retreat through the bottom end of the village. Bob Haynes, the company commander, had been hit in the thigh, so I took over his company and positioned the platoons. We dug in. Later I was sent on a patrol down the track by which the Japanese had retreated, but finding no Japanese, reached a position from which I had a good view of the battle at Kohima.

As a result of the assiduous propagation of the Christian faith to the Nagas since the nineteenth century by missionaries, it was rare for villages not to have a 'separate' Christian village next to the old, animist one, the two communities living alongside each other, the animists angrily rejecting the new religion and forcing converts to construct their own villages away from the old. Before being called up, Philip Brownless had been training for the Christian ministry at Cambridge University. In the middle of the fighting for Nerhema, the Essex Commanding Officer, Lieutenant Colonel Walker asked him, as the Essex columns had no chaplain, if he would take a service. Brownless agreed:

> We sat on the reverse slope with the enemy just over the ridge within earshot. Half the congregation were British soldiers and the other half were Nagas, a devoted Christian people. The old Naga headman and I agreed – with no common language – to share the service. I started with a prayer in English, and then the wizened old man, red headman's blanket around his shoulders, read one in his language. We bowed to each other and then each read a piece from the Bible, he reading his with great vehemence, then more prayers and the Grace. We did not rise to hymns for lack of hymnbooks but that did not stop the Nagas: they were described by one of our chaps, a Welshman, as 'fairly bashing out them 'ymns'.

~

The Japanese were now being challenged for control of the villages that lay along the track running from Kohima to Bokajan, and which passed through Merema, Cheswema and Phekekrima. After their defeat at Phekekrima they had moved to build defensive positions in the nearby village of Nerhema. These would need to be destroyed before the Japanese were forced to relinquish control of the track. The job was given to 44 Column. 'The enemy were dug in on two mounds just outside the village,' recalled Philip Brownless, 'and their patrols used to creep up and fire and throw grenades at us at night. I always slept with my rifle just beside me, and when it started I used simply to roll over into the firing position.' A number of attacks had failed to move the Japanese from their positions:

> I led an attack on the Japanese position through jungle and secured the left hand mound. The other two platoons were held up attacking the other mound. There were several casualties, including Peter Comber, the Company Commander, shot through the knee. A further attack by 56 Column also failed, resulting in a number of wounded and killed who included Lieutenant Keith Mann. A third attack was laid on, but was called off because the planned air support was cancelled at the last minute.

A fourth attack was planned, which was to include twelve Hurribombers and the combined mortars of 33 and 76 Columns. On the morning of the attack the Japanese could be seen from Chechama wandering around the village unconcernedly. Then, in the distance and flying at 10,000 feet, the tiny dots of the incoming Hurricanes showed themselves to the expectant soldiers. The mortars opened up on Nerhema to lay smoke on the target to guide in the fighter-bombers:

> The mortars were accurate. The aircraft plunged on the village and unleashed their bombs in a screaming dive. One by one, they came in, pulling out at an incredibly low altitude, almost appearing to brush the hill-side with their wing-tips.
>
> Bombs gone, the Hurricanes swept in for the second phase of the attack – cannon-strafing. The watching British saw the tracer and heard the four cannon of each machine rattle the tune every soldier hates.

The Japanese survivors fled. When a patrol entered Nerhema the following day the village was littered with their dead. 'The stench,' recalled Wilcox, 'was awful.' These battles set the scene for the engagement over the next three months between the Chindits and men of the Japanese 124th Regiment. The British objective was to dominate the villages and tracks in the region and deny them to the enemy while destroying Japanese positions and bases wherever they were found. Desperate to remove this thorn in their side, the Japanese attempted to hunt the Chindits down. So developed a battle of endurance and wits, in which ambushes and intense, though small-scale, actions were fought between the Japanese and British patrols. In late May a typical encounter took place involving men of Corporal Stanley Hutson's 60 Column near the Naga village of Nungphung, south of Jessami on the track that wound its way over the mountains to Somra. Too small ever to feature in any history of the campaign, it was an example of the type of engagement that characterized this exhausting, bloody and unreported war.

The battle of Nungphung 'probably started because of an ambush that went wrong two days previously,' Hutson recounted:

[Thirteen] Platoon had been sent to give support to 14 Platoon of 60 Column on an ambush. We had picked a good position but as a large group of Japs – probably twice our number – started to enter the trap a little Gurkha couldn't wait for the officer's first shot. He shot one Jap, but it gave the others a chance to re-group and counter-attack. After skirmishing for about half an hour, our officer realized it was an unprofitable situation and gave the order to withdraw. We left the Japs looking for us and set off for Nungphung about five miles away. We arrived at the base of a hill on which the village stood in total darkness and torrential rain. It was assumed that the heavy rain would wash away our tracks but in fact this was not so. The following day sections were sent out scouting for any Japs that could have followed us. They found nothing. We realized later that they had found our tracks heading for the hill but had kept well clear for a day to lull us into a feeling of false security.

That night, after the usual section patrol at 'Stand To', the perimeter guard was put out as always. The rest of the men slept in the centre. As the night wore on about 150 Japanese Imperial Guards crept up towards us. Dawn began to break [on 31 May 1944] and a low mist swirled on the ground when, just before 'Stand To', the Japs bumped the perimeter guard. Sten and Bren–gun fire soon had the column wide awake and in position to fight off an attack. I remember feeling very cold and wet. I also felt afraid and the swirling mist at knee height made everything seem unreal. I couldn't see any Japs to fire at, but every time I sat up a burst of automatic gunfire splattered bullets about an inch over my head. The firing got more intense then suddenly from out of the mist came a long line of huge Japs with fixed bayonets. Realizing we were not in the best of positions I waved to the rest of the section to fall back. This was done in an orderly fashion but as I looked around for the ideal place to make a stand I became aware that I had lost a sergeant and gained a Gurkha Bren gunner. The Gurkha waved me to take the men further up the hill, then settled down to hold the enemy on his own. The Gurkha's courage and initiative gave me time to reach an ideal spot on the edge of the village where the enemy would have to cross open ground to reach us.

As soon as I had deployed the men I went back with one man to give covering fire to get the Gurkha out. The three of us rejoined the section and we all waited quietly. We made not a sound as the advancing Japs passed on instructions from their officer. We couldn't see them or the officer but we knew they had stopped as the officer became aware of the open space and realized what we had in store for them. He continued to shout orders from the bottom of a tree. I moved quickly amongst the section and told them to wait until I gave the signal and then to throw grenades at the base of the tree. The next time the officer shouted I gave the signal. We never heard him again and later found him in bits. Open space or not, it wasn't long before the Japs decided to attack. Using automatic weapons and the small mortars their infantry had strapped to their legs, over they came. We were ready for them and fortunately I had acquired another Bren gunner from another section. The firepower we produced stopped the line of Japs before they had covered half the open space. The ones that weren't killed wavered and dropped back. Five minutes later they burst out from the trees to try again. The same result. If the Japs hadn't realized that we had nowhere else to go and were certainly not going to be taken prisoner, they did now!

I anticipated they might make a sneaky attack on the flank. I was right. I had just joined a Yorkshireman on the left flank when six or seven Japs burst out of the trees firing automatic weapons. They were met by bullets from our Sten guns and though some of them dropped in their tracks the others came on. Suddenly I became aware that my companion's face had disappeared and I was staring down at his brains on my shirt. In a daze I carried on firing until my numbed brain indicated that there was nothing left to fire at – they were all dead … [the remainder of the] Imperial Guard decided they had had enough and they melted away. The battle for Nungphung was over and for the loss of three killed and four wounded, we had come out of it by far the best …

~

As April wore on the first signs of the impending monsoon approached. The rain lashed down at night, the men curling up on the ground in their waterproof capes, if they had them. The weather changed the operating environment significantly. Airdrops of supplies were much more difficult than before, as the cloud cover over the mountains was now much more intense. There was nothing more depressing than sitting at a dropping zone under thick cloud, listening to the drone overhead of the unseeing Dakota searching for a gap in the clouds in which to carry out the correct identification procedure to allow the supply drop to begin. Failing to find a suitable gap would mean the Dakota heading reluctantly for home, and the hungry Chindits below tightening their belts and arranging for another delivery – perhaps several days later – when the weather improved. The terrain became much more precipitous as the columns travelled east from Kohima towards the north-easterly track to Jessami.

The constancy and fury of the rain made each step a difficult one. With the monsoon at its height the rain poured down in steady streams, day after day, hour after hour. There was occasionally some respite during the day, but it was rare for it to be cloudless, and the damp heat made it impossible to get dry, except for those glorious occasions when the fire in a Naga hut made it possible to strip off and for clothes to be dried. The relentless deluge turned the tracks into slippery, muddy quagmires and muddy riverbeds into raging torrents. It was in these appalling conditions that 76 Column was sent to attack the Japanese in a village close to the road between Kohima and Imphal. Moving south-east of the Jessami track in a march against the grain of the country towards the Naga village of Phezachedama the strong patrol made first for the village of Runguzumi, due east of Kohima and deep within Japanese territory. Through flooded valleys, across muddy *padi* fields and swollen streams, the column marched, sweating in the heat despite the plenitude of water that surrounded them. Finally, they reached the slopes of the hills beneath Runguzumi. How Wilcox cursed the fact that all Naga villages were sited on the topmost peaks!

> We were now so wet and miserable that even when we halted for a rest we could not be bothered to take off our back-pack since the weight when it was replaced clamped the cold shirts on our sweat-heated bodies and gave us chills. We simply sank to the ground and lay on our loads amid the streaming rivulets of rainwater. Higher up the mountain we were in cloud and we marched – or rather, limped – through the soupy mass until we reached the summit where we found a track which led to the village.

In pouring rain the column moved off again the following day, Wilcox noting that their Naga guide, Mr Kumbo, a Kohima schoolmaster, was carrying one of the soldier's packs, and an umbrella, upon which the 'driving, swirling rain beat a tattoo and dribbled off onto his drenched shirt'. The villages along this route were visited regularly by Japanese patrols, and some were occupied, and it soon became apparent that the Japanese had become aware by then of the British presence, and were planning to do something about it. Ambushes were a constant threat. For Lieutenant Desmond Early of 1st Essex 'the jungle was a difficult place in which to operate, since one often only found the enemy when they opened fire and even then you were never sure where they were'. After another two days of sweaty exertion the column reached their objective, Phezachedama village.

The Japanese tried to lull the forty men of 76 Column into a false sense of security by not attacking immediately. It was two days after the patrol's arrival that they launched their first attack on the village. At dawn, a rifle shot broke the silence. It came at the end of 'Stand To' when the soldiers had been lying quietly in the drizzling rain, watching and keeping guard during the dangerous half hour between darkness and dawn. An eerie period of silence followed the rifle shot, the Chindits' fire discipline preventing them from firing at anything other than a clearly visible target. News then came back in whispers to the centre of the village: some sixty Japanese soldiers were lining up on the north side of the slope, preparing to attack. Now, Sten guns began occasionally to chirp, sometimes followed by the distinctive crack of a British Lee Enfield .303 rifle, probably from the perimeter sentries guarding the steep approaches to the village, but for the most part the position was quiet, the men crouching low in their slit trenches awaiting the inevitable. Then silence fell again, this time for two long hours, the rain driving relentlessly, hitting the ground around them with such force that each drop bounced visibly, creating a double haze at ground level and a hum that drowned out all but the loudest sounds. Still the men waited, stretching legs slowly when they could to maintain circulation, but keeping their heads low. The sun had risen by now and the rain ceased. Suddenly, they heard the shrill voice of the Japanese officer, this time from the opposite direction, the southern slope. Then Wilcox heard voices from every direction: they were surrounded.

The Japanese officer screamed a command and a heavy volley of rifle fire hit the position, but did little damage. It did, however, provide the prelude to the arrival of a series of sharp explosions in the village: the

Japanese had brought up a mortar, a lethal weapon against slit trenches as its high trajectory allowed its devastating rounds to drop from the sky:

> The noise was terrific. The crack, crack of rifles and the vicious buzz of the missiles like a swarm of angry bees was punctuated with the heavier thud of the mortar. It lasted nearly fifteen minutes in this fashion and then died in intensity ... [Then the] Jap officer's voice screamed again from the north side and then bedlam let loose. The trees disgorged a howling pack of Japanese and they came at a run towards our thin green line of Chindits, firing wildly into our midst.

The charge faltered on the Chindit trenches, and the survivors fled back to the tree line, leaving six dead Japanese sprawled on the ground. The Japanese for a while resorted to sniping from the trees and mortaring the positions, sending shrapnel whistling overhead and into the sodden earth but before long the Japanese officer screamed, and a volley was fired from the tree line before they charged again:

> The noise was unearthly. They came, slipping from tree to tree, sunlight flashing on the bare steel bayonets, howling like a savage pack of wolves ...
>
> A hysterical wail started up behind us and our south side defenders fired into the attack which started on that side. The Brens rippled out short staccato bursts into the frenzied mobs as they came in at the front and rear of our camp.

Once again, the Japanese were cut down by the determined, unflinching defenders. After what had happened to the Essex at Phekekrima the 'Dukes' were not going to be taken prisoner by the Japanese. 'We were swearing and sweating and the weapons were hot in our hands. Steel for steel and bullet for bullet, the bloody contest was fought and won.' It was now midday, and the sun was beating down fiercely. The Chindits had lost two men dead, but untidy heaps of Japanese bodies lay dotted across the open ground and amongst the trees where they had fallen. No fanatical *banzai* charge would budge the Chindits from their positions. At Phezachedama, however, the Japanese needed to do nothing but keep the Chindits holed up until they ran out of ammunition or starved and, accordingly, after further hair-raising adventures, the patrol managed to extricate itself, in darkness and heavy rain, through the Japanese cordon and several days later, back to the relative safety of Runguzumi village.

By late-May the Chindits were operating far to the east of Kohima in the area of Jessami and Kharasom, close to the Chindwin river. In a typical column action three platoons of 55 Column, accompanied by their RMO, Captain Harry Good, moved to destroy the Japanese positions in and around the largely Christian village of Phekekedzumi ('Phek', not to be confused with Phekekrima, north of Kohima), where Flying Officer Ray Jackson had received sanctuary. A two–day march brought the Chindits to the village, two platoons setting up roadblocks outside the village and the Headquarters platoon, commanded by Major Douglas Scott, launching roving patrols to attack Japanese positions identified in the locality. It was like stirring up a hornets' nest: the Japanese reacted with fury. While the British laid a number of highly effective ambushes on tracks in the area – Japanese movement discipline in the jungle was often remarkably poor, chatting being an unforgivable sin to Chindits who were trained only to communicate by whisper – the Japanese repeatedly attempted to overwhelm the British patrol and column bases by means of frontal attack. They never once succeeded. In the various engagements around Phek, recorded Good, some thirty Japanese were killed and ten wounded, at a cost of two British casualties.

> The column commander, Major Scott, was wounded in the arm and, as I was dressing his wound, we were fired upon by a machine gun from the top of the hill. As we were not now in touch with the two platoons on roadblocks, and as I was not an infantry officer and Major Scott was wounded, it was decided to withdraw as the party was no longer large enough to carry out an assault on the strongpoint on the hill from which the LMG fire had come. After we had travelled a mile or two from the village, Major Scott said that there was a wounded NCO left in the village and would I return there with a section of ten men and try to recover him. We set off up the hill to join a track running into the village. As we rested before finally stepping up onto the track, a Naga hillman came up and said 'Japani'. We looked up and saw a Japanese officer looking down at us. We immediately realized that we were almost caught in an ambush, so, at the double, we made for the rice *padi* fields at the side of the track in the direction of a secondary jungle area 100 yards or so lower down. Thanks to the step-like formation of the *padi* fields, where we jumped down every few yards, and to the poor marksmanship of the Japanese, we arrived without any casualties in the jungle, for the Japanese opened up with everything they had – rifles, machine guns, mortars and grenades.

They escaped, but there is no record of the fate of the wounded British soldier left in the village.

# Chapter 7

# The Battle of Kohima

After five days of cramped and uncomfortable train travel that had taken them nearly 2,000 miles across India from their starting point at Ahmednagar, south-east of Bombay, Harry Swinson of the 7th Battalion Worcestershire Regiment (Worcesters) and a gaggle of other officers from 5 Brigade, the lead formation of the British 2nd Infantry Division (4, 5 and 6 Brigades) – including Tom Hughes, Keith Halnan, Charles Barker and 'Boggie' Allen – awoke to find themselves, on the morning of Friday 31 March, parked in a station twenty miles outside Calcutta. The local newspaper, purchased for a couple of *annas* from a lad on the station, reported that three Japanese columns were moving into Manipur. With somewhat pompous authority the newspaper asserted that enemy ambitions were clear, namely that 'cutting our road of communication North and South of Imphal, to force our withdrawal from the Naga Hills ... would enable the Japs to threaten the railways in Eastern Assam which are carrying supplies not only to the central front, but to General Stilwell's army in North Burma'.

This was the first public explanation the men had received about the reason for the sudden dash of the entire division (nine infantry battalions, a machine-gun battalion, reconnaissance regiment, three field regiments of artillery (25-pounders), an anti-aircraft/anti-tank regiment and masses of supporting services) across the length and breadth of India. Their journey had been a surprise, not just to them but to their divisional commander, Major General John Grover, who only two weeks before had been told by General Giffard in New Delhi that there could be no possibility of using his formation in 1944. Only four days after this meeting Grover received a signal from Slim ordering him to mobilize his division and get it to Chittagong. Only when on the move – on 27 March – were they told to make for Assam instead. Soon after crossing the Brahmaputra and transferring to a train on a different gauge on Saturday 1 April, a slow moving ambulance train travelling back towards Calcutta gave the fresh troops of the division food for thought.

> The tail end of it stopped opposite us for a few minutes and I looked down at the rows of weary men. Some sitting up smoking, others lying quite still, but all with a glazed, hollow look in their eyes. It does you no good seeing ambulance trains – not when you're on your way to the front, it doesn't. If I hadn't remembered how tough it was going to be it would definitely have spoiled my lunch.

Colour Sergeant Fred Weedman of the Worcesters – one of the three battalions in Brigadier Victor Hawkins' 5 Brigade, and one of two Territorial Army (TA) battalions in 2nd Division – travelled on the same train, recalling the 'uncomfortable wooden carriages, pulled by an ancient steam engine from which we drew hot water whenever we stopped to 'brew-up''. Mike Ball, an American civilian volunteer who was part of the American Field Service, driving big three-ton Chevrolet ambulances and attached to 161 Brigade, could not recall much of the journey. Memories of Poona were 'clouded by gin and orange' and the train journey to Dimapur 'was one horrendous binge. It's a wonder no one fell off the slow moving train'. That evening the train crawled into Dimapur. The atmosphere of the place appeared riven with panic. Harry Swinson:

> The Japs seem to be well on the way to Kohima … The whole place is in one big flap. The chair-borne troops in the L. of C. Area are digging and wiring themselves in their offices and pioneers are putting slit trenches round the Rest Camp.

He wasn't the only one to sense the fear that the unexpected Japanese thrust deep into the Naga Hills had wrought. Lieutenant Lentorn 'Snagger' Highett, a platoon commander in 2nd Battalion, Dorsetshire Regiment (Dorsets) – also in 5 Infantry Brigade – was horrified at the state of nervous panic that seemed to have engulfed Dimapur, but made the most of the confusion:

> The Japs were only forty miles away. There were huge supplies of stores, which nobody seemed to be too bothered about. There are few things more unpleasant than a base in a flap. It was full of people who never expected to fight, and who couldn't wait to get out. 'Take what you like,' they said, 'just give us a signature if you've got the time.' We were pretty arrogant in 2 Div and were not impressed. I acquired two armoured cars, which proved very useful. We picked up masses of stores, ammo, food, drink etc.

Swinson, however, was encouraged by the calm professionalism exhibited by the troops of the division as they arrived into Dimapur in dribs and drabs over the coming days. The day after his own arrival he went to see a train with 1st Battalion, Queen's Own Cameron Highlanders (Cameron Highlanders) pull in. 'They looked so calm and orderly amidst the confusion around us that I blessed the sight of them.' The plan at this early stage was for 2nd Division to protect Dimapur, whilst 161 Brigade did what was necessary to defend Kohima which, it was confidently expected, the Japanese would not reach until 6 April at the earliest. But two days later, as 2nd Division continued to arrive into Dimapur in dribs and drabs, the panic had, if anything, increased. On both sides of the road to Kohima Swinson

> saw large dumps of ordnance stores, petrol, ammunition, vehicles, medical supplies, and food supplies. Found the best stocked canteen have seen in years. The *babu*[25] in a flap was letting masses of stores go. Let me have four bars of chocolate without argument. The size of this base emphasizes the importance of holding it. If the Japs take Dimapur they will have enough stores for a march on Delhi.
>
> The flap continues and the speed of the vehicles roaring north (empty) is steadily working up to a crescendo. Have heard no news from the front, which is just as well.

At first light on Wednesday 5 April Harry Swinson was shaving when a rather dishevelled American officer walked in, said he was from Kohima, and asked for a wash. 'I pointed to my canvas bucket and told him to use it. He stripped off his leather jacket, took the soap I handed to him, and commenced to wash. When he was clean:

'Are they going to hold Kohima?' he said.

'I hope so. Why?' I replied, somewhat startled.

'I've just come from there and I've never seen such confusion in my life. There's about 2,000 *babus* there and only about 200 fighting men.'

'They're sending the Royal West Kents back there today, I believe,' replied Swinson.

The Japanese arrival in Kohima the previous night and during that day galvanized Stopford, Grover and Ranking, all of whom were rattled by the sudden turn of events. Why was it that the Japanese always seemed to be able to surprise the British so that we were always on the back foot? This was the first time that most of the men of 2nd Division had encountered the Japanese (although some of 6 Brigade had already learned of their enemy from painful experience in Arakan in 1943): they were going to learn fast. Ranking sent Warren's 161 Brigade back into Kohima from Nichugard, and the Worcesters and the Cameron Highlanders accompanied by a battery of 25-pounders – the advance guard of 5 Brigade – prepared to move into the hills to block the road that ran the forty-six miles from Kohima down into Dimapur. The remainder of 5 Brigade was warned to prepare for a minimum of a seven-day battle, at the news of which Swinson observed in his diary, 'Most optimistic'. As the days unfolded and Sato built up his strength at Kohima, Grover did likewise at Dimapur, although 2nd Division was not assembled in its entirety until 11 April. By Sunday 9 April a Worcester patrol had bumped a Japanese roadblock at the village of Zubza, which lay astride the Dimapur-Kohima road at Milestone 36. Two days later two companies of the Worcesters attacked this Japanese position but were repulsed in their baptism of fire. Swinson watched the aftermath:

> Soon the wounded came back in jeeps ... Gave them cigarettes and tried to cheer them. They weren't badly wounded, but were palpably shocked. Their eyes looked watery and there was an uncontrollable tremor in their voices. Met two men from 18 Platoon, one shot in the shoulder, the other in the arms. Told me they had attacked a small woody hill, but the covering fire had proved insufficient. The Japs got them at short range with LMG fire. 'Mr. Watkins was the first to be killed,' they said.

On Friday 14 April an attack by the Cameron Highlanders after a twenty-minute bombardment by 25-pounders and two 5.5-inch guns that had been found without an owner in Dimapur and 'adopted' by the division drove the Japanese from the hill they had occupied at Milestone 37.5. That night Colour Sergeant Fred Weedman's company occupied the high ground overlooking Zubza to protect what was fast becoming the divisional administration area. In the area that day had arrived three Lee Grant tanks, cut off from their colleagues in Imphal. Their first night in action for these Territorial Army infantry made them bless the thoroughness of their training and the cool professionalism of their commanders.

> With the utmost caution, and paying all due respect to the sniping abilities of the Japanese, barbed wire was run out around the two positions at a distance of six yards from the box perimeter. A telephone line was also run from the main position to 15 Platoon in

their own small isolated position. All the preparations that could be done to make the position less vulnerable were quickly carried out. The clearing of fields of fire, making trip wires and fastening cans to the barbed wire, elbow rests in the trenches and making ledges to line up grenades for immediate use, preparations that proved to be invaluable.

We were not disappointed, for that night a Japanese jitter party prodded our defences and 15 Platoon had a short skirmish, without any casualties. [Later that] night the Japanese made a determined sortie to over-run the position, this time concentrating their attack against the main body of the Company, namely 13 and 14 Platoons and Company HQ.

At approximately eleven thirty, Corporal Stevens came crawling over to the command post to report that he had heard enemy movement outside the perimeter. Orders were issued quickly and quietly for everyone to stand-to, a procedure that was carried out in complete silence by the pulling of bedding ropes running from trench to trench around the perimeter. There was no moon and visibility was nil. Eyes were strained to pierce the blanket of darkness and each sound was interpreted as hostile, but nobody moved. The most weird of all the noises in the surrounding jungle, was the tap, tapping of the woodpecker … or was it the Japanese signalling to each other? The climax was reached when the 'twang' of the wire being cut broke into the other sounds. A quiet order from the Section Commander and the men in the forward positions threw their grenades in the darkness towards the unseen enemy. The night was split asunder.

The deafening explosion was followed by the screams of wounded Japanese. Bren guns on the flanks opened up and swept the undergrowth with bursts of .303 fire. A Japanese Taisho machine gun with its peculiar staccato sound joined in the confusion of noises. Bullets flew over the position with their singing whine, some hit the branches of the trees ricocheting into the darkness like angry bees. The steady sound of small-arms fire continued as those in the forward trenches probed suspicious shadows. The answering 'ping' of Japanese bullets proved that though they had withdrawn, it was only to lick their wounds before making another attack.

Silence eventually reigned and everyone remained tense, waiting for the next attack. It came at two o'clock in the morning when a Japanese machine gun opened up on the left flank, intended as a diversion from the attack that materialized from the right. This time there was no attempt at silence and with loud shouts and blood-curdling yells they attempted to over-run the position. At that moment our lives were in the hands of that thin line of fellows who defended the right flank.

Major Burrell passed a message to the cooks, clerks and batmen of Company HQ to fix their bayonets and charge if the Japanese broke through at any point. During the whole of this operation which lasted for over half-an-hour, grenades fell intermittently into the box. Private Blair and his beloved 2-inch mortar returned two shells for every one of theirs.

The night wore on and except for one half-hearted attempt to gain the position, it passed without further incident. It was only when the daylight came that the full extent of the attack could be appreciated; rifles, equipment, and dead bodies were strewn on the ground. At no place had the Japanese been allowed to penetrate the forward positions although the wire had been cut in several places. Seventeen rifles strewn in various places proved that the wounded had been carried away in the darkness. A body that was lying about twenty yards down the slope was seen to move. It was identified as a Japanese officer. A puff of smoke came from his chest and [he] curled up his body. He smouldered for the rest of the day and slowly burnt himself to death.

Three days of subsequent fighting by men of the Cameron Highlanders and 2nd Battalion, Durham Light Infantry (Durhams) opened up the road all the way to Warren's HQ and the gun lines at Jotsoma. The Lee Grants fired in support of the Cameron Highlanders' attack, protected by the infantrymen of Sergeant Frederick Hazell's 18 Platoon, D Company, 2nd Battalion, Royal Norfolk Regiment (Norfolks). Three of his men were wounded in the melee:

One of them had been wounded in France, during the retreat to Dunkirk he got shot in the backside. As he passed me on his stretcher he sort of sat up, beamed at me and said, 'I've been shot in the arse again!' I wondered if it was his custom to stick his arse in the air to get it shot at.

On the hill Company Sergeant Major Tommy Cook of C Company, Cameron Highlanders (later to die on Point 5120) seized a sword from a Japanese officer and killed its owner, along with several others. Dick Reynolds was a Sapper in 5 Field Company, Royal Engineers, given the task with his section of clearing up 'Bunker Hill', as it was now dubbed, following the attack, and of clearing Japanese corpses of booby traps. Captain Harry Swinson had walked up to watch Reynolds and his sappers at their work as they sorted through what was left of the Japanese position: looting was a favourite pastime of soldiers. The men prized Japanese flags and the remarkably explicit pornographic postcards which many Japanese carried, incongruously alongside photos of, and letters from, their loved ones, the British soldiers 'bursting with laughter when they found a 'filthy' one ... There were soldiers' pay-books too, surprisingly like ours in character. One sapper, seeing a figure entered in red, exclaimed: "My God, the little bugger's in debt!"'

~

Five and 161 Brigades joined hands for the first time on 16 April, offering hope of imminent relief to the defenders of the parachute-garlanded Garrison Hill two miles further on. In the meantime the three Lee Grants trundled back to the relative safety of Zubza, protected by the bayonets of Sergeant Fred Hazell's 18 Platoon. The following day Hazell went to investigate a report from one of his NCOs that 'Indian' troops were approaching, and nearly ran into what he assumed was a Japanese patrol, winding its way through the heavily-forested Zubza nullah. 'When I looked there was a bloody great Jap officer, big broad fellow and behind him I could see all these little hats bob-bobbing up and down.' Fortunately, he was not seen and rushed back to warn his men. He managed to get his platoon in a position overlooking the track below but he had miscalculated the size of the enemy 'patrol'.

> I was thinking there were nine of them at that stage. I said, 'Nobody fire until I give the word'. I got my rifle and waited for the 'nine' to appear. It became nine, ten, eleven, twelve, thirteen. In the end we had 100 of them lined up. As the first one started to disappear from view into the woods again, I fired and everyone joined in with rifle and Brens.

His men later counted thirty Japanese corpses. Hazell and his men had no difficulty obeying the special order that came on Friday 14 April from Major General John Grover to 'KILL JAPS, and to KILL AS MANY of them as we damned well can' but to do so 'without unnecessary casualties to ourselves. One well-aimed bullet is all that any JAP wants.' It seemed the natural thing to do. The Japanese were not, to the British soldier at least, a natural enemy, one with the same passion for life as themselves. If the Nip wanted to die, they surmised, it was their duty to help him on his way. But it made the Japanese a formidable and often, literally, an immoveable foe.

From the moment the men of 2nd Division arrived in the hills they were struck by the warmth of the welcome they received from the Nagas, who saw in their arrival the first fruits of Pawsey's promise that the British would defend their ancestral hills from the depredations of the invader. On Wednesday 19 April Swinson came into close contact with them for the first time. He was impressed by their hardiness, and self-evident willingness to fight the invader on the side of the British.

> A group of twenty or so Nagas came in during the morning. They were the first I had seen at close quarters, so I took a good look at them. A fine group of men they were, with dark, smooth-skinned limbs and a manly bearing. From the broad grins that traversed their faces you would never have guessed they'd had trouble with the Japs. Their dress... consisted firstly of a short, tight-fitting, skirt of some rough black material ... Their knees were covered by a series of bangles, piled one over the other. Their torso was left quite bare, though some older men wore bright red coatees ... Except for a cloth around their shoulders, that was all the dress proper, but Carmen Miranda herself was never more loaded with bangles, rings, necklaces, beads, ear-rings, charms, nick-nacks, and jew-jaws. These hung in great festoons from the ears, neck, and arms. Some men, I noticed, had white shells hanging down the nape of the neck. To complete the picture was their jet black hair, cut pudding-basin wise, and decorated with flowers, and, to spoil it, their black umbrellas ...

The Nagas were muscular, erect, proud, clad only with short woven skirts and wearing pudding basin haircuts. Metal-tipped spears rested in the crooks of their arms, while dull-metalled fishtail *daos* hung from their hips. They had a quiet enquiring yet unhurried courtesy that belied their recent history as head-hunting warriors of fearsome potency. Their children tumbled and squealed as they played, the very young strapped tightly to their mothers' backs in the colourful shawls of their tribe, each slightly different to each other but nevertheless shot through with red, a colour that seemed more than any other to represent the Naga people as a race. The British, who had instituted the post of *gaonbura*, had decreed that he, and he alone, could wear an entirely red blanket as a sign of his rank and authority. Woebetide any attempt to usurp this privilege. Swinson's account continued:

Elderfield, the Field Security Officer, received the Nagas. He motioned them to sit, which they did, solemnly in a circle, their headman stepping forward to make his speech. He spoke eloquently like a French politician, making quick, nervous gestures with his hands. I listened intently, but, except for catching the word 'Japani' understood not a thing.

After the proceedings had been translated into Urdu, Elderfield turned to the Brigade Major and said, 'What they want is rifles. The Japs have been coming to their village for food and, if they are refused, start to loot. They say that if the white sahibs will give them rifles, they'll be only too glad to shoot the Japanese and bring in their heads.' And rifles they got, Brigadier Hawkins agreeing wholeheartedly to the request. After all, there were plenty spare. 'A couple of hours later I saw them trekking away to the hills, their Japanese rifles carried proudly at the slope.'

Fred Weedman described the help provided to his battalion by the Nagas as 'beyond value or praise'. He recognized that without their support the battle would have been much prolonged, if it had been won at all. The people of the hills demonstrated their support to the British in a myriad of practical ways. On Thursday 27 April Harry Swinson watched a column of 5 Brigade wounded coming into Zubza after crossing the deep nullah on their journey from the Merema ridge on the left-hand side of the valley, heading for the Dressing Station at Milestone 42:

It was a precarious journey as a heavy shower of rain had rendered the precipitous tracks unnegotiable. Saw the slow, winding column come up to the road, the casualties lying quite still, obviously exhausted. Here they were transferred to ambulance cars, each car moving off as it received its four stretchers. The doctors were full of praise for the conduct of the Nagas. When the odd mortar bomb came over they had put the stretchers down under cover, and fanned the wounded men with branches till they could move on again. A great show this. I could see the [Medical Officer] was pleased. Had the Nagas shown they couldn't take it, a most difficult situation would have arisen; there aren't enough troops to do the job.

~

With the relief of the original garrison on Kohima Ridge, Grover now formulated a plan for the recapture of the entire Kohima area and the destruction of 31st Division, which held positions in a horseshoe shape, each side of which faced the British advance and the right side of which rested on the Merema ridge. His idea was that, whilst holding Zubza and Periphema to the rear, Brigadier John Shapland's 6 Brigade (1st Battalion, Royal Welch Fusiliers (Welch Fusiliers), 1st Battalion, Royal Berkshire Regiment (Berkshires) and the Durhams) would attack the Japanese in the centre, and gradually push them back on the southern and south-western flanks of the Kohima Ridge. At the same time, he planned two simultaneous flanking movements, one to the left (north) by Brigadier Victor Hawkins' 5 Brigade and one to the right (south) by Brigadier Willie Goschen's 4 Brigade. To the north he planned to roll up the long arm that Sato had thrown out along the valley side that ran from Naga Village along the ridge to Merema. To his right he planned something even more dramatic, namely to come at the Japanese far behind the mountain range that towers over Kohima's southern flank.

It was immediately clear to Grover, when he first saw the terrain at Zubza, looking up the valley to the dramatic ridge 'stopping the bottle' on the distant horizon, that the situation he faced entailed fighting many simultaneous, small-scale, infantry-dominated battles across a wide area. The heavily-jungled Naga hills swallowed large numbers of soldiers without trace, and single sections deeply dug into carefully-camouflaged bunkers could hold off companies for days; platoons could resist battalions and company positions were well nigh impregnable without many days and nights of direct and coordinated attack from the ground, by artillery and from the air, as well as by the deliberate starvation of the defenders through encirclement. The struggle for Kohima, which was now to consume his division for the next forty-seven days, was not a single set-piece engagement, but a desperate close-quarter infantry and artillery battle against tough and determined Japanese soldiers holding no ambition other than to die for their Emperor, and to trade their lives for the highest price. The entire duty of a *samurai* was to die in the service of the Emperor. Surrender was the ultimate humiliation: only death was sufficient to assuage the profound embarrassment of failure on the battlefield. Time and again British troops were confronted by the spectacle of a hopeless – and sometimes pathetic – *banzai* attack launched by Japanese troops for whom death at the hands of their enemy was the only honourable exit to an otherwise impossible predicament. Sato's division, when it moved from the attack to defence, dug itself deeply into many hundreds of small but interlocking defensive positions hidden in the jungle undergrowth across the entire Kohima area. It would be extremely difficult to dislodge them.

To cap it off, the monsoon had also begun. The rain belted down in buckets for long stretches of both day and night, turning roads and tracks into quagmires, filling trenches and bringing with it weeks of wet discomfort. The only saving grace of the monsoon was the low rain-laden clouds that clung to the hillsides like damp blankets and which gave a modicum of protection, for periods of time, from the omnipresent Japanese sniper.

On the left flank of 2nd Division Brigadier Hawkins despatched the first element of his brigade – a company of the Worcesters, with Naga guides – across the deep Zubza nullah to the Merema Ridge on the evening of 18 April, to cut the Kohima-Merema-Bokajan road. It was this column that was encountered by Aviü and the other refugees heading south from Biaku to Khonoma across the Zubza nullah. The journey entailed several hours of hard physical exertion, described in detail by Captain Ian Spalding.

> C Company, under Major Burrell MC, was chosen for this task and at eight o'clock at night we set out. The pace was necessarily slow because we had to move along goat tracks slippery with mud. As the crow flies, I don't suppose the journey was more than four or five miles and we reckoned it would take us till about midnight, but midnight came and we were still plodding along. Time passed and the company commander began to grow anxious; then at two o'clock word came back that the Naga guides had lost the track and could not go on. Detecting a certain shakiness in front, I went up to see if there was anything wrong. The column had broken and one platoon had disappeared into the blue, or rather the black. Dawn was rapidly approaching and suddenly a burst of machine-gun fire came from our left. I heard a voice I knew – that of our company sergeant major. He was a link between the broken halves of the company. Dawn was breaking and still we had not reached the road, so the company commander decided to stay where we were on a round-topped, jungle-covered hill, lie low till dark and then push on. We couldn't be very far from our objective, but the risk of travelling by daylight was too great.
>
> It was a pretty grim situation and the men were fully aware of its seriousness. Nevertheless, though tired, they were quite cheerful. The CSM had slipped down the cliff side, bruised his back and, worse still, broken his false teeth. There we lay for what seemed like endless hours. The sun came up, water bottles were emptied and by midday our throats were parched. Tentative crawlings revealed the road only three hundred yards away below us. One patrol spotted half-a-dozen Japs not more than 10 yards away.

It was obvious that there was water in the deep nullah on the other side of the road, so I took a patrol loaded with as many water bottles as we could carry. We reached the bottom of the hill and then had to dive for cover. Nearly a company of Japs were marching past, three or four deep, with mules and full kit. That ended all attempts to get water. We knew that if we were discovered the Brigade would be imperilled. Guides went back for the main body, and early next morning they moved in. The company commander and I went to investigate. They were Japs, quite oblivious to the fact that we were there too – cooking breakfast in a huge aluminium dixie and talking and laughing.

Major Burrell, armed with pistol and grenades and accompanied by one man, went round the left, and I, accompanied by another man, to the right. A full view revealed half-a-dozen Japs and as many mules and loads of kit. It was obviously a supply point on the route. We wriggled our way to within a few yards. Major Burrell contributed his grenades towards the breakfast and we let go with all we had. It was all over in a twinkling. The mules were brought back alive and everyone in the company had souvenirs varying from Jap riding boots to regimental flags.

In the following days the remainder of 5 Brigade made the journey across the valley, in single file and cutting across the front of the Japanese positions on Kohima Ridge. Not a man was lost. Within minutes of arriving at the road on the morning of 21 April, Lieutenant Arthur Carbonell of the Cameron Highlanders, later to die of wounds sustained on Naga Hill, encountered a Japanese sergeant major riding in the direction of Merema on a bicycle. The man was shot, his satchel revealing the orders to 1/138th Regiment to make its way to the south of Kohima and from there to assist Yamauchi's struggling 15th Division in the capture of Imphal, an order precipitated by the failure to secure Nunshigum. These orders had been received from Mutaguchi three days before. With the increasing pressure being placed on him by the arrival of 2nd Division, however, Sato saw no way of acceding to this demand, regarding it as evidence of Mutaguchi's ignorance of conditions on the Kohima battlefield. Although he assembled three battalions on the Aradura Spur in preparation for a move south, he made no other move to obey Mutaguchi's order, as it would, in his judgement, have dangerously reduced his own ability to secure a decisive advantage at Kohima.

Relations between the two men, never good, were now disintegrating.

Believing that he had been promised that at least 250 tons of resupplies would arrive by 8 April Sato testily demanded food and ammunition. In fact, very few supplies ever reached 31st Division from Burma, the men having to survive on what they had brought with them, what they could beg or steal from Naga villages, or what 'Churchill Rations' they could capture from British stockpiles. Sergeant Major Imanishi crossed the Chindwin with 270 cattle but reached Naga Village with only fourteen. 'The remainder are dead, worn out on the journey or fell down into the valley,' he reported despondently. Lieutenant Masao Hirakubo was the quartermaster to 3/58th Regiment, responsible for feeding 1,000 men. He suspected that the supply situation would become difficult and after discovering twenty warehouses in Kohima Village full of rice and salt on his arrival on 5 April determined to recover all of it, despite the exhaustion of the men.

> I thought it essential to secure the food and asked the battalion commander to lend some men to carry out rice from the warehouses during the night. The adjutant bluntly refused, as all the soldiers were fast asleep after the hard march in the mountains and the work could be done the next day. So I argued and fought with him and the commander finally supplied me with fifty soldiers. I took command of the men and carried as much rice and salt as possible to a valley. Next morning many British planes bombed the warehouses and everything was turned to ashes. I regretted not to have carried more.

Such was Lieutenant Hirakubo's foresight that when the retreat began on 1 June 'we still had some rice left which we divided among all the men in the battalion'. Unfortunately for the Japanese, there were far too few supply officers in 31st Division with the prescience of the young Lieutenant Hirakubo.

Sato's fury at the lack of promised supplies reaching Kohima was fuelled by his belief that 31st Division was being let down by Mutaguchi's abject failure to break into Imphal. In response to Mutaguchi's demand that he send troops to assist in the Imphal battle, on 20 April Sato sent the first of a number of increasingly tetchy signals to the Army Commander, 'We captured Kohima in three weeks as promised. How about Imphal?' Mutaguchi replied, 'Probable date for capture of Imphal April 29 [the Emperor's birthday].' Sato plainly did not believe him. Mutaguchi's physical and mental remoteness from the battlefield (he was in Maymyo, far away in the cool hills east of Mandalay) combined with a fatal unwillingness by his staff to give him unpalatable news, meant that he never properly understood the true situation at Kohima. On 30 April Sato signalled again: '31st Division at the limit of its endurance. When are you going to destroy Imphal?' He received no reply.

With no knowledge of Sato's developing difficulties, by 27 April the entirety of Hawkins' 5 Brigade was safely ensconced on the Merema ridge, threatening the right flank of Sato's horseshoe.

~

Meanwhile, in the centre the long struggle for the Kohima Ridge showed no let-up with the relief of the original garrison of the siege. The Berkshires, Dorsets and Durhams occupied Garrison Hill, the Berkshires and Dorsets overlooking the Tennis Court and the Durhams facing south out to Kuki Picquet. Major Francis Boshell commanded B Company of the Berkshires:

> To begin with I took over an area overlooking the Tennis Court, although only my left forward platoon could see the Court. The Dorsets were responsible for the position closest to the court itself. The lie of the land made it impossible to move by day because of Japanese snipers. We were attacked every single night. On the worst night they started at 1900 hours and the last attack came in at 0400 hours the following morning. They came in waves: it was like a pigeon shoot. Most nights they overran part of the battalion position, so we had to mount counter-attacks. When part of my right-hand forward platoon was overrun, we winkled them out with the bayonet. I lost two platoon commanders, but good sergeants took over, and did better. Water was short and restricted to about one pint per man per day. So we stopped shaving. Air supply was the key, but the steep terrain and narrow ridges meant that some of the drops went to the Japs. My company went into Kohima over 100 strong and came out at about 60.

The relief of the Royal West Kents between 18 and 20 April meant that Sato now recognized that it would be better to go onto the defensive, forcing the British to attack, rather than continuing to waste increasingly scarce men on the British position that had now held out for nearly three weeks, and which, despite its fragility, showed no signs of falling. He observed to Colonel Yamaki, his Intelligence officer, 'We're losing so many troops this way that before long we'll be too thin on the ground to achieve anything.' One last attack on Garrison Hill was launched on the night of 23

April. It coincided with plans for the Durhams to launch their own attack on Kuki Picquet early the following morning. Lieutenant Shosaku Kameyama:

> On the night of 23 April the remnant, thirty men of 7th Company, attacked Garrison Hill supported by machine guns and only a few shells of the mountain gun, and captured the front-line position. But when a company of 138th Regiment went ahead to the hilltop, petrol drums stored by the enemy caught fire and all advance routes were blocked by the spreading flames, lighting up the battlefield like daytime. As the attackers were shot at from the hilltop, the commander had to give up the attack.

Corporal Bob Blenkinsop of the Durhams was preparing to attack Kuki Picquet when the Japanese attacked.

> I was in a raiding party ready to attack a Japanese position at dawn. [A]s I and the rest of the party were doing our last-minute checks, the call went up that the Japanese were attacking us. We rushed to meet them coming forward. The battle was very intense and very bloody. I found myself in the middle of hand-to-hand fighting with a Japanese soldier. I knew if I did not kill him, he would kill me without another thought so my survival instinct came to the front and I plunged my bayonet into the Japanese soldier and moved on to the next. There were a lot wounded but we could not help them as we had to keep fighting. This lasted until the sun started to shine at the first glimpse of dawn.

The Japanese used phosphorus grenades to clear each trench they encountered. CSM Martin McLane of C Company of the Durhams was woken by shouts from his company commander, Major Roger Stock (who was soon to be killed), to see

> green phosphorus was pouring into one end of the trench, I was covered in the stuff, which causes deep penetrating burns. I was rubbing the stuff off me with earth, then the Japs came in yelling and shouting. They were in among us and just ten yards away there was a fearsome looking man waving a sword. But we did for him.

Lieutenant Pat Rome remembered climbing into a trench the night before with Sergeant Brannigan and his batman, Private Joe Wilson. Pulling a groundsheet over the trench, lighting up cigarettes, they considered that with a good hole and the prospect of a night's sleep they were having a good war. They were awakened in the early hours by the unmistakeable sounds of an attack. Each man grabbed his weapon and inexplicably climbed out of the trench. It was the wrong thing to do, Brannigan and Wilson being killed almost immediately. Later, caught in a shower of grenades, the Japanese ones distinctive by the little tail of blue light sailing behind through the air, Rome was knocked flat by a blast, his arm broken. He spent the rest of the day crawling from trench to trench with Bren-gun magazines, his useless arm, limp but numb and painless, resting in a makeshift sling.

The attacking Japanese were illuminated by the fires, and shot down en masse. Kameyama recorded that the failure of this attack reduced the size of the battalion to a skeleton. 'After the attack our rifle companies which originally had 180 men each were reduced to four in the 5th, four in the 6th, sixteen in the 7th and none in the 8th. Machine Gun Company had thirty-five and Battalion Gun Platoon fifteen. With such small numbers of men we were not able to attack any more.' But British casualties were also heavy, McLane noting that his 'company commander, the runners, and the signallers were all dead. A shell had landed right into a shell hole they were standing in'. The Durhams lost fifteen officers and over 100 men. Captain Sean Kelly, the commander of A Company, Durhams was astonished at the courage of the stretcher-bearers.

> Every now and then there would be a crack and nearly always a groan or cry for help and the stretcher-bearers would rush forward, kneel where the man had been hit, dress him, and carry him off! What cold-blooded courage! It's nothing to charge in hot blood, but to kneel and do your job where a man has just been hit, and where you must be hit too, if another comes, is the bravest thing I know.

Two stretcher-bearers were recommended for the award of the Victoria Cross. Major Alexander Wilson recorded,

> In A, C and D Companies there was a total of four officers left. Of the original 136 men in A Company, only sixty were left. The pioneer and carrier platoons also lost many killed and wounded. The fighting there was hand-to-hand. Men were kept going by training, regimental pride, and the will to survive.

The discordant noise of desperate battle was incessant, a constant bass orchestra of artillery and mortars reverberating around the valley, the sounds of the weapons firing at Zubza and Jotsoma mixing with the reports of the explosions two miles away on the Kohima Ridge. The British 25-

pounder gun/howitzer was an ideal weapon in this terrain, as it boasted a high elevation of fire that meant it could engage targets relatively close by. There was plenty of ammunition available at this stage of the battle, although later battles were startlingly deficient of fire support as supplies ran low. Major 'Tank' Waterhouse, the commander of C Company of the Durhams recalled the fire support on to Kuki as 'first class', 3.7s, 25-pounders and mortars firing 1,300 rounds and causing the Japanese heavy casualties. The belting staccato of machine guns added a different tone to the cacophony, as did the almost constant sound of aircraft – British ground attack and transport aircraft, and Japanese fighters making forays from across the Chindwin. On Monday 24 April Swinson watched RAF Vengeances attack Garrison Hill, followed by a supply drop by lumbering and vulnerable Dakota transport planes.

> A dozen of them, and they dived, straightened out, bombed, and climbed again. It was the first air-strike the troops had seen ... As the Vengeances flew away over came the supply planes. Very low and cumbersome, they steered for Hospital Hill. The parachutes came down, two or three at a time, glinting white in the afternoon sun. The planes flew in a circle, each dropping in turn; apparently it takes six or more runs to empty a plane load. IGH Spur, which is already flecked with white like the hide of a cheetah, will soon look completely snow-capped. The parachutes are lodged up in the trees and it is not yet possible to salvage them.
>
> Heard later the drop was only 35 per cent successful, the bulk, presumably, having gone to the Japs. If we go on like this, they'll be holding out for months.

The bitter battles on Kohima Ridge continued inconclusively for the following two weeks. Increasingly desperate attacks on the extreme northern edge of the Ridge – around the Tennis Court – took place in late-April to open up the road that led left from the TCP, to allow access for a troop of Lee Grant tanks to lumber up the back (i.e., western) end of Naga Hill in order to provide armoured support for 5 Brigade as it advanced slowly along the left flank from Merema. On Garrison Hill the Dorsets and the Berkshires fought to defend their water-logged trenches from repeated Japanese assaults and the regular exchanges of grenades across the few yards that separated both sides. Major Geoffrey White of the Dorsets was appalled at the sight of Garrison Hill when he saw it for the first time, recording that

> in some places where the Jap had put in a '*Banzai*' attack his dead lay piled deep where they had fallen in their assault on our positions.

In a steep gully not forty yards from the club square, at the top of which lay one of our posts, were piled high the bodies of about a hundred and fifty of the enemy who had perished as they made one of their suicidal attacks against the Royal Berks.

The plan to get tanks onto the back of Naga Hill by driving through the Japanese positions overlooking the TCP finally succeeded on 27 April, the Lee Grants trundling along the track, wary of mines, but taking the Japanese entirely by surprise at this stroke of legerdemain. Peppered on all sides futilely by bullets, they joined 5 Brigade on Naga Hill, albeit at the cost of twenty-eight Dorset dead, who had kept intense pressure on the TCP end of the Kohima Ridge to distract the Japanese during the operation.

In the fighting for control of the Tennis Court no means of overcoming Japanese bunkers could be discovered using infantry alone, and attempts were made to bulldoze a path up to the remains of the Deputy Commissioner's bungalow to allow a Lee Grant tank to move onto the Tennis Court and engage the bunkers directly with its 75mm gun. As Geoffrey White suggested, 'if we could only get a medium tank on to the tennis court, serving some pretty fast balls from the north end, the Nip would not stay to finish the set.' Unhappily, the first effort failed when the Lee Grant went into reverse, pulling the bulldozer to which it was attached back down the steep slope in a heap of crashing, twisted metal. Four days later a similar attempt with a Stuart light tank of 45th Indian Light Cavalry also failed, as the Japanese had brought up a 37mm anti-tank gun that put the tank out of action, fortunately with no loss to the crew. It was now time for the forward companies to be relieved. On 3 May, White watched with 'a large lump in my throat' as the remnants of Major John Bowles' once-100-man A Company were relieved after five days' fighting to keep the road open to 5 Brigade. The twenty-eight 'blackened and red-eyed' survivors, who had 'hung on by the skin of their teeth against almost overwhelming opposition' for five and a half days, made their way back into battalion reserve under the cover of a smoke screen.

~

While Hawkins' 5 Brigade was moving into the left flank and Shapland's 6 Brigade was battling away on the parachute-shrouded Kohima Ridge, on the right flank, Brigadier Willie Goschen's 4 Brigade, consisting of 1st Battalion, Royal Scots (Royal Scots) and the Norfolks had been ordered to carry out a daring flank march to the south of Kohima to cut the Imphal Road below the Aradura Spur, beginning on the night of 25 April. This was a distance of seven miles on the map, three or four times that on the ground, and it was estimated that it would take four days. It was a journey that even Pawsey's Nagas insisted was, if not impossible, then certainly not one that they or their forefathers had ever undertaken. They would give it a try, nevertheless, if the British believed it necessary. The terrain is the most intimidating and hostile of the entire region, comprising deep, almost vertical, jungle-covered gullies falling between the rear of Mount Pulebadze and the face of Mount Japfü, underneath a canopy of green through which the sun never penetrates. The third battalion in the brigade, 1/8th Lancashire Fusiliers (Lancashire Fusiliers), were on loan to 5 Brigade on the division's left flank, so 4 Brigade had been reinforced by 143 Special Service Company, originally formed for amphibious operations in the Arakan, and stronger than a normal company, together with A Company of 2nd Battalion, Manchester Regiment (Manchesters), the divisional machine-gun battalion. Captain John Howard was the Intelligence Officer of 4 Brigade.

> The country was difficult and for the final stage, we knew that there were no trails and that we should have to cut our own way through the forest which covered the seven-thousand-foot ridge over which we should have to climb to reach the Aradura. Three hundred Naga porters carried the heavier loads of wireless sets and mortars and rations; when we arrived we were to be supplied by air.

Sergeant Fred Hazell was amazed at the loads the 'merry, gentle, courageous and apparently tireless' Nagas were able to carry, watching incredulously 'men, women, young lads and even young girls carrying ammunition and water'. Despite the help provided by the Nagas, every soldier was still heavily laden.

> We were issued with 100 rounds of ammunition in addition to what we already had. This we carried in two bandoleers. Blankets were cut in half, and rolled up on top of our packs. Every third man was given a shovel, every third man a pick, and the other third two carriers of mortar bombs [a total of six bombs, each weighing 10lb].

Sergeant Bert 'Winkle' Fitt, who commanded 9 Platoon, B Company of the Norfolks, spoke for everyone else at the start of the brigade's extraordinary journey when he remarked, 'We didn't expect the climb and the march to be quite as fierce as it was.' For Lieutenant Sam Horner, the Battalion

Signals Officer, the physical demands of the march through what was soon dubbed 'Death Valley' were extreme.

> The physical hammering one takes is difficult to understand. The heat, humidity, altitude and the slope of almost every foot of ground combine to knock hell out of the stoutest constitution. You gasp for air which doesn't seem to come, you drag your legs upwards till they seem reduced to the strength of matchsticks, you wipe the sweat out of your eyes. Then you feel your heart pounding so violently you think it must burst its cage; it sounds as loud as a drum, even above the swearing and cursing going on around you. So you stop, horrified to be prodded by the man behind you or cursed by an officer in front. Eventually long after everything tells you should have died of heart failure, you reach what you imagine is the top of the hill; to find it is a false crest, and the path still lies upwards. And when you finally get to the top, there is a hellish climb down. You forget the Japs, you forget time, you forget hunger and thirst. All you can think of is the next halt.

On day three, after covering four miles on the map, the brigade lay deep in the valley between Pulebadze and Mount Japfü, a miserable, wet and gloomy world hidden under the jungle canopy, lit only by the glowing phosphorescence of rotting vegetation, when a message arrived from Stopford. Instead of attempting to carry on to the Aradura Spur, the brigade was ordered to climb left over the Pulebadze Ridge and come down on the Kohima side to fall against the Japanese positions on the GPT Ridge, which were proving a serious hindrance to the troops of 6 Brigade attempting to overcome the defiant Japanese defenders on Kohima Ridge. The brigade accordingly turned left, climbing up and over the Pulebadze Ridge and beginning the slow descent through the jungle down onto the Kohima side. A prominent pimple above the GPT Ridge, known as Oaks Hill, sitting at 6,000 feet, was occupied by the Norfolks and 143 Company on 1 May, the presence of British troops 1,500 feet above the Japanese positions becoming known to them for the first time.

The heavy jungle on the slopes of Mount Pulebadze meant it was almost impossible to tell where one was, however, and judging where the Japanese position might be on GPT Ridge could not be considered an exact science. Four Brigade had to make its uncertain way down the slopes, therefore, feeling its way, in torrential rain, alert for the Japanese. 'We could see absolutely bugger all,' recalled Captain John Howard,

I suppose we were a couple of miles from the [Kohima-Imphal] road and immediately below one was heavy jungle. I know it was clear [of trees] down by the road, but they were all reverse convex slopes and you couldn't see what was beyond the slope. It was too far away. I saw two chaps walking along the road, but even with binoculars you couldn't tell whether they were soldiers, Japs or Nagas – they might have been anybody.

The Royal Scots stopped and occupied Oaks Hill, the brigade artillery back in Jotsoma on standby to pound any Japanese positions the Norfolks, who were pressing on down the ridge, encountered. The Japanese, alert now to the dangerous presence of enemy troops above them, moved up against Oaks Hill and fought hard to expel the Royal Scots during that first night, with no success. The morning that followed a night of screaming, fear-inducing attacks found the jungle undergrowth littered with Japanese bodies. It was usual practice for the Japanese to take away their dead and wounded, but on this occasion there were too few Japanese survivors for the task.

On 4 May the Norfolks found themselves in a position to assault the topmost slopes of GPT Ridge, led by their dynamic CO, Lieutenant Colonel Robert Scott. Despite the fighting the previous night at Oaks Hill above them, the Norfolks achieved almost complete surprise during their aggressive and fast-moving attack. But the Norfolks managed to seize only the topmost bunkers. They had secured the upper part of GPT Ridge while, simultaneously, Indian troops of 161 Indian Brigade captured the area south-east of Two Tree Hill, offering the possibility of linking Jotsoma with 4 Brigade on the forward slopes of Pulebadze for the first time. But the Japanese bunker complex on GPT was much more substantial than the British had expected, with literally dozens of small, carefully-sited bunkers littering the entire area with interlocking arcs of fire, while the entire position was also covered by Japanese machine guns further to the east on Aradura Spur. No sooner would one be discovered and attacked, than another would open up against the attackers from somewhere else. Until the entirety of GPT was cleared, Goschen's Brigade could not enjoy the short-cut through to Jotsoma via Two Tree Hill, the road to Imphal remained in Japanese hands and their machine guns continued to spray fire on 6 Brigade's exposed right flank.

~

The other operations by 2nd Division on 4/5 May were less successful, however. In the centre, attacks by 6 Brigade on Kuki Picquet and FSD Ridge did not meet with any material success. Fighting went on throughout the day and the attacking troops suffered heavy casualties. In their attack on Kuki Picquet the Welch lost two company commanders, three platoon commanders and some sixty killed. The Durhams, whose task had been to drive round the ridge on Bren carriers (supported by Lee Grant tanks) and to attack from the western edge of the ridge, also lost heavily, although by the evening of Thursday 4 May they had obtained a precarious toe-hold on FSD, which was to hold firm for a further week. Major David Wilson was ensconced with his brigade commander in a dug-out on Garrison Hill, when a Hurribomber mistook its target and landed a bomb on top of his position.

> It exploded with a loud report, but luckily did no physical damage to anyone. John Shapland was furious, and rang up our RAF liaison officer at Divisional Headquarters to complain. He did not get much change: 'I'm terribly sorry, Brigadier,' said the liaison officer. 'Quite disgraceful; I shall report him at once. Did you get his number?'

On the left flank 5 Brigade made slow but painful progress, the Cameron Highlanders and Lancashire Fusiliers securing a small part of Naga Village during the night of 4 May after discarding their heavy hobnailed boots for quieter gym shoes, which allowed them successfully to bypass enemy positions on Merema Ridge and seize Church Knoll and Hunter Hill. Attempts at the end of April by the Lancashire Fusiliers to capture Japanese fortified positions along the ridge from Merema had ended in failure, and Hawkins decided that it would be best to bypass them, allowing them to wither on the vine while he concentrated his efforts on the main Japanese position, and Sato's HQ on Naga Village. Unfortunately, the Cameron Highlanders did not have time to consolidate their success by digging in, heavy Japanese mortar fire at daylight forcing the Jocks back to the western edge of the hill. Here Hawkins had them dig to secure the ground that had been seized and the Worcesters, who had protected the flanks of the night advance, were called up to help build a defensive position able to resist counter-attack. 'C Company dug in on Church Knoll,' recorded Weedman, 'which consisted of a ridge which overlooked 'Treasury' [to the south] where the Japanese had constructed bunkers. Each one provided cover for another and so made it very difficult for such a position to be assaulted.'

The rain was by now constant. Fred Weedman was constantly

'drenched to the skin, slipping and slithering, as we floundered in water-logged trenches, like the army of a generation before. On the steep hillsides, the tracks were turned into treacherous mudslides.' The next morning the Japanese Air Force made one of their occasional forays into the deep valley which flowed out of the Kohima Ridge westward. Harry Swinson watched four Zeros which came

> flying low and swept down the valley through the flak that was already filling the sky, to strafe Div H.Q. and the forward gun positions. A quick wheel before Kohima Ridge and they came roaring down on us, their cannons blazing. The flak by this time was thicker than ever, but the Zeros seemed equipped with immortality. Ten seconds and they were on us, so low that I felt I could reach up and pluck them out of the sky.

Unfortunately the huge barrage of small-arms ammunition sent skywards failed to hit their target.

~

Meanwhile, on the green slopes of Pulebadze on 6 May, B Company of the Norfolks, commanded by Captain Jack Randle, was ordered to seize the remaining part of the bunker position at the bottom of GPT Ridge, while 4/1st Gurkhas of Brigadier Freddie Loftus Tottenham's newly arrived 33 Indian Brigade (which had begun to replacing the battered British 6 Brigade on Kohima Ridge, having arrived by Dakota from Arakan between 5 and 9 April), assisting the breakthrough in the centre against Kohima Ridge and Jail Hill, were to attack the lower, western slopes of GPT. In these attacks the Norfolks were to seize the remaining Japanese bunkers but at high cost, in which Captain Randle was awarded the VC posthumously. The Norfolks remained in the positions they had seized and, after a night of heavy rain, a further attempt to attack the remaining Japanese positions was made at first light on the morning of 7 May by the 4/1st Gurkhas and the Royal Scots. It was important that this operation was successful, as at 10.30 a.m. an attempt was to be made by 1st Queen's – part of 33 Indian Brigade, who had arrived at Kohima exhausted and malaria-ridden from Arakan the day before – on Jail Hill. If the machine-gun nests on GPT could be wiped out *before* the Queens attacked they would enjoy a much higher chance of success. The only achievement on GPT that day, however, was bloody stalemate, with both Lieutenant Colonel Hedderwick of 4/1st Gurkhas and Brigadier Goschen being shot dead by snipers. The Queen's, aware that 4 Brigade had not managed to secure GPT, nevertheless went in against Jail Hill as planned, and were slaughtered. In retrospect the attack was premature, but Stopford continued to demand speed to remove the Japanese stranglehold on Kohima in order to relieve beleaguered Imphal.

There was a belief in some higher quarters – in particular by those whose only experience of the terrain came from reading a map in the comfort of a headquarters tent in the rear – that 2nd Division's offensive lacked pace. These accusations, to the hard-pressed men on the ground, were preposterous. It was impossible for commanders and staff officers in the rear who could not see the ground to understand how a small piece of jungle-topped hillside could absorb the best part of a brigade; how a small group of well-sited bunkers could hold up an advance until every single one – together with every single occupant – had been systematically destroyed; how only medium artillery (the 5.5-inch medium gun) could penetrate the roof of a Japanese trench; how only direct and short-range sniping by Lee Grant tanks was guaranteed to defeat a Japanese bunker; how the desperate terrain, incessant rain and humidity led even the fittest men quickly to tire and what an extraordinarily determined opponent they faced. With few exceptions, the Japanese only gave in when they were dead. Every conscious man who could lift a weapon fought until he collapsed. An officer of the Japanese 58th Regiment recalled,

> Even the invalids and the wounded were driven to the front to help supply manpower. Even those with broken legs in splints were herded into battle, malaria cases too. I have seen these going forward with yellow faces, the fever still in their bodies. I saw one man, whose shoulder had been shattered by a bullet, stagger forward to the front. Some of the wounded who were over forty fondly hoped that they would be sent home, but even they were sent forward.

As the early dawn began to break on the morning of 7 May Major Michael Lowry, the Officer Commanding B Company, 1st Queen's, lay on the ground observing Jail Hill, listening to 'the screech and thunder of battle'.

> As we peered through the rain, the low clouds and smoke from the artillery and mortars, we were looking at what appeared to be a dozen different battles going on in front of us. There were the sustained noises of belting machine-gun fire, the cracks and zips of sniper bullets, punctuated by the shrieks and crumps of artillery and mortar fire. At this stage we did not know whose firing was the heavier, or from where.

With his company in battalion reserve, Lowry was forced to watch first the men of D Company, and then those in A, being cut down in large numbers as they attempted to attack the hill, struck by machine-gun and rifle fire from the right (GPT) flank.

> By 11.40 a.m. our artillery concentrations on Jail Hill had lifted and D Company had begun their climb up the spur just this side of the road. As the haze and smoke of the bombardment lifted they soon came under very heavy cross-fire from DIS and FSD on their left and from their right by machine guns firing straight down the road, probably from positions on GPT. Through my field-glasses I could see D Company moving with determination, but I could also see what a terrible time they were having as men were hit and dropped to the ground, they were getting casualties before they crossed the road. Then they moved up the hill itself, one platoon to the right and one up the left. Over the wireless set the CO gave the OK to A Company to go [at 1.20 p.m.].

Before long, however, it was clear that the Queen's were unable to make a toe-hold on Jail Hill, and Lieutenant Colonel Duncombe, the Commanding Officer, ordered the battalion back, Lowry's B Company going forward under smoke to help recover the wounded.

~

This day was described by Swinson as the 'Black 7th' and 'probably the most depressing for the Allies in the whole battle'. At its end, after thirty-four days of some of the toughest fighting experienced anywhere during the Second World War, the Japanese still held all the key ground, together with all of that, and more, which they had seized since 4 April. British morale was edging lower as the men struggled to contemplate how the intransigent Japanese might be moved from their bunkers. The Japanese feat of arms at Kohima was a miracle of defensive tenacity rarely matched anywhere else in the annals of war. Despite their lack of supplies Sato's troops dug themselves in with skill and imagination, ensuring that each bunker was mutually supported. Sato's defensive technique, while it was not going to enable him to break through Kohima by dint of offensive action, was designed to do the next best thing: to draw the enemy onto defences of great complexity and depth and to break them there, both physically and morally. In so doing, his troops had to withstand the sort of conditions few other soldiers in history could have survived. They did so, and very nearly succeeded in persuading Stopford that battering through Kohima was an impossible task. Between the 4th and 'Black 7th', for instance, the thirty-eight 3.7-inch mountain guns dug in around Jotsoma fired over 3,000 rounds, the forty-eight 25-pounders fired over 7,000 rounds and the big 5.5-inch guns of the medium artillery had fired more than 1,500 shells at the Japanese positions, not to mention the almost continuous salvos from the massed 3-inch mortars of the infantry battalions and the constant strafing and bombing by Hurricanes and Vengeance dive-bombers. In spite of this almost endless torrent of fire and steel, Sato's troops continued to fight back doggedly and skilfully, boasting little more than their courage and resolve as, with virtually no air support, only a few artillery pieces and anti-tank guns, they repeatedly kept even the most determined British attacks at bay. Their strength of mind and willingness to fight to the death demonstrated the highest physical and moral courage and gained the grudging admiration of their enemies.

In the weeks that followed, 5 Brigade on the left flank, 6 Brigade on Garrison Hill, 33 Indian Brigade on the southernmost slopes of the Kohima Ridge, and 4 Brigade (now under the command of Robert Scott of the Norfolks after Brigadier Theobalds, Goschen's successor, was himself mortally wounded), ate away slowly at the Japanese defences. Nowhere were sudden gains made, but by gradual perseverance and the application of focused firepower the Japanese were destroyed, bunker by bunker, trench by trench. Rarely did the Japanese run, or retreat, remaining to die where they fought. Lieutenant Lintorn Highett of the Dorsets considered the Japanese to be magnificent trench warriors.

> Every army in the world talks about holding positions to the last man. Virtually no other army, including the Germans, ever did – but the Japs did. Their positions were well sited and they had a good eye for the ground. They relied on rushing and shouting in the attack. We thought they were formidable fighting insects and savages. We took few prisoners – about one or two in the whole war. We wanted prisoners, but wounded men would have a primed grenade under them, so stretcher-bearers were very careful.

But for Lieutenant Kameyama, being on the defensive was a lonely and depressing existence:

> Although we kept fighting it was very lonely and miserable to stay isolated in a foxhole on the mountain in the situation when a chance of winning seemed too remote. We ran out of ammunition and food, so sometimes we went out to attack an enemy position at night, and

when the enemy ran away after firing several rounds, we collected rations, bullets and grenades, and used them the next day. In this way we held out stoutly day by day, but inevitably someone got hurt or killed, so only a few, maximum seven to eight, men defended a position. It was heartbreaking that even if one did his best, nothing could help. And it was even more heartbreaking that one's comrade had to do more work if one became unable to move. If he were heavily injured he would regret over-taxing his mates. Those men passed away saying, 'Excuse me. I regret dying.' They died apologizing and weeping. The battlefield takes the life of such brave men, and there is no way of helping them.

We were short of food, but most distressing was that we did not have bullets. Still we did not give up and never thought of running away.

Talking of the struggle on Naga Hill between 5 and 15 May, Colour Sergeant Fred Weedman described the Japanese as

fanatically stubborn defenders. Artillery attacks and Hurricane and Vengeance bombers had little positive effect. The British and Japanese were hopelessly intermingled. One side would attack, the other counter-attack: neither would give way. During daylight they fought ferociously ten or fifteen yards apart, and at night they crept even closer attacking with grenades and bayonets.

The fighting was so close, so intense, that bullets were no respecter of rank. Second British Division lost four brigadiers in the Kohima battle, two killed and two wounded. On 12 May Brigadier Victor Hawkins was wounded on Naga Hill, being shot (in David Wilson's words) 'through his right hand and his scrotum (without serious damage to either). Let that be a lesson to you, David,' [Hawkins] said 'waving goodbye with his damaged flipper; "Never scratch your balls in the face of the enemy!"'

~

But British progress, though slow, remained sure, even though, to the troops on the ground, it seemed as if this battle would go on for ever. Four Brigade cleared GPT Ridge on 11 May, by which time further costly attacks by 6 British and 33 Indian Brigades had finally forced the Japanese to relinquish their hold on Pimple Hill, FSD and Jail Hill, the last of which was captured by the Queen's and C Company, 4/1st Gurkha Rifles. 'Each Japanese position had to be individually dealt with,' recalled David

Wilson, 'and this was a very slow business. We were slowly strangling them with our air and artillery power, but starving or not, 31st Division was not in any mood to give in.' Lowry's company had marched through the night to reach its forming-up point just short of the Japanese positions. At 5.00 a.m., following a twenty-minute artillery bombardment, the Queen's rushed the first bunkers and within the hour had reached the summit, isolating and grenading each bunker one by one. Then, as the dawn light exposed them to fire from the GPT flank, Lowry called for smoke, enabling his company to carry on down the reverse slope, hurling grenades.

> It was the nearest approach to a snowball fight that could be imagined. The air became thick with grenades, both theirs and ours. We were all scurrying about trying to avoid them as they burst. This duel appeared to go on non-stop for an unreckonable time.

Under the cover of smoke and low-lying monsoon mist, the Queensmen frantically dug themselves in. By 6.45 p.m. two officers and twenty-eight soldiers of Lowry's company remained, from the seventy who had started early that morning. By nightfall, too, 4/15th Punjab and D Company, 4/1st Gurkha Rifles managed, in their second attempt that day, to capture DIS, and to cling on to their precarious hold under intense fire that night. For several hours, however, it was touch and go. Major Arthur Marment of 4/15th Punjab was not sure that his men could retain their grasp on the position.

> It was extremely difficult ... we were being hit from FSD and Jail Hill and had taken 130 casualties. It was impossible to move because snipers seemed to be everywhere, and we could not make much impression on the main bunker. We were digging with our hands, grabbing every tin to fill, and getting as tight to the ground as we possibly could.

But they did. The tide was slowly – and painfully – beginning to turn. On the days that followed the positions seized on 11 and 12 May were carefully consolidated, the remaining Japanese being exterminated one by one, sniper by sniper and gun by gun. No one could ever assume that a position was fully cleared until every body, every trench, every clump of undergrowth or pile of rubbish had been painstakingly checked over as sometimes, days after a position had been apparently 'captured', a corpse in his foxhole might pop up and fire off his last remaining rounds or throw a grenade at an unsuspecting soldier. The Berkshires cleared FSD on 12

May, discovering that the Japanese had honey-combed the hill with tunnels, creating an elaborate underground fortress that included a battalion headquarters, repair shop, ammunition storage dump and hospital. Fortunately, the monsoon rain reduced visibility dramatically, bringing with it cloud that worked as effectively as smoke as an obscurant, acting dramatically to reduce the volume of sniper fire which, until the last, remained a pestilential curse across the battlefield. Those Japanese bunkers on the western edge of the ridge that remained out of reach of the British artillery could now be engaged directly and at point-blank range by the Lee Grants, trundling up the road that divides DIS and Jail Hill. They did so to the cheers of the British and Indian infantry, who often found themselves hugging the ground as the 75mm smashed the enemy foxholes only yards from them, the ground shaking and the shockwave of the blast sucking out their breath and showering them with dirt and debris.

On the northernmost edge of Kohima Ridge on 13 May the sorely-depleted Dorsets finally captured the smouldering remains of Pawsey's bungalow. On that day a final attempt to get a Lee Grant onto the Tennis Court succeeded. The tanks of 150th Regiment RAC under the command of Major Ezra Rhodes were accompanied and protected by men of the Dorsets, fire from the lumbering leviathans allowing the infantry to close with the bunkers. Richard Sharp, a BBC correspondent, was on hand to report the scene of the Dorsets' triumph, albeit one that had cost the lives of seventy-five men. When it was broadcast a few nights later it was the first time that an audience in the United Kingdom had had any news of the dramatic struggle high in the Naga Hills brought into their homes. He was not allowed to mention the Dorsets by name but

> The men who took it came from a battalion of a West Country regiment. They've been plugging away at that Tennis Court for sixteen days, and when I got there at noon they were on it at last. In these sixteen days they'd become personal enemies of the Japs there, who used to taunt them at dusk, calling across the tennis court: 'Have you stood-to yet?' ... Here's hoping that they hold the tennis court through the night.

They did. The capture of the southern end of the Kohima Ridge a full thirty-seven days after the first arrival of Sato's men enabled Rhodes' Lee Grant tanks finally to trundle their way around the road and to use their guns against the remaining bunkers on the lower slopes of both Pimple Hill and GPT Spur. The Norfolk Bunker which had cost the life of the gallant

Jack Randle was finally taken by the Royal Scots with support from the tanks. Then, on 15 May, patrols from 5 Brigade moved down from Naga Hill, secured Treasury Hill and met up with the victors of Kohima Ridge on the Imphal road.

The capture of the Kohima Ridge was a remarkable triumph for the men of the British 2nd and the Indian 7th Divisions, following those who had held on so grimly under Richards' command at the start of the siege. But across the rest of the Kohima area lay a string of other Japanese positions, all of which remained to be eliminated: there was never any expectation that they might surrender, and they needed to be cleared by hand, inch by inch. Two principal redoubts remained: Point 5120 on Naga Hill and the Aradura Spur, the last remaining barrier on the road to Imphal.

~

On Sunday 14 May Harry Swinson went forward from the Brigade rear HQ position at Zubza to cross the valley in order to visit the three battalions (Lancashire Fusiliers, Worcesters and Cameron Highlanders) on Naga Hill. He was shocked by the filth of the place and the strained, unkempt look of his friends. The relentless monsoon rains made conditions appalling for the troops in their forward dug-outs. 'Apart from flooding roads and rendering Jeep tracks unjeepable, it has a bad effect on the morale and condition of the troops,' he wrote. 'The infantry, as usual, get the worst of it. Living in water-logged slit trenches, their clothes soaked, their boots sodden, their food when they get it often cold and mushy, life rapidly becomes almost insupportable.' The following day he arranged bathing facilities for his battalion. Fred Weedman:

> We wrapped our razors, combs and bits of soap in our ragged towels, and were marched to the Dimapur–Imphal road where the unit was waiting for us. It was parked on the road and had some means of heating water. Here we were told to 'strip off' and in our nakedness, were each directed to a sawn-off half drum of warm water ... A brief hair-cut by one of our C Company lads and we then enjoyed the luxury of being issued with clean battledress and underwear, our old kit being removed. As we marched back down the road, we met D Company. They were covered with dirt and filth and we held our noses as we passed them.

Five Brigade, now under the command of Brigadier Mike West, whom

Captain Gordon Graham first met in a bunker on Naga Hill 'bare-chested and bush-hatted', was preparing to launch coordinated set-piece attacks on the remaining, intransigent Japanese positions on Naga Hill (Point 5120) on 19 May. Previous attempts had failed. An attack by the Cameron Highlanders on Hunter's Hill on the night of 15 May was hurled back. Swinson recorded the common belief that this time round, with the overwhelming firepower involved, the attack should be successful: 'With six batteries of 25-pounders, three of 3.7s, two of 6-pounders, one of 5.5s, a troop of [Lee] Grants, and a couple of squadrons of Hurribombers to harry them, the Japs should feel depressed, to say the least of it.' In preparation for this attack bulldozers were used to cut a track up Naga Hill for the tanks, 'snorting and roaring at an angle of about 60 degrees from the horizontal, ... cutting thousands of tons out of the hillside. I've never seen anything like it.' However, Swinson's evaluation did not tell the whole story, namely Grover's desperate shortage of artillery ammunition for the whole of his division, a problem exacerbated by the fact that, in mounting three simultaneous brigade offensives, demand for artillery support for all attacks far outstripped the amount available, particularly after heavy expenditure of ammunition in bombardments earlier in the battle. Lieutenant Norman Havers of the Dorsets observed that the division's 3.7-inch howitzers 'were so short of shells that they were silent for days on end'.

When, at 8.15 a.m. on Friday 19 May the attack went in it was again repulsed. The weather was too poor for the promised air support, and the Japanese bunkers were laid out in considerable depth. When the Worcesters had taken eight bunkers they were faced with devastating fire from a further unheralded group of bunkers on the reverse slope that the artillery could not touch. 'Bertie Woodward was killed leading his platoon on to their third bunker, the first two having been dealt with successfully,' wrote Swinson in his diary that night. 'Rather shaken at this.'

~

Lieutenant General Montagu Stopford now reorganized his forces in an attempt to maintain the greatest possible pressure on the Japanese. On 23 May Major General Messervy's 7th Indian Division[26] took responsibility for what had been 5 Brigade's area of operations on the left flank, 4/15th Punjab, Queen's and 4/1st Gurkhas withdrawing from the scene of their triumph on DIS and Jail Hill to see what they might be able to do with the otherwise unbending defenders of Hunter's Hill. This switch allowed

Grover to concentrate the remainder of his tired division for an attack on the Japanese positions on Aradura Spur. Both sets of attacks, first on Japanese defences around Point 5120 (Church Knoll and Hunter's Hill) by Messervy's 7th Indian Division on the left of the battlefield, and then of Aradura Spur by Grover's 2nd Division on the right, turned out to be miserable failures. On Naga Hill heavy attacks by Hurribombers were made from the air during the 24th and 25th but the Japanese remained firmly entrenched and resolutely immovable. The proud 4/15th Punjab suffered a bloody reverse in these assaults, losing eighteen officers and 443 casualties for not a single yard of ground in return. No combination of attacks from the air, artillery strikes, tanks, flame-throwers, infantry or mortars could shift what Swinson described with some awe as 'this incredible Japanese infantry'. Nothing seemed to be working, the troops were tiring and their morale – as a result of repeated failure to break the most stubborn defences imaginable – was plummeting. Indeed, Gordon Graham, about to win the first of two Military Crosses in the campaign, called the situation 'chaotic'. It was clear that if success were not achieved soon, morale might reach the point of no return. The British were now fighting as much against the dark night of the warrior's soul, that fog of depression in which lies fear of imminent death or maiming, and failure against a seemingly unconquerable foe, as against the Japanese.

The Japanese were, however, at this time beginning to recognize the limits of their own endurance. On 23 May Sato, in an exhortation entirely unimaginable to a British army, had ordered his men, 'You will fight to the death. When you are killed you will fight on with your spirit.' But by now Sato realized that he was not going to be able to force the British from Kohima, or even to hold on indefinitely to what little he had gained. On 25 May he sent a signal to Mutaguchi which veiled an appeal to allow him to withdraw what remained of his division, on the premise that it had run out of rations and the effect of the heavy monsoon rains required it 'to move to a point where he could receive supplies by 1 June at the latest'. Reading between the lines Mutaguchi replied bluntly three days later:

> It is very difficult to understand why your division should evacuate under the pretext of difficult supply, forgetting its brilliant services. Maintain the present condition for ten days. Within that time I shall take Imphal and reward you for your services. A resolute will makes the Gods give way.

~

Sato's final defence of Kohima was based on holding the two remaining bastions, one on Aradura Spur to the extreme right and the other on Hunter's Hill to the left. His last chance was that the British would exhaust and demoralize themselves in repeated attacks on positions that they had not demonstrated any propensity thus far to penetrate, let alone overcome. Lieutenant Kameyama observed that the British and Indians were far less persistent in the attack than the Japanese. He put this down, correctly, to their determination not to waste lives. 'It was fortunate for us that the enemy respected human life,' he wrote. 'They came attacking our position, but when we sniped at them they retreated … when we shot them 'bang, bang', they went back. If they came close we were sure to be killed. But as they did not charge like Japanese, we had little fear of being killed; as long as we were in the foxholes we would survive unless we got a direct hit.' The British policy made sense, reflecting Grover's order on 14 April, an instruction interpreted by Swinson to be based on the view that the best way to fight the Japanese was to

> knock hell out of him with every gun and round you've got before the infantry go in. A gun or a tank can be made in a week, but your infantryman is twenty years a-growing. And when he's killed, none of him can be salvaged for use again; neither his body, his experience, his skill, his fighting spirit, nor his great heart. It's all gone forever.

But the British could not simply ignore Sato's bastions, nor could they be bypassed if the road to Imphal was to be reached, and used to bring relief to the beleaguered IV Corps. Accordingly, Grover ordered simultaneous assaults on both to take place on 27 and 28 May. On the right the Royal Scots and Norfolks were to attack the north-east end of Aradura Spur, while 6 Brigade were to take the south-west, where their objectives were named 'Matthew', 'Mark', 'Luke', and 'John'. When launched, however, the 6 Brigade attack on 28 May failed miserably. The weather was poor, the terrain atrocious and the morale of the exhausted 2nd Division as low as it had been since its arrival. The obstinate Japanese just did not know when they were beaten, and British soldiers begrudged having to lay down their lives merely to teach them this lesson. Major David Wilson, an experienced pilot, had been sent up in a light aircraft to see whether aerial observation might help. It did not. He saw nothing because the Japanese positions were too well camouflaged. 'The Japanese Army could have been back in Japan for all the trace I could find of them round Kohima,' he recalled. However, flying back over Naga Hill he spotted the flash and smoke of one of 31st Division's mountain guns and a regimental shoot of twenty-four guns was called up in support of 7th Indian Division. On Aradura Spur, Wilson remembered, everything seemed to go wrong. The Japanese ambushed the advancing troops of the Durhams, Berkshires and Royal Welch from high ground above, the Brigade Commander, Brigadier Shapland, being wounded by a bullet in the neck. The Berkshires managed to reach the top of the spur but the remainder of the brigade was in chaos. The attack by the Norfolks and the Royal Scots on the north-west spur met the same fate as the luckless 6 Brigade. Lieutenant Horner's heart sank when, with all the other officers of the brigade, they were shown the ground from the vantage point of Treasury Hill.

> This is a straightforward nonsense from start to finish. There was a very steep hill, we knew the Japs were on top, we knew they'd be in a reverse slope position, and we were going to assault straight up the front – not a hope in hell.

He was right. The Norfolks were now down to fourteen officers and 366 men, many exhausted and ill and, despite the remarkable leadership of Lieutenant Colonel Robert Scott and above average morale, the Japanese positions looked typically impervious to anything other than a direct tank round into each bunker, which of course was not possible in the steep, jungle-matted hillsides. Company Sergeant Major Gilding was with B Company, the leading company, when he saw Robert Scott get hit in the backside by grenade fragments. He was carried off the hillside cursing loudly. It signalled the end of the attack, and the brigade withdrew, bringing its wounded with it. It is no understatement to say that the failure of 2nd Division to secure the Aradura Spur was perhaps the lowest point of the long battle for Kohima. Yet again the Japanese had demonstrated their immovability, defying the odds despite their increasing weakness. The British troops were wet, exhausted and some units reduced to skeleton numbers while, in at least one other, the Welch Fusiliers, morale had reached the point at which Brigadier Shapland was forced to remove the commanding officer.

Meanwhile, on the left flank, likewise, 33 Indian Brigade had not managed to find a way to break the Japanese defence of Point 5120. Stalemate once more threatened. Until, that is, the newly-appointed twenty-seven-year-old commanding officer of 4/1st Gurkhas – Lieutenant Colonel Derek Horsford – decided to do things slightly differently, capturing Gun Spur at the extreme eastern edge of Naga Hill by a night infiltration on 27 May that took the Japanese entirely by surprise. This allowed tanks to approach the Japanese positions and by 1 June an attack by the Queen's discovered that the Japanese were pulling back.

~

Sato's sense of alienation from HQ Fifteenth Army had not diminished during May. He was in no doubt that it was Mutaguchi's abject failure to send supplies through the mountains that had forced him to undertake the kind of passive defence in which his division was now engaged, preventing him from continuing offensive operations. On 27 May Sato signalled Major General Tazoe, commander of 5th Air Division, 'Since leaving the Chindwin, we have not received one bullet from you, nor a grain of rice. We are still under attack by the enemy. Please send us food by plane.' Tazoe was personally sensitive to Sato's plight but perhaps acute embarrassment led to him not sending a response. Waiting in vain for any positive communication from Tamu, to where Mutaguchi had finally taken HQ Fifteenth Army, four days later Sato reported that the position was hopeless, and that he reserved the right to act on his own initiative and withdraw when he felt that it was necessary to do so, so as to save what remained of his battered division from inevitable destruction. In fact, later that day he signalled Mutaguchi,

> We have fought for two months with the utmost courage, and have reached the limits of human fortitude. Our swords are broken and our arrows spent. Shedding bitter tears, I now leave Kohima.

Apoplectic with rage and astonished at his subordinate's blatant disobedience, Mutaguchi ordered Sato to stay where he was. Sato ignored him and on receipt of Mutaguchi's threat to court martial him, replied defiantly, 'Do as you please. I will bring you down with me.' The angry exchange continued, with Sato the following day sending a final angry message to Mutaguchi in which he declared, 'The tactical ability of the Fifteenth Army staff lies below that of cadets.' Sato then ordered his staff to close down the radio sets. The die was cast. Mutaguchi or no, he now began a fighting withdrawal with the remnants of his division. In an attempt to save face and to show that the withdrawal from Kohima was planned and under control, Mutaguchi published an Order of the Day:

> Withholding my tears and painful as it is, I shall for the time being withdraw my troops from Kohima. It is my resolve to reassemble the whole army and with one great push capture Imphal ....

ON THIS ONE BATTLE RESTS THE FATE OF THE
EMPIRE ... Everyone must unswervingly serve the THRONE and
reach the ultimate goal so that the Son of Heaven [i.e., the Emperor]
and the Nation may be forever guarded.

But rhetoric could not hide the bitter reality of Sato's defeat at Kohima.
Sato's withdrawal demonstrated this truth, but it was a fact that Sato was
sure that neither Mutaguchi nor any of his gilded staff officers back in the
safe areas truly understood. Only those who had fought at Kohima could
appreciate the intensity of the fighting, the desperate nature of the bloody,
hand-to-hand struggle in some of the most inhospitable campaigning
country on earth, in the full unrelenting fury of the monsoon, a struggle
that for the Japanese, with the seemingly inexhaustible resources available
to the enemy, had by now only one obvious outcome: withdrawal, or death.

Ignorant of Sato's dilemma, but harried by Stopford (and Slim's)
urgent demands to make progress towards Imphal, Grover thrust troops
from the newly captured Naga Hill south-east across the valley that runs
east of the Kohima Ridge to seize a series of prominent ridges – Dyer Hill,
Pimple and Big Tree Hill – to outflank Miyazaki's rearguard from 124th
Regiment on Aradura Spur and to bring 2nd Division's embarrassment to
an end. Now, the Aradura Spur was itself cut off and Sato, recognizing the
inevitable, began to withdraw south on 4 June.

The battle for Kohima could now be said to be over, although the road
stretching down to besieged Imphal needed to be peeled open. The most
desperate and bloody struggle in the entire war on the south Asian land
mass had ended. It had lasted sixty-four days, had seen some of the most
obdurate fighting of the war and cost the British around 4,000 men and the
Japanese over 7,000. Around Kohima, recalled Mike Ball, 'the spirits of the
troops soared. You could feel the elation. People talked out loud, joked,
laughed. Ours was a different army. Even the 'brass' seemed more human.'
As if to signify the turn in British fortunes, Swinson recorded that on 6
June news swept the division of the landings in Normandy. More
importantly, the sun broke through the clouds and bathed the weary
warriors below in the warmth of its embrace. 'What a place to be told this
news!' he wrote. 'The sunlight was streaming across the mountains,
stretched west and south as far as the eyes could see ... Great, green,
untamed country, almost as unaware of man's presence on the earth as the
day God created it ... all the troops have been coming up to our signallers
asking 'How's it going? How are they doing in France?'

The move to cut off the Japanese on Aradura Spur worked, although it then took, to some at least, an unconscionable period of time for XXXIII Corps to organize itself to pursue the Japanese with vigour in the direction of Imphal. Ten full days were to pass before, on 17 June, an armoured column began to make its way south, past untidy piles of blackened, bloating corpses littering the roads and tracks south, to brush aside the feeble opposition Miyazaki was able to establish at various ambush positions on the road. This long delay, evidence of the disorganized state of both 2nd (British) and 7th (Indian) Divisions following the extraordinarily tough and relentless battles around Kohima, which reinforced perceptions that 2nd Division had not pressed its opportunities with proper vigour earlier in the battle, was to cost Grover his job. Slim and Giffard had regarded 2nd Division's move into the hills to have been unnecessarily tardy and placed pressure on Stopford – who in turn demanded pace from Grover – not just because of the need to relieve Imphal before the full weight of the monsoon reduced the airlift of supplies through Operation STAMINA to a trickle, but because they knew that if 2nd Division slowed it would lose the initiative and be ground down by Sato's brilliant defensive grinder. The first elements had arrived in Dimapur on 1 April and were complete by 11 April, while the garrison on the Kohima Ridge were first engaged by the Japanese with real intensity on the 5th. Yet the vanguard of one of Britain's proudest and best-trained and equipped infantry divisions only reached Warren's headquarters at Jotsoma on 16 April, with the relief of the exhausted survivors only being effected on 20 April. As with much British military experience in countless wars, success – or rather, the avoidance of defeat – was achieved by the merest whisker. With the 'odds and sods' of the Assam Rifles, Assam Regiment and the Dirty Half Hundred fighting for their lives in the mud and gore of the Kohima Ridge, the measured arrival of 2nd Division smacked to many in Fourteenth Army as over-caution. However, these same critics – Slim being one of them – failed to acknowledge that the disorganized state of Dimapur was the responsibility of Ranking's 202nd Line of Communication Command – part of Fourteenth Army – and not that of the bewildered 2nd Division at all, and had forgotten that the division, when first entrained, were despatched initially to Chittagong, diverting to Dimapur only at the last minute. It is perhaps more reasonable to argue that this measured advance ensured that 2nd Division did not over-reach itself, and arrived on the battlefield in a fit state to engage a powerful, well-led and aggressive enemy. Equally, in the days before the armoured column left for Imphal on 17 June, the Poor Bloody Infantry of Grover's division had been battling to remove Miyazaki's stubborn rearguard at Viswema and all points before. Whatever the truth, Grover was punished for the perception of failing to move with the alacrity his masters demanded. His men were angered by the manner in which he was dismissed, and veterans today harbour great bitterness against those who removed 'their' general from command at the pinnacle of his achievement in winning one of the most dramatic struggles of the entire war. It was certainly unfair, but Grover went uncomplainingly, speaking nothing of it to his death. His response was a disciplined, loyal, even 'stiff upper lip' silence, which proved a dramatic contrast to the vitriolic exchanges that were to pass between Mutaguchi and Sato many years after the end of the war, right to their respective graves.

In fact, comparatively rapid progress was achieved down from the hills on the Imphal road between 17 and 22 June once the Camerons and Worcesters had fought through the final obstinate defences at Viswema. The route was a defensive paradise on which an army any stronger than Sato's ragged, starving and emaciated troops could conceivably have held up the British advance indefinitely. Sato's rearguard fought determinedly. Often a few men with an artillery piece, grenades and a machine gun, would take up positions on the high ground above tracks, ambushing the British advance guards before melting away to repeat the performance a few miles further back or, as was often the case, remaining obstinately in their positions until they were killed. Few were free from disease and fatigue, but surrender played no part in these men's vocabulary: they fought on till overtaken by a British bullet or bayonet or, more often, by starvation and exhaustion. But 31st Division had literally fought itself to death. Exhausted men lay in pits unable to defend themselves, suicide squads with anti-tank mines tottered towards the advancing Lee Grants and Stuarts to be mown down by accompanying infantry, or obliterated by shell-fire. The advancing troops now had their tails up: the Japanese blocks at Maram and then Viswema were swept aside with a fraction of the time and effort, and a tiny proportion of the blood and treasure, that had been expended to overcome the Japanese defences at Kohima. All of a sudden the war, or at least the long struggle to defeat the thrust against Kohima, appeared to be nearing its end. On Thursday 22 June Harry Swinson's diary caught the drama of the final surge that linked the men of 2nd Division with the defenders of the Imphal pocket:

> The sun was shining as we rode forward … The whole Army was surging forward with the knowledge that the Japs were beaten and soon, soon, there would be rest. Nights spent in comfort unbroken

by a sentry-go; time to dry clothes; time to bath; time to write letters home; time to become human again; and, most of all, time to sleep. You could hear the troops singing on the crowded trucks.

At Milestone 108, Captain Sean Kelly of the Durhams saw the tanks accompanying the advance guard of his battalion identify

> movement away forward where elephant grass gave way to trees and began to brass it up properly.[27] Soon they stopped. A plaintive message relayed through many sets had reached them: we were brassing up the advance elements of 5th Indian Division of the beleaguered [IV] Corps. Imphal was relieved. We sat alone in the sunshine and smoked and ate. Soon the staff cars came pouring both ways. The road was open. It was a lovely day.

A few days after the road was open, Swinson accompanied the brigade into Imphal. In a corner of A Mess at HQ IV Corps he had something of a surreal experience.

> In a corner I found a solitary subaltern: I didn't know him, but I fell on his neck like a long-lost brother. He was the only officer within three ranks of me. We introduced ourselves.
>
> 'Good morning,' he said, 'will you have a beer?'
>
> 'A beer?' I echoed. 'I thought you were besieged and we were relieving you.'
>
> 'Besieged?' he asked in a pained voice. 'Whatever made you think that? We've been all right. Do have a beer. There's plenty in the Mess.'
>
> I accepted with alacrity. It was good stuff when it arrived, and I said 'Cheerio' and swigged it down. Then unaccountably (to the subaltern) burst out laughing.
>
> 'What's the matter?' he asked. 'Anything wrong?'
>
> I thought of the weary, beerless months we'd spent trying to relieve these people.
>
> 'No, nothing wrong,' I said, 'but it's a bloody funny war, isn't it?'

Swinson's young interlocutor was either profoundly ignorant of the realities of the situation or was spinning a line. Edward Lydall, the President of the Manipur State Council, recalled that the only alcohol available during the siege was *zu*, the locally brewed rice beer. When the siege was lifted 'the first convoy of lorries to enter the beleaguered town contained three months' arrears of drink rations for us all, and at one stroke the Commander [Stopford] became 'our most popular general''. The young officer in the mess with Swinson was also demonstrating profound ignorance of the importance of the road, without which the defenders of the Imphal pocket were dependent on a diminishing air resource, one made increasingly tenuous as the monsoon made flying conditions extremely difficult. The onset of the wet season in late-April meant that deliveries of supplies would not match the quantity required to sustain Scoones' four divisions in the pocket. Indeed the IV Corps staff had calculated that if the road remained unopened by 15 June the ration scale, already reduced, would have to be cut still further, beyond even the half rations on which men were subsisting.

Swinson had also stumbled on one of the profound realities of the fighting within the Imphal pocket, namely the gap between the appalling privations of the troops on the front line and the relative comforts enjoyed by the headquarters staff in Imphal. David Atkins watched the immediate consequence of the lifting of the siege: the vast influx of trucks driving over the Naga Hills from Dimapur, carrying food, fuel and ammunition, 'Like rain on parched soil, the food renewed everyone's energies and determination which had been undermined by months of hunger ... In the same way as the food revived the men, the ammunition flowed up to the guns. They began to fire not six rounds a day but as many as their commanders wished.'

~

Meanwhile, back in Khonoma hundreds of displaced Nagas, including the thirteen-year-old Neidelie, were now free to return to their villages for the first time in three months.

> So we happily retraced our way back. We travelled in a great company spending one night at Jotsoma and progressing slowly onward the next morning. We were elated at the thought of going back home. But on the way back, we saw many dead Japanese soldiers ... After some time, I grew tired of counting and looking at the dead soldiers all of whom looked alike now that they were bloated and decomposing by the roadside. We gathered some of the rifles from the dead. The Japanese rifles were very long, almost a

man's height in length and the officers always carried what the villagers thought were spears, actually, very long swords.

Every few steps of our journey home, we found dead Japanese. Some hung out of trees, shot as they sat on their sniping perches in trees, others still clung to the barbed wire fences, their decomposing hands clasping the fences in desperate gestures of men who had vainly tried to flee death. The group that we were travelling with was a large body of our villagers so we buried the dead bodies when we came upon them on our way. But after some time, we gave up this effort because there were just too many dead Japanese for us to bury all ... Dead bodies were strewn over the countryside and the stench from the bodies was more than anyone could bear.

# Chapter 8

# The Battle for Imphal

By the middle of May, with the Japanese now on the defensive and with Scoones' IV Corps pushing aggressively against the Japanese in the north, south-east and south, Slim's worst anxieties about the prospect of Imphal falling to Mutaguchi were over. The Japanese were everywhere showing signs of faltering, despite fighting tenaciously to hold ground they had seized, and attempting still to break through at Bishenpur in the south and on the Shenam Ridge to the south-east. Consequently, Slim's priorities changed: his primary concern was no longer the relief of Imphal but rather first to seek a means of ensuring that Mutaguchi could not escape the close battle to which he was now committed. This meant the prospect of a battle of attrition, but one in which the British enjoyed the overwhelming advantage in the air and on land in terms of resources and firepower. Slim's objective now became the destruction of Fifteenth Army. He could see clearly that, by extending his forces deeply and boldly into Manipur on multiple lines of attack, Mutaguchi was playing directly into his hands. By early-May the Japanese had suffered fearsome casualties across each part of the front, losing irreplaceable experienced fighting men, while all the time Fourteenth Army was strengthening daily, in experience, reinforcements and supplies. With the monsoon in full flood, the physical strength of Japanese troops began to break down.

Imphal was defended sufficiently strongly for Slim to be confident that Scoones had the resources to deal with any eventuality. The only urgency was to ensure that Imphal did not run out of supplies. The airlift would improve that situation in part but the monsoon meant that the flying programme was severely disrupted. Accordingly, in early-May, Slim determined that Scoones would have to re-open the road to Kohima by the third week of June to prevent the possibility of the 118,000 men and 1,000 animals still in the pocket from running critically short of essential supplies, such as artillery ammunition, fuel and food.

Despite this, more nervous voices could still be heard in the corridors of power urging the need to 'relieve Imphal'. On 1 June Wavell wrote in his diary,

> I don't feel altogether happy about the Assam and North Burma [Chindit] operations. There is not much progress being made anywhere, especially in the vital task of reopening the Kohima–Imphal road. Meanwhile the supply by air to Imphal and to the 3rd Division columns [the Chindits in Operation THURSDAY] in North Burma is causing anxiety.

Likewise, five days later Field Marshal Sir Alan Brooke, the CIGS in London, could still talk in his diary of a potential disaster at Imphal and at this time also Lieutenant General Henry Pownall, Mountbatten's Chief of Staff in HQ SEAC in Kandy was reportedly unable to sleep because of worry about the fate of the surrounded IV Corps. Indeed, pressure was placed on Mountbatten from London to make the opening of the Kohima road and thus the relief of Imphal his priority. However, Slim's immediate boss, General Sir George Giffard at 11 Army Group, refused to be hustled. 'Neither General Giffard nor I was as anxious as they appeared about Imphal's power to hold out,' wrote Slim; 'we knew that IV Corps would shortly take the offensive.' To his credit, Mountbatten, thus persuaded, backed his subordinates to the hilt, and directed that the road be opened by mid-July. 'I was grateful to him for not being stampeded by more nervous people into setting too early a date,' Slim recalled. 'I intended that the road should be open well before mid-July, but I was now more interested in destroying Japanese divisions than in 'relieving' Imphal.'

~

During the land battles for the Imphal Plain air power provided the essential lubricant in Scoones' defensive machinery, a crucial ingredient in eventual British success. The role played by fighters in securing air superiority was critical in preventing Japanese attacks on the lumbering transports that provided daily supply runs into the Imphal airfields over the endless green hills that rolled like ocean waves between Assam and Manipur. British air activity over the entire battlefield was intense and comprised defensive sorties to protect the airlift and the airfields, offensive ground attack sorties in support of the fighting troops, reconnaissance flights and offensive air sorties designed to hunt down and destroy the 220 Japanese aircraft flying against Manipur and Assam from Burma. In fact, the numbers of British sorties declined as the battle progressed, in part because of the reducing numbers of missions launched by the Japanese as a result of their own rapidly dwindling numbers. The massive air operation in support of Operation STAMINA across the period of the siege was a remarkable success. By 30 June the operation had flown in 19,000 reinforcements, 14,317,000 pounds of rations, 1,303 tons of grain for animals, 835,000 gallons of fuel and lubricants, 12,000 bags of mail and 43,475,760 cigarettes, an average of 250 tons of supplies being delivered each of the seventy-six days of the siege. At its height in the second half of April the airlift employed 404 aircraft from fifteen squadrons. As each month went by the contribution by the Royal Air Force and Indian Air Force were demonstrated starkly by the mathematics of war: in April 1944 there were at least 7,372 separate sorties by Spitfires, Hurricanes, and Vultee Vengeances. During the month twenty-four aircraft were lost, eight were damaged and thirty men killed. In May 5,873 sorties were flown with twenty-two aircraft lost and in June 3,938 sorties were flown. Thus, in the three months between April and June, 17,183 sorties were conducted by fighter and dive-bomber aircraft alone: the total number of air sorties, including transport flights, directly in support of Imphal and Kohima exceeded 30,000. The Japanese air force remained aggressive and persistent throughout the long months of the siege, flying formations of aircraft against targets when they could get away with it, and darting single or pairs of aircraft through the cloud or at tree-top height to avoid the British warning radar to strike at the airfields on the plain when they could, which meant that resupply by air for Mutaguchi's forward troops was only ever a distant dream. But the greatest deficiency of Major General Tazoe's 5th Air Division was in transport and bomber aircraft. Nor could he replace those aircraft he lost: Tazoe's limited aircraft numbers could mount a mere 1,750 sorties over the battlefields during this time, and by the end of July only forty-nine aircraft remained in the Japanese inventory.

Attacks from the air by Hurribombers and Vultee Vengeances on ground targets were always dangerous affairs, as the aircraft had to come in low and were vulnerable to return fire on the pull-out after an attack. On Tuesday 30 May Warrant Officer G. F. MacMillan's Hurricane was hit by ground fire as he came into his final steep bombing run over Shenam, his aircraft turning onto its back and crashing in flames. The low-lying cloud made the pilots' tasks particularly difficult, but more often than not they pressed on in aid of their earth-bound comrades in spite of the obvious dangers posed by the enemy, the weather and the terrain. On 7 June Flying Officer Bill Brittan, flying a Hurricane IID of 20 Squadron, armed with tank-killing 40mm cannon, was sent in against a cluster of Japanese tanks on the Tiddim road south of Bishenpur. This squadron successfully destroyed twelve Japanese tanks in June, but on this occasion Brittan's aircraft was hit by ground fire on its approach to the target, and blew up on striking the ground.

Squadron Leader Peter Bray of 31 Squadron flew Dakotas into Imphal during the siege, flying from Agartala airfield in Assam, dropping supplies direct to the troops on the ground.

> Typically, crews would be called at 4.30 a.m. for breakfast at 5. Take off would be around dawn at 6 a.m. Flying eastwards one would see the paddy fields soon replaced by the inhospitable and uninhabited [sic] Chin Hills running in ridges north to south, rising at first to a few hundred feet and gradually to 6,000 feet, each ridge with a correspondingly deep valley, much of which was covered by deep jungle.
>
> Briefing before take-off was provided by an Army Liaison Officer who defined the DZ with great care so that we would be able to find it from some prominent feature on our large-scale map – about 15 miles to the inch. DZ code letters were given to prevent supplies going to false DZs created by the Japs. The pilot would make a straight approach on the DZ giving the 'stand by' light to the dropping crew in the back of the aircraft, followed by the 'drop' light when he judged the aircraft position to be right. When the load was clear the pilot made a steep turn to the left to observe the accuracy of the drop so as to know the correction to make for the subsequent drops.

Night flights against ground targets also increased in number during the siege. The Japanese nicknamed the quiet, low-flying Bristol Beaufighter nightfighters 'whispering death' for their penchant for appearing at low level with very little warning. Troops or transport caught in the open could expect no mercy. On 24 May Warrant Officer Pat Bowen 'flew right down the Tiddim Road and we attacked six or eight Jap vehicles that were moving, and got about four of them – they really went up in flames'. A week later a pair of Beaufighters caught more transport on the Tiddim road and on 4 June he and Squadron Leader Brocklehurst caught a train near Tamu, sending it crashing off the rails, before strafing road convoys and river boats. Squadron Leader 'Dave' Davies of 607 Squadron was hunting targets along the Tiddim road on 12 June, and found and strafed a truck hidden among some trees, followed by attacking a Japanese supply dump south of Churachandpur. The Japanese were extremely good at camouflaging both men and transport, and it was rare to catch them off guard, but Davies devised an effective system to destroy an otherwise moveable target when he would normally have to fly back to base to replenish his ammunition after an initial attack. By the time he returned to continue the strafe, the Japanese would have disappeared.

> [The Japanese] were masters of camouflage. Therefore I called up base and told them to send out another pair [of aircraft] while we kept circling so the Japs wouldn't move, until the second pair arrived. That was the only way to do it for the Japs were fantastic. How they got their vehicles off the road and how they managed to camouflage them I just don't know. Even on one occasion I set one on fire right in the middle of the road [but] when the next pair went out, the damn thing had disappeared – in less than 20 minutes. What they'd done with it I couldn't imagine.

On another occasion, after a fruitless night sortie, Squadron Leader Guy Hogan of 5 Squadron was returning to base in his Hurricane:

> Making my way back I was following a road just as the sun was coming up. Suddenly, right ahead of me on the road were four Jap soldiers, rifles slung casually over their shoulders. They saw me at the same moment that I saw them. Before they had a chance to make any move I had brought my sights on and let them have it.

~

Away from the outer defensive 'crust' surrounding the Imphal perimeter, where the fighting conditions were often appalling, men's experience of the siege differed considerably. Inside the Imphal defences morale on the whole remained high, especially when it became clear that, despite the desperation of the fighting and the panics of the early weeks when the Japanese appeared to be close to breaking in at multiple points, the enemy were being held back and were suffering tremendously in the battle of attrition on the Kohima road, the Ukhrul Track, the Shenam heights and Bishenpur. Major David Atkins:

> We were very aware that on all sides the enemy were attacking daily and that we were enclosed in an area of about thirty miles by twelve. Confidence, however, remained strong. This confidence was helped when Noel Coward and George Formby were both flown in. They gave concerts well within the fighting zones at Bishenpur and Palel. The staff officer back in India was always fair game for those in the forward areas and Noel Coward's songs on the fashionable life in Delhi were wildly applauded:

> Sticking it out at the Cecil,
> Doing our bit for the war,
> Going through hell at Maidens Hotel,
> Where they stop serving drinks prompt at four.

Inside Imphal there were wide variations in the quality of life. For some, especially those on the Corps and Garrison staff the war appeared not much more than an irritation. Edward Lydall, British President of the Manipur State Council, lived in the 'Citadel' box along with the sub-area headquarters, the Residency and the State Offices, and remarked on the discomforts suffered by those forced to live behind the barbed wire. Tennis was available but on the whole 'entertainment was inevitably on a much reduced scale and carried on under increasing difficulties'. Indeed the noise produced by the artillery finally got on the nerves of the Political Agent [Mr C. Gimson]. 'Damn those Japanese!' he testily exclaimed one Sunday evening. 'How the hell do they suppose I can hear the gramophone if they make that filthy row?' Fighting men are always suspicious that those in the rear have a 'cushier' life than they do. Lance Bombardier Ron Bunnett, surviving in the mud and rain of the 5th Indian Division front north of Imphal was chagrined to discover after the battle that over 43 million cigarettes had been flown in during the siege. 'What happened to them, and where did they go?' he mused,

> None of them came our way, not even the noxious and notorious 'Victory Vs' which were reputedly made with mule dung, and shunned by even the sepoys. We certainly had none, and were told that there were none. There was a small supply of pipe tobacco – Capstan Full Strength, strong enough to make your hair curl – but as nobody possessed a pipe it was all a bit academic. The more enterprising among us tried to make pipes out of green bamboo, whittled with the standard issue knife, but in this they were unsuccessful, and would probably have poisoned themselves anyway. So, we went without, but I doubt the 'basewallahs' did.

Whether or not Bunnett's suspicions were true, life inside the defensive boxes was immeasurably better than those experienced by the combat troops in the hills surrounding the plain, but was nevertheless uncomfortable. The arrival of the full force of the monsoon meant that canvas roofs quickly became saturated and leaked, and duck boards in the trenches only helped to a limited extent, the more poorly-constructed trenches not allowing effective drainage. For Squadron Leader 'Buck' Courtney the tents and bashas used for accommodation away from the airstrip boxes 'were adequate, even comfortable, until it rained. The sheer misery of living in a tent or leaky basha during a monsoon has to be experienced to be believed'. Toilets were dug in rows outside the perimeter but in sight of the sentries. Made from petrol drums with the top cut off, and placed over holes dug deep into the ground, they could only be used during the day, as any movement at night outside the perimeter was regarded as suspicious and could be shot at. Only in an emergency would someone go out to use the thunderbox at night, and only after agreeing with the sentry not to shoot. Keeping the latrines free of flies was a never-ending battle. Flying Officer Ken Lister of 34 Squadron RAF watched 'Paddy' Fee, the squadron's Irish doctor, attempting to use 100-octane petrol as a fly-killer when the normal supplies of disinfectant ran out.

> Because of the risk of fire every toilet carried large 'No Smoking' signs in prominent positions. Unfortunately a visitor, not knowing the reason for the notices, ignored them and dropped his fag end into the trench. The result was a loud explosion, a rapid evacuation, and five people with an amazed expression at one end and a singed bum at the other!

The airfield at Palel was very close to the edge of the hills in the south-eastern corner of the Plain, and in sight of the Japanese. A Spitfire squadron occupied each end of the strip, and the aircraft were kept at night behind high earth bunds. The airstrips were regularly shelled, especially as aircraft were flying in or taking off. The Japanese would often 'lay down a barrage as we were taking off,' recalled Flight Sergeant C. M. G. Watson, a Spitfire pilot of 615 Squadron. 'In these conditions we staggered the take-offs but I don't believe anyone was ever hit, though there were some fairly narrow escapes.' Flying overhead, Squadron Leader Guy Hogan saw Palel under bombardment on 18 May, and Imphal Main would receive incoming rounds regularly. The Japanese made a number of attempts to destroy aircraft on the ground. Palel was attacked on several occasions by small patrols trying to get through the perimeter to destroy the parked aircraft. On 1 May, with torrential rain hammering down, a patrol of about thirty Japanese attempted and failed to get through but, on the night of 3/4 July, a small party under the command of Captain Inoue managed to penetrate the defences, destroying or damaging seven aircraft in a last-gasp effort against the aircraft that had helped IV Corps to prevent the Japanese achieving their objectives. The Japanese planted blast bombs in the air intakes underneath the engines and most of the party managed to get away in the confusion that followed.

With the pocket cut off by land, the supply of food became severely restricted, and the diet monotonous. Rationing was implemented from the outset of the siege, tightening as the siege wore on. Food became an obsession with everyone, recalled Major David Atkins, who lost one and a half stone during the siege.

> When the Japanese attacks on Box Bull [at Palel] eased up we were moved back to the Bishenpur Road. Up to that time rations had been full for the infantry and two-thirds for the support troops. Now they were cut to two-thirds for the divisions and we were cut to half – quite reasonable in the circumstances. We were all getting thinner by the day. At dinner I would carve a small tin of bully beef between seven officers. We had enough rice but as we had little else we were all losing weight fast and meals were eagerly awaited.

His company had a small herd of ten goats which, as time went on, became pets. Understandably, the men refused to eat them but, as hunger began to bite, the men's resolve also began to wane, and only two animals survived the siege. The rest found their way into the communal pot. By mid-April Private Jack Clifford of the Northamptons, fighting on the Bishenpur front, could attest that 'hunger became a general complaint here, to which we learned, rations may have to be cut further'. For Sergeant F. H. Thomas 'bully beef, and the never to be forgotten sausage supreme – the soya link' were the culinary mainstays of the diet of those caught within the siege, along with the delights of dehydrated vegetables and powdered egg. Private Ron Parker of the Northamptons on the Silchar Track came to detest the sight of bully beef. 'You name it, we had it – bully beef cold – bully beef hot – bully beef fried – bully beef boiled – bully beef sausages – bully beef stew – bully beef rissoles – bully beef steaks – bully beef sandwich…' Likewise, Major David Atkins cursed the wretched British staff officer who had been conned into ordering soya links from America, noting that American troops were not forced to eat them. 'Taste soya link sausages once, they were tolerable, twice and you just got them down, three times and one could never touch them again.' Major Gerald Hanley described them as 'a piece of chemical composition shaped like a sausage and possessing a taste so flat and boring that it is quite impossible to face it after three days' trial'. Lieutenant Peter Toole of 20 Field Company recalled the 'hard tack' provided to the men while on operations away from a fixed base.

> These sorties tended to last two or three days and the small force often had to carry all the supplies needed on a small detachment of mules. Fires for cooking could give our position away so all rations

were dry rations. Having taken a breakfast snack of a third of a tin of some unknown species of fish together with a third of a packet of biscuits wrapped in the thinnest paper imaginable, we had to carry the 'Unexpired portion of the day's ration' (as it was called) rattling around in our haversacks. The condition of the food and the haversack worsened as the day wore on and the evening meal could best be described as a 'fishy biscuity mash'.

Necessity – or perhaps hunger – was the mother of invention in the Imphal pocket. Atkins supplemented his rations by shooting the large fruit bats the size of small chickens which hung during the day from the large mango and karnikar trees in the foothills of the Tiddim Valley. Their flesh, he observed, was not unlike chicken. Flying Officer Ken Lister and his colleagues went duck and pigeon shooting with two of the squadron's 12-bore shot guns to supplement their diet around Logtak Lake, where large flocks of ducks and geese resided on a migration path from Siberia. John Henson, a keen shot, recalled that when in flight during the evening their numbers would darken the sky like an eclipse of the sun. There was also plenty of fish. To catch one, recalled Atkins, one merely had to dam up two ends of a stream and bail out the water. For the six weeks of the siege there was no beer, but the aircrews flying in and out of the pocket found ingenious ways of getting alcohol into Imphal. The Hurricane crews of 34 Squadron, when returning from flights out of the Plain, would return with bottles of gin and rum secreted inside the overload tanks under the wings, which had been suitably modified by the squadron engineers.

Every unit contributed to the defence of the boxes. In late April 1944 David Atkins' Transport Company was assigned a defensive role in Box Bull at Palel, an area that included the airfield. He had all sorts of odd companies under his command, including a bakery section and a disinfection unit. The Japanese attacked the Box each night, and regularly penetrated the defences, where they fired 'from the paddy fields in the centre of the box where no troops were camped'. The Japanese fired artillery daily into Atkins' box from the surrounding hills, but with surprisingly little effect, given the fact that several thousand men were hunkered down in trenches across the area.

~

To the north of Imphal during June, Briggs' primary focus was to open the road to Kohima while at the same time reducing the freedom of movement for Japanese troops in the mountain vastness skirted in the south by Wakan,

Mapao and Runaway Hill. Salomon's 9 Brigade therefore joined Evans' 123 Brigade in unstitching each part of the Japanese defensive tapestry as it stretched mile after agonizing mile along the road, terrain ideally suited to delaying tactics, as every curve and culvert was overlooked by Japanese-held hillocks, each of which had to be prised, painfully, from their grasp. Crowther's 89 Brigade took over responsibility for the hilly terrain to the east. The battle for the road consisted of many small actions repeated, seemingly endlessly, often at section, platoon or sometimes company level. A hill, defile or bridge would be isolated and attacked in the traditional way by artillery if available (given the grave shortages of ammunition by this time), by battalion 3-inch mortars, by Hurribombers or Vengeances, possibly a Lee Grant or Stuart tank firing main armament from the road, but principally by infantry closing on the enemy bunkers with bayonet and grenade. Enemy blocks sometimes comprised infantry armed with mines and a heavy anti-tank gun, but most contained a few determined men armed with little more than bullets, bayonets and raw, fanatical courage. British and Indian battalions were, by mid-June, now advancing beyond their supply lines, and often received urgent stores by air. Sometimes it was necessary for the Sappers to construct tracks up and around hillsides to bring up tanks against Japanese positions, winches being used on occasions to inch tanks up the heavily-wooded hillsides. Each day was a grind of hard physical exertion under heavy packs (and on half rations) up and down impossible hillsides awash from the torrential rain.

At the end of each day the brigade staff would collate their casualty numbers, battalions then having to rebalance platoons and companies to take into account these losses in preparation for the next day of fighting. Every day it was the same story: nine killed and twenty-eight wounded here; twenty-three killed and forty-two injured there. On days where large-scale attacks were mounted the casualty figures easily doubled these. On every occasion the only Japanese captured were those so severely wounded that they were unable of their own volition to take their own lives. Captain Anthony Brett James provides an example of this type of fighting by 3/9th Jats who on 13 June moved north from one hill called Squeak, to another nicknamed Wilfred.

> Three days' rain had made the very steep slopes of this ridge slippery. It was impossible to supply the leading companies by mule. Trees grew thickly on the hills, and even where the jungle had clearings, these were covered in high elephant grass that impeded our progress. The leading Jat company under Major Sanson drove

some enemy outposts off a knob called Bye. And when C Company passed through to occupy Button, another thousand yards farther north along the ridge, the enemy offered no resistance.

Jat patrols now crept through the jungle to probe the defences of the main hill along this ridge, Liver. There seemed to be little opposition. But this supposition proved to be false, when an attack was made at half-past two by Captain Muskett's guerrilla platoon and a platoon of Rowling's B Company, led by a newly-joined officer named Armstrong. The Japanese on Liver threw down scores of grenades. Their four machine guns took a saddening toll. Armstrong and his jemadar were killed, Muskett was wounded by a grenade, and the B Company platoon suffered in all twenty-four wounded and two killed out of a strength of twenty-seven.

All the while the monsoon deluge continued. It was impossible for the troops in the hills or on the road far below to stay dry. Streams that had trickled and gurgled in the dry season now angrily smashed their way through every obstacle before them in raging brown torrents that drowned men and mules and swept away bridges and vehicles. The grey, dripping wet misery of the terrain was reflected in the overcast darkness of the sky which only spasmodically opened to allow through the reluctant rays of a half-forgotten sun.

Attacks on Liver continued, but were repelled by showers of grenades. Along the road tanks inched while infantry outflanked, but at a high cost in killed and wounded. At times it appeared that 5th Division was not making any progress and tactics being perfected in Arakan were copied in order to inject pace into the advance northwards. Wide hooks through the jungle allowed British units to emerge on the road behind the Japanese blocks, and occupying high ground on Japanese lines of communication, isolating their mountaintop positions from resupply, forced them to choose between starvation or withdrawal.

These tactics did not obviate the requirement for hard fighting, however. The weather, terrain and tenacious defence by the Japanese in their many positions in the hills overlooking the road made Briggs' advance a prolonged and bloody affair. By mid-June, after two months of fighting, the forward troops of Salomon's 9 Indian Brigade had only reached a point sixteen miles north of Imphal. In fierce fighting to clear the hills around Liver between 19 and 21 June, for instance, Lieutenant Colonel Gerty's incomparably brave 3/9th Jats had lost thirty-three men killed, and 111 wounded in the fighting. However, on the morning of 22 June the battalion found that Liver had been abandoned. The Japanese had had enough: the tactics of isolation, heavy bombardment from artillery and air, and repeated assaults with bayonet and grenade had eroded their will to continue fighting. This was a new phenomenon on the Imphal battlefield, but mirrored the collapse further north at Kohima at the start of the month, a sign that what had once been a seemingly unbreakable martial confidence was now considerably more fragile and, in parts, collapsing. Later that day men of 1/17th Dogras met troops of 2nd British Division at Milestone 109 on the Kohima road. The road was open, the first major stitch in Mutaguchi's plan to seize Imphal had been undone.

~

Along the Shenam Ridge Yamamoto's force was now unable to maintain consistent pressure on the defenders in their muddy, bomb-cratered defences, with the result that the fighting came now in intensive spurts. Between 20 and 24 May desperate struggles developed along the ridge between Gibraltar and Malta, held by Brigadier Marindin's strengthened 37 Brigade, with the Japanese securing a toe-hold on the former and cutting off the latter. Simultaneously, Brigadier King's 1 Brigade struggled to eject the Japanese from positions they had secured on a series of features dominated by one that 1st Seaforth Highlanders dubbed 'Ben Nevis', which threatened to open up a means of outflanking Shenam in the north. On Gibraltar fierce counter-attacks with grenade and kukri finally told with the Japanese streaming away down Gibraltar, having suffered at least 150 dead; the Japanese were also driven from Ben Nevis. These actions so exhausted the Japanese that Yamamoto was forced to build up his strength before his next major offensive on the Shenam Ridge, against Scraggy, was launched on 9 June. The period between these major actions was taken up with intensive patrolling by both sides, a difficult task given the precipitous nature of the terrain and the torrential rain which made living in these conditions a debilitating nightmare. The Japanese, poorly supplied, suffered terribly.

Then, late on 9 June, the Japanese attacked again, in a last-ditch attempt to push the small force from 3/3rd Gurkha Rifles holding Scraggy. The attack was preceded by a massive artillery bombardment, considered by some to have been the most intensive of the entire campaign. As the Gurkhas watched, swarms of desperate Japanese clambered through the mud up the now naked hillside. It was clear to the defenders, crouching in their slit trenches in the pouring monsoon rain, that this was a last 'do or die' attempt to capture the ridge. Despite inflicting severe losses on the assaulting Japanese infantry, the Gurkhas themselves suffered thirty-six casualties in the fighting – almost their whole strength were killed or wounded – and, short of ammunition and out of grenades, the survivors were pushed back from part of the hill. Ouvry Roberts, recognizing the desperation of the Japanese decided not to attempt to retake Scraggy as it would only lead to many more casualties, concluding that the Japanese would be too exhausted to advance beyond the territory they had gained. He was right. Exhausted by their exertions and depleted sorely by the losses inflicted on them, the Japanese had not the energy to make any further progress towards Imphal.

The fighting along this stretch of mountains took on the attritional characteristics of the fighting elsewhere: furious Japanese assaults on British positions, followed by even more furious defence of these positions against British counter-attack. On 22 June 5/6th Rajputana Rifles (the Raj Rifs) attacked Japanese positions on a hill on the Shenam Ridge, supported by the 25-pounders of 158th Field Regiment and the 5.5-inch guns of 8th Medium Regiment. The twenty-two-year-old FOO accompanying the Raj Rifs, Lieutenant Dick Channer, described the moment his regiment's guns fired in support of the attack.

> There was a 'whoosh' like the sound of an express train whipping through Clapham Junction [as 40 rounds came in]. There was a huge pall of smoke and the shells seemed to rip the hill apart. The 'Raj Rifs' in a tricky manoeuvre traversed round the steep side of the hill and gained a wider ridge on the far side, where they fixed bayonets. The attack took the enemy in the rear as [Major 'Bunny'] Dubois led with a Tommy gun under his right arm and a Gurkha kukri in his left hand. The surprise worked. The objective was taken …
>
> Over a period of two hours the Japs mounted three counter-attacks but the Raj Rifs and the gunfire ground them down. At dusk Dubois felt secure and went to check his layout. He returned saying, 'We've counted eighty-eight Japs dead. We've lost thirty dead and thirty are wounded, (out of 100). The forward platoon has only nine men left, (out of thirty).

On the track to Ukhrul similarly difficult terrain confronted Gracey's 20th Indian Division, following its switch from the Shenam fighting, as it sought to clear the Japanese from the territory they had captured after the struggle for Sangshak at the end of March. The regimental historian of the Mahrattas provides a taste of the enormity of the task faced by infantry battalions as they attempted to shift the Japanese from the deeply-dug positions into which they had withdrawn. On 15 June 6/5th Mahrattas, supported by two Stuart troops of 7th Light Cavalry, were tasked with ejecting the Japanese from a strong position on a high ridge overlooking the Ukhrul road on which previous attacks had made no impression. The light tanks were winched up hillsides by bulldozers.

> Following a not very effective artillery concentration and air strike A and B Companies, preceded by the three light tanks and with D Company in support, moved forward in pouring rain up the slope of the ridge. Almost immediately coming under heavy fire from all infantry weapons, and shelled by enemy artillery, the attack was pressed home despite heavy casualties, which included the two forward Company Commanders killed, and penetrated the Japanese forward defences with considerable loss to the enemy. Here, however, the assault was held up by murderous automatic and medium machine-gun fire at close range from well-sited and strongly constructed enemy bunkers while numerous tree snipers and heavy mortar fire added to the stream of casualties passing to the rear.

All three tanks were soon out of action (one had its tracks blown off on a mine, the second became bogged in a collapsed enemy bunker and the third had its turret jammed by a direct hit from an anti-tank gun). Several hours of stubborn infantry fighting among and even on top of the bunkers still failed to dislodge the defenders and, in the teeming rain, and after suffering 130 casualties, including two company commanders, the battalion withdrew disconsolately. The regimental historian recounts that an 'indication of the intensity of the enemy fire may be had from the fact that Major A. F. S. Wilson in the space of a few minutes had the stock of his rifle shattered by an enemy bullet, his equipment and grenade pouch torn away by another, and was wounded in the hand by a third'. Three days later the same position was again attacked by 6/5th Mahrattas, this time accompanied by air, artillery and tank support, but to their amazement the Japanese had fled, their morale shattered, before the infantry assault went in. A diary taken from a corpse on the Tamu Road demonstrated the gradual reduction in Japanese strength. The dead man was the Medical Officer of 1/60th Regiment:

> 3 Apr 44. We have crossed the Arakan and set foot on the soil of India. Already Lieutenant Goto and 9 others have been killed. I am sure they will become the guardian deities of our country. We out in the front line are too busy to pay our respects to the spirits of the

departed, for we too owe everything to the Emperor to carry out our duties to the utmost.

19 Apr 44. From the chilling of the stomach and the cold nights in camp arise many cases of diarrhoea and dysentery, and there are many cases of beri-beri. Still the willpower of the Japanese soldier is high, and he can withstand this with ease.

25 Apr. 5,000 feet up in the mountains there is no water. We cannot fight without water. Days pass when you only get rice and salt to eat. Sweat soaks through your underwear, and the stench of your body is appalling.

6 May. Bombing by a large enemy formation is mortifying.

18 May. Am I the only MO left? More than ever then I must try to do my utmost.

23 May. God, I hope it doesn't rain tonight. I'll never forget this life of slopping around in the slime of filthy streams and drinking foul waters. Well I've got amoebic dysentery now. My wound is discharging pus, but if I weaken and fail what is going to happen? Am I not the only MO left now? Come on now, I must put all my efforts into it.

~

The struggle for Bishenpur did not lessen in its violent intensity as June arrived. Indeed, of the five Victoria Crosses awarded during the battle, four were won on this front. Angered by Yanagida's inability to break through, Mutaguchi accused him of timidity and at the end of May replaced him with Lieutenant General Tanaka Nobuo[28] who was rushed from Thailand to take over the job. Japanese command relationships, weak from the outset of the campaign, were now unravelling fast. Tanaka could not bring himself to believe that the task of capturing Imphal was as difficult as Yanagida had made out. 'The officers and men were more exhausted than I had expected,' he recalled when he first met them, 'but their haggard faces did not make me pessimistic about the prospect of battle.' In any case, unwilling to accept publicly the possibility of failure (even though he confided to his diary that he fully expected his division to be wiped out, his men having fought for over a hundred days with little food), and stamping his own robust authority on a division which he feared had grown too pessimistic about the chances of success, Tanaka promulgated a Special Order on 2 June ordering his men to fight on until they were overtaken by either victory or annihilation.

The coming battle is the turning point. It will denote the success or failure of the Greater East Asia War. You men have got to be fully in the picture as to what the present position is; regarding death as something lighter than a feather, you must tackle the task of capturing Imphal. For that reason it must be expected that the division will be almost annihilated. I have confidence in your firm courage and devotion and believe you will do your duty, but should any delinquencies occur you have got to understand that I shall take the necessary action ... in order to keep the honour of his unit bright, a commander may have to use his sword as a weapon of punishment, exceedingly shameful though it is to have to shed the blood of one's own soldiers on the battlefield. Fresh troops with unused rifles have now arrived and the time is at hand – the arrow is about to leave the bow. The infantry group is in high spirits: afire with valour and dominated by one thought and one thought only – the duty laid upon them to annihilate the enemy. On this battle rests the fate of the Empire. All officers and men fight courageously!

This rhetoric pleased Mutaguchi, who added some encouraging words of his own to the exhausted, hungry and malaria-ridden troops desperately struggling to stay alive in the rain-sodden quagmires of Shenam, Kohima and Bishenpur:

The struggle has developed into a fight between the material strength of the enemy and our spiritual strength. Continue in the task till all your ammunition is expended. If your hands are broken fight with your feet. If your hands and feet are broken use your teeth. If there is no breath left in your body, fight with your spirit. Lack of weapons is no excuse for defeat ... There must be no room for historians of the future to say we left something undone which we ought to have done.

Such determination against all odds deeply impressed Slim. 'Whatever one may think of the military wisdom of thus pursuing a hopeless object,' he commented, 'there can be no question of the supreme courage and hardihood of the Japanese soldiers who made the attempts. I know of no army that could have equalled them.' This stubbornness, however, as Slim had calculated, and as events were beginning at last to show right across the Manipur front, was also to prove their downfall. During June Tanaka repeatedly threw his weakened units forward against the hills overlooking Bishenpur and into Ninthoukhong, over which both sides struggled at fearsome cost. Once again it was the courage and stamina of the individual soldier, on both sides, which allowed the fighting to continue in spite of every impediment nature could throw at them. An attempt to seize the British-held part of Ninthoukhong on the night of 7 June by tanks and infantry failed only by virtue of the extraordinary bravery of Sergeant Harold Turner of 1st West Yorkshires, who won a posthumous Victoria Cross repelling the men of Lieutenant Araki's company from 1/67th Regiment as they attacked with tanks and automatic weapons. The struggle for the village continued until 12 June, Rifleman Ganju Lama of 2/5th Gurkhas repeating his performance at Torbung by destroying two Japanese tanks with a PIAT despite being severely wounded in the legs. He was awarded the Victoria Cross for his valour. This desperate fighting was reinforcing the Japanese reputation for foolhardy bravery, but it was not bringing them the strategic success that Mutaguchi demanded, and Tanaka so desired. Instead, with no reinforcements 33rd Division was rapidly reaching a point at which it would no longer exist. Following the attacks on Ninthoukhong 1/67th Regiment had no officers left, and only thirty-eight men alive. By 30 June the Japanese 33rd Division had lost 12,000 men, 70 per cent of its strength. Second Lieutenant Taiso Nishikawa bemoaned the Japanese failure to resupply the fighting divisions.

> The whole [of 33rd] Division, including the Divisional Commander, fought ten days without rice, and, because of things like this, the date of the general offensive, originally 10 June, was postponed ten or twenty days, and left indefinite. We felt it bitterly, this need for aircraft and motor transport. We wanted to shout to the people at home, 'Send more aircraft to the battle fronts'. The enemy stands firm, having plenty of weapons, ammunition and food. His attacks with tanks and mortars are something terrific — so are his air raids, and we can do nothing.

Along the Silchar Track, John Randle, of 7/10th Baluch, described the nature of the struggle for the high ground, which included a surprise attack on the Baluch position on Water Picquet on 20/21 June by 3/151st Regiment as part of a last-ditch attempt to break through the British positions.

> I was the controller of the fire support, guns, mortars, 25-pounders, and 5.5-inch mediums, also some AA guns in the direct fire role. We shared a Command Post with 5th Gurkhas.
> Water Picquet, Mortar Bluff, etc were pimples or hills occupied

by companies or even platoons, and mutually supporting. Subedar Netrabahadur Thapa on Water Picquet called for fire through me. Spoke in Gurkhali, but switched to Urdu when realized he was not talking to Gurkha officer. He was overrun – got a VC.

In fact there were only five Gurkha survivors of Water Picquet when it was overrun, four of whom were wounded. Lieutenant M. J. G. Martin told the story,

> Mortar Bluff was held by a platoon reinforced to a strength of forty-one men under Subedar Netrabahadur Thapa. At about 8 p.m. in pitch dark and torrential rain, the Japanese attacked. There were good communications to Battalion HQ, and the attack was broken up by supporting fire. In the early hours of the morning another attack came in and succeeded in penetrating the position. Savage and confused fighting followed, and the Subedar called for defensive fire from guns and mortars, but the position was almost overrun. Arrangements were made to send up reinforcements with extra ammunition, but they were wounded carrying it up, although some ammunition was retrieved. The Subedar had been killed by a grenade leading a counter-attack. Only six unwounded men remained on Mortar Bluff. These, collecting as many wounded as possible, withdrew to BP Picquet. When the Subedar's body was recovered his kukri was found embedded in a Japanese.

The Japanese occupation of Water Picquet isolated the British companies on Wireless Hill. Private Jack Clifford's platoon was part of the counter-attack by No 2 Company, Northamptons, which went in at 5.00 p.m. on the 21st, following a bombardment by 270 shells.

> This meant a bayonet attack, an order I and most soldiers dreaded. We moved off tired, hungry, and in horror of what lay before us, as we trudged the muddy tracks, the random shells and machine-gun fire all added to the tension. By the time we arrived, the enemy had occupied the picquet for at least three hours, and were well entrenched. I looked up at the barbed wire I had helped to strengthen, and wondered how we could surmount it under fire, some of the steel stakes were bedded in rock; we were given rum, then waited our time to go over. The artillery barrage started and sounded as if nothing could survive it. A corporal said, 'Doesn't that make you feel better?'
> He meant well but the barbed wire was still intact. The charge

went in as soon as the barrage ceased. It was slow going up the slippery slope. One corporal was way out in front, he kept looking back, urging us on, he went as far as he could and lay down about two yards from the wire. I joined him a yard to his right, the rest of the platoon joined us along this line, the air above our heads was thick with machine-gun bullets, the officer leading (Captain Michael Nott) tried to rally a final assault over the barbed wire but had his steel helmet shot off. To stand up is suicide; the defenders kept up a hail of machine-gun fire, every second our casualties were mounting, the corporal who had led gasped, 'Oh! they got me in the spine', the corporal who tried to inspire us was already dead, blood foaming from his mouth ...

The 2/5th Gurkha Rifles successfully retook the position – containing Mortar Bluff and Water Picquet on one of the ridges running up to Point 5846 – four days later. John Randle watched the counter-attack:

Next day 2/5 RGR got another VC, Agansing Rai, only time I've seen Gurkhas go in with the kukri. An awe-inspiring sight. They were counter-attacking the position and took it back. It was the most close fighting I ever saw in Burma.

Japanese attacks tended to come up and close the last few yards with bayonets. In a counter-attack we gave enemy positions a really good pasting, then fought our way in, clearing enemy positions with grenades, Tommy guns, Gurkhas with kukris, and our chaps used a bayonet. Casualties were high in this period. The 1/4th Gurkhas had 300 per cent officer casualties. There were twelve officers in a battalion, so they had thirty-six officer casualties.

The physical condition of the troops was now a serious cause for concern. The half rations on which men were subsisting was wholly insufficient to keep them fighting fit and well nourished in the appalling conditions of the monsoon, where the cold and wet sapped the morale of even the most motivated men. Private Ron Parker of the Northamptons recalled of Point 5846 that conditions were absolutely awful.

Everyone without exception developed a form of dysentery, but unless one was actually passing blood ... there was no question of reporting sick ... The latrines were a swimming mass of yellow excreta with thousands of flies and bluebottles buzzing around. It was a traumatic experience just having to relieve oneself.

Despite the huge quantities of water sluicing down the hillsides fresh water

remained a serious problem for the men on the hilltops. As a result there
was no shaving or washing. 'After a while some strange beards started to
appear,' recalled Captain Michael Nott, 'some of them a different colour
from a man's hair, and odd shapes.' Across the entire Imphal pocket men
were on half rations, but on the front line it was often much less. Private
Denis Short of the Northamptons recalled that in June they were down to
quarter rations. For Private Jack Clifford hunger remained 'the main
source of misery, everyone being under weight, rumours abounded daily,
that on such and such a day we would be replaced, all turned out to be
wishful thinking'. At the end of June he noted in his diary,

> By now I had not washed or shaved for three months and in sympathy
> with everyone else have lice. Hunger, tiredness, and exhaustion is
> taking over, how long can I keep going? The Dimapur road has been
> open for over a week, but no extra food has arrived here yet.

The British never ceased to be astonished at the fighting determination of
their enemy, despite their obvious suffering. At least for the British, food of
sorts was getting through to the fighting men. The Japanese were by now
living off leaves, roots and grass. Lieutenant Colonel Ted Taunton of the
Northamptons considered that few back home in Britain would ever believe
the savagery of combat against the Japanese.

> How few will believe that when he attacks (nearly always at night and
> throughout the night) you will beat him off all right, but you will hear
> and see him at daylight dug in within fifty yards of your perimeter
> wire. And there he will stay two days at a time, digging away until he
> has tunnelled out a veritable rabbit warren. He dies in scores and
> hundreds by fanatical attacks and fanatical hanging on to any ground
> he had gained – I have known them fight on for three days without
> food, come out completely dazed to attempt to recover, and then go
> back to fight on (if not killed before they get back). No German would
> stand and fight, whether in attack or defence, like these savages.

The casualties suffered by IV Corps bear stark testimony to the ferocity of
the fighting. As but one example, the three months of fighting for the
Silchar Track cost the Northamptons 76 per cent of their starting strength
in terms of killed, wounded or missing. Four hundred and fifty began the
battle in April but only 107 marched back to Imphal in July. But every one
of these men was sick, lice-ridden and hungry. They were also desperately
tired and there seemed no end in sight.

## Chapter 9

# Armageddon

But the Japanese were by now close to exhaustion. By early-June 1944 Operation C was near collapse, the fighting during the following six weeks merely prolonging the death agonies of the once proud, all-conquering Fifteenth Army. Despite desperate attempts, Yamamoto had failed to evict first 20th Indian Division and then 23rd Indian Division from the Shenam ridge. With casualties mounting with every attack he could do little else during the latter half of June but attempt to hold the ground that he had managed to seize, the life blood draining from his exhausted column. Yamauchi's 15th Division was fighting a bloody and tenacious delaying action against Briggs' 5th Indian Division which was moving inexorably if slowly along the Kohima Road, but by this time the result was never seriously in doubt. In the far north Sato's evacuation of his Kohima positions was by no means a headlong flight for safety, however. Thirty-first Division, desperately short of supplies and suffering fearsome casualties, fought an organized and tenacious withdrawal over the ensuing six weeks as the survivors struggled to make their way to the Chindwin over the same rugged hills whence they had come three months before. They now had the monsoon, starvation, physical exhaustion and the bitter taste of defeat with which to contend. In the south, determined not to relax his pressure, Tanaka's two weak regiments had attempted one last effort in late-May to break through the Bishenpur defences but at staggering cost. In obedience to Tanaka's orders, 33rd Division held on desperately, although the difficulties faced by his exhausted troops were made considerably worse by the fury of the monsoon. Unable to advance and unwilling to withdraw, the attacking Japanese were trapped and systematically destroyed.

By 22 June, however, the time for pretence was gone, Mutaguchi signalling Kawabe for permission to retreat back into Burma. The British had by this time broken through the final blocks on the road between Kohima and Imphal: what remained of Mutaguchi's army was by now in desperate straits, starving and demoralized, no match for the growing strength of Slim's Fourteenth Army building up in Imphal and flooding through from Dimapur on the now open Kohima Road. But Mutaguchi's anguish was not yet over. Kawabe, seeking higher permission for his actions, passed on Mutaguchi's request to Terauchi in Saigon, and it was not until 8 July that Mutaguchi at last received permission to retire. Even then Mutaguchi attempted to control the fighting withdrawal of what remained of his divisions. It was only on 20 July, formalizing what was already happening to his shattered army, that Mutaguchi ordered a general retreat across the Chindwin.

At the same time Slim ordered Stopford and Scoones to pursue Mutaguchi with such vigour that Fifteenth Army's defeat was turned into a rout. But the conditions conspired against a rapid British counter-offensive. Disease and malnutrition had weakened many and exhaustion was widespread. The extreme ruggedness of the terrain made progress difficult and slow. Many of Scoones' troops had fought continuously in appalling conditions for eight months. Slim's counter-offensive nevertheless got underway. While 7th Indian Division pressed 31st Division through the Naga Hills from the north-west, 80 Brigade of Gracey's 20th Indian Division[29] moved north towards Ukhrul during June to cut the line of communication and withdrawal routes for both 15th and 31st Divisions. The Japanese still held the positions they had secured for themselves in this mountain vastness, and proved stubbornly resistant to British attempts to remove them.

As the 80 Brigade column wound its way deeper into the tangled Naga Hills, the wild country forced them onto resupply by air. The drone of the twin-engined Dakotas winding their way up the valleys to drop their loads with remarkable accuracy on tiny drop zones on the top of steep ridges and in the narrow confines of deep valleys became as welcome and soothing as the sound of the bells of the local church in far-distant Britain. Rain continued to fall relentlessly as the heavily-laden troops sweated up hills and across valleys, exhausting the fittest man. Most of the activity in June revolved around small-scale patrol actions against support troops of 15th Division who were protecting their line of communication back to the Chindwin. Emulating the resourcefulness of their enemy, the column used elephants on a number of occasions to take the wounded to the rear. Towards the end of June the brigade, spread widely and thinly like a net across a vast swathe of hilly country, began to encounter large numbers of Japanese troops retreating east as the remnants of Sato's 31st Division flooded back from the north-west, and 15th Division withdrew from the

Kohima Road to the west. At the start of the withdrawal from Kohima units attempted to march back in an orderly and disciplined manner but by July signs of complete collapse became increasingly evident. The war correspondent Shizuo Maruyama, withdrawing with Sato from Kohima, wrote angrily,

> We had no ammunition, no clothes, no food, no guns ... the men were barefoot and ragged, and threw away everything except canes to help them walk. Their eyes blazed in their lean bodies ... all they had to keep them going was grass and water ... At Kohima we were starved and then crushed.

Because they were so few in such large country, British tactics concentrated on ambushing roads, tracks and river crossings, although deliberate attacks on Japanese-held villages dominating the road to Ukhrul were undertaken when necessary. On 5 July A Company of the Devons, for example, attacked Lambui, a village covering the road at a point on the Ukhrul Road which the Japanese had decided to hold in strength. Part of the village was captured in the attack but the Japanese did not relinquish their hold on the entire position until five days later when a heavy aerial bombardment put paid to the last defenders. Over the intervening days, accurate and heavy Japanese artillery fire fell on the Devons, killing and wounding a number of men, including the temporary Commanding Officer. The Japanese fought hard to push their withdrawing columns through the ambushes and road blocks placed in their way by 80 Brigade, furiously counter-attacking whenever and wherever they were attacked with the desperation of men knowing they were using up their last reserves of life to escape the clutches of the enemy and the unforgivable trauma of capture.

While conditions were bad for the British they were infinitely more so for the Japanese. For the men of both 15th and 31st Divisions, starvation, exhaustion and the savage monsoon rains daily extracted their toll, many hundreds dying on the endless, cloud-covered mountain ranges that flowed like angry waves on a mighty ocean all the way to the Chindwin. The Japanese began to call the trail of rotting bodies the 'bleached bones road'. 'There were dead bodies everywhere,' remembered Private Masaoki Okoshi,

> We couldn't even rest. We were retreating in the dark, and I'd get tired and would sit down to rest, but then would notice something soft underneath, and I'd realize it was a dead body. There were that many dead bodies all along the way. All along the road as we

travelled back. They all collapsed and died by the roadside. There would be a dead body every twenty metres or so. So it was impossible to stop for a rest. Wherever you stopped for a rest, you'd feel something soft and limp.

After being issued with a small amount of rice Private Sakae Sekiguchi observed that for his group of soldiers there

> was only one cupful (about 150 grams) of rice to last a whole company a week. In one company, there were twenty or thirty men. To go a whole week with just one cupful of rice was impossible. It was literally a few grains or a pinch of rice each. Because there wasn't enough to eat everyday, we'd have vegetables, or rather, grasses and weeds we'd find in the jungle, and mix them with the rice to make gruel. We'd be lucky to have three grains of rice. We'd say how bitter it tasted but we had no choice, as there was nothing else to eat.

The absurdly optimistic risks taken at the outset of the campaign, which provided support for an offensive lasting only twenty days, now began to demand their deadly payment. The pursuing British troops came across countless putrefying bodies, skeletons and abandoned weapons and material littering the jungle paths that led back through the hills to the Chindwin. 'On patrol near Ukhrul,' recalled Ken Cooper of 2nd Borders (part of 100 Brigade),

> amid tall, dripping jungle and dark menacing shadows, we heard the cries and screams of the Japanese wounded. In one clearing, not far from the Company positions, there was a lotus pool, blasted by the monsoon torrent: it was full of Jap corpses rotting, emaciated yellow hands clutching at the empty sky.

As 2nd Borders advanced eastward they were shocked to discover the extent of the disaster that had overtaken the Japanese army, as its detritus lay scattered across the jungle floor – corpses in their hundreds, equipment, weapons, burnt vehicles – and also its barbarity, including the body of a British officer nailed to a tree with Japanese bayonets. Disease, starvation and despair were accompanied in places by cannibalism. Private Nobuyuki Hata remembered fighting over what food was available, and Private Zenta Makioka observed the brutal facts of life in this fight for survival,

> Basically, in order for you to live, you want rice, and if you notice

that some guy has rice, you kill him to get the rice, and you eat it and stay alive. That was how it was. If you looked like you had rice, you'd get killed. So you couldn't appear to be carrying any rice. Many people were killed that way.

Yet, despite their predicament, still they fought. Japanese trucks and mule trains flowed back towards the Chindwin in considerable numbers, so much so that it was often impossible for the scattered British units in the hills to counter them all. Moving east along the Ukhrul road, 100 Brigade joined forces with 80 Brigade in early-July near Litan. On 12 July the Devons, part of this newly-amalgamated force, spread their net across the valley of the Thoubal river where, two days later, a small force of escaping enemy were intercepted, ten being killed and three taken prisoner. The following day the bag was thirteen killed and four prisoners.

The fact that an increasing number of enemy soldiers was being taken prisoner was a distinctive feature of the fighting at this time. Outside the frantic, stabbing, chaotic frenzy of close combat, and for all their hatred of the unnatural barbarity often demonstrated by the Japanese, many British troops came to feel sorry for the ragged specimens of humanity they now came across, helped perhaps by the rarity factor of these occasions. Lieutenant Peter Toole on the Tiddim Road with 20 Field Company heard the excited buzz that a Japanese soldier had been taken prisoner, and watched the event with interest. 'One day word came that a prisoner had been taken. This capture was rare and we had not until now seen a live Jap. The soldier was a sorry sight, small, in tatters, emaciated, scared stiff and bowing left, right and centre, being escorted to the rear.' Antony Brett-James recounts a story about the attitude of British soldiers to their defeated foe. Troops were clearing the Japanese from the villages leading north from Kohima in June 1944. A Japanese soldier 'was seen skulking in a bush near Jessami, by the side of the track. Out leapt the soldiers and seized him,

> "Shall we kill the little bastard? It's what he and his like deserve ..."
>
> "Oh, no, we can't. We'll take him back with us."
>
> After a few hundred yards – "Ere, Tojo, you look pretty miserable, 'ave a fag."
>
> A mile farther on they had a puncture, and it was "Come on, Tojo, give us a hand."
>
> By the time Kohima was reached, Tojo was a mascot, if not a friend.

Not all Japanese prisoners received such treatment. Mike Ball of the

American Field Service despatched a wounded Japanese prisoner in a truck from Kohima to the Field Hospital in Dimapur, accompanied by an armed guard. A couple of hours later he was chastised over the radio 'for sending in a dead Jap, shot through the head … the prisoner had been killed either by the guard or the driver or both'. On subsequent shipments a reliable Gurkha guard was appointed for the task, and only one severely-wounded Japanese prisoner was lost, succumbing to his injuries.

Meanwhile the advance by Messervy's 7th Indian Division began on 23 June and was led by 33 Brigade. Starting from a point fifteen miles south of Kohima the brigade's task was to march overland to Ukhrul, to converge on this sprawling mountain village with 80 and 100 Brigades who were advancing from the south. The 1,760-strong brigade comprised Major John Shipster's company of 7/2nd Punjab, the under strength 1st Queen's, 4/1st Gurkha Rifles, a battery of mountain guns, a company of Royal Engineers and a detachment from a field ambulance unit, including a mobile surgical team. The march was hugely demanding, both mentally and physically. Crossing swollen torrents with heavily-laden men and mules was a task in itself, without the challenges posed by the terrain. Mules fell off tracks into steep ravines, the tracks acting as riverbeds for the ever-flowing rain water seeking to make its way downhill. Progress was painfully slow, but there were few face-to-face encounters with the Japanese. What the men did come across, however, were large numbers of dead bodies, some hit by strikes from aircraft and some dead of exhaustion or starvation, or both. Ukhrul was captured on 8 July against only light resistance and the brigade struggled on in the wake of the Japanese retreat towards the Chindwin river. By now, Shipster recalled, the

> rigours of the march had put a great strain on men and mules, most of whom were tired, weak and sick. The health of the Brigade was beginning to deteriorate rapidly and 1st Queen's were almost too weak to fight. The Gurkhas, with their amazing stamina, still remained remarkably fit. The mules were also in a poor state, for disease was rife among them and a number had died. Plans had been based on reaching Ukhrul and little margin remained. Many men were too weak to digest or retain their food and chronic diarrhoea was rife. For days on end many officers and men lived on a diet of rum and hot tinned milk, which was all they could manage.

This advance was accompanied, far to the east, by part of Brigadier Perowne's Chindit brigade marching deep into the Somra Tracts in an attempt to cut off the Japanese retreat to the Chindwin. It proved to be one of the most physically demanding challenges of the entire campaign. The men of 1st Essex, deep on the eastern flank of 2nd Division near Somra, moved along an elevated track which (at 6,000 feet) ran round the inside curve of these ranges almost at the top of some enormous mountain ridges: it was nicknamed Death Valley as so much of the monsoon rain drained into it. Lieutenant Philip Brownless:

> The weary column of men and mules which made up 44 Column plodded down and then up the slippery mountain tracks, waded through torrents, trudged for miles through thick mud. It was here that some began to suspect the extent of the defeat being inflicted on the Japanese army. An occasional corpse or the carcase of a dead pack pony had been a fairly common sight, but here the column was marching over corpses, corpses sunk into the mud, with a helmet or a piece of equipment or a limb showing, and past an almost continuous line of dead pack animals ... This continuous line of dead stretched for twenty to thirty miles.
>
> The extreme misery of the march is impossible to describe. The incessant rain and the monotonous drips from the trees were relieved very occasionally by the crash of some great tree falling in the jungle below. The men staggered through the mud and up the slopes, borne down by the weight of their great packs. All were tortured by exhaustion because all were sick. We were so upset that few could eat the already short rations. Many were marching with temperatures and tick typhus had begun to break out. We had been sodden for weeks, were covered in mud, and we stank. Hollow-eyed, wasted, hungry, and yet incapable of eating more than a minute meal, we talked of nothing else but food. Towards the end of the march the food supply became precarious and even a small ration difficult to maintain. Some tried to fill the aching void with stewed leaves. Two small monkeys were shot and a number shared them. A myten (buffalo-type animal) was shot and divided among the Column. Each afternoon for five days a supply drop had been arranged, and each afternoon a hungry battalion waited in position listening to the drone of the supply planes as they circled above the clouds, loaded with food and searching anxiously for a break in the heavy cloud. Food and food alone was the subject of all conversation.

But by mid-July it was clear that British victory, in the triangle of hills between Jessami, Somra and Ukhrul, was unequivocal and the Chindit columns were withdrawn back to Imphal and Kohima, for their journey to a rehabilitation centre and hospitals in Dimapur. It was only now that the desperate condition and precarious health of many of the men became apparent. Flight Lieutenant Wilcox, his body a mass of sores, was evacuated on a Naga bamboo stretcher to Kohima, escorted by a section of men, as lone but fanatical Japanese soldiers still loitered along the jungle tracks. Finally reaching the Casualty Clearing Station at Kohima he was given a mirror, and was shocked to find himself 'looking at a strange sub-human with sunken, dirty cheeks covered in a black hirsute growth, whose dark hair lay matted and thick on its neck'. When his little party had reached Kohima, pressing their way through a throng of sepoys (they had brought with them a bound and suicidal Japanese prisoner, who excited some interest given the rarity of such creatures), Wilcox recalled his first encounter with civilization after four months living rough in the jungle.

> An RAMC officer pushed through the Indians and approached us. He looked harassed, sweated copiously. He said:
>
> 'Who the hell are you?'
>
> 'Doctor Livingstone. Who the hell are you?'
>
> He stared for a moment and then relaxed in a smile.
>
> 'I'm a doctor.'
>
> 'And I'm an RAF officer – believe it or not.'
>
> The ice was broken. He said:
>
> 'Where've you come from? God, you're in a mess!'
>
> I pointed to the hills behind the Japs.
>
> 'From there.'
>
> 'Bale out?'
>
> 'No – I've been in with 23 Brigade.'
>
> 'Marching?'
>
> 'Marching.'
>
> His jaw hung loose.
>
> 'My God! What's the Air Force coming to?'

The exhausted and malaria-ridden men of the Border Regiment marched to Imphal where they were placed in trucks to begin the journey back to Dimapur, and thence by Dakota to rest camps in India. On the way back they passed through the wreckage of Kohima. The rapidity with which normality could settle over the battlefield was astonishing. Dr Harry Good recalled the scene.

> Passing through Kohima was like viewing a scene of Flanders in the 1914–18 war with skeletons of trees with no leaves on them. Amongst all this chaos we noticed a guard mounting of the Durham Light Infantry, complete with blancoed equipment – this within a week or so of one of the bitterest battles of WW2.

Lieutenant Philip Brownless, likewise ending this phase of operations near Ukhrul, marched into Imphal. He, too, was surprised at the reception the column of bedraggled fighters received.

> At the end of the campaign, as we approached Imphal and hopes of some vestiges of civilization, we came upon a surprising sight – a very clean, rosy-faced military policeman. As we approached he shouted, 'Where have you come from, mate?' My batman … didn't even deign to look at him: he just said, 'We've been doing this for four … effing … months!' It was a simple expression of everybody's feelings.

~

Likewise, 33 Brigade were ordered to give up their chase on 16 July, the evidence of profound Japanese defeat all around them, and their own troops weakening in the challenging conditions, causing Stopford to recognize that there was now little value in continuing the pursuit: the Japanese were a broken reed, and dying in vast numbers of their own accord, without the intervention of the British. One of the Japanese soldiers being followed by John Shipster's men was Senior Private Manabu Wada, one of only a hundred or so survivors of 3/138th Regiment. The horror of the retreat from Kohima through these matted hills was indescribable.

> Without shelter from the rains, with boots that had rotted and had to be bound with grass, we began to trudge along the deep mud paths carrying our rifles without ammunition, leaning on sticks to support our weak bodies. Our medical troops slipped and slid as they carried the sick and wounded on stretchers or supported the 'walking wounded'. Some of the orderlies were themselves so weak that they fell to the ground again and again until their physical and

moral endurance was at an end, so that when a sick man cried out in pain they simply said, 'If you complain we'll just let you go, and throw you and the stretcher down the cliff side.'

Icy rain fell mercilessly on us and we lived day and night drenched to the skin and pierced with cold. I remember how we longed for a place, any place at all, where we could take shelter and rest. Once we found a tent in the jungle; inside it were the bodies of six nurses ... In another tent we found the bodies of three soldiers who had killed themselves. How could one ever forget such terrible, distressing sights as the dead nurses, and the soldiers who had taken their own lives?

Our path to safety lay beyond these Arakan Mountains [sic] covered in dense jungle. In the rain, with no place to sit, we took short spells of sleep standing on our feet. The bodies of our comrades who had struggled along the track before us lay all around, rain-sodden and giving off the stench of decomposition. The bones of some bodies were exposed. Even with the support of our sticks we fell amongst the corpses again and again as we stumbled on rocks and tree roots made bare by the rain and attempted one more step, then one more step in our exhaustion.

Thousands upon thousands of maggots crept out of the bodies lying in streams and were carried away by the fast-flowing waters. Many of the dead soldiers' bodies were no more than bleached bones ... We walked and walked endlessly along a road littered with corpses. With almost nothing to eat and our feet aching and legs weary, we used sticks to support ourselves until at last, several days later, I don't know how many, we reached Tonhe. Although there were three or four houses there we found no villagers and assumed they must be hiding somewhere.

~

While these events were taking place in the hills around Ukhrul, on the Shenam front in mid-July Roberts' 23rd Indian Division was ordered to drive Yamamoto's remnants to Tamu, 49 Brigade cutting off the Japanese line of communication with a flanking march through the hills to the north, while the two remaining brigades attacked frontally the Tengnoupal defences. The men were exhausted after months of fighting, and the monsoon rains still belted down with inconvenient consistency, but for five days the 49 Brigade column weaved its way slowly through the hills before arriving at Sibong, 2,000 feet above the bridge on the Lokchao river, which was heavily defended by the Japanese, with dug-in tanks and copious quantities of barbed wire hidden in the long grass. A fierce struggle developed for Battle Hill, a prominent feature overlooking the road, but, without artillery, even the most resolute attack had little chance of prising the Japanese from their positions. Instead, the weak 4th Mahrattas (now numbering fewer than 200 men) moved out from Sibong before first light next day, 26 July, in an attempt to create a road block a few miles north of Tamu. Their arrival stirred up a hornets' nest, the Japanese rushing against the improvised block with angry fury from both directions. The block could not be held, and the survivors withdrew that night. But simultaneously, in the east along the Tengnoupal position the remainder of 23rd Division had thrown itself against the rapidly-weakening defenders, and at long last the flood gates broke, the Japanese abandoning the position and pouring east over jungle tracks in disorder to escape the British advance. Artillery came up with the advancing division and 6th Mahrattas occupied Battle Hill on 31 July with little opposition.

Staff Sergeant Yasumasa Nishiji, of 20th Independent Engineer Regiment, withdrew with the remains of his unit from the Shenam Ridge with this exodus.

> From March 1944 the platoon to which I belonged was in the front line on the Palel road. When all Japanese troops retreated in July, I and ten relatively healthy men selected from the company operated boats and ferried soldiers across the Yu River which was flowing with great turbulence due to the heavy monsoon rainfall. When all the soldiers had crossed the river we struggled through muddy mountain passes to make our way to the east of the Chindwin River. In our position at the very rear of the retreating troops I saw many exhausted men unable to keep up with their units, and their comrades too weary to help them … Almost all of them, tens of thousands, perished. We called the road the 'Human Remains Highway'. What happened here was beyond the bounds of acceptable human behaviour. It was a vision of hell … It became a routine that a soldier who was emaciated and crippled, with no hope of recovery, was given a grenade and persuaded, without words, to sort himself out … It often occurred that soldiers took their own lives in pairs. They embraced, placing a grenade between them. We called it double suicide.

There even began a trade in hand grenades, explains Private Zenta Makioka,

I think it got up to about 10 yen for one hand grenade. People would ask others to sell them their grenades. To kill themselves. They wanted hand grenades so they could commit suicide. They didn't have any weapons because they had discarded them. So even if they wanted to shoot themselves, they no longer had their rifles. And so in the end, they would use hand grenades. If they didn't have their own, they'd give money to buy one and then die.

Twenty-third Indian Division pushed Yamamoto's limping columns into Tamu, before they were replaced by 2nd Division, the fresh 11th East African Division, preparing for the push down the Kabaw valley, following thereafter. The Irish travel writer Gerald Hanley, serving as a War Correspondent attached to the East Africans, was shocked to see the devastation of the Japanese retreat at Tamu in July as 23rd Division mopped up the town.

The smell of Tamu came to us as we drove down into the mouth of Khabaw Valley. It was a smell that was sweet and terrible … (it) gave off a smell of dead that reached for miles around it.

Over five hundred Japanese corpses were packed inside this small village of blackened sticks and rubble. The jungle had been torn down, ripped away, and blasted into splinters, exposing the frameworks of the enemy hospital buildings, barracks, and offices. In the ruins of these buildings the enemy lay dead in rows, in heaps, in pieces. They choked the village. Many had killed themselves with grenades, and these lay like horrible broken dolls.

The dead lay in bullock carts, under houses, in trees, craters and trenches, half dressed, fully equipped and naked … Some were alive, half demented by hunger and fever, who turned to fight like animals on the last tremor of the electric fanaticism that had brought them here. These were cut down by bullets. Some tottered around in circles, mumbling, out of their minds.

Tamu, pest and charnel-house, was evil and ghastly, and you drove through it swiftly, for the smell stayed on your clothes.

~

Meanwhile, south of Bishenpur, Cowan's division pushed hard against the shattered remnants of Tanaka's division, which fought back from strongpoints and defended villages with undiminished tenacity. When its own withdrawal was reluctantly ordered it did so carefully and deliberately, mining roads, blowing up bridges and delaying the advance of 5th Indian Division (who had taken responsibility for the pursuit) along the Tiddim Road through the use of stay-behind parties who ambushed the road and only pulled back when their own position became imperilled. This was a task in which the combat engineers rebuilt the road, often under fire, and made it fit for travel for the Lee Grants, Stuarts and heavy trucks which followed behind the vanguard troops, while the ubiquitous infantry out-flanked Japanese positions through the hills, and protected the men on the road below. When the weather allowed, Hurribombers swooped in from above to attack these stay-behind positions with cannon fire and 250-pound bombs. The pattern was described by Lieutenant Peter Toole, whose 20 Field Company found itself repeatedly in the direct line of fire,

> There was one incident where a crater had been blown at a very sharp bend round the nose of a hill. The scissors bridge came forward and was so heavily engaged by fire that it had to retire with its crew wounded. The West Yorkshires made an encircling movement the next day, the enemy retreated, the scissors got the tanks across and we repaired the road and we all moved on again.

The Japanese were desperately short of stores, but improvised effectively. One problem for the slowly advancing 5th Indian Division was the improvised anti-tank mine. Toole:

> We were called forward to clear mines which had been spotted on a sharp bend. No vehicles had been along the stretch of road leading to the site and I was detailed to sit on the jeep bonnet with my feet on the bumper and be driven slowly along to examine the road for more mines. On arrival at the bend the jawans were dealing with the problem in true text-book fashion, on their bellies and using prodders. The mines themselves were very poor, consisting of two flat primerless mines one above the other separated by an impact-type hand-grenade, and were easily dealt with.

By such means the exhausted, emaciated survivors of Tanaka's 33rd Division managed their withdrawal back over the tangled hills whence they had rushed so expectantly in March. Briggs' pace was equally slow, this being less a pursuit than a methodical clearance but, with the exhaustion of the troops, the narrowness of the front (it being limited to the width of the road and its immediate hinterland) and the challenges of the terrain, this was all that could be managed. It was on 12 November that the Division marched, finally, into Kalemyo, meeting up with 11th East African Division which had completed its clearance of the Kabaw valley.

This advance proved to be the final chapter in the ignominious destruction of the Fifteenth Army. During July its entire command structure had disintegrated, men and units being left to fend for themselves in the life-and-death struggle to evade the clutches of the slowly advancing Fourteenth Army: by the last day of July 1944 the battle for India could be said to be over. The extraordinary commitment of Mutaguchi's benighted troops in battering away at Imphal until they lacked even the energy to retreat was remarkable, but ultimately pointless. The power of bushido could not make up for the reality, observed by Arthur Swinson, that the 'Japanese commanders had bungled at the start [and had] quarrelled at the end'. The staggering disunity of command displayed across the whole of Fifteenth Army repaid poorly the commitment, often to the death, of those who had blindly to carry out the incoherent orders of their masters. So perished Mutaguchi's army and, with it, Japanese dreams of victory in India. Of the 65,000 fighting troops who set off across the Chindwin in early–March 1944, 30,000 were killed in battle and a further 23,000 were wounded, a casualty rate of an unprecedented 81 per cent of combat forces, and 46 per cent of the total size of Fifteenth Army. Only 600 allowed themselves to be taken prisoner, most of them too sick even to take their own lives. Some 17,000 pack animals perished during the operation and not a single piece of heavy weaponry made it back to Burma.[30] The battle had provided the largest, most prolonged and most intense engagement with a Japanese army yet seen in the war. 'It is the most important defeat the Japs have ever suffered in their military career,' wrote Mountbatten exultantly to his wife on 22 June 1944, 'because the numbers involved are so much greater than any Pacific Island operation.' The extent of the disaster that befell Fifteenth Army is captured by a comment by Kase Toshikazu, a member of the wartime Japanese Foreign Office, who lamented, 'Most of this force perished in battle or later of starvation. The disaster at Imphal was perhaps the worst of its kind yet chronicled in the annals of war'. The latter might better have included the caveat 'Japanese' to avoid charges of exaggeration, but his comment captures something of the enormity of the human disaster that overwhelmed Fifteenth Army. It might more fairly be described as the greatest Japanese military disaster of all time. When considered with the defeat of Twenty-eighth Army in Arakan, Fourteenth Army's substantial – even extraordinary achievement – can be seen. Not only had it destroyed five divisions and inflicted some 90,000 casualties on the enemy, something that would have been considered inconceivable only five months before, but in so doing it had severely degraded the fighting power of the Burma Area Army. The Indian, Gurkha, African and British troops of this remarkably homogeneous organization had also decisively removed any remaining notions of Japanese superiority on the battlefield. The cost? Fourteenth Army had suffered 24,000 casualties in Arakan, Kohima and Imphal, many of whom recovered under Fourteenth Army's medical care.[31]

~

The battles for Imphal and Kohima had been a triumph for Bill Slim, at the time a relatively-unknown lieutenant general fighting on the very edge of an empire that – had he but known it – was about to collapse of its own accord. The plan for battle had been his, as were its assumptions, risks and mistakes. Given his bitter experience of the Japanese in 1942 and 1943, he believed that he knew what he had to do to defeat Mutaguchi and he accordingly developed a plan of battle to turn that theory into reality, building on the rigorous training programme he introduced in 1943. The plan was unconventional and, with the resources in hand, unproven. But it proved successful. Withdrawing IV Corps onto the Imphal plain, transferring firstly 5th Indian Division and then 7th Indian Division by air to the Manipur and Kohima battlefields and relying on air supply to maintain the besieged IV Corps were all phenomenal risks and yet undoubtedly shifted the balance of the battle in Fourteenth Army's favour. His self-belief allowed him to deflect the fears of those less certain than himself, especially those few who misinterpreted his risk-taking at the start of Operation C as recklessness.

In particular his recognition of the power of air supply and battlefield air support proved the lifeblood of his defence in Arakan, Kohima and Imphal. And by firmness of conviction and strength of character he was able to bind to his cause the most important senior commander in the theatre, Mountbatten. It was this relationship which was to prove to be *the* relationship of the war in the Far East. It was indisputably Slim's concept of battle, and Slim's plan for the destruction of Fifteenth Army, that Mountbatten adopted as his own and represented upwards to Churchill and Roosevelt and revealed a dramatic contrast to the relationship the hapless Mutaguchi enjoyed with Kawabe.

Likewise, although the troops of Fourteenth Army – Indian, British and East and West African alike – might still claim that they were the 'Forgotten Army', by 1944 there was no doubt about the strength and depth of the hard-won *esprit de corps* that now lay at the heart of the army; a sense of moral power that was sealed in the heat of battle and the realization of victory. They had taken on the most fearsome enemy the British Army had ever encountered in its history, and had conquered. Slim had stared disaster in its face during those first desperate weeks of the Imphal-Kohima battle and by his calm and careful handling of the various crises as they arrived brought about their successful resolution. Crucially, he had earned and retained the respect and confidence of his corps and divisional commanders. He made mistakes, but was the first to admit them, concentrating his effort on solving problems rather than apportioning blame. By the end of these battles General Slim had become 'Uncle Bill', a soubriquet soon in universal currency in Fourteenth Army, and which was to remain with him for the rest of his days.

Slim, of course, was helped in the achievement of his victory by the mistakes of his enemy. Mutaguchi's poor relationship with Sato had the greatest strategic impact of all on his plans for a successful offensive. Sato's failure to strike against Dimapur cost the Japanese the chance of seizing this jewel in the British strategic crown: its loss would have been a catastrophic blow to the British, leading inevitably to the collapse of Imphal. But his biggest failure was to fail adequately to supply Sato's division. Mutaguchi believed that the advance into India would be rapid and decisive and that captured British supplies would remove the need to bring large quantities of stores across the Chindwin to supply his army, especially if Sato were able to reach Dimapur. Mutaguchi was also convinced that Sato's troops could forage sufficient supplies from the native villages through which they passed, and never believed the reports that subsequently filtered back that 31st Division was starving. However, Sato's hatred of Mutaguchi meant that he was never seriously going to act on his superior's strategic vision (by advancing on Dimapur) in contravention to Kawabe's direct orders. In the circumstances, it is difficult not to accept that Sato's ultimate disobedience of Mutaguchi's orders, and his decision to withdraw from Kohima, was the correct thing to do, even though Mutaguchi knew that 31st Division had been within a whisker of capturing Dimapur, an act that would have dealt a devastating blow to the British and at the same time refuelled his army.

Mutaguchi's failure was compounded by a number of other factors. While an advance into India in 1944 was a distinctly different prospect from 1942, in Mutaguchi's eagerness to launch an offensive he failed to appreciate the nature of the changes that had taken place in British warfighting capabilities during the period, and indeed his own weaknesses. The problem in 1944 was that he was prepared to secure this military glory on the assumption that nothing had changed in British training, techniques and capabilities since 1942. Even so, despite the preponderance in men, equipment (especially artillery and armour) and aircraft enjoyed by the British in 1944, there was still no guarantee that the British could defeat the Japanese in a straight fight. There was every possibility that they could yet again be defeated by the daring, risk-taking Japanese. There were many things that could go wrong for Slim, not least of which was the loss of Dimapur. Nevertheless, Mutaguchi's excessive optimism and high hopes made his failure in Assam more likely and put at risk a sound strategic idea. In the first place, Japanese knowledge of what the new Fourteenth Army was building up in terms of capability and strength unseen beyond the Chindwin was negligible, although a number of audacious long-range patrols had been carried out, deep into Manipur. The dramatic improvements to the quality of the British forces in India could have been surmised, but were not. Lieutenant General Naka, Burma Area Army's Chief of Staff, told 15th Division, for instance, that it would not need any anti-tank weapons because the British did not have any tanks. They would find in fact that Scoones of IV Corps had two regiments of heavy tanks at Imphal, and many successful British counter-attacks in the coming weeks were framed around the effective British use of armour.

Indeed, there was an almost criminal lack of intelligence in the Japanese Burma Area Army about the transformation overtaking India in its preparation for war. The disastrous British showing in Arakan in May 1943, which ended when Mutaguchi was pressing the merits of an Imphal offensive on his superiors, served merely to reinforce existing prejudices that the British would, yet again, run for the rear in the face of Japanese aggression and decisiveness. On past experience of his British enemy, the odds, Mutaguchi believed, were clearly in his favour. 'The British Army is weaker than the Chinese,' he declared to his staff at the Maymyo conference in December 1943. 'If you surround them, they run away!'

But these odds were changing, the first evidence of which was the defeat of Major General Sakurai Tokutar's bold offensive in Arakan in February 1944. That the British had stood and fought, refusing to be panicked into a hasty withdrawal, was a new phenomenon in Japanese experience, but Mutaguchi took no notice of it. As it transpired, Operation Z in Arakan began too early, as it took Mutaguchi longer than expected to muster all his troops on the Chindwin ready for the advance against Imphal. This allowed a dangerous hiatus to elapse between the demise of Operation

Z in February 1944 and the launch of Operation C in March, a delay that allowed Slim quickly to move two Indian divisions directly to the threatened area by air. Instead, he took comfort from the fact that Slim had been forced to divert his reserves away from Imphal, where his own attack was now about to fall, to Arakan. Mutaguchi consistently overestimated his chances of success. He airily dismissed the repeated concerns of Sato and Major General Tazoe, Kawabe's air commander, for instance, and ordered, ten days after the initial advance began, that the entire complement of Fifteenth Army's prostitutes, or comfort girls, were to be despatched to Imphal, so as not to waste any time before his men could be rewarded for their arduous endeavours, once Imphal had been reached. Mutaguchi refused to be separated, even on operations, from his own geishas, a group of whom accompanied Headquarters Fifteenth Army from Maymyo into India.

But he was wrong to discount the new realities presented by Slim's Fourteenth Army. In Arakan during February 1944 the British had decisively bettered the Japanese in weeks of hard, desperate fighting. Success was total. Mutaguchi should have paused to consider the hard lessons taught to the Japanese during Operation Z but instead, because of his airy assumptions about the cowardly British, Operation C was launched weak in weapons and firepower, especially in 15th and 31st Divisions. The force was stripped of its medium artillery and had it replaced with lightweight mountain guns which, while easier to transport across the hills, were nevertheless hopelessly inadequate compared to the weight of firepower able to be put down by the British. Likewise, Japanese air power was diminishing rapidly. Although able to concentrate aircraft for short periods of time over the battlefield (and for occasional aggressive sorties against the Hump airlift), overwhelming air superiority was enjoyed by the British in the skies above Manipur and the Naga Hills. The disparity between British and Japanese air strength grew more marked every day. In the period between 10 and 31 March 1944, 5th Air Division could only put up an average of forty-one fighters a day. The British could boast ten times this number of fighters, together with 224 bombers and thirty-one reconnaissance aircraft. A significant Japanese weakness lay in the fact that most of their aircraft were fighters: Tazoe possessed no transport capability and only a tiny bomber force that was frittered away early in the fighting. One of Tokyo's worst miscalculations in 1944 was failing to anticipate the combined strength of Allied air forces, without which the defence of India would not have been possible. Both Kawabe and Mutaguchi saw the invasion of India as an exercise in ground warfare and in their assessments (if, indeed, they ever made them) of Allied air power they failed grievously to appreciate this war-winning capability enjoyed by their enemy, and their own dramatic weakness in this regard.

Mutaguchi's swift onslaught against Imphal might have worked if he were facing a less resolute enemy. In 1944, however, his stratagem failed because he was unable to concentrate his forces. Mutaguchi's rationale for at least five widely-dispersed and separate attacking columns made much sense in the context of any enemy that was expected to run away on first contact, frightened by the prospect of engagements on multiple fronts. When the British, however, failed to do so, and instead remained to fight, this dispersal became a devastating weakness, as the Japanese were denied the opportunity to concentrate their forces at a single point, and by sheer weight of numbers and firepower to overwhelm the defenders. Mutaguchi desperately tried to reorganize his troops where he could, especially by transferring 14th Tank Regiment to Bishenpur in mid-May, but this was too little (it now had forty serviceable tanks remaining from an initial sixty-six), too late. The British, by contrast, could quickly move units around the plain to support vulnerable locations when required.

Mutaguchi also made the mistake of not being forward with his divisional commanders from the very beginning, driving, influencing and making sure that his plan was followed, only moving his HQ forward from Maymyo in May. To the end he remained in obstinate denial of the crisis facing his army, talking still of breaking through into the Imphal Plain despite the battering his three divisions were each receiving at Bishenpur in the south, on the Shenam heights to the south-east and at Kohima in the north, despite the huge casualties he had sustained, and despite the collapse of the rickety line of communication over the Chindwin. The onset of the monsoon in April added to the misery of his starving troops. Mutaguchi's new headquarters' location in Tamu did not materially improve his understanding of what was happening on each of his three fronts. As the news from each division got progressively worse, the staff of HQ Fifteenth Army increasingly resisted passing bad news to their commander for fear of the rage that would ensue. Even when the truth was stated plainly to him (such as by Sato, for instance, or Yanagida), his own pride prevented him from accepting the truth for what it was. Considerations of 'face' meant that it was not only Mutaguchi who was embarrassed publicly to admit defeat. Prime Minister Tōjō himself had already had the opportunity to call back Mutaguchi's army on 15 May but, according to Major Iwaichi Fujiwara he 'bottled' the decision. General Hata, Tōjō's Deputy Chief-of-Staff in Tokyo, had visited Saigon and Rangoon between 28 April and 1

May and concluded that it would be better to suspend operations in India. Tōjō, when informed of this news on 15 May, agreed privately with Hata but strangely refused publicly to countenance the prospect of failure and refused to call back Mutaguchi's army. Equally, the demands of *bushido* prevented Mutaguchi from publicly admitting that his offensive had been halted and was on the verge of defeat, although he was later to admit that, on 6 June 1944, he met with Kawabe and tried to tell him that he believed that his army should withdraw. Mutaguchi found it impossible to talk plainly about the need to retreat, and hoped that some kind of extra-sensory perception by Kawabe would enable him to understand the crisis he faced. It did not work, and Kawabe remained unaware of Mutaguchi's desperate desire to call off the offensive. Instead, Kawabe offered him more troops, and for a further month Mutaguchi and his three divisions struggled on against the enemy, the climate, the terrain, and each other. So the Japanese army fought on, destroying itself in the process because the senior generals concerned could not bring themselves to communicate openly on the subject.

Kawabe later argued that he was also motivated by the need to give every opportunity to Subhas Chandra Bose to succeed in fomenting rebellion across India. This is a tortuous excuse. By early-June it was plainly evident to all that no such nationalistic conflagration was either possible or probable and that the quality of the contribution made by the INA was insufficient to rouse rebellion amongst their erstwhile comrades who chose to continue fighting for the Raj. The statistics speak for themselves. Of the 6,000 men in the two deployed Regiments of the INA Division in March 1944 about 400 were killed in battle, 1,500 died of disease, 800 surrendered and 714 deserted or were captured before July.

It was clear that Mutaguchi's greatest failure was the over optimism that led to the extraordinary logistical risks he was prepared to take. One of the many lessons that Orde Wingate had learned from the first expedition into Japanese-held Burma (Operation LONGCLOTH in March and April 1943) was that he needed air supply to ensure that his troops were supplied and casualties evacuated. Mutaguchi believed that Wingate had demonstrated that the mountain range could be broached by an invading force, but he failed to understand the lesson that Wingate had learned about logistics, namely that without supplies his force would rapidly wither on the vine. This lesson was only to become apparent to the Japanese in the logistically-induced disaster of Operation C. The startling fanaticism of *bushido* provided all that the Japanese needed in terms of spiritual strength but was wholly insufficient to feed what Fifteenth Army required materially, serving only to add an uncertain glory to the final sacrifice of thousands of Japanese soldiers as the campaign's last breath was slowly strangled from them.

In his excitement Mutaguchi entirely neglected to consider the possibility of failure. The consequences of not capturing Imphal, once he had committed himself to an offensive, were dire. At worst, it would create a vortex that would act to suck the British back into Burma. At best, it would extend Japan's defensive barrier on the frontier with British India to breaking point. But Mutaguchi did not fill his mind with such baleful thoughts, believing that he could not fail. Not preparing for this possibility, however, was a serious mistake. While Allied strategy was to avoid entanglements in Burma, both Slim and Stilwell were convinced that the re-occupation of Burma (rather than merely its bypassing, as Churchill urged) was possible. Until the invasion of France had taken place in June 1944 and released large quantities of landing craft for use in Asian waters, the only way in which the country would be taken from the Japanese was overland from India or China. In Slim's mind, this opportunity would be greatly enhanced if the Japanese advanced in force into Manipur, as a Japanese defeat would open the door to the re-occupation of Burma. Both Mutaguchi and Slim knew this, but Mutaguchi was content to ignore it as a risk that he was certain would remain unfulfilled. He was wrong.

Laurels are awarded to the victor. On 15 December 1944, Wavell knighted Slim at Imphal on behalf of King George VI, alongside his three corps commanders, Christison,[32] Stopford and Scoones. Together they had not only defeated the invasion of India, but had inflicted upon the Japanese the greatest defeat in their country's history. In so doing Fourteenth Army had also completely changed the strategic landscape in South East Asia Command as, at last, the possibility of an Allied offensive into Burma presented itself. The battle for India was over, and that for the reconquest of Burma about to begin. This, of course, is another story.

# Epilogue

Of all the invading armies of history, it is hard to think of one that was repulsed more decisively, or more ignominiously, than the Japanese Fifteenth Army launched against India in March 1944. Its defeat was not the fault of the Japanese soldiers, who fought courageously, tenaciously and fiercely, but of their commanders, who sacrificed the lives of their troops on the altar of their own hubris.

The importance of this victory was overshadowed at the time, and downplayed for decades afterwards, by the massive victories which brought the Second World War to an end in Europe and the Pacific. But only as the generation which witnessed and participated in it passes away does the cool light of history begin to reveal that the battles in India in 1944, epitomized in the fulcrum battle at Kohima, were an epic comparable with Thermopylae, Gallipoli, Stalingrad, and other better-known confrontation battles where the arrogant invader became, in time, the ignominious loser. It is clear that Kohima/Imphal was one of four great turning-point battles in the Second World War, when the tide of war changed irreversibly and dramatically against those who initially held the upper hand. The first was at Midway in June 1942 when the US Navy successfully challenged Japanese dominance in the Pacific. The second was at Stalingrad between August 1942 and January 1943 when the seemingly unstoppable German juggernaut in the Soviet Union was finally halted in the winter bloodbath of that city, where only 94,000 of the original 300,000 German and Rumanian troops survived. The third was at El Alamein in October 1942 when the British Commonwealth triumphed against Rommel's *Panzerarmee Afrika* in North Africa and began the process that led to the German surrender in Tunisia in May 1943. The fourth was the battle at Kohima and around Imphal between March and July 1944 when the Japanese 'March on Delhi' was brought to nothing at a huge cost in human life, and the start of their retreat from Asia began. Adjectives such as 'climactic' and 'titanic', struggle to give proper impact to the reality and extent of the terrible war that raged across the jungle-clad hills during these fearsome months. Lord Louis Mountbatten called Kohima 'one of the greatest battles in history, of naked unparalleled heroism, the British/Indian Thermopylae'.

Yet the victory was hailed at the time more with relief – because it was not a defeat – than with triumph because it was a victory. It was also seen as giving the Allies a new headache: the practicality of an offensive directly into Burma, which the Chiefs of Staff in London had long resisted. In 1944, in south-east Asia, the Allies were unified in the objective of defeat of the Japanese (provided it was *after* the defeat of Germany) but they were seriously divided on the means by which victory should be achieved. The exclusive purpose of American strategy in south-east Asia was to support China so that it might continue to hold Japan at bay. To support China effectively required operations in Burma to restore the supply lines that had previously run from Rangoon into Yunnan. The British, however, following on from the bitter defeats in Malaya and Burma in 1942 and the débâcle in Arakan in 1943, regarded the prospect of a long and slow jungle campaign to retake Burma from the north with intense reluctance. It would be akin, Churchill said, to 'going into the water to fight the shark' or (as Field Marshal Alan Brooke reported another of Churchill's sayings) to 'eat the porcupine quill by quill'.

The alternative strategy proposed by London was to launch amphibious attacks against the Japanese along the vulnerable littorals in Burma, Malaya and Sumatra, thus avoiding becoming embroiled in long and expensive land campaigns. On the basis of this reasoning, an entanglement in Burma could be avoided altogether. South East Asia Command's core strategic ambiguities were ultimately resolved both by a severe impoverishment of resources and by the Japanese defeat in Assam. Plans for an amphibious invasion of northern Sumatra, from whence an attack on Singapore could be launched across the Malacca Straits, did not survive 1943. Other seaborne plans went the same way, sinking on the rocks of inadequate shipping and the need for amphibious craft in Europe. Even a small operation against the Andaman Islands, together with a resurrected amphibious assault against Akyab, did not get beyond outline planning.

Amphibious warfare was abandoned despite the insistence of Chiang Kai-shek that the *sine qua non* for Chinese help in the reconquest of Burma was the recovery of British naval control of the Bay of Bengal. Chiang Kai-shek also demanded that the British make every possible effort to seize Mandalay and Rangoon immediately to facilitate the building of a new road to China. Unless he had assurances to this effect, together with a commitment to deliver at least 10,000 tons of supplies a month over the 'Hump', he was not prepared to move his forces any further south than Lashio. His approach to strategic dialogue was based on brinkmanship and blackmail, and quickly exhausted the patience of the Allied war leaders unable to find a practical way of meeting these demands even if they had the political will to achieve them.

The dramatic success of Slim's Fourteenth Army in Assam by July 1944 therefore opened up for the first time the prospect of the reconquest of Burma by land. And this, in 1945, is precisely what, against every expectation, it achieved. The 1944 victory thus not only was a turning point in the war against the Japanese, but precipitated the reconquest of Burma in 1945.

The Churchill government had been deeply apprehensive about the political consequences of defeat in 1944. The fact that they did not trumpet the victory was also partly political. The less said about anything connected with India, given Roosevelt's public hostility to the British Empire, the better. The growth of 'The Forgotten Army' legend was thus not only caused by the fact that Burma was seen as a strategic backwater but was also a deliberate act of censorship by the British.

The invasion of India was not only Japan's last bid for victory, but its last imperial land grab. It was also the last time Britain was forced to defend its empire (Suez in 1956 and the Falklands in 1982 were hangovers). New and old empires collided in India in 1944. In the searchlight of history, neither had any right to be there. However, the British victory was profound. It did not, as some had feared, strengthen British determination to bolster her empire, at least by military means, but rather confirmed its perception that the time was approaching when it should give up. In the short term, it made a dramatic impact on the morale of the Allies fighting back the tide of fascist militarism that had appeared unstoppable. Strategically, it made little impact on the final outcome of the war against Germany and Japan. Politically, it removed any claim that India was ripe for civil war. The possibilities available to the militant Bengali nationalism of Subhas Chandra Bose were never a match for the peaceful and powerful drive for political self-determination led by Gandhi and Nehru. It also demonstrated forcefully to the Japanese the harsh reality of defeat, for there was no doubt that Japan had been comprehensively – even profoundly – beaten. Their earlier defeats had ousted them from, or destroyed them in, territories which they had captured. They suffered this defeat when attempting to advance. In the physical defeat of the Japanese in Asia in 1944 and 1945 the hard lesson was taught to a nation previously drunk on expansionist ambition that aggression of this type had no long-term reward and belonged to a previous, less intelligent, age.

Even when compared with the other great turning point battles of the

Second World War, and of history, repulse of the Japanese invasion of India had unique features. The terrain dictated that there was no alternative to head-on combat between foot soldiers. It also limited the effectiveness of heavy ground and aerial armament. It demonstrated how aerial supply can both aid defence and facilitate attack.

It was also a battle in which no mercy was shown. Very few prisoners were taken. Surrender was not an option. On the Japanese side, death in battle was inculcated as an honourable, even desirable, fate, and, on the Allied side, killing the Japanese was seen as the only possible response to an enemy which had incurred detestation through its savage treatment of prisoners of war.

Presiding distantly over this confluence of explosive ingredients, the high commands in London, Washington and Tokyo all failed to evolve unqualified objectives. The Japanese government was talked into the invasion of India against its better judgement. Washington's sole interest in the theatre was to maintain a supply line from India to China. The British were motivated partly by the shame of their earlier defeats, but were divided by the propriety of restoring their lost Asian empire, a goal with which their American allies had no sympathy. All of this made a combination of forces and counter-forces without precedent and a recipe for disaster for one of the two sides. The odds were against the Japanese in the long term, but in the short term they could have, and almost did, achieve a damaging masterstroke. While fighting each other, both sides were promoting a fading ideal. Future wars would be ideological or civil, haunted by the spectre of atomic mass slaughter, an apocalyptic vision unimaginable by the floods of emaciated Japanese soldiery as they limped back into Burma from their ill-fated expedition, the collapse of which signalled the death-knell of Japanese militaristic ambitions in Asia.

*Appendix 1*

# British Infantry Structure

A battalion (commanded by a lieutenant colonel) had a War Establishment of about 800 men (although it was often very much less when deployed or in action), with the following structure:

- 4 'Rifle' Companies (each commanded by a major)
  ° each of which had three platoons (commanded by a second lieutenant/lieutenant)
    - each of which had three sections of ten men commanded by a lance corporal/corporal.

- 1 Headquarters Company with
  ° Six platoons including
    - One Signals
    - One Quartermaster
    - One Defence
    - One Mortar
    - One Transport
    - One Machine-Gun
    (although some battalions differed in their HQ Company composition)

Two or three battalions made up a brigade, which was commanded by a brigadier.

Two or three brigades made up a division, commanded by a major general.

Two or three divisions made up a corps, commanded by a lieutenant general.

Two or three corps made up an army, commanded by a lieutenant general/general.

# *Appendix 2*

# The Indian and Gurkha Infantry Regiments of the Indian Army

In 1939 the twenty infantry regiments of the Indian Army were:

1st Punjab Regiment
2nd Punjab Regiment
3rd Madras Regiment
4th Bombay Grenadiers
5th Mahratta Light Infantry
6th Rajputana Rifles
7th Rajput Regiment
8th Punjab Regiment
9th Jat Regiment
10th Baluch Regiment
11th Sikh Regiment
12th Frontier Force Regiment
13th Frontier Force Rifles
14th Punjab Regiment
15th Punjab Regiment
16th Punjab Regiment
17th Dogra Regiment
18th Royal Garwhal Rifles
19th Hyderabad Regiment/Kumaon Regiment
20th Burma Rifles

The following were raised during the war:

The Indian Parachute Regiment
The Bihar Regiment
The Assam Regiment
The Sikh Light Infantry
The Mahar Regiment

1st Afridi Battalion
The Ajmer Regiment
The Chamar Regiment
1st Lingyat Battalion
1st Coorg Battalion

Each pre-war regiment contained a number of battalions, which increased dramatically as the Indian Army expanded in 1940. The various battalions of each regiment were shown in abbreviated form, for example the Fifth Battalion of 1st Punjab Regiment was 5/1st Punjab; the Second Battalion of 6th Rajputana Rifles as 2/6th Rajputana Rifles, and so on.

The eleven Gurkha Regiments were:

1st King George V's Own Gurkha Rifles (The Malaun Regiment)
2nd King Edward VII's Own Gurkha Rifles (The Sirmoor Rifles)
3rd Queen Alexandra's Own Gurkha Rifles
4th Prince of Wales's Own Gurkha Rifles
5th Royal Gurkha Rifles (Frontier Force)
6th Gurkha Rifles
7th Gurkha Rifles
8th Gurkha Rifles
9th Gurkha Rifles
10th Gurkha Rifles
11th Gurkha Rifles

*Appendix 3*

# Major Combat Formations & Units
# March – July 1944[33]

**British**

HQ SEAC (Vice Admiral Lord Louis Mountbatten)
11 Army Group (General Sir George Giffard)
Fourteenth Army (Lieutenant General William Slim)

**Arakan**

• 5th Indian Division (Major General Harold Briggs) [to IV Corps, 19 May]
    ° 9 Brigade (Brigadier Geoffrey Evans; Salomons)
        • 2nd West Yorkshire Regiment
        • 3/9th Jat Regiment
        • 3/14th Punjab Regiment

    ° 123 Brigade (Brigadier Winterton; Evans)
        • 2nd Suffolk Regiment
        • 2/1st Punjab Regiment
        • 1/17th Dogra Regiment

    ° 161 Brigade (Brigadier 'Daddy' Warren) [to XXXIII Corps, 5 April]
        • 4th Queen's Royal West Kent Regiment
        • 1/1st Punjab Regiment
        • 4/7th Rajput Regiment

**Manipur**

IV Corps (Lieutenant General Geoffrey Scoones)

• Corps Troops

- ° Infantry
  - • 9th Jat Regiment [Machine-gun Battalion]
  - • 15/11th Sikh Regiment
  - • Chin Hills Battalion
  - • 3rd Assam Rifles
  - • 4th Assam Rifles
  - • Kalibahadur Regiment (on loan from the Kingdom of Nepal)
  - • Gwalior Infantry (1 Company)

- ° Artillery
  - • 9th Field Regiment Royal Artillery [25-pounders]
  - • 8th Medium Regiment Royal Artillery [5.5- inch guns]
  - • 67th (York and Lancaster) Heavy Anti-Aircraft Regiment
  - • 78th Light Anti-Aircraft Regiment
  - • 15th Punjab Anti-Tank Regiment

- ° Engineers
  - • 75 Field Company Royal Engineers
  - • 424 Field Company Royal Engineers
  - • 16th Battalion Indian Engineers

- • 17th Indian Infantry (Light) Division (Major General D. T. 'Punch' Cowan)
  - ° 48 Infantry Brigade (Brigadier Cameron; Hedley)
    - • 9th Border Regiment
    - • 2/5th Gurkha Rifles
    - • 1/7th Gurkha Rifles

  - ° 63 Infantry Brigade (Brigadier Cumming; Burton)
    - • 1/3rd Gurkha Rifles
    - • 1/4th Gurkha Rifles
    - • 1/10th Gurkha Rifles

  - ° 1st West Yorkshire Regiment [Support Battalion]
  - ° 7/10th Baluch Regiment [Reconnaissance Regiment]
  - ° Artillery
    - • 129th Field Regiment Royal Artillery (Lowland) (TA)
    - • 1st Indian Field Regiment
    - • 82nd Light AA/A-Tk Regiment

- 21st Indian Mountain Regiment
- 29th Indian Mountain Regiment

- 20th Indian Infantry Division (Major General Douglas Gracey)
  - 100 Brigade (Brigadier 'Jimmy' James)
    - 2nd Border Regiment
    - 14/13th Frontier Force Rifles
    - 4/10th Gurkha Rifles

  - 80 Brigade (Brigadier 'Sam' Greeves)
    - 1st Devonshire Regiment
    - 9/12th Frontier Force Regiment
    - 3/1st Gurkha Rifles

  - 32 Brigade (Brigadier David Mackenzie)
    - 1st Northamptonshire Regiment
    - 9/14th Punjab Regiment
    - 3/8th Gurkha Rifles

- 23rd Indian Infantry Division (Major General Ouvry Roberts)
  - 1 Brigade (Brigadier King; McCoy)
    - 1st Seaforth Highlanders
    - 1/16th Punjab Regiment
    - 1st Patiala Regiment

  - 37 Brigade (Brigadier Vivian Collingridge)
    - 3/3rd Gurkha Rifles
    - 3/5th Gurkha Rifles
    - 3/10th Gurkha Rifles

  - 49 Brigade (Brigadier Esse)
    - 4/5th Mahratta Light Infantry
    - 6/5th Mahratta Light Infantry
    - 5/6th Rajputana Rifles

- 50 Indian Parachute Brigade (Brigadier Hope-Thomson)
  - 158th Jungle Field Regiment Royal Artillery
  - 15 (Jhelum) Battery, Indian Mountain Artillery
  - 152nd Indian Parachute Battalion
  - 153rd Gurkha Parachute Battalion

° Machine-gun Company

• 254 Indian Tank Brigade (Brigadier Reginald Scoones)
    ° 3rd Carabiniers
    ° 7th Light Cavalry
    ° C Squadron, 150th Regiment Royal Armoured Corps (10th Bn, York & Lancaster Regiment)
    ° 3/4th Bombay Grenadiers

**The Naga Hills**

XXXIII Corps (Lieutenant General Montagu Stopford)

• Corps Troops
    ° Infantry
        • 1st Burma Regiment
        • 1st Chamar Regiment
        • 1st Assam Regiment
        • The Shere Regiment (on loan from the Kingdom of Nepal)
        • The Mahindra Dal Regiment (on loan from the Kingdom of Nepal)

    ° Armour
        • 149th Regiment Royal Armoured Corps (7th Bn, King's Own Yorkshire Light Infantry)
        • Detachment, 150th Regiment Royal Armoured Corps (10th Battalion, York and Lancaster Regiment)
        • 11th Prince Albert Victor's Own Cavalry (11th Frontier Force) [reconnaissance regiment]
        • 45th Cavalry (Stuart light tanks)

    ° Artillery
        • 1st Medium Regiment RA
        • 50th Indian LAA/A-Tk Regiment
        • 24th Indian Mountain Regiment

    ° Engineers
        • 429 Field Company Indian Engineers
        • 44 Field Park Company Indian Engineers
        • 10th Battalion, Indian Engineers

- 202nd Line of Communication Area (Major General R. P. L. Ranking)
- 2nd British Division (Major General J. M. L. Grover)
  - ° Divisional Troops
    - Infantry
      - 2nd Manchester Regiment [Vickers machine-guns]
      - 2nd Reconnaissance Regiment
      - 143 Special Service Company

    - Royal Artillery
      - 10th Field Regiment
      - 16th Field Regiment
      - 99th (Buckinghamshire Yeomanry) Field Regiment
      - 100th LAA/A-Tk Regiment.

    - Royal Engineers
      - 5 Field Company
      - 208 Field Company
      - 506 Field Company
      - 21 Field Park Company

  - ° 4 Brigade (Brigadiers Willie Goschen (KIA); Theobalds (KIA); Robert Scott (WIA))
    - 1st Royal Scots
    - 2nd Royal Norfolk Regiment
    - 1/8th Lancashire Fusiliers
    - 4th Field Ambulance RAMC

  - ° 5 Brigade (Brigadier Victor Hawkins (WIA))
    - 7th Worcestershire Regiment
    - 2nd Dorsetshire Regiment
    - 1st Queen's Own Cameron Highlanders
    - 5th Field Ambulance RAMC

  - ° 6 Brigade (Brigadier Shapland)
    - 1st Royal Welch Fusiliers
    - 1st Royal Berkshire Regiment
    - 2nd Durham Light Infantry
    - 6th Field Ambulance RAMC

&deg; 23 Long Range Penetration Brigade (Brigadier Perowne)
- 60th (North Midland) Field Regiment Royal Artillery
- 12 Field Company Royal Engineers
- 2nd Duke of Wellington's Regiment
- 4th Border Regiment
- 1st Essex Regiment

~

**Air Command South-East Asia 1944 at the time of Operation C**

**Air Command South-East Asia – Kandy** (Air Chief Marshal Sir Richard Peirse)

- **Eastern Command – Calcutta** (Major General George Stratemeyer USAAF)

&deg; Strategic Air Force – Comilla. (Major General Howard Davidson USAAF)
&deg; Troop Carrier Command – Comilla (Brigadier William Old USAAF)

| | | |
|---|---|---|
| • 31 Squadron | – | Dakota |
| • 62 Squadron | – | Dakota |
| • 99 Squadron | – | Wellington X |
| • 117 Squadron | – | Dakota |
| • 194 Squadron | – | Dakota |
| • 215 Squadron | – | Dakota/Wellington |
| • 216 Squadron | – | Dakota |

&deg; 3rd Tactical Air Force – Comilla (Air Vice Marshal John Baldwin)
- 224 Group RAF – Chittagong (Air Commodore A. Gray)
- Northern Air Sector (USAAF)
- 221 Group RAF – Imphal (Air Commodore S. F. Vincent)

| | | |
|---|---|---|
| • 5 Squadron | – | Hurricane IIC |
| • 11 Squadron | – | Hurricane IIC |
| • 20 Squadron | – | Hurricane IID |
| • 28 Squadron | – | Hurricane IIC |
| • 34 Squadron | – | Hurricane IIC |

| | | |
|---|---|---|
| • 42 Squadron | – | Hurricane IIC |
| • 60 Squadron | – | Hurricane IIC |
| • 81 Squadron | – | Spitfire VIII |
| • 84 Squadron | – | Vengeance |
| • 110 Squadron | – | Vengeance |
| • 113 Squadron | – | Hurricane IIC |
| • 123 Squadron | – | Hurricane IIC |
| • 136 Squadron | – | Spitfire VIII |
| • 152 Squadron | – | Spitfire VIII |
| • 176 Squadron | – | Beaufighter VIF |
| • 607 Squadron | – | Spitfire VIII |
| • 615 Squadron | – | Spitfire VIII |
| • 1 IAF Squadron | – | Hurricane IIB/C |
| • 7 IAF Squadron | – | Vengeance |
| • 9 IAF Squadron | – | Hurricane IIC |

~

## Order of Battle, Kohima Garrison on 4 April 1944

### Infantry

1st Assam Regiment
One Company, 3/2nd Punjab Regiment
One Company, 1st Garrison Battalion, Burma Regiment
One Company, 5th Burma Regiment
Two Platoons, 27/5th Mahratta Light Infantry
3rd Assam Rifles (minus detachments)
Detachments of V Force
Detachment, Shere Regiment (Nepal)

### Artillery

One 25-pounder with gun detachment

### Engineers

Commander Royal Engineers, and staff
Garrison Engineer, Kohima, and staff

**Signals**

221 Line of Communication Construction Section
Detachment, Burma Signals
Detachment, IV Corps Signals
Detachment, Line of Communication Signals

**Medical**

80th Light Field Ambulance
Detachment, 53rd Indian General Hospital
19 Field Hygiene Section

**Service Corps**

46 General Purpose Transport Company
36 Cattle Conducting Company
87 Indian Field Bakery Section
622 Indian Supply Section

**Labour**

1432 Company Indian Army Pioneer Corps

**Miscellaneous**

24th Reinforcement Camp
Administration Commander, Kohima, and staff

~

**Japanese**

Burma Area Army (General Kawabe Masakazu)

Fifteenth Army (Lieutenant General Mutaguchi Renya)

31st Infantry Division (Lieutenant General Sato Kotuku)
     • Infantry Group (Major General Miyazaki Shigesaburo)
     • 58th Regiment (Colonel Fukunaga)[34]
          ° I Battalion[35]
          ° II Battalion
          ° III Battalion

- 138th Regiment (Colonel Torikai)
    - ° I Battalion
    - ° II Battalion
    - ° III Battalion
- 124th Regiment (Colonel Miyamoto)
    - ° I Battalion
    - ° II Battalion
    - ° III Battalion
- Mountain Artillery Regiment
- Field Gun Battery
- Field Engineer Battalion
- Signals Battalion
- Field Hospital
- Transport Battalion

33rd Infantry Division (Lieutenant General Yanagida/Tanaka)
- Infantry Group (Major General Yamamoto)
- 213th Regiment (Colonel Miyawaki)
    - ° I Battalion
    - ° II Battalion
- 214th Regiment (Colonel Sakuma)
    - ° I Battalion
    - ° II Battalion
- 215th Regiment (Colonel Sasahara)
    - ° I Battalion
    - ° II Battalion

15th Infantry Division (Lieutenant General Yamauchi)
- 51st Regiment (Colonel Omoto)
    - ° I Battalion
    - ° II Battalion
- 60th Regiment (Colonel Matsumura)
    - ° I Battalion
    - ° II Battalion
- 67th Regiment (Colonel Yanagizawa)
    - ° I Battalion
    - ° II Battalion
- Field Artillery Regiment

14th Tank Regiment (Colonel Ueda)

Indian National Army (Colonel Zaman Kiani)
- 2nd (Gandhi) Regiment
- 3rd (Azad) Regiment

5th Air Division (Major General Tazoe)
- 50th Sentai    –    Ki43 Oscar
- 64th Sentai    –    Ki43 Oscar
- 87th Sentai    –    Ki43 Oscar
- 204th Sentai   –    Ki43 Oscar
- 8th Sentai     –    Ki48 Lilly
- 12th Sentai    –    Ki21 Sally
- 62nd Sentai    –    Ki49 Helen
- Unknown        –    Ki46 Dinah

# Appendix 4

# Common Abbreviations and Usage

| | |
|---|---|
| AA | Anti-Aircraft |
| Ack Ack | Anti-Aircraft |
| ADMS | Assistant Director of Medical Services (in a Division) |
| ADS | Advanced Dressing Station |
| ALFSEA | Allied Land Forces South East Asia (replaced 11 Army Group) |
| AP | Armour-Piercing |
| APM | Assistant Provost Marshal (Military Police) |
| AT | Anti-tank |
| Angami | The Naga tribe who live in Kohima |
| Basha | Native hut usually covered with bamboo fronds |
| Bund | Earthen embankment |
| BGS | Brigadier General Staff (the 'Chief of Staff' in a divisional HQ) |
| BOR | British Other Rank (as opposed to an IOR, Indian Other Rank) |
| Chaung | A river gulley, often dry outside of the monsoon |
| CIGS | Chief of the Imperial General Staff (Field Marshal Sir Alan Brooke, in London) |
| CO | Commanding Officer (of an infantry battalion or an armoured, artillery or support regiment) |
| CRA | Commander Royal Artillery (in a Division) |
| CRE | Commander Royal Engineers (in a Division) |
| CRASC | Commander Royal Army Service Corps (in a Division) |
| CSM | Company Sergeant Major |
| DAG | Deputy Adjutant General |
| DAQMG | Deputy Adjutant & Quartermaster General |
| Dao | Naga machete |
| DC | Deputy Commissioner (Indian Civil Service) |

| | |
|---|---|
| DCM | Distinguished Conduct Medal |
| DIS | Daily Issue Stores (on Kohima Ridge) |
| DLI | Durham Light Infantry |
| DSO | Distinguished Service Order |
| DZ | Drop Zone (for supply aircraft) |
| ECO | Emergency Commissioned Officer |
| FFR | Frontier Force Regiment (the 'Piffers') |
| FF Rifles | Frontier Force Rifles |
| FOO | Forward Observation Officer (Artillery) |
| FSD | Field Stores Depot (on Kohima Ridge) |
| G3 | General Staff Officer, Grade 3 (GSO3) |
| Gaonbura | Naga village chief |
| GHQ | General Headquarters |
| GOC | General Officer Commanding (a Division) |
| GPT | General Purpose Transport (on Kohima Ridge) |
| Gunner | Private soldier in Royal Artillery |
| HE | High Explosive |
| IAF | Indian Air Force |
| IO | Intelligence Officer |
| IGH | Indian General Hospital |
| INA | Indian National Army |
| JIF | Japanese Indian Forces (the INA) |
| LMG | Light Machine gun |
| LofC | Line of Communication |
| LRP | Long Range Penetration (used to refer to Chindit operations) |
| MDS | Main Dressing Station (Medical) |
| MC | Military Cross |
| MM | Military Medal |
| MMG | Medium Machine Gun (Vickers) |
| MS | Milestone |
| MT | Motor Transport |
| NCO | Non-Commissioned Officer |
| Nullah | Valley |
| OP | Observation Post |
| PoW | Prisoner of War |
| QM | Quartermaster |
| RAC | Royal Armoured Corps |
| RAMC | Royal Army Medical Corps |
| RAP | Regimental Aid Post |

| | |
|---|---|
| RMO | Regimental Medical Officer |
| RA | Royal Artillery |
| RE | Royal Engineers |
| Sapper | Engineer; also private soldier in Royal Engineers |
| SEAC | South East Asia Command (commanded by Mountbatten) |
| TCP | Traffic Control Point (the road junction between Kohima Ridge and Treasury Hill |
| USAAF | United States Army Air Forces |
| VC | Victoria Cross |
| VCO | Viceroy's Commissioned Officer (Indian Army) |
| WOI | Warrant Officer Class 1 |
| WOII | Warrant Officer Class 2 |
| Zu | Naga rice beer |

# *Appendix 5*

# British and Indian Rank Structures

| British | Indian Infantry | Indian Cavalry |
|---|---|---|
| Private | Jawan (Sepoy) | Sowar |
| Lance Corporal | Lance Naik | Acting Lance Daffadar |
| Corporal | Naik | Lance Daffadar |
| Sergeant | Havildar | Daffadar |
| Staff Sergeant | – | – |
| Warrant Officer Class I | – | – |
| Warrant Officer Class II | – | – |
| | Jemadar (VCO) | Jemadar (VCO) |
| | Subedar (VCO) | Risaldar (VCO) |
| | Subedar Major (VCO) | Risaldar Major (VCO) |

All other commissioned ranks remained the same, viz:

Second Lieutenant
Lieutenant
Captain
Major
Lieutenant Colonel
Colonel
Brigadier
Major General
Lieutenant General
General
Field Marshal

# Select Bibliography

While I have some sympathy for Max Hastings' observation that formal bibliographies can often become 'merely an author's peacock display' I have nevertheless often found them to be of immense help in identifying works for my own research. The literature of the Burma Campaign (such title, of course, includes the battles for Arakan, Imphal and Kohima) is vast (and growing), so what I list here are the books and papers that I have found most useful in my preparation of this book. For dedicated students of the campaign the first step must be a visit to the Burma Campaign Memorial Library, the most comprehensive collection of sources on the war in Burma and India probably anywhere in the world and the brainchild of Major Gordon Graham MC, which is housed in the library of the School of Oriental and African Studies, Thornhaugh Street, Russell Square, London WC1H 0XG. Other excellent collections are held in the London Library (which is membership only, but well worth the investment), and the Prince Consort's Library, Aldershot.

### Manuscript Sources

The Liddell Hart Centre, King's College, University of London (the papers of General Sir Ouvry Roberts, Lieutenant General Sir Frank Messervy, Lieutenant General Douglas Gracey and Major General John 'Tubby' Lethbridge)

The Churchill Archives, Churchill College, Cambridge (the papers of Field Marshal Lord Slim)

The Hartley Library, University of Southampton (the papers of Admiral Mountbatten)

The Centre for South Asian Studies, University of Cambridge (the papers of Sir Charles Pawsey and Mr C. Gimson)

The Imperial War Museum, London (veterans' reports and narratives as well as the papers of Major General Geoffrey Evans)

The Kohima Museum, York (various manuscripts, including Major General Grover's diary)

The Second World War Experience Centre, University of Leeds

BBC Peoples War Archive (online)

The Museum of the Worcestershire Regiment (Harry Swinson's diary and Fred Weedman's narrative)

The Burma Campaign Memorial Library, School of Oriental and African Studies (SOAS), London

The National Archives, Kew (Divisional, brigade and unit war diaries held under WO 172, and Interrogations of Captured Japanese Commanders in WO 106 5895/6)

The British Library (India Office Papers under L/Mil/17 and L/WS/1)

The National Army Museum

### Official Publications

Giffard, General Sir George, *Operations in Burma and Northeast India from 16 November 1943 to 22 June 1944* (*London Gazette*, London, 1951)
Kirby, S. Woodburn, *The War Against Japan*, Volume II (HMSO, London, 1958), *The War Against Japan*, Volume III (HMSO, London 1962)
Mountbatten of Burma, Admiral the Earl, *Report to the Combined Chiefs of Staff, 1943-1945* (HMSO, London, 1951)
Prasad, Bisheshwar, *Official History of the Indian Army Forces in the Second World War: Campaigns in the Eastern Theatre Reconquest of Burma Volume 1* (Orient Longmans, Calcutta, 1958)

### Books and Monographs

Anon, *History of the 7/10th Baluch Regiment in Burma* (MS, 1945)
Anon, *History of the 7th Light Cavalry in Burma* (2 vols, 1944/5)
Anon, *History of 17 Indian Division, July 1941 to December 1945* (Thackers Press, Calcutta, nd)
Allen, Louis, *Burma, the Longest War* (Dent, London, 1984)
Annett, Roger, *Drop Zone Burma* (Pen and Sword, Barnsley, 2008)
Arnold, Ralph, *A Very Quiet War* (Rupert Hart-Davis, London, 1962)
Atkins, David, *The Forgotten Major* (Toat Press, Pulborough, 1989)
Barclay, C. N., *The Regimental History of the 3rd Queen Alexandra's Own Gurkha Rifles, Volume II, 1927 to 1947* (William Clowes, London,1953)
Barker, A. J., *The March on Delhi* (Faber and Faber, London, 1963)
Bickersteth, Anthony Charles, *ODTAA* (Aberdeen University Press, Aberdeen, 1953)
Blight, Gordon, *The Royal Berkshire Regiment* (Staples Press, London, 1953)
Brett-James, Antony, *Report my Signals* (Hennel Locke, London, 1948),
     –*Ball of Fire* (Gale and Polden, Aldershot, 1951)
      –& Evans, Geoffrey, *Imphal* (Macmillan, London, 1962)
Graham Bower, Ursula, *Naga Path* (John Murray, London, 1952)
Callahan, Raymond, *Burma 1942-45* (Davis-Poynter, London, 1978)
Campbell, Arthur, *The Siege, A Story from Kohima* (George, Allen and Unwin, London, 1956)
Chaplin, J. B., *Action in Burma* (Privately printed, London, 1984)
Colvin, John, *Not Ordinary Men* (Pen and Sword, Barnsley, 1994)
Condon, W. E. H., *The Frontier Force Rifles* (Gale and Polden, Aldershot, 1953)
Connell, John, *Wavell: Supreme Commander* (Collins, London, 1969)
Cross, John, *Jungle Warfare: Experiences and Encounters* (Arms and Armour Press, London, 1989)
Doulton, A. J. F., *The Fighting Cock* (Gale and Polden, Aldershot, 1950)
Edwards, Leslie, *Kohima: The Furthest Battle* (The History Press, Stroud, 2009)
Evans, Geoffrey, *The Desert and the Jungle* ((William Kimber, London, 1959)
Evans, Charles, *A Doctor in XV Army* (Pen and Sword, Barnsley, 1998)
Fay, Peter Ward, *The Forgotten Army, India's Struggle for Independence 1942-1945* (University of Michigan Press, Ann Arbor, 1993)

Forty, George, *XIV Army at War* (Ian Allan, London, 1982)

Franks, Norman, *The Air Battle of Imphal* (William Kimber, London, 1985)

Freer, Arthur, *Nunshigum* (Pentland Press, Durham, 1995)

Grant, Ian Lyall, *Burma: The Turning Point* (Zampi Press, Chichester, 1992)

Graham, Gordon, *The Trees Are All Young on Garrison Hill* (Kohima Educational Trust, Marlow, 2006)

Griffen, J.A.A. (ed), *The History of the Tenth Foot 1919–1950* (Gale and Polden, Aldershot, 1953)

Grant, Peter, *A Highlander Goes to War: A Memoir 1939–1946* (Pentland Press, Edinburgh, 1995)

Hallam, John, *The History of the Lancashire Fusiliers 1939–1945* (Sutton, London, 1993)

Hanley, Gerald, *Monsoon Victory* (Collins, London, 1946)

Hart, Peter, *At the Sharp end: from Le Paradis to Kohima* (Pen and Sword, Barnsley, 1998)

Havers, Norman, *March On! An infantry battalion in England, India and Burma* (Square One Publications, Worcester, 1992)

Henslow, John, *A Sapper in the Forgotten Army* (John Henslow, Petersfield, Sussex, 1986)

Hickey, Michael, *The Unforgettable Army: Slim's XIVth Army in Burma* (Spellmount Limited, Tunbridge Wells, 1992)

Hudson, John, *Sunset in the East* (Pen and Sword, Barnsley, 2002)

Irwin, Anthony, *Burmese Outpost* (Collins, London, 1945)

Iwaichi Fujiwara, *F. Kikan: Japanese Army Intelligence Operations in Southeast Asia During World War II* (Heinemann, Singapore, 1983)

Keane, Fergal, *Road of Bones: The Siege of Kohima 1944* (Harper Collins, London, 2010)

Kemp, P. K., *The Red Dragon: The Story of the Royal Welch Fusiliers 1919–1945* (Gale and Polden, Aldershot, 1960)

Latimer, Jon, *Burma: The Forgotten War* (John Murray, London, 2005)

Lebra, Joyce, *Jungle Alliance* (Asia Pacific Press, Singapore, 1971)

— *Japanese Trained Armies in Southeast Asia* (Columbia, New York, 1977)

Leyin, John, *Tell Them of Us* (Lejins Publishing, Stanford-le-Hope, 2000)

Lewin, Ronald, *Slim: The Standard Bearer* (Leo Cooper, London, 1976)

Lydall, Edward, *Enough of Action* (Jonathan Cape, London, 1945)

Lyman, Robert *Slim, Master of War* (Constable, London, 2004)

— *The Generals. From Defeat to Victory: Leadership in Asia 1941-45* (Constable, London, 2008)

Lowry, Michael, *An Infantry Commander in Arakan and Kohima* (Gale and Polden, Aldershot, 1950)

— *Fighting through to Kohima* (Leo Cooper, Barnsley, 2003)

Martin, Thomas, *Essex Regiment* (The Essex Regiment Association, Brentwood, 1951)

McCann, John, *Echoes of Kohima* (John McCann, Oldham, 1989)

— *Return to Kohima* (John McCann,, Oldham, 1993)

McKelvie, Roy, *The War in Burma* (Methuen, London, 1948)

McLynn, Frank, *The Burma Campaign* (The Bodley Head, London, 2010)

Moxon, Oliver, *Bitter Monsoon* (Robert Hale, London, 1955)

Molloy, Terence, *The Silchar Track* (Melrose Books, Ely, 2006)

Mullaly, Brian, *Bugle and Kukri* (Blackwood, Edinburgh, 1957)

Neild, Eric, *With Pegasus in India* (Jay Birch and Co, Singapore, 1970)

Oatts, Lewis, *I Serve* (Jarrold and Sons, Norwich, 1966)

Owen, Frank, *The Campaign in Burma* (HMSO, London, 1946)

Painter, Robin, *A Signal Honour* (Pen and Sword, Barnsley, 1999)

Pearson, Michael, *The Burma Air Campaign* (Pen and Sword, Barnsley, 2006)

Perrett, Bryan, *Tank Tracks to Rangoon* (Robert Hale, London, 1978)

Philips, C. E. Lucas, *Springboard to Victory: Battle for Kohima* (Heinemann, London, 1966)

Probert, Henry, *The Forgotten Air Force* (Brassey's, London, 1995)

Randle, John, *Battle Tales from Burma* (Pen and Sword, Barnsley, 2004)

Rissik, David, *The DLI at War: The History of the Durham Light Infantry 1939–1945* (The Durham Light Infantry, Durham, 1952)

Roberts, Michael, *Golden Arrow: The Story of the 7th Indian Division in the Second World War 1939–1945* (Gale and Polden Ltd, Aldershot, 1952)

Robertson, G. W., *The Rose and the Arrow: A life story of the 136th Field Regiment Royal Artillery 1939–1946* (136th Field Regiment Royal Artillery Old Comrades Association, 1986)

Rooney, David, *Burma Victory* (Cassell, London, 1992)

Sandes, E. W. C., *From Pyramid to Pagoda: The Story of the West Yorkshire Regiment in the War 1939–1945 and afterwards* (F. J. Parsons, London, 1951)

Seaman, Harry, *The Battle at Sangshak* (Leo Cooper, London, 1989)

Shears, Philip, *The Story of the Border Regiment* (Nisbet, London, 1948)

Shipster, John, *Mist Over the Rice Fields* (Pen and Sword, Barnsley, 2000)

Shores, Christopher, *Air War for Burma* (Grub Street, London, 2005)

Slim, William J., *Defeat into Victory* (Cassells, London, 1956)

Steyn, Peter, *History of the Assam Regiment* (Orient Longmans, Calcutta, 1959)

Street, Robert, *Another Brummie in Burma* (Barney Books, Grantham, nd)
     –*The Siege of Kohima* (Barney Books, Grantham, 2003)

Stripp, Alan, *Code Breaker in the Far East* (Oxford University Press, Oxford, 1995)

Swinson, Arthur, *The Battle of Kohima* (Cassell, London, 1966)

Tamayama, K., & Nunneley, J., *Tales by Japanese Soldiers of the Burma Campaign 1942–45* (Cassell, London, 2000)

Taylor, Jeremy, *The Devons: A History of the Devonshire Regiment 1685–1945* (White Swan Press, Bristol, 1951)

Thompson, Julian, *The Imperial War Museum Book of the War in Burma 1942–1945* (Pan, London, 2002)

Toshikazu, Kase *Eclipse of the Rising Sun* (London: Jonathan Cape; 1951)

Toye, Hugh, *Subhash Chandra Bose: the Springing Tiger* (Jaico Publishing House, Bombay, 1991)

Turnbull, Patrick, *The Battle of the Box* (Ian Allen, London, 1979)

Vincent, S. F., *Flying Fever* (Jarrolds, London, 1972)

Warwick, Nigel, *Constant Vigilance* (Pen and Sword, Barnsley, 1997)

White, O. G. W., *Straight on for Tokyo* (Gale and Polden, Aldershot, 1953)

Wilcox, W. A., *Chindit Column 76* (Longmans, London, 1945)

Williams, J. H., *Elephant Bill* (Rupert Hart-Davis, London, 1950)

Wilson, David, *The Sum of Things* (Spellmount, Staplehurst, 2001)

# Notes

1 A guerrilla group made up from British officers and loyal villagers.
2 Japanese divisions (although not Yamauchi's *15th Division*) had, in addition to the divisional commander, a Major General who commanded the divisional infantry.
3 A private soldier in an armoured regiment.
4 Nishida Susumu survived the war and in due course became President of the 58th Regiment Association and a keen supporter of reconciliation with his erstwhile enemies.
5 Lock was killed at Sangshak several days later.
6 The site of the current Imphal Airport.
7 Flight Lieutenant W. J. N. (John) Lee DFC of 5 Squadron RAF, who died in a flying accident on 27 March 1944. Boyes was shot down and killed on 24 April 1944.
8 In 1944 the Naga Hills were managed by New Delhi through a resident Deputy Commissioner. Nagaland became a separate state in the independent India in 1963.
9 161 Brigade (Brigadier Warren) was diverted by Slim to Dimapur for the defence of Kohima while 123 Brigade (Brigadier G. C. Evans) and 9 Brigade (Brigadier J. A. Salomons) were flown into Imphal as planned.
10 Donald Easten MC was able to revisit Kohima, aged 90, in 2008.
11 A fish-tailed native machete.
12 Almost certainly troops of 7th Worcesters making the journey between Zubza and Merema.
13 Both 9 and 123 Brigades were flown into Imphal, while Warren's 161 Brigade was diverted to Dimapur for operations at Kohima.
14 '*Munshi*' in Hindi means 'Teacher'. Cree was bald, which gave him a schoolmasterly appearance.
15 Meaning 'wood' in Urdu, 'Lakri' was a common nickname for British officers with this surname in the Indian Army, similar to 'Chalky' White, 'Spud' Murphy or 'Smudger' Smith in the British Army.
16 B Squadron, Royal Scots Dragoon Guards, the successor regiment to 3rd Carabiniers in the modern British Army, celebrates 'Nunshigum Day' each year by parading without its officers, under the command of the Squadron Non Commissioned Officers.
17 There were in fact two roads, roughly parallel to each other, one for east bound traffic and one for west bound.
18 The Japanese named the hills after the officers who led the assault on them. Scraggy was named after Major Ito, of 213th Regiment.
19 'India for ever! On to Delhi!'
20 This RAC unit was formed by re-roling 10th Battalion, The York and Lancaster Regiment.
21 Lieutenant James Evans survived, and travelled with the author back to Burma in 2005.

22 Oldham shortly afterwards took up command of 2/5th Royal Gurkhas, when he was wounded. He died on 30 May when his ambulance was struck by shells during the evacuation of 48 Brigade wounded from Potsangbam.

23 Projector, Infantry, Anti-Tank.

24 Each of the sixteen separate Naga tribes speaks its own language. Vepopa could not speak anything other than the dialect used in his village.

25 A Hindi term for 'Mr', but used derogatorily by soldiers of civilians and clerks.

26 Eighty-nine Brigade from 7th Division was now fighting with Briggs' 5th Indian Division in Imphal, while Messervy's division was reinforced by Warren's 161 Brigade following its brief period of recovery after the siege.

27 To 'brass' something up was a colloquialism meaning 'to shoot at' or 'to fire at'.

28 Not to be confused with Colonel Tanaka Tetsujiro, the 33rd Division Chief of Staff, who ran affairs until Lieutenant General Tanaka Nobuo arrived from Thailand in late May.

29 32 Brigade remained attached to 17th Indian Division on the Tiddim Road.

30 Fifteenth Army consisted of 115,000 troops, 50,000 of whom were support, line-of-communication and administrative troops. Of this number, 15,000 were lost, in addition to 53,000 fighting troops. Fifteenth Army overall, therefore, lost 65,000 of its original strength.

31 8,000 casualties in Arakan, 4,000 at Kohima and 12,000 at Imphal.

32 Commander XV Corps, Arakan

33 This list is not meant to be exhaustive, but to provide a summary of the major combat units involved on both sides during Operations U and C.

34 A Japanese Regiment was the same size as a British Brigade.

35 Battalions were commanded by a Major.

# Index